DISCOVERING AMERICA
1700–1875

The

New American Nation Series

EDITED BY

HENRY STEELE COMMAGER

AND

RICHARD B. MORRIS

DISCOVERING AMERICA

1700 ★ 1875

By HENRY SAVAGE, Jr.

ILLUSTRATED

1817

HARPER & ROW, PUBLISHERS

NEW YORK, HAGERSTOWN, SAN FRANCISCO, LONDON

Grateful acknowledgment is made for permission to reprint the maps on pages 98 and 259 from *Army Exploration in the American West* by William H. Goetzmann. Copyright © 1959 by Yale University Press, Inc. Reprinted by permission of Yale University Press, Inc.

The map on pages 138–39 is reprinted from *Zebulon Pike: The Life and Times of an Adventurer* by John Upton Terrell. Copyright © 1968 by John Upton Terrell. Reprinted by permission of Julian Bach Literary Agency, Inc.

FIRST EDITION

Library of Congress Cataloging in Publication Data

Savage, Henry, date
    Discovering America, 1700–1875.
    (New American Nation series)
    Bibliography: p.
    1. United States—Description and travel—To 1783. 2. United States—Description and travel—1783–1848. 3. United States—Description and travel—1848–1865. 4. Natural history—United States. I. Title.
E162.S26 1979   973   78-20113

ISBN 0-06-013782-7   79 80 81 82 83 10 9 8 7 6 5 4 3 2 1

ISBN 0-06-090740-pbk   79 80 81 82 83 10 9 8 7 6 5 4 3 2 1

To Elizabeth:
My wife and full partner
in enterprise

Contents

Illustrations

MAPS

Editors' Introduction

WE ARE accustomed to thinking of the discovery of America in terms of Columbus, De Soto, Verrazano, Cabot, and Henry Hudson or of the Norse who discovered Vinland or even, if we are gullible, of Prince Madoc who settled a colony of Welshmen in the Upper Missouri three centuries before Columbus. And of course it was Columbus, and his followers and successors, who "discovered" America in the traditional meaning. But their discovery was, in a sense, like the "discovery" of a new land by aerial reconnaissance. The task of discovering America, its climate, its soil, its rivers, its mountain passes, its flora and fauna, came later and engaged the mind and energies of ten generations of explorers, surveyors, map-makers, hunters, fur traders, soldiers, botanists, ornithologists, en-tomologists, ethnologists, archeologists, farmers, and settlers for three centuries; indeed the process is still going on.

The whole process of discovery was a kind of anticipatory vindica-tion of Robert Frost's insight, that "the land was ours before we were the land's." The land was indeed ours, by conquest or, as many Americans believed, by Manifest Destiny: Americans fell upon it, cultivated it, exploited it, ravaged it. All this involved discovery. It is *this* discovery which is the theme of Mr. Savage's book. While the latitude and longitude of the book encloses a map of the country that was to be the United States, the theme is rather how Americans discovered, exploited, and, ultimately, accommodated their society and economy to the land that—as they assumed—it was their destiny to occupy.

The process of discovery embraced three themes of compelling interest. The first, that America was not Europe, nor merely an extension of Europe, but a "strange new world" came first as a shock, then as a challenge, then—in the eyes of men like Franklin and Jefferson—as a blessing, for it seemed to promise that America would develop its own character and potentialities. The second was that suggested by Crèvecoeur, "two hundred miles formerly appeared a great distance; it is now but a trifle." For here was the fateful impact of the concept of infinity—just what Jefferson nourished when he spoke, in his Inaugural Address, of "land enough for our descendants to the thousandth and thousandth generation." What that meant was the illusion of infinite resources, infinite variety, and infinite potentialities. The third was that the New World was indeed different from the Old; it was not—as legions of European naturalists and philosophers and theologians had argued—inferior. Jefferson, who had done more to "discover" America geographically, economically, politically, and morally than any other statesman, saw that, and in his *Notes on Virginia* vindicated American superiority so convincingly that the century-long dispute ended abruptly.

In his *Discovering America,* Mr. Savage has brought together all the strands of discovery. Here are the familiar figures—from Catesby and Bartram, Wilson and Audubon, to Schoolcraft and Catlin, Pike and Frémont; here, too, are many who are less familiar than they should be—Le Page du Pratz, who hit on new cures for old and new diseases, or André Michaux, who explored equally the American West and Madagascar, or members of the natural history circle in Philadelphia that somehow was large enough to embrace Collinson in England and Banks of the Royal Society and Linnaeus up in Uppsala and Buffon at the Royal Garden in Paris; and here is the "boatload of knowledge" that floated down the Ohio to the Utopian colony at New Harmony, carrying a dozen naturalists and philosophers, from the geologist-philospher William Maclure to the eccentric Constantine Rafinesque, whose scientific activities spanned two continents.

Discovering America is a volume in the New American Nation Series, a comprehensive, cooperative survey of the area now embraced in the United States. Other aspects of the material covered by Mr. Savage are found in the volumes by Wilcomb E. Washburn, David B. Quinn, Louis B. Wright, W. J. Eccles, Russel B. Nye, and Ray A. Billington.

HENRY STEELE COMMAGER
RICHARD B. MORRIS

Preface

THE word "discovering" in the title of this book is used in its most literal sense—the act of uncovering or revealing the unknown; and the term "America" refers to the area within the forty-eight contiguous states of the United States. Essentially, the work is an account of the development, piece by piece, of a mosaic image of the physical nature of America—its geography, its pristine fauna and flora, and its native people—an image given to the world through countless explorations, observations, and studies made largely between 1700, when our cultural forebears as yet knew little of the interior of the country beyond its Atlantic and Gulf Coast areas and a narrow thread along the Mississippi and Great Lakes, and the period memorable for the driving of the golden spike to mark the completion of the transcontinental railway, and the establishment of Yellowstone National Park.

Obviously the exigencies of an assignment so extensive and comprehensive, both geographically and temporally, demanded the exercise of drastic selectivity in choosing materials from the boundless wealth available. Though perhaps only the brush of a Breughel could do justice to so crowded a canvas, nevertheless an attempt has been made here to present all the most significant figures. In the process of selection, many varied criteria were applied. Priority of revelation, for instance, took precedence over priority of physical encounter, though many contestants qualified on both counts. The extent and range of public exposure, and the degree of absorption into the American cultural heritage, were often decisive factors.

Sometimes the glamour of an expedition and contemporary interest in its achievements proved quite sufficient to qualify its leader as a substantial contributor to the image of America. Some made their way into these pages through a revealing brush or camera lens. Still others, without venturing the perils of the wilderness, derived materials from those more daring, and fashioned books that contributed so substantially to the vast picture that they are of necessity included in this account.

Finally, a word about the painful process of exclusion, demanded by limitation of space. The intrepid Spanish explorers of the Southwest, for instance, have been considered only as background material on the basis of the cultural isolation imposed by imperial Spain during the significant years of this study, and the overwhelmingly British, and to a lesser extent French, nature of our cultural heritage. Books as popular in Europe as Hector St. John de Crèvecoeur's *Letters from an American Farmer* (1782) have been regretfully eliminated as dealing with areas already revealed by the time of their publication. Since the primary purpose of this study was to present an account of those who first effectively made known the physical face of America, the dramatis personae are, for the most part, explorers, botanists, ornithologists, geographers, ethnologists, and artists; the reader will look in vain for social scientists, such as the incomparable Alexis de Tocqueville, or lesser commentators on the social scene such as Harriet Martineau or Mrs. Trollope. The same restrictions made it necessary to turn away resolutely from the rich and inexhaustible field of America revealed in legend, poetry, and fiction, for this too is another story.

Most of the extensive research required in the preparation of this volume was done at the University of South Carolina libraries. I take this opportunity to express my gratitude to the libraries' administrators for making their resources available to me and to their personnel for countless instances of generous assistance. And to the Harvard University libraries I owe a debt of gratitude for courtesies extended to me during my visits to Cambridge.

To the series editors, Henry Steele Commager and Richard B. Morris, I tender my profound gratitude for valuable guidance. Professor Commager has been involved with me in this project from the day of his invitation to me to undertake the present volume to its going to press. His advice, encouragement, and editorial suggestions through the intervening years have been of inestimable value. And Corona Machemer of Harper & Row has given most helpful assistance throughout the preparation of the manuscript for the press.

HENRY SAVAGE, JR.

DISCOVERING AMERICA
1700–1875

CHAPTER 1

Retrospect, 1700

IN mid-May 1607, almost five months after leaving London, three tiny ships, aggregating less than 200 tons, dropped anchor off the north bank of Virginia's James River. When the 140 surviving passengers left their cramped shipboard quarters and once again set foot on *terra firma,* they little reckoned the extent to which this American *terra firma* would prove *terra incognita* as well. On that tidewater peninsula Europeans, at frightful cost, were to learn yet another bitter lesson in the strangeness and inhospitality for the untutored alien of the great forest wilderness of North America.[1]

Repeatedly, for almost a century before Jamestown, Englishmen, Frenchmen, and Spaniards had made futile efforts to establish settlements on these shores, only to have them end in disaster. Until 1607 the only lasting fruit of all those efforts was St. Augustine,[2] still little more than the garrisoned citadel Spain had erected on the Florida peninsula to guard the narrow Gulf Stream seaway followed by her treasure fleets homeward bound from Central and South America, which had proved far easier to subdue and vastly more profitable. Illustrative of the contrast is the fact that by 1607 the University of Mexico, one of seven flourishing universities in Spain's southern domains, had been conferring degrees in law and

[1]Oscar Handlin, "The Significance of the Seventeenth Century," in James M. Smith (ed.), *Seventeenth Century America* (Chapel Hill, N.C., 1959), pp. 6–9.

[2]Herbert I. Priestley, *The Coming of the White Man* (New York, 1929), pp. 77–78; David B. Quinn, *North America from Earliest Discovery to First Settlements* (New York, 1977), pp. 262ff.

1

theology for more than half a century.[3] Now, however, in part sparked by Jamestown, came in rapid succession Quebec, Santa Fe, and a Dutch trading post on the Hudson River.[4] But many years would come and go before the great temperate forest wilderness of the North became *terra cognita* for Europeans.

Between 1500 and the establishment of these first permanent settlements, European explorers had sailed many expeditions up and down the Atlantic coast and into the Gulf of Mexico. They had explored the Chesapeake Bay, the Hudson to the site of Albany, and, far to the north, the St. Lawrence to the rapids above Montreal. Samuel de Champlain had joined a Huron war party and campaigned up the Richelieu River into Lake Champlain, and later carried his explorations beyond the rapids of the St. Lawrence, before returning to France to prepare a popular account of his experiences which, soon after its publication in Paris, was translated and published in London as well.[5]

From Florida, in the early decades of the sixteenth century, the Spanish had launched expeditions into the great forests of the South in search of treasure. Pánfilo de Narváez had led a band from Tampa Bay up the West Coast to disaster in the Gulf Coast wilderness. Survivors built boats in the futile hope of going by sea to Mexico. Three of them, marooned on the Texas coast, undertook to continue on foot, emerging after six years of wandering in northwest Mexico. A few years after Narváez's failure Hernando de Soto, at the head of a great expedition launched from the same part of Florida, set out to find rumored golden cities. His vast congregation of men and beasts—including cattle and swine to supply meat in a wilderness teeming with deer, bear, and buffalo—struggled north into the southern Appalachians, thence to the Mississippi and beyond. Even that brave effort to defy the great wilderness became a fruitless disaster with negligible historical impact. Eventually, after the Mississippi had received the weighted corpse of their leader, fewer than half of those who had set out with De Soto made their way by improvised craft down the river and along the coast to

[3]Herbert E. Bolton and Thomas M. Marshall, *The Colonization of North America* (New York, 1920), p. 76.

[4]Priestley, *Coming of the White Man* p. 309; Quinn, *North America*, pp. 406–407, 507–510, 410–411.

[5]Priestley, *Coming of the White Man*, pp. 86–88; W. P. Cumming, S. Hillier, D. B. Quinn, and G. Williams, *The Exploration of North America, 1630–1776* (New York, 1974), pp. 29–31; Quinn, *North America*, pp. 479–485.

Spanish towns in Mexico, ending what had developed into little more than a four-year struggle for survival.[6]

Even as De Soto's expedition was engaged in its fruitless roaming through the forests of the South, another intrepid treasure-seeking Spanish soldier of fortune, Francisco Vásquez de Coronado, was leading his column northward from Mexico through the Pueblo country of the Southwest, thence across the southern plains all the way to western Kansas, on an equally futile search for the fabled seven golden cities of the West. Other less ambitious and historically all but fruitless expeditions into both the Southeast and Southwest continued to be launched until the potency of overextended Spain began to fail in the later years of the century.[7]

Despite a full century of such efforts, in 1600 America remained virtually *terra incognita*. Of its 3 million square miles, only a minuscule bit had been explored by Europeans; such discoveries as were made had been given little currency abroad, and were soon all but forgotten. In the measure of time, the marks of passage of Narváez, De Soto, Coronado, and others through the forests, across the deserts, and over the prairies of wilderness America were scarcely less ephemeral than the wakes of the ships that had brought them to these alien shores. (Except, let it be noted here, for the horses that strayed from their camps. Two centuries later, in the hands of Plains Indians, the progeny of those strays were to play substantial roles in the resistance of the red men to white encroachments.) Indeed, so faint was the trace of De Soto's incredible trek that Louis Joliet and Jacques Marquette, when they set out down the Mississippi more than a century after its waters had hidden his body, failed to associate their river with his, despite the fact that De Soto's wanderings had by then been published in Lisbon, and in London by no other than Richard Hakluyt.[8]

In retrospect it is difficult to understand why a land we are accustomed to regard as exceptionally bountiful and healthful, where the natives lived with a minimum of labor, should have proved so hostile to the efforts of Europeans to establish themselves on its shores. It is particularly hard to explain the British failures, when we recall

---

[6]Priestley, *Coming of the White Man*, pp. 41–42; Quinn, *North America*, pp. 148–151, 207–222.

[7]Priestley, *Coming of the White Man*, pp. 44–45; Quinn, *North America*, pp. 196–205.

[8]F. B. Steck, *The Joliet-Marquette Expedition* (Washington, D. C., 1927), p. 14; Walter Prescott Webb, *The Great Plains* (New York, 1931), p. 57.

that, thanks to Richard Hakluyt's enthusiasm for accounts of travel and exploration and for the colonization of America by his country, much had already been published in England descriptive of Virginia (in its original larger sense, embracing those regions between New York and Spanish Florida) and its inhabitants. Most notable perhaps were Arthur Barlowe's description of Carolina based on his observations with Walter Raleigh's reconnoitering voyage to Roanoke Island in 1584, and Thomas Hariot's and Ralph Lane's accounts of the first settlement attempt there. Hariot's account, including descriptions of the natural history, natives, and products of the region, had been republished in 1590 with the by then familiar Théodore de Bry engravings of the natives and their activities, prepared from the exquisite watercolors John White had painted while he was with the short-lived settlement.[9]

Nevertheless, even with the substantial assistance wrung from their easy-living Indian neighbors, a mere handful of those who came ashore from the *Susan Constant, Godspeed,* and *Discovery* would survive more than a few months in their strange new environment. By the spring of 1610, of the 900 who had joined the settlement at Jamestown, only 150 remained alive. Inept leadership and the distractions of imaginary gold finds partly account for the decimation, but it is impossible to regard them as wholly responsible for the colony's trying years: under better leadership and without the gold chimera, most of the early settlement attempts in the region encountered similar difficulties of accommodation to this bountiful but strange new world.[10]

After playing a major role in saving that feeble settlement on the James, the doughty Captain John Smith returned to England in the fall of 1609. There he added to the store of knowledge of Britain's America with the publication, in 1612, of *A Map of Virginia, with a Description of its Commodities, People, Government, and Religion.* In 1614

[9]John E. Pomfret and Floyd M. Shumway, *Founding the American Colonies, 1583–1660* (New York, 1970), pp. 13–18. For reprints of all the works referred to in this paragraph together with those of Jacques le Moyne and Nicholas le Challeux, beautifully presented, see Stefan Lorant, *The New World* (New York, 1946); Quinn, *North America,* pp. 325–333; Thomas Harriot, *A Briefe and True Report on The New Found Land of Virginia* (London, 1588; Ann Arbor, Mich., 1931).

[10]Bolton and Marshall, *Colonization,* pp. 116–118ff.; Wesley Frank Craven, *The Southern Colonies in the Seventeenth Century, 1607–1789* (Baton Rouge, La., 1949), pp. 65–74ff.; Quinn, *North America,* pp. 447–459.

he returned to explore the coast to which he gave the name New England. He sailed up and named the Charles, and prepared a map that he included in his *Description of New England; or, Observations and Discoveries in North America,* published in 1616, in time to be of immense service to the Pilgrims and Puritans when they came to settle that stern and rockbound shore.[11]

Those religiously motivated people were scarcely well settled before they resorted to the written and printed word beyond the measure of Virginians, and of any of the sister colonies as they eventually came into existence; but with few exceptions their early publications were concerned either with God, the theocracy they were building, or their special relationships with the Almighty.[12] Among the rare exceptions during New England's early years was *New England's Prospect,* a sprightly and interesting little book of 100 pages plus a map of southeast New England, published in London in 1634. Its author, William Wood, set out to present "a true, lively and experimentall description of that part of America called New England . . . laying down that which may both enrich the knowledge of the mind-travelling Reader, or benefit the future Voyager," an aim in which he was successful enough to justify three editions to meet the demand for his honest description of the area, its geography, wildlife, and native inhabitants.[13] Accounts of pigeon flights with neither "beginning nor ending, length or breadth," continuing for four or five hours, of easily securing a half-dozen turkeys weighing up to 40 pounds in a morning, and of killing "twelve score" plover in two shots, were balanced by reluctant confessions of the New Englanders' troubles with the "ravenous wolves" invading their barnyards and the rigors of the winter weather. What Wood had to say of the Indians of the area reflected the condescending tolerance of the Squanto era, when the neighboring natives were

[11]John Lankford (ed.), *Captain John Smith's America* (New York, 1967), pp. xvii–xxii; Quinn, *North America,* pp. 385, 559.

[12]William Bradford's moving and eloquent history, *Of Plymouth Plantation,* was not published in full until the nineteenth century, although parts were included in *A Relation or Journal of the Beginning and Proceeding of the English Plantation Settled at Plymouth in New England* (London, 1622), sometimes known as "Mourt's Relation" for its preface by G. Mourt; and in Nathaniel Morton's *New England's Memorial* (Cambridge, Mass., 1669). The best modern edition of Bradford's history is that edited by Samuel Eliot Morison (New York, 1966).

[13]Louis B. Wright, *The Cultural Life of the American Colonies, 1607–1763* (New York, 1957), p. 157.

regarded as God-sent instructors of the art of survival on those "hideous and desolate"[14] shores—as beneficent a wonder, working in the interest of His people, as the providential epidemic that had cleared the region of nine-tenths of New England's native populations while preparations for the settlement were being made.[15]

Although before the close of the seventeenth century British settlements extended along the coast from Maine to lower South Carolina and up many of the rivers to the fall line, there had been no commensurate growth in knowledge of the Indian country beyond the settled fringe. Until the far-ranging Carolina Indian traders appeared on the scene during the latter years of the century, the exploratory forays of the English were few and modest, a far cry from the daring penetrations of the wilderness so typical of the Spanish conquistadors, or the Frenchmen's talent for adopting the native's way of life in the wilderness and enlisting his cooperation. While the British were contenting themselves with a few modest expeditions along new-found Indian paths or buffalo trails across the Appalachian wall west of their waterbound settlements, the Cross and Fleur-de-lis, in effective working partnership, had penetrated nearly 2,000 miles into the American wilderness. True, as each new English settlement was established, the shores and waterways in its environs were investigated, but usually only far enough into the interior to locate desirable sites for expected accretions to the colony. (With that intent Captain John Smith, the first summer after the landing at Jamestown, even as the settlement's life hung in precarious balance, had explored most of the estuaries of Chesapeake Bay and sailed up the James to its falls. Later comers in due course did much the same, as the several settlements were established.)

Rare indeed, therefore, are any contemporary accounts or surviving seventeenth-century records of expeditions from the English settlements far into the hinterland. One of the few, published in London in 1672, was that of a German doctor, John Lederer, who in 1670, under the sponsorship of Governor William Berkeley, made several forays from the Virginia settlements into the unex-

[14]Morison (ed.), Bradford: *Of Plymouth Plantation*, p. 62.

[15]William Wood, *New England's Prospect* (facsimile edn., Amsterdam, N.Y., 1968), pp. 4ff., 26ff., 44ff., 56ff.; J. S. Barry, *The History of Massachusetts* (3 vols., Boston, 1855), vol. 1, pp. 25ff.; Alvin M. Josephy (ed.), *The American Heritage Book of Indians* (New York, 1961), pp. 170–173; Wilcomb E. Washburn, *The Indian in America* (New York, 1975), p. 52.

plored backcountry. The first of these took him up the Pamunkey to the Blue Ridge where, seeing only an endless array of mountains to the west and unable to find a pass that horsemen might employ, he turned back in disappointment.[16] Undeterred, Lederer set out again, southwestward across the Roanoke River and over the Carolina piedmont, where his account becomes fantastic. Although his reports of the Indians he encountered along the way are valuable, modern authorities are unable to account for some of his tales of the region—of a great lake "ten leagues broad" upon which lived people whose women were Amazonian fellow warriors with their braves, of men who could walk unharmed on live coals, and of great stores of unbored pearls. Reflecting the current concept of the width of North America in that latitude, Lederer reported having met along the way

four stranger-Indians whose bodies were painted in various colours with figures of animals whose likeness I had never seen and by some discourse and signs which passed between us, I gathered that they were the only survivors of fifty, who set out together in company from some great island, as I conjecture, to the northwest; for I understood they crossed a great water, in which most of their party perished by tempest. . . .

To Lederer, the most reasonable conjecture was "that these Indians might come from the Island of New Albion or California from whence we may imagine some great arm of the Indian Ocean or Bay stretches into the Continent towards the Apalatean Mountains. . . ." Lederer's return route led through a "barren sandy desert" before he arrived at the villages of the Tuscarora, then seated in the Sound region of North Carolina.[17]

The fantastic portions of Dr. Lederer's account are, in a way, more enlightening than those parts regarded as reliable observation, for they strikingly demonstrate how little Virginians, even after two generations in America, knew about the country beyond their settlements. Surely Lederer would not have submitted his report to Governor Berkeley, and later for publication, without full confidence that his great "Lake Ushery" actually existed where the maps of the day showed it in the South Carolina piedmont, a fantasy of

[16]William P. Cumming (ed.), John Lederer: *The Discoveries of John Lederer* (Charlottesville, Va., 1958), pp. viii, 15; Cumming, *et al.*, *Exploration*, pp. 83–85, 102–103.

[17]Lederer, *Discoveries*, pp. 19–33; C. W. Alvord and Lee Bidgood, *First Explorations of the Trans-Alleghany Region by the Virginians (1650–1674)* (Cleveland, 1912), pp. 64–69; Cumming, *et al.*, *Exploration*, pp. 84–85.

the mapmakers that persisted well into the next century when it was last shown as Lake Ashley.

Lederer's was but one of many reflections of another persistent geographical fantasy involving the same region, Verrazzano's Sea, which had its origin far back in the history of American coastal exploration. Reporting his voyage of 1524, the Florentine navigator Giovanni da Verrazzano claimed to have found in the latitude of Cape Hatteras "an isthmus a mile in width and about 200 long, in which, from the ship, we could see *el mare orientale* . . . the same which flows around the shores of India, China and Cataya. . . ." Of course by Lederer's day, people no longer thought that only a mile-wide strip of soil separated the Atlantic and the Pacific, but the notion persisted that North America was nothing like as wide as it later proved to be,[18] and during the latter half of the seventeenth century the idea that the "South Sea" probably washed the western ramparts of the Appalachians continued firmly fixed in the minds of many Virginians. Agreeable to the belief of the day too were Sir William Talbot's sentiments in the dedication of Lederer's book to Lord Ashley: "From this discourse it is clear that the long looked-for discovery of the Indian Sea does nearly approach. . . ."[19]

That preconception was further indicated in the reports of the first known passage beyond the Appalachian divide by an expedition from the British colonies—one sent out in 1671 by Abraham Wood from his Virginia frontier trading post on the Appomattox River, where Petersburg now stands. Wood's men, Thomas Batts and Robert Fallam, followed up a tributary of the Roanoke River to its headwaters, and crossed through a pass they found there to New River, a north-flowing tributary of the Kanawha. Although they had thought themselves the first whites to penetrate so deeply into the western wilderness, beside the buffalo trail they followed over the divide they found blazed trees and the initials of unknown predecessors. When they reached the valley beyond, they set a stake in the river at the water's edge. It soon indicated a fall in the water level, which they interpreted as a tidal ebbing. That, and a glimmer of water to the west seen through a pervading fog, convinced them that they had indeed "reached the tidal waters on the confines of the Western Sea." Before turning homeward they too blazed trees beside the forest path; on one they carved the royal insignia of Great

[18]W. P. Cumming, "Geographical Misconceptions of the Southeast," *Journal of Southern History,* IV (1938).

[19]Lederer, *Discoveries,* p. 4.

Britain and formally proclaimed: "Long live Charles the Second, by the Grace of God, King of England, Scotland, France, Ireland and Virginia and all the Territories thereunto belonging."[20]

Now to set in focus the incipient struggle for mastery of the emerging North American continent, we have but to return to a day in June before Batts and Fallam had proclaimed the king of England monarch of "Virginia and all the Territories thereunto belonging." Far to the northwest, upon a hill overlooking the swift-running waters of the Sault connecting Lake Superior and Lake Huron, a crowd of Indians had gathered at the behest of their new-found mentors, the "black robes," who represented themselves to be emissaries of the great king across the great water as well as an even greater one in the sky above. The natives had been summoned there to receive a message from their great father across the water, brought to them by Daumont de Saint-Lusson, the central figure in a group of French interspersed with black-robed Jesuit fathers. With pageantry, chants, prayers, and orations, a great wooden cross was raised, and beside the cross was planted a massive cedar post to which was affixed a metal plate bearing the arms of France. Standing beneath these companion symbols of empire, facing the broad, flowing Sault Ste. Marie, Saint-Lusson, gorgeously attired in the silks, furs, and velvets of the court of Louis XIV, read a proclamation declaring that by those symbols the king of France had become the supreme ruler of "all countries, rivers, lakes and streams contiguous and adjacent thereunto . . . in all the length and breadth, bounded on the one side by the seas of the North and West, and on the other by the South Sea. . . ." The tide of France was approaching its full flow.[21]

Even as Saint-Lusson presided over his pretentious wilderness pageant, plans were well under way to give more substance to the claims he was making on behalf of his distant king. These plans centered on two men engaged in trade with the Indians of the Great Lakes, Robert Cavelier, sieur de la Salle, better known to American history as LaSalle,[22] and Louis Joliet. Separately they were being encouraged to undertake explorations of the "great water" re-

[20]Alvord and Bidgood, *First Explorations*, pp. 19, 70ff., 188–192; Cumming, *et al.*, *Exploration*, pp. 84–85.

[21]Alvord and Bidgood, *First Explorations*, p. 17; Cumming, *et al.*, *Exploration*, p. 85; John Bartlett Brebner, *The Explorers of North America, 1492–1806* (New York, 1933), pp. 207–208. For the developments in New France leading up to the ceremony at Sault Ste. Marie, see W. J. Eccles, *France in America* (New York, 1972), pp. 60–89.

[22]Francis Parkman, *La Salle and the Discovery of the Great West* (Boston, 1869).

ported to lie but a few days journey beyond Lake Superior. In both Paris and New France these projected expeditions were being given great encouragement in the belief that this Great Water might be the long-sought passage to the South Sea and the riches of the Orient. The wishful thinking of the Verrazzano Sea persisted among Frenchmen as stubbornly as among Virginians. Almost a century and a half earlier, in 1535, Jacques Cartier had sailed 700 miles up the St. Lawrence Estuary in search of a parallel myth, the Northwest Passage. Eighty years later the same persistent chimera lured Samuel de Champlain up the Ottawa River and down the French River into Lake Huron, which he persuaded himself "could be nothing else but the South Sea." Now, another half century later, hope flamed anew that the elusive waterway to the Orient was, at last, relatively near at hand.

The Indian trader and experienced voyageur Louis Joliet was one of those who attended the ceremony at Sault Ste. Marie and listened to Saint-Lusson's bold proclamation. Two years later, in the summer of 1673, Joliet and the Jesuit missionary Jacques Marquette added support to Saint-Lusson's territorial claims and gained for themselves a notable place in history by their attempt to carry out the instructions given to Joliet by Governor Frontenac "for the discovery of the South Sea by . . . the great river which they call the Mississippi, which is believed to disembogue in the sea of California."[23] The expedition of Joliet and Marquette took them from Lake Michigan's Green Bay up the Fox River, across a portage to the Wisconsin and down it to the Mississippi, which they followed as far as its confluence with the Arkansas. There they were impelled to turn back, fearful of the ferocity of the Indians beyond, and by then fully convinced by the river's course that it would carry them not to the Vermilion Sea (Gulf of California) but to the Gulf of Mexico, where they feared a Spanish prison might well await them.

Although LaSalle had shared with Joliet the wishful belief that the Mississippi's flow might carry one to the South Sea, Joliet's disappointing discovery, reported in 1674, gave him little pause. The leaping imagination of that daring entrepreneur was now fired by

[23]Letter from Frontenac to Colbert, Francis Borgia Steck, *The Joliet-Marquette Expedition, 1673* (Ann Arbor, Mich., 1971), p. 147. See also Louise Phelps Kellogg (ed.), *Early Narratives of the Northwest, 1634–1699* (New York, 1917); and for a readable account of both the Joliet-Marquette and LaSalle expeditions, see Timothy Severin, *Explorers of the Mississippi* (New York, 1968), Chaps. 4–7.

the dream of an empire for France in the heart of America, with the great river as its main street. After years of struggle in the face of an incredible series of disasters and delays, the relentlessly driving LaSalle set out from Fort Frontenac at the mouth of Lake Ontario in 1679. Leaving fortified posts at strategic points all along the way, he finally arrived at the mouth of the river, which, although long known to the Spaniards as Rio del Espiritu Santo, he now named the Colbert in honor of the French king's powerful minister. Near its mouth, far out in the Gulf where the marshes of the delta meet the open water, LaSalle presided over a modest simulation of Saint-Lusson's ceremony at the Sault and that of the Virginians on the headwaters of the Kanawha, laying claim to the same wilderness realm. There by the turbid river LaSalle's men raised a column proudly inscribed: "Louis Le Grand, Roy de France et de Navarre, règne; le neuvième Avril, 1682," which LaSalle augmented by proclaiming in a loud voice to his men and their Indian companions that Louis Le Grand was ruler over the whole great wilderness drained by the mighty "river Colbert, or Mississippi." This done, a cross—the traditional companion of the regal column—was raised to stand guard over the entrance to the river. Although LaSalle would not live to see his dream take shape, he had more than earned his place in the topmost rank of the world's great explorers.[24]

While the French in Paris and Quebec were planning the expeditions of Joliet and LaSalle, plans were also being laid in London with an eye on the same strategic territory. Even as the French despatched canoes across the Great Lakes and down the Mississippi to secure its main artery, the British were already establishing a strongly supported settlement on the Carolina coast. Although primarily intended to prevent faltering Spain from further attempts to take physical possession of territory north of Florida, the venture was fraught with historical consequences affecting the Mississippi Valley, for in that latitude the Appalachian barrier fell away to permit easy access to the West. Only through the Mohawk Valley of New York was there another geographically practical passage; but

[24]In a later attempt to plant a settlement at the mouth of the Mississippi, LaSalle was murdered by one of a disaffected group of his command. An earlier companion who had set out with LaSalle on his descent of the Mississippi, the mendacious Recollet friar Louis Hennepin, in later years sought to undermine LaSalle's reputation and belittle his accomplishments, going so far as to fabricate an account in which he represented himself as having anticipated his leader in navigating the river to its mouth.

there, from the early days of the Dutch, the Five Nations of the Iroquois had claimed for themselves the position of middlemen in the westward trade, and had consequently proved a barrier to westward British movement as effective as the mountains elsewhere.

Almost immediately after its settlement in 1670 Charles Town had become a trading town, with deer hides providing its principal export. Through the use of intertribal paths extending westward around the southern flank of the mountains all the way to the Mississippi, traders out of Charles Town, emulating the ways of their rival *couriers de bois,* had firmly established themselves before the turn of the century all across the Gulf plains, and in the Valley of the Tennessee to the Mississippi. Though for competitive reasons they were a secretive lot and, with few exceptions, unlettered,[25] they became pathfinders in that vast region, facilitating its later disclosure by more literate travelers, much as, a century and a half later, the "mountain men" of the Great West paved the way for those who will appear later in these pages as its "discoverers."[26]

[25] A notable exception was James Adair, whose remarkable and charming book *The History of the American Indians* (London, 1775) became a prime source of knowledge of the trade and the ethnology of the Gulf Indians.

[26] Readers of Verner Crane, *The Southern Frontier, 1670–1732* (Ann Arbor, Mich., 1929), and Bernard DeVoto, *Across the Wide Missouri* (Boston, 1947), will be impressed by the parallel. More brief accounts of the Carolina traders may be found in Henry Savage, Jr., *River of the Carolinas: The Santee* (New York, 1956), Chap. 8, and in Cumming, *et al., Exploration,* pp. 94–95.

CHAPTER 2

Robert Beverley and John Lawson

"I am an *Indian* and I don't pretend to be exact in my language: But I hope the Plainess of my Dress, will give him the kinder Impressions of my Honesty, which is all I pretend to." With that appraisal of himself as a native American, Robert Beverley, Virginia-born Englishman, addressed the reader of his *History and Present State of Virginia*, which first appeared in London in 1705.[1] Scion of one of the leading families of the emerging Virginia aristocracy, widower of the daughter of the elder William Byrd, Beverley at thirty-one followed a simple way of life on his own extensive plantations where even the household furnishings were homely productions of plantation hands,[2] in sharp contrast with the baronial grandeur of the Westover estate of his brother-in-law, William Byrd, II, so dark and dashing he was known as the Black Swan. Beverley's apology for his plainness was quite unnecessary. Tested in the crucible of time, his *History* has become a classic of American historical literature—perhaps without a peer in the eighteenth century.[3]

[1]Louis B. Wright (ed.), Robert Beverley: *History* (Chapel Hill, N.C., 1947), p. 9; subsequent citations to the *History* are to this edition.

[2]The diary of John Fontaine in "Memoirs of a Hugenot Family" describes a visit of several days in 1715 to Robert Beverley's home, Beverley Park, in King and Queen County. "This man lives well," Fontaine writes, "but, though rich he has nothing in or about his house but what is necessary"—quoted in John McGill, *The Beverley Family of Virginia* (Columbia, S.C., 1956), p. 533.

[3]Beverley, *History*, Wright's introduction, pp. xi–xxxv; Richard S. Dunn, "Seventeenth Century English Historians of America," in James Morton Smith (ed.), *Seventeenth-Century America* (Chapel Hill, N.C., 1959), pp. 217–222.

Beverley's work is significant on several counts. His history of the first century of his native colony, recounted in lively and readable style, salted with prejudices and peppered with wit and satirical humor, is followed by a comprehensive description of the Virginia country, its natural history, and its aboriginal inhabitants. Happily, this feast is served up in a work that is self-consciously American in spirit and outlook.[4] Beverley's professed intent is to try to do justice "to so fine a country . . . because it has been so misrepresented to the common people of England as to make them believe that the servants in Virginia are made to draw in cart and plow, as horses and oxen do in England, and that the country turns all people black who go to live there, with other such prodigious phantasms." Such misapprehensions of a country he regards as the most blessed under heaven distress him, but he is even more provoked by the failure of his fellow Virginians to make the most of its bounties. His book is a rapturous paean to Virginia's blessings, with sharp criticisms of a people who are too prone to

depend altogether upon the Liberality of Nature, without endeavouring to improve its Gifts, by Art and Industry. They spunge upon the Blessings of a warm Sun, and a fruitful Soil, and almost grutch the Pains of gathering in the Bounties of the Earth. I should be asham'd to publish this slothful Indolence of my Countrymen, but that I hope it will rouse them out of their Lethargy . . . and if it does this, I am sure they will have the Goodness to forgive me.[5]

The Virginia of Beverley's day was a vast territory of indeterminate bounds except for that portion east of the Appalachians. Beverley confesses that little was then known of its western reaches;[6] he confines his attention therefore to the coastal and piedmont regions of the present state of Virginia, excepting only a brief account of Captain Batts's 1671 glimpse of transmontane Virginia, where he found an "infinite quantity of Turkies, Deer, Elks, and Buffaloes, so gentle and undisturbed, that they had no Fear at the Appearance of

[4]Beverley, *History,* p. xxi.
[5]*Ibid.,* pp. xvii, 319.
[6]Evidence of this is Lieutenant Governor Spotswood's much-publicized expedition, made up of some dozen gentlemen romantically dubbed the Knights of the Golden Horseshoe, who set forth in 1716, with an array of servants and a military convoy, to explore the Western mountains and open up the Valley of Virginia for settlement. Beverley was a member of the party—McGill, *Beverley Family,* p. 534; W. P. Cumming, *et al., The Exploration of North America, 1630–1776* (New York, 1974), p. 86.

Men.["7] "And since that," Beverley reports, "there has never been any such Discovery attempted from Virginia." His chronological history of the colony concludes with a biting criticism of Sir Francis Nicholson, then royal governor, an attack that served effectively to end Beverley's own political career in the colony.

Following his chronological history, which occupies but a third of the book, Beverley moves on to catalogue the "Natural Product and Conveniences of Virginia in its unimproved State, before the English went thither." Although his Virginia was severely limited to the part with which he was familiar, even that area provided a rich catalogue of "blessings."[8] The reader is given descriptions of rich meadows "wherein are hundreds of acres without any Tree at all," covered with "Grass of incredible Height," of forested swamps with "Trees, as vastly big, as I believe the World affords," of earths for potter's wares, and of "Coals," about which Beverley comments that "it is not likely they should ever be used there in anything but Forges and great Towns, if ever they happen . . ." for "Wood grows at every Man's Door so fast, that after it has been cut down, it will in Seven Years time, grow up again from Seed, to substantial Fire-Wood. . . ." There, too, good iron ores and lead mines were to be found.[9]

Beverley, honest reporter that he is, does not fail to mention Virginia's less appealing attributes: "very loud and surprizing Thunder," excessive heat two or three times a year, and "troublesome Vermin"—"Frogs, Snakes, Musketa's, Chinches, Seedticks or Red-Worms." But he softens the impact of this formidable list with assurances that Virginia never suffers an earthquake and has very short winters.[10]

Of the fruits of its forests and meadows Beverley confesses but little knowledge, "because I never went out of my Way, to enquire after any Thing of this Nature," and so ventures descriptions only of the better sorts, "not designing a Natural History."[11] Persimmons, chestnuts, mulberries, walnuts, wild grapes, sugar maples,

[7]Beverley, *History*, pp. 73–74.

[8]One of Beverley's purposes in writing his *History* may have been to attract French Huguenot and other European settlers. In any case, his book had wide circulation and served that purpose, with two eighteenth-century printings in English and four in French on the continent—Wright's introduction, p. xx.

[9]*Ibid.*, pp. 124–126.

[10]*Ibid.*, pp. 299–300.

[11]*Ibid.*, p. 129.

and wax myrtles get more than passing attention, along with the food plants cultivated by his Indian neighbors: Indian corn, peas, beans, potatoes, tobacco, musk-melons, watermelons, and pumpkins.

In the teeming wildlife of Virginia's woods and waters nature was even more extravagant. Of fish and shellfish, "no Country can boast of more Variety, greater Plenty, or of better in their several Kinds" than the bountiful waters of Chesapeake Bay and its tributary streams. Even in Beverley's day these waters seasonally abounded with herring, shad, rockfish, and sturgeon, crabs, oysters, and shrimp; but "Before the Arrival of the English there, the Indians had Fish in such vast Plenty, that the Boys and Girls wou'd take a pointed Stick and strike the lesser sort. . . ." For the larger sorts, the Indians made weirs in the tidal waters and fish dams with trapped openings on the streams. Sturgeon were roped in the narrow streams, while other species were hunted at night with torch and spear. To illustrate these fishing methods, Beverley brings in here the first of his fourteen engravings adapted from Theodore de Bry's 1590 edition of Thomas Hariot's *Virginia.* These engravings, in turn, were made from the splendid watercolors John White had painted at ill-fated Roanoke Island. In this particular engraving Beverley had his engraver, Simon Gribelin, replace the birds flying overhead in the background with a sequence showing the piratical propensities of the American bald eagle, saying he had "often been pleasantly entertain'd by seeing these [Ospreys] take Fish out of the Water, and as they were flying away with their Quarry, the bald Eagles take it from them again." One morning he and a friend frustrated an eagle that had forced an osprey to drop its prey, and thereby profited by a 2-foot rockfish for dinner.[12]

With the advent of winter the fecund waters of the Bay harbored multitudes "of Swans, Geese, Brants," and ducks of all sorts: "The Plenty of them is incredible," twenty sometimes being had at a single shot. At the interior plantations there were "Wild Turkeys of incredible Bigness, Pheasants [grouse], Partridges, Pigeons," as well as "Bears, Panthers, Wild-Cats, Elks, Buffaloes and Wild Hogs."[13]

All this "and a great deal more was the natural Production of that Country, which the Native Indians enjoy'd, without the Curse of Industry, their Diversion alone, and not their Labour, supplying their Necessities." Their minds uncorrupted by "the Desire of

[12] *Ibid.,* pp. 146–148, xxxv, 151.
[13] *Ibid.,* p. 153.

Hoarding up Treasure: They were without Boundaries to their Land; and without Property in Cattle; and seem'd to have escaped, or rather not to have been concern'd in the first Curse, Of getting their Bread by the Sweat of their Brows; For, by their Pleasure alone, they supplied all their Necessities. . . ."[14]

In contrast to Beverley's confessed ignorance and indifference toward the Virginia plant life, he was thoroughly intrigued by his red neighbors, of whom he had actively sought to learn everything he could. He had studied what had been written of them by such early English adventurers as Arthur Barlowe, Ralph Lane, John White, and John Smith, as well as the less reliable and less pertinent accounts of more distant aborigines furnished by Louis Hennepin and Baron Lahontan. And he could measure what those writers had reported against what he himself had learned through his acquaintances among those natives yet remaining near the English, and others he chanced upon. Consequently, Beverley spoke with well-earned authority of the Powhatans and the related Algonquin Indians of his Virginia.[15]

In his eyes they were physically admirable people, being "of middling and largest stature of the English: They are straight and well proportion'd, having the cleanest and most exact limbs in the World: They are so perfect in their outward frame, that I never heard of one single Indian, that was either dwarfish, crooked, bandy-legg'd, or otherwise mis-shapen."[16] Beverley was almost as generous and uncritical of the Indians' moral standards and customs, which in every age and aspect of their lives, from birth to death, were commonly at variance with English ways.

Instead of the soft cradle and coverlets awaiting an English baby, the newborn Indian was greeted in very different fashion:

the first thing they do is to dip the Child over Head and Ears in cold Water, and then bind it naked to a convenient Board, having a hole fitly plac'd for evacuation; but they always put Cotton, Wool, Furr, or other soft thing, for the Body to rest easy on, between the Child and the Board. In this posture they keep it several months . . . and then let it loose . . . to crawl about. . . .

[14]*Ibid.,* pp. 156, 17.

[15]John R. Swanton, *The Indians of Southeastern United States* (Washington, D.C., 1946), p. 10, and generally on Beverley's Indian material. Beverley's *History* is without rival as a sourcebook for our knowledge of the Algonquin Indians of Virginia. "It was the first attempt by a colonial American to write a 'complete' account of the nature of the Indian"—Roy Harvey Pearce, *Savagism and Civilization* (Baltimore, 1953), pp. 42–43.

[16]Beverley, *History,* p. 159.

Thus bound, the child could be leaned up erect, carried on the mother's back, or dangled conveniently away from vermin.[17]

When the boys reached their middle teens, by way of initiation into manhood and warrior status they were subjected to a trial by ordeal known as the *huskanaw*. According to Beverley, the huskanawing discipline involved caging the youths in isolation from the village and forcing upon them quantities of a nauseous plant brew intended to induce forgetfulness, so that, if they survived their ordeal, they might emerge men free of impediment by their childhood ways. "Thus they unlive their former lives, and commence Men," says Beverley.[18] For girls there was no parallel initiation into womanhood. On the contrary, perhaps by way of advance payment for the traditional toil of the Indian woman, he reports that "the maidens are entirely at their own disposal, and may manage their persons as they think fit. . . . The Indian Damsels are full of spirit. . . . The excess of Life and Fire makes them frolicksom, but without any real imputation to their Innocence." Later he recounts the widely observed Indian custom by which notable guests were given temporary wives, selected from the unattached maidens without their "suffering in their Reputation for this Civility."[19]

Before being provided with such "civility," the visitor would already have experienced the Indians' "peculiar way of receiving Strangers, and distinguishing whether they come as Friends or Enemies . . . by a singular method of smoking Tobacco," in which ritual formalities were strictly observed. Beverley details those peace pipe formalities step by step until the ceremony is ended and the feasting and dancing can begin.[20]

Space precludes more than bare mention of Beverley's highly readable descriptions of the Indians' dwellings, villages, and fortifications, their ways of war, their foods and cookery, their sports and pastimes. The Indians' religion and superstitions, however, were of particular interest to him, perhaps partly because of the reluctance of the red men to discuss such matters with outsiders. One day when abroad in the country, Beverley met an Indian of "extraordinary Character . . . Ingenuity and Understanding" who, with the aid of generous potions of "strong Cyder," was induced to expound the Indians' religious beliefs. The savant explained in detail their faith

[17] *Ibid.*, p. 171.
[18] *Ibid.*, pp. 207, 208.
[19] *Ibid.*, pp. 171, 189.
[20] *Ibid.*, pp. 186–187.

in a "universally beneficent" God, "whose Goodness reach's to the Earth beneath," who "is the giver of all good things . . . but they are shower'd down upon all Men indifferently without distinction; that God do's not trouble himself with the impertinent affairs of Men. . . ." Consequently it served "no purpose either to fear, or Worship him: But on the contrary, if they did not pacify the Evil Spirit, and make him propitious, he wou'd take away, or spoil all of these good things that God had given . . . ," and this evil spirit "expected Adoration and Sacrifice from them, on pain of his displeasure. . . ." This brought to Beverley's mind an earlier expedition during which, while "ranging in the Woods," his party had come upon a native temple or *Quioccosan* set in a circle of posts, each carved with a human head. All the Indians being away "at another place, to consult about the bounds of the Land given them by the English," and curiosity overcoming fear and feelings of impropriety, they had removed the barricade from its door and examined the two-room, 18- by 30-foot cabin "temple" and its arcane contents. In the dim light provided by the single door and the smoke-hole in the roof they had examined the bundles of human bones, sewed up in woven mats and stored on shelves along a wall, a store of decorated tomahawks, and the parts of a dismantled idol and its attire—all that that holy shrine contained. Recalling that visit to the *Quioccosan,* Beverley now turned the conversation to the apparently crude idolatry it indicated. The old Indian confessed: "It is the Priests—they make them believe."[21]

From his discussion of the natives and their ways, Beverley moves on to provide the reader with an account of the "Present State of Virginia," its laws and government, husbandry and improvements, and other colonial ways. After the appearance of Beverley's *History,* almost every significant book dealing with the American scene throughout the eighteenth century would follow to a substantial degree the same format of a book made up of sections dealing with diverse but related subjects. The pattern became so pronounced that in the latter years of the century books of the genre sometimes were veritable literary potpourris.

In December 1700 a young Englishman named John Lawson, destined to make the first significant attempt to describe the natural history of Carolina, set out from Charleston, then the only English

[21] *Ibid.,* pp. 200–201, 195–196.

town south of the Virginia settlements, on what seemed a quixotic voyage.[22] With five other Englishmen, three Indian men, the wife of one of them, and Lawson's spaniel bitch, all packed into a cypress dugout canoe, he left Charleston, planning, in spite of the inclement season, to make his way along the coast to the mouth of the Santee and up the river, through an unexplored wilderness, into the back-country.

Nothing is known of John Lawson before the spring of 1700 when fate, in the form of a chance meeting in London, turned him toward the New World. Being at that time of a mind to travel, he "accidentally met with a Gentleman, who had been abroad. . . . [H]e assured me, that Carolina was the best country I could go to; and that there then lay a ship in the Thames, in which I might have passage."[23]

A few hints of Lawson's background may be gleaned here and there from his writings. His professed English-gentleman status is supported by his obvious familiarity with the ways of gentry, and his good education by the standards of the day. His reference to the color of Dutch ditchwater and his knowledge of French and Italian viniculture imply some acquaintance with the continent. Perhaps also one might infer a north of England background from his frequent use of the physical aspects of Yorkshire as standards of comparison for his observations, though he shows an intimate acquaintance also with London.

Whatever life he left behind in England, the young man who stepped ashore in Charleston in late summer 1700 brought with him a cargo of personal qualities well adapted to the challenges of the new land: physical stamina, an observant eye, an inquiring mind,

[22]John Lawson: *A New Voyage to Carolina; Containing an Exact Description and Natural History of that Country; Together with the Present State thereof and a Journal of a Thousand Miles, Travel'd thro several Nations of Indians, giving a particular Account of their Customs, Manners, etc.* (London, 1709). My citations are to the Chapel Hill edition of 1967, edited by Hugh Talmage Lefler. Other editions of Lawson's work appeared under the title of *Lawson's History of North Carolina.* Several editions, including French and German translations, followed the first London publication in rapid succession. William Byrd II, who had served with Lawson in the planning stages of the famous survey of the boundary line between Virginia and Carolina, copied out most of the natural history of Lawson's work, carefully deleting all his less favorable observations, and sent it to a Swiss promoter of a proposed settlement on a vast tract of land Byrd had acquired on the Roanoke River in the Virginia backcountry. Translated into German and published in Switzerland, it was translated back into English years later and republished as *William Byrd's Natural History of Virginia* (Berne, 1737; Richmond, Va., 1940).

[23]Lawson, *A New Voyage*, p. 7.

and a love of adventure. After only three months in the port city, he set out on his expedition through uncharted and perilous lands —a voyage described nine years later in his fascinating chronicle, *A New Voyage to Carolina.*

Characteristically, Lawson tells us nothing of the purpose of this journey, nor of his intended destination; nor does he identify his companions save by sex and nationality. After leaving Charleston, the party made their tortuous way northward through the tidal creeks behind the low-lying sea islands to Bull's Island, where for two days they were held captive by gale winds, and by night plagued by "Musketoes and other troublesome Insects." There the travelers encountered "Plenty of Fowl, as Curleus, Gulls, Gannets, and Pellicans, besides Duck, and Mallard, Geese, Swans, Teal, Widgeon, etc.," presaging the island's destiny as part of the Cape Romain National Wildlife Refuge. Upon leaving Bull's Island they entered the Santee River, which was then in flood, its waters spread out for miles through the bordering forests of giant cypresses. Against the current of the swollen stream progress was painfully slow; so slow and difficult that after a few days of discouraging progress they abandoned their dugout and took to the Indian path, which ran along the edge of the river's vast flood plain, into the Carolina backcountry, which few white men, other than an occasional anonymous Indian trader, had ever seen and none had described. Along the way most nights were spent where sleep was often disturbed by the sounds of the surrounding wilderness, "the dismall'st and most hideous Noise that ever pierc'd my Ears." It "was customary to hear such Musick along that Swamp-Side, there being endless Numbers of Panthers, Tygers, Wolves, and other Beasts of Prey . . . coming out in Droves to hunt Deer," and flocks of turkeys "coming out of the Swamp" at sunrise. On other occasions inclement weather forced them to accept the ready and generous hospitality of an Indian village and suffer the discomforts of excessive heat, smoke, and the ever present company of surly dogs and myriads of fleas that likewise had taken refuge in the oven-shaped, bark-covered hovels. The weather was often cruel and travel arduous; so much so that one of their number could take no more. This "poor, dejected Traveller with Tears in his Eyes" left them, "to travel back again over so much bad Way. . . ."[24]

[24]*Ibid.*, pp. 13–33.

At one point along the way they were astonished by "a great Noise, as if two Parties were engag'd against each other, seeming exactly like small shot." This great noise proved to be the sounds of the exploding canes of the American bamboo, which grows abundantly through the rich alluvial riverbottoms of the South. The Indians had set them on fire in a band across the neck of a meander of the river to trap the resident game between the encroaching flames and the river's waters—a simplified form of the common Indian practice of fire hunting, by capturing game within an ever-diminishing circle of fire. Further along they stopped at a village of the Congarees, where large "cranes," either American ibises or sandhill cranes, were kept as domestic fowl. At another village they were shown the art of stalking deer by employing a mask and shoulder cover fashioned from the head and forepart of an antlered buck, by which means the hunter may "go as near a Deer as he pleases, the exact Motions and Behaviour being so well counterfieted. . . ."[25]

The travelers' way northward along the Wateree and Catawba rivers often crossed extensive clearings—abandoned Indian fields no longer needed by the natives' sadly diminished numbers, a consequence of susceptibility to many of the white man's contagions to which Indians had little or no inherited resistance. At a town of the Waxhaws, near the present boundary between the Carolinas, the entertainment provided by the "king" for Lawson and his companions was largely a lamentation of that sad decline. "The Burthen of their Song was, in Remembrance of their former Greatness and the Numbers of their Nation, the famous Exploits of their Renowned Ancestors . . . that had (in former Days) been perform'd. . . ." Lawson was impressed by the extraordinary stature of the Waxhaws, tall, straight Indians with their heads flattened, fore and aft, by binding during infancy; thus their eyes were forced to protrude, which gave them, it was said, a frightening appearance and strengthened the eyesight for hunting.[26]

As the small band traveled northeastward across the North Carolina piedmont, there were many wonders to note. It was probably the Valley of the Yadkin that provided these observations:

This Valley afforded as large Timber as any I ever met withal . . . where we saw plenty of Turkies, but pearch'd upon such lofty Oaks, that our Guns

[25]*Ibid.*, pp. 17, 35, 29.
[26]*Ibid.*, pp. 40, 44–45.

would not kill them, tho' we shot very often. . . . Some of our Company shot several times, at one Turkey, before he would fly away. . . .

In the same region were clouds of passenger pigeons, "so numerous in these Parts, that you might see Millions in a Flock; they sometimes split off the Limbs of stout Oaks . . . upon which they roost o' Nights." To Lawson this was superlative country, evoking the conclusion that "The Savages do; indeed still possess the Flower of Carolina, the English enjoying only the Fag-end of that fine Country."[27]

By spring he and some of his ever anonymous companions (others having left to follow the Virginia path northward) had reached the place where the Neuse and the Trent rivers join to become an estuary of Pamlico Sound; there, a few years later, Lawson would establish the city of New Bern (named for its Swiss settlers), one of the two earliest towns in North Carolina, both products of his versatile energy. A few days after his arrival he joined the sprinkling of settlers from Virginia, who had established their raw clearings along the Pamlico River to the north, where Lawson was to make his home, and where he would found the town of Bath, the first town in North Carolina. There he ended the expedition that was the subject of his memorable account, an arduous midwinter trek of 600 miles through the Carolina wilderness.[28]

Lawson begins *A New Voyage to Carolina* with a charming and sprightly narration of this journey, followed by a formal description of the settled parts of North Carolina, before launching into his "Natural History of Carolina," which occupies nearly two-thirds of the book. He gives first a catalogue of the native trees, shrubs, and vines, noting the outstanding qualities of each; next the "Beasts of Carolina" are presented, beginning with the buffalo, bear, and panther, and continuing downward in bulk to mice and moles; his list of the "Insects of Carolina" likewise follows a sequence of diminishing bulk—from alligators to small snakes and lizards. Except for a map of the eastern portions of Carolina, which represented a marked advance over earlier representations, the only illustrations gracing Lawson's *New Voyage* are a buffalo, a bear catching mullet, a big cat attacking a deer, and a raccoon fishing for crabs using his tail for bait!

Lawson's natural history reaches its high point with his bird sec-

[27] *Ibid.*, pp. 50, 51, 61.
[28] Lawson himself called it a 1,000-mile journey.

tion, which represented a major advance in revealing the richness of American bird life. Here he describes some 110 species, about equally divided between land and waterfowl. For many he has anecdotes, such as the visitation in 1707 of the passenger pigeons, the fatal penchant of "mischievous" parakeets for the seeds of the ripening fruit in the settlers' orchards, the piratical ways of the bald eagle, the wonderful flight and artful nest of the hummingbird, the ways of the plentiful droves of turkeys, and the ever varying song of the mockingbird.

Later observers would elaborate and improve upon Lawson's descriptions of the natural history of his part of America. But no later observer has diminished the value of the part of the *New Voyage to Carolina* devoted to its Indians. His "Account of the Indians of North Carolina" is honest and objective, and remains the most complete and authoritative source work on them. Lawson was as generous in charity for what he perceived as the Indians' faults and weaknesses as in his praise for those qualities in which they impressed him as being superior to the white man. "We look upon them with Scorn and Disdain," he wrote, despite the fact that "for all our Religion and Education, we possess more Moral Deformities, and Evils than these Savages do." And he added that "we make way for a Christian Colony through a Field of Blood, and defraud, and make away with those that one day may be wanted in this World."[29]

Early in 1709, Lawson sailed for England to arrange for the publication of his book. After busy months in London seeing his work through the press, conferring with the Carolina Proprietors, receiving from them his commission as surveyor-general, meeting with one of England's foremost naturalists, apothecary James Petiver, a member of the Royal Society, and arranging to become one of his field collectors of specimens in America, Lawson sailed in company with 650 Palatine settlers for the town he had laid out at the confluence of the Neuse and the Trent. It was a terrible voyage. Fewer than half the settlers lived to reach their destination, to which they gave the name New Bern.

The year and a half that Lawson survived after his return to America was a time of equally intense activity. He was laying plans

---

[29] *Ibid.*, pp. 243, 246. Lawson, like Beverley, had an uncommonly generous and enlightened attitude toward the American natives, in marked contrast to William Byrd, Cadwallader Colden, and Lewis Evans—Pearce, *Savagism and Civilization*, pp. 43–46.

to prepare a work on all facets of the region's natural history, collecting and shipping specimens to Petiver,[30] performing the duties of his survey position, supervising his own plantations, and exploring. It was the last activity that led to his doom. On an expedition up the Neuse to determine how far it was navigable, he and his companions were taken captive by Tuscarora Indians; although his companions were released, Lawson, friend and champion of the Indians, suffered death at the stake at their hands.[31]

Lawson's death left unresolved the mystery of the man who, during a mere decade in America, had shed so much light on the Carolina wilderness. It is passing strange that a man who established North Carolina's first two towns, served as surveyor-general under the Lords Proprietors of Carolina and as correspondent and field collector for one of England's foremost scientists, and produced a book successful in several countries, should have left no identifiable record of his life prior to his sudden decision to take passage to Carolina on a boat that lay in the Thames.[32] The knowledge he displays of the geography, the natives, the flora and fauna of his adopted country is remarkable. Unless he arrived in America already trained in natural history, agriculture, land surveying, and mapmaking, one wonders how he garnered the information with which his book is packed.

Lawson had hoped to write a complete natural history of America,[33] and, had he lived, would no doubt have been one of the great naturalists of his time. As it was, he laid a sound foundation for those who were to follow, whose work he himself anticipated: "As to a right knowledge thereof, I say, when another Age is come, the Ingenious then in being may stand upon the Shoulders of those that went before them, adding their own Experiments to what was delivered down to them by their Predecessors, and then there will be something towards a complete Natural History. . . ."[34]

[30]Lawson, *A New Voyage,* introduction, pp. xli–xliv, and appendix, pp. 267–273; Raymond P. Stearns, "James Petiver, Promoter of Natural Science," *Proceedings of the American Antiquarian Society,* new series, LXII (1952), 243–265.

[31]Lawson, *A New Voyage,* pp. xxxi–xxxvi.

[32]For a more complete discussion of Lawson's ten years in America, see Hugh Leffler's introduction to the Chapel Hill edition; see also Henry Savage, Jr., *Lost Heritage* (New York, 1970), Chap. 2.

[33]Lawson, *A New Voyage,* p. xliii.

[34]*Ibid.,* p. 139. Mark Catesby was to be the successor John Lawson anticipated— see Chapter 4 below.

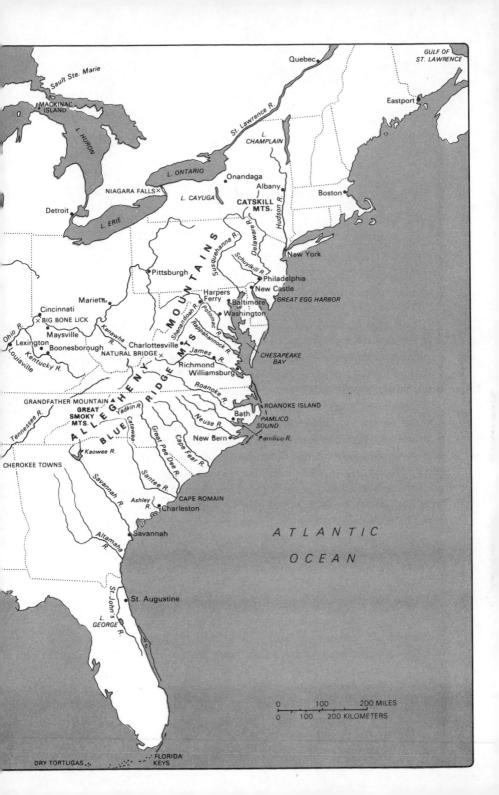

CHAPTER 3

The Discovery of the Mississippi, 1720–1776

DURING the first two centuries of the European discovery of America, its waterways were the only highways available to the explorer.[1] The expeditions of those such as De Soto and Coronado, who had dared to seek freedom from the limitations inherent in these natural highways, had proved of little historical consequence. The trackless forests of the South closed in and obliterated De Soto's trails only a little more slowly than the rains effaced from the plains the hoofprints left by Coronado's vast caravan. Through the years waterways provided the carriage for trade goods destined for the interior and for the essential tools and supplies of those seeking homestead sites in the hinterland. Herein lies the key to the striking contrast between the slowness of the westward progress of English exploration and settlement *vis-à-vis* the giant strides of the French. The rivers of the English colonies were relatively short and, except in New York where the way west was blocked by the Iroquois, they were highways that ended beneath the montane shadows of the evening sun. In marked contrast the St. Lawrence–Great Lakes waterway was a vast natural throughway into the fur-rich northwest wilderness, where a man might quickly garner a fortune.

As early as 1634, a mere quarter century after their first settlement at Quebec, there were Frenchmen settled in the interior as far

[1]The influence of rivers in the development of regional history became the idea behind the "Rivers of America" series, launched in 1937 by Constance Lindsay Skinner to develop the theme, river by river, that "the American nation came to birth upon the rivers."

as Green Bay on Lake Michigan. From the outset the lure of pagan souls, whose salvation inspired the selfless dedication of the Society of Jesus[2] for more than a century, was powerfully augmented by the stimulus of rich harvests of pelts in the western wilderness. In another half century Jesuits and fur traders, conducting in concert their disparate searches, had made their way down the Mississippi to the Gulf of Mexico and affixed the Cross of the Church and the royal seal of France upon the vast heart of America from the Appalachians westward—a domain too boundless and too remote to be assimilated without concentrated effort. Louis XIV, although convinced of the great potential of this imperial domain, found himself too overextended by war and burdened by debt to devote the requisite attention and money to securing his tenuous hold upon it. In the hope of achieving the desired result without expense to the crown, he resorted to grants of colonial proprietorship, a plan similar to that then being used by the British in Maryland, Pennsylvania, and Carolina. In return for generous concessions a wealthy financier, Antoine Crozat, first undertook the settlement of the Mississippi country. By 1717 he confessed failure and surrendered his privileges to his successor, entrepreneur John Law, a Scottish financial genius, then the French king's finance minister. To undertake the settlement and development of Louisiana and the Mississippi Valley, Law organized the Compagnie des Indies, better known in America as the Company of the West. The great public confidence in Law's financial genius, coupled with glowing reports from the region, set off a boom that, as booms have a way of doing, soon burst—a débâcle that earned for Law's company its lasting sobriquet, the Mississippi Bubble.[3]

Among the motley many who, in response to Law's promotion, soon set out for that combination of Eden and El Dorado known as Louisiana, were two men who in the years to come were to make major contributions to the substitution of fact for fiction in the minds of people in France and England. With contrasting backgrounds, these two reporters almost simultaneously entered upon their disparate assignments in Louisiana, appropriately enough,

[2]The Jesuit order founded by Loyola in 1534 to carry the gospel to the heathen —see Francis Parkman, *The Jesuits in North America in the Seventeenth Century* (Boston, 1908); John Bartlett Brebner, *The Explorers of North America, 1492–1806* (New York, 1933), pp. 151–162, 197–213.

[3]W. J. Eccles, *France in America* (New York, 1972), pp. 163–166.

from opposite directions. Young Antoine Simon Le Page du Pratz was a Dutchman with a background of service in the French army; Pierre François Xavier de Charlevoix was a highly educated Jesuit priest of aristocratic birth, who had seen previous service in New France but who, at the time he was selected to explore the Mississippi country, was back in Paris teaching in a Jesuit college.[4] Le Page du Pratz came to America as an official of the Company; Charlevoix as an emissary of the crown. While du Pratz's assignment was commercial, Charlevoix's, though no less material, was on the more exalted level of empire and international rivalry. Nevertheless, years later when the two came to write of Louisiana, the effects of those contrasts seemed minimal in the impressions of Louisiana and the Mississippi they conveyed to their readers.[5]

In 1718, in an initial effort to transform the Company of the West from mere words on paper to more tangible men on land, three ships bearing 800 settlers left La Rochelle for Louisiana. Le Page du Pratz, one of the settlers, was described as an "overseer or director of the public plantations."[6] After three months spent on low, sandy Dauphine Island, at the mouth of Mobile Bay, he and his hired servants departed for the neighborhood where the new governor, sieur de Bienville, was in the process of laying out New Orleans.[7] By small craft they coasted westwardly through the passage into Lake Pontchartrain and along the south shore of the lake to the site of the new capital. New Orleans was marked only by a hut, covered with palmetto leaves, which the commandant had built for his own lodging. Not far from the embryonic New Orleans du Pratz chose a spot for his

[4]Pierre François Xavier de Charlevoix, *Journal of a Voyage to North America* (Paris, 1744); this and subsequent citations are to the Caxton Club edition (2 vols., Chicago, 1923), edited by Louise Phelps Kellogg, p. xiv.

[5]Charlevoix, *Journal*, and Antoine Le Page du Pratz, *The History of Louisiana or the Western Parts of Virginia and Carolina* (2 vols., London, 1763), a translation of the original 3-volume Paris edition of 1758, and a revised, single-volume London edition, 1774. Much of du Pratz's material had appeared earlier in Georges Butel-Dumont, *Mémoires sur la Louisiana* (2 vols., Paris, 1753), Butel-Dumont having had access to du Pratz's manuscript in the preparation of his work—see *Mémoires*, vol. 1, pp. 118–119; Bernard DeVoto, *The Course of Empire* (Boston, 1952), pp. 66, 412. My citations of Le Page du Pratz are to the undated Pelican Press (New Orleans) edition, edited by Stanley Clisby Arthur, the text and illustrations of which are a reprint of the 1774 London edition with its editor's preface.

[6]Du Pratz, *History*, preface, p. i.

[7]Jean Baptiste le Moyne Bienville, sieur de Louisiana (1680–1768), governor of Louisiana (1701, 1717), and founder of New Orleans (1718).

own residence, a hut built near Bayou St. John, to which he moved his menage.[8]

Although du Pratz described his site near New Orleans as convenient to his business and having good soil, his residence there was brief—perhaps only a matter of months—before reports of much more desirable country further upriver set the restless Dutchman on the move again. After augmenting his household with an Indian slavegirl and two newly arrived black slaves, he set out up the Mississippi by dugout, aiming for the greener pastures of Natchez. As they pushed upstream, the supply of game was incredibly bountiful: ducks, geese, flamingos, and alligators—one 19 feet long was shot for the slaves to feast on its tail.

At the Natchez Bluffs the French had built Fort Rosalie, a palisaded post overlooking the river. Nearby, on the path leading to the neighboring Natchez village, du Pratz selected his new plantation of rich black soil, fine forest groves, and a native hut. Through a Natchez interpreter he negotiated the purchase of this tract, which he described as being larger than Paris. There, in close association with the Natchez, he was to spend most of the ensuing eight years —leaving only for business expeditions downriver and explorations upriver and westward to the plains.

Shortly after his arrival among these people who were so soon to be exterminated, his acquaintance with them ripened into admiration and gratitude. During his first summer there he was stricken with pains in his thighs, and the cures prescribed by the New Orleans physicians had proved so ineffectual he was contemplating returning to France. In desperation he accepted the proffered ministrations of the Natchez conjurers, "who are both surgeons, devines and sorcerers." By employing scarifications and poultices, they effected in eight days a complete cure of the crippling affliction that had tormented him for months. Later du Pratz recounts an equally effective treatment of a fistula in his eye.

When his superiors in the Company learned of these cures and others in like vein, du Pratz was asked to seek out the "simples" by which such cures were accomplished and to collect any other plants that might be sources of dyes. In response, he "transplanted in earth, put in cane baskets, above three hundred simples, with their numbers, and a memorial, which gave a detail of their virtues,"

[8]Du Pratz, *History*, pp. 16–20.

which he tells us, were eventually "planted in a botanic garden made for the purpose by order of the Company."[9]

Although the chronology of du Pratz's activities as recorded in his *History* is obscure, it is possible that this impressive collection of plants was among the goods he carried down for shipment from Biloxi early in 1722, when he "met with a large pettyaugre,[10] which belonged to F. Charlevoix the Jesuit, whose name is well known in the republic of letters." He traveled back to New Orleans on this vessel—New Orleans having by then (so Charlevoix's *Journal* tells us) become an aggregation of "two hundred persons, who have been sent out to build a city, and who have settled on the banks of a great river, thinking of nothing but putting themselves under cover . . . and waiting till a plan is laid out for them."[11]

Le Page du Pratz's sixteen years of experience, "with the advantage of being overseer or director of the public plantations, both when they belonged to the company, and afterwards when they fell to the crown," inevitably demanded extensive travels up and down the river where settlements were springing up. His active interest in the discovery and collection of useful plants, and his even more intense interest in the Indians, plus a yen for exploration and mineral discoveries, all meant that he acquired a rare familiarity with much of the Mississippi country. The two maps that appear in his *History,* one covering the lower reaches of the river and the other embracing the entire valley, are ample evidence that he utilized his opportunities to the full. The *History* provides a running description of the country passed in navigating upstream from the marshes of Belise—then the French outpost at the river's most utilized mouth —all the way upstream past New Orleans to Baton Rouge, where the cypresses were so tall they "could never be measured," and the red color of their wood gave that place its name; then higher up the river, beyond the mouth of the Red River, to the Natchez, "so fine and good a country, the natives so obliging and familiar, and the women so amiable"; and on again, past the Yazoo country, with its superior air and soil, to the Arkansas, where the soil is so fertile one need never "manure" it, and the "beauty of the climate" renders its inhabitants "at the same time very gentle and very brave." Further

[9] *Ibid.,* pp. 21–27, 42–45.

[10] These canoe-like vessels, fashioned by hollowing out a large log, were generally the canoe of the Mississippi where submerged snags made bark canoes impractical.

[11] Charlevoix, *Journal,* vol. 2, p. 273; Du Pratz, *History,* pp. 27–30.

upstream at the Chickasaw Bluffs du Pratz reported finding outcroppings of both coal and iron ore, and the country "beautiful, and of excellent quality, abounding with plains and meadows."[12] His knowledge of the river ended with the settlement of Canadians at the mouth of the Illinois.

Du Pratz's contribution to disclosing the Mississippi Valley went far beyond a mere scanning of the banks and immediate environs of the Mississippi. His *History* includes two of the earliest published accounts of expeditions into the western prairie country. One of these was an expedition led by Étienne Veniard, sieur de Bourgmond, a French officer who, in 1723, had established a post on the Missouri about 150 miles above its mouth, and who later visited nations of Plains Indians as far away as western Kansas. The other was one he himself made in company with a band of Indians up the St. Francis River of Arkansas and Missouri.[13]

De Bourgmond's narrative describes a region heretofore unknown. Setting out early in July 1724, from Fort Orleans on the Missouri, he aimed for the country of the Padoucas,[14] Plains Indians who were even then at war with most of the nearer nations friendly to the French. It was a strange array that set out westward into unknown country on a journey that would take four months to complete: a hundred Missouri Indians including their grand chief, sixty-four Osages, a few Frenchmen, and, as a peace offering, two Padouca slaves de Bourgmond had ransomed. His retinue burgeoned as they went along. After three weeks it included 300 warriors, another 300 women, about 500 young people, a handful of Kansas chieftains, and at least 300 dogs.[15] The women and the dogs, to the astonishment of the French, carried prodigious burdens, the dogs dragging along their loads by travois, on poles. On the way there were frequent interruptions as new bands were met with and prolonged peace pipe rituals played out. Progress was slow; the country strange and beautiful. In mid-October along the Kansas River de Bourgmond reported "beautiful meadows, covered with herds of elks and buffaloes," and hills in the distance having the

[12]Du Pratz, *History*, pp. 45–58.

[13]DeVoto, *Course of Empire*, p. 177; John Bartlett Brebner, *The Explorers of North America, 1492-1806* (New York, 1933), p. 283. In Du Pratz' account in his *History*, pp. 59–71, the French officer is identified merely as M. de Borgmont.

[14]Comanches; DeVoto, *Course of Empire*, pp. 184–185.

[15]Du Pratz, *History*, p. 60. A far more full account appeared in the original French edition, vol. 3, Chap. 9.

appearance of ancient castles. Sometimes these "meadows" were so thickly covered with buffalo, elk, and deer that "one could scarcely distinguish the different herds," and along the streams there were "enchanting groves, adorned with grass underneath." "Besides the larger game, these groves afforded a retreat to flocks of turkeys."[16]

Upon entering the Padouca country, the two ransomed slaves were sent forward as messengers to herald de Bourgmond's approach and vouch for his peaceful intent. Consequently, as the caravan neared the main Padouca town, it was welcomed by smoke signals, then by a greeting party that rode out at full gallop, so surprising de Bourgmond that he at first feared he was under attack. Flag ceremonies followed, and then a final punctilious sealing of the welcome by the ritual smoking of the calumet, after which the guests were mounted and escorted into the town.

De Bourgmond's journal tells us that the village's 140 shelters housed some 800 warriors, 1,500 women, and 2,000 children. Polygamy was common, some of the men having as many as four wives. The Indians had no previous acquaintance with firearms and were much frightened by the discharge of those brought by the Frenchmen.[17]

The Padoucas, like most other Plains Indians, placed little or no dependence on agriculture, cultivated no grain, and lived only by hunting. Periodically bands of hunters, often accompanied by their families, traveled out from the town on hunting expeditions of several days duration, with buffalo their usual quarry. Acting in concert, bands of mounted hunters chased small herds into a state of exhaustion, when the young cows could be selected for slaughter. Buffalo supplied most of their needs—food, fresh and dried for later use, skins for bedding, clothing, moccasins, covering for their hunting lodges and for the bullboats they used for river crossings, even the armor to cover their horses in time of war.[18]

In late October, his diplomatic mission accomplished, de Bourgmond set out to return to Fort Orleans. When his party reached the Missouri, they adopted the way of the Plains Indians, fashioning canoes of buffalo hides to carry them downstream to their post. For Le Page du Pratz the most significant revelations of de Bourgmond's journal were that Louisiana maintains its good qualities

[16]Du Pratz, *History,* p. 63–64.
[17]*Ibid.,* pp. 65–66.
[18]*Ibid.,* pp. 66–69.

throughout, and that "the natives of North America derive their origin from the same country, since at bottom they all have the same manners and usages, as also the same manner of speaking and thinking." But he hastened to except from that generality his beloved Natchez, to whom he had become so warmly attached.[19]

Perhaps it was de Bourgmond's glowing account that determined du Pratz to see for himself regions distant from the Mississippi, for he soon launched his own expeditions west into the St. Francis River region of Arkansas and Missouri and eastward into the Chickasaw country of Tennessee—precisely where we do not know, for he had discovered valuable metal deposits and so covered his tracks carefully.

To accompany him, he "pitched upon ten Indians," they being inured to hardship and endowed with patience beyond that of other men. In September, after the annual prairie fires had made travel through the tall grass country much less difficult, they set out on foot. They headed north, crossing the Mississippi several times in the Indian manner by means of rafts made of bundles of canes laid across each other, "a kind of extemporaneous pontoon." To broaden his coverage, du Pratz deployed three scouts, one a league in advance and the others a league distant on either side, periodically communicating with them by smoke signals. The system provided him with a constant and bountiful supply of game.

Along the way one of his scouts reported sighting a flock of

[19] *Ibid.*, pp. 69, 283. Based on his observation of several Indian nations, perhaps as many as a dozen, du Pratz had become convinced that they were of Tartar ancestry. But the Natchez, he believed, were descended from Phoenicians. When Chateaubriand used du Pratz for his background material in his prose epic of the Indian, *The Natchez*, his Natchez powerfully reflected du Pratz's partiality.

James Adair, a native of Ireland who came to Charleston in 1735 and for several decades was engaged in the Indian trade with the Gulf and Mississippi Indians, had a different belief as to the origin of the American Indians. Based upon thirty years residence among the Cherokee, Chickasaw, and Choctaw, the well-educated and articulate Adair energetically championed his thesis that the American Indians were the descendants of the Lost Tribes of Israel—*History of the American Indians* (London, 1775). Other well-known supporters of that belief included John Eliot, Roger Williams, Cotton Mather, and William Penn—*ibid.*, p. vii.

Somewhat earlier, Père Lafitau in his *Moeurs des Sauvages Américains Comparées aux Moeurs des Premiers Temps* (Paris, 1724) had undertaken to prove that the American Indians were the descendants of the ancient Greeks and Romans—a belief Edmund Burke subscribed to. Other fanciful views of the origin and nature of the native American are discussed in Henry Steele Commager's *Jefferson, Nationalism, and the Enlightenment* (New York, 1975), pp. 39–43.

turkeys from which, for want of a dog, he had failed to bag even one. Du Pratz records the sequel:

I went with him and took my dog along with me. On coming to the spot, we soon descried the hens, which ran off with such speed, that the swiftest Indian would lose his labour in attempting to outrun them. My dog soon came up with them, which made them take to their wings, and perch on the next trees. . . . I came near their place of retreat, killed the largest, (and) a second. . . . We might have killed the whole flock; for while they see any men, they never quit the tree they have once perched on. Shooting scares them not, as they only look at the bird that drops, and set up a timorous cry, as he falls.[20]

It was a leisurely expedition. Coming upon a beaver colony, they stopped for several days to observe that creature's amazingly ordered society.[21] Resuming their way, they came upon a herd of buffalo to the windward and approached it with but little caution, the eyesight of buffalo being as poor as their sense of smell is keen. Du Pratz was able to approach close enough to a fat bull to bring him down with a single shot, only to be rewarded with ridicule from his native companions for his ignorance in choosing a bull when he might have taken a cow. To reduce the Indians' wasteful preference for killing cows only, du Pratz explained that he had taken a bull to show them that, if properly prepared, its meat was as edible as that of the cow. To convince them, he prepared "a soup that was of exquisite flavour, but somewhat fat, of the broth boiled from the marrow-bones of this buffalo, the rest of the broth serving to make maiz-gruel, called sagamity, which to my taste surpassed the best dish in France; the bunch on the back would have graced the table of a prince."[22]

The food provided by this wilderness country was not the only thing that pleased the author of the *History*. To gainsay those who might belittle the value of Louisiana, he catalogued the products it could furnish: hides, myrtle wax, timber, pitch and tar, saltpeter, saffron, hemp, cotton, indigo, tobacco, sassafras, sweetgum, maize, peas, rice, and birds. For du Pratz was convinced that Louisiana was

[20]Du Pratz, *History*, pp. 119–121. John Lawson had reported this peculiar turkey propensity in Carolina.

[21]By way of experiment they breached the beavers' dam to see its internal construction and observe the colony's repair activities. They worked in pairs, each apparently at an assigned task. The living quarters, too, were partially dismembered to enable sketches to be made of its construction—*ibid.*, pp. 127–131.

[22]*Ibid.*, pp. 122–123.

superior to any other part of America; after all, "a country fertile in men, in productions of the earth, and in the necessary metals, is infinitely preferable to countries from which men draw gold, silver, and diamonds."[23]

In the manner of Beverley's and Lawson's books, the latter third of du Pratz's work is largely given over to catalogues and brief descriptions of the plants and animals of Louisiana and to an account of its native human inhabitants. His botanical account is mostly of those plants reputed to have medicinal values, according to the plant wisdom of his Indian friends. It is rife with inaccuracies and its illustrations crude, but these deficiencies are readily forgiven when we come to his account of the Indians of Louisiana.[24]

Although du Pratz professed to treat of the several Indian nations of Louisiana, it was the Natchez, among whom he lived for half his sixteen years in America, who dominated his account. In his eyes they were so superior to all other Indians he knew, he was persuaded that they were descendants of Phoenicians who were said to have crossed from Africa to Brazil. This theory was belied by his own account of the similarities between the culture, manners, and customs of the Natchez and those of Beverley's Algonquins and Lawson's Siouans. Indeed, what emerges most strikingly from du Pratz's account is that people of such diverse environments and linguistic stocks, separated by vast wilderness areas across which there was minimal communication, could resemble each other to the degree they obviously did. This is not the place to go into the details of those resemblances; suffice it to say that in almost every aspect of their lives—artifacts, housing, games, peace pipes, sexual customs, and ways of war—there was remarkable uniformity throughout the whole region east of the Mississippi. Perhaps du Pratz's belief that the Natchez were unique can be accounted for by the fact that he knew them intimately and admired them greatly, whereas his acquaintance with others was generally slight or based on hearsay, often prejudiced.

Chief of the differences persuading du Pratz that the Natchez were unique among the American natives was their worship of the sun, symbolized by the eternal flame they maintained in their crude temples, which in other respects—crude idols, chieftain's bones, and all—closely resembled the temple Beverley had surreptitiously

[23] *Ibid.*, pp. 178–186.
[24] *Ibid.*, pp. 200–239.

inspected in Virginia.[25] And while their Great Spirit, the sun god Coyococop-Chill, could do no wrong, there were evil gods who constantly required propitiation through ceremonies or the good offices of a medicine man. All this helped to give rise to the common belief among the partially informed that Indians were devil worshippers.[26] Another Natchez characteristic du Pratz thought unique was the slaughter of their own people, including children, to accompany a deceased king or "sun" to the next world. There is a drawing in the *History* depicting one of these funereal multiple sacrifices, which he witnessed. This custom, which augmented the continuing havoc wrought among the Indians by the white man's diseases, presaged the destruction of the Natchez.[27]

Upon the arrival of a new governor in 1734, du Pratz's position as overseer of plantations was abolished. Later that year he returned to France.[28]

Like Le Page du Pratz's *History*, Charlevoix's *Journal of a Voyage to North America* did not appear until more than two decades after the voyage he described, when interest in Louisiana was again on the rise after the great disillusionment that followed the bursting of the Mississippi Bubble. But upon its appearance it was an immediate and sustained success—a success amply justified by its charming literary style. Charlevoix employed a popular literary device of the day, shaping his account into the form of a series of letters to a French duchess, so skillfully done that they have the verisimilitude of genuine correspondence. The result is an entertaining description of a vast, strange, and exotic region, one with which Frenchmen

[25] *Ibid.*, pp. 312–313.
[26] John R. Swanton, *The Indians of Southeastern United States* (Washington, D.C., 1946), pp. 742ff.
[27] Du Pratz, *History*, pp. 335–339.
[28] Du Pratz's *History* did not appear until 1758, when interest in the American dominions of France was running high in both France and England. English translations appeared 1763 and 1774. The unsigned preface of the latter, reflecting England's special interest in Louisiana, is in substance a brief for its acquisition by Britain, proclaiming, in effect, that acquisition to be the manifest destiny of the English. Its author warns that "they who are possessed of the Mississippi, will in time command that continent," and that its fertile plains "are more valuable than all the mines of Mexico." He urged that the English possess that heartland "at the forks of the Mississippi, where the Ohio falls into that river; which, like another ocean, is the general recepticle of all the rivers that water the interior of that vast continent"— du Pratz, *History*, pp. vi–x.

had bonds of empire and on which Britons were casting covetous eyes.[29]

In the early spring of 1721, even before winter had loosed its grip on the land, Charlevoix's small party had set out up the St. Lawrence in two heavily laden bark canoes aiming for little known regions far to the west, beyond the Great Lakes. Ostensibly, they went to inspect the Jesuit missions beyond the Great Lakes. Actually, Charlevoix sought information that might lead to the long-sought water passage to the South Sea and the fabled Orient, and, additionally, to report to the French crown his assessment of its great new domain in the American heartland.

They soon encountered the scenic highlight of their voyage—the stupendous falls of the Niagara—which Charlevoix described as "the noblest cascade perhaps in the world."[30] He refuted Father Hennepin's typically exaggerated report, which had put the height of the falls at 600 feet, scaling it down to 140 or 150 feet, some 50 less than modern measurements. He also deflated Hennepin's stories of fish being swept over the falls to their death and birds being sucked into them, saying flatly that he "saw nothing of the sort."[31]

By midsummer Charlevoix's party was on Lake Michigan, approaching the French outpost on Green Bay. At Mackinac in the strait leading into Lake Michigan, the newly appointed commandant of Green Bay had joined them. Apparently word of their approach had preceded them, for the Sauk village near the post had prepared an impressive welcome, one that to a marked degree resembled that accorded de Bourgmond at about the same time on the far distant plains of Kansas. As the canoes approached the lakeside village, they were met "with great demonstrations of joy." The natives saluted the new commandant "with a discharge of their muskets," waded out "up to their middle . . . and received him on a large robe composed of several skins of roebucks well sowed together . . . and carried him to his apartment."[32] A four-hour ceremonial welcome ensued. In the esplanade between the Sauk village and the French post the festivities began with the dance of the calumet. In Charlevoix's words:

[29]Kellogg's introduction to Charlevoix, *Journal,* vol. 1, p. xxiii. The *Journal* was so popular that three editions appeared in Paris in 1844 alone, and beginning in 1761 three editions in English appeared in rapid succession.
[30]Charlevoix, *Journal,* vol. 1, p. 336.
[31]*Ibid.,* p. 338.
[32]*Ibid.,* vol. 2, pp. 59ff.

this is properly a military festival in which the warriors are the sole actors.
. . . All those . . . dancing, singing and beating the drum and chichikoue,
were young persons equipt as when they prepared to take the field; they had
their faces painted with all sorts of colours, their heads were adorned with
feathers . . . and the calumet was also adorned with them and was set up
in the most conspicuous place . . . [where it] made a very pretty appearance.
They had erected a post, to which at the end of each dance a warrior came
and gave a blow with his battle-ax [and] proclaimed some of his own
valorous achievements.

At the conclusion, they engraved "a serpent upon the stalk of the
Pipe," and near it placed a plate upon which figures were drawn
representing the alliance or peace, and skins bearing pictographs in
similar vein, some painted on the surface and some worked in with
the hair of porcupines.

With that account Charlevoix begins a long series of descriptive
passages and anecdotes dealing with the Indians he encountered.
That they derived in a large measure directly from previous publications detracts little from their value.[33]

"The Indians," he reported, "are generally well made . . . it is
extremely rare to meet with any who are decrepet, or who have any
external deformity. . . . Their imagination is a sort of prodigy."
Should a forest be

ever so vast or untrodden they will cross it without wandering out of their
way. . . . They are born with this talent. . . . Their eloquence has a strength,
nature and pathos which no art can give. . . . Most of them have really a
nobleness of soul and a constancy of mind, at which we rarely arrive, with
all the assistance of philosophy and religion. . . . Their constancy in torments is beyond all expression. . . . In fact [they are] more estimable and
ought to be looked upon as true philosophers [in] that the sight of all our
conveniences, riches and magnificence affects them so little, and they have
found out the art of easily dispensing with them.[34]

At Green Bay, Charlevoix, finding the season was too advanced
to consider continuing westward beyond Lake Superior, was com-

[33]Most of Charlevoix's borrowings were from the *Jesuit Relations*—reports of
brother Jesuits that, beginning in 1632 and continuing until 1673, had been published annually in France with very limited circulation, mostly among the Jesuits
themselves—R. G. Thwaites (ed.), *Jesuit Relations and Allied Documents, 1610–1791* (73
vols., Cleveland, 1896–1901). See also Edna Kenton (ed.), *The Jesuit Relations and
Allied Documents* (New York, 1925).

[34]Charlevoix, *Journal*, vol. 2, pp. 72–93. Charlevoix contributes here to the concept
of the "Noble Savage." See, generally, Albert Keiser, *The Indian in American Literature*
(New York, 1970); H. N. Fairchild, *The Noble Savage* (New York, 1928); and Benjamin
Bissell, *The Indian in English Literature* (New Haven, 1925).

pelled to defer his primary expedition until the following year. In the interim he decided to journey down the Mississippi to the Gulf —a daring resolve in the face of warnings that whatever route he chose to follow from Lake Michigan to the Mississippi he would encounter furious wars between the Sioux and the Outagamies.

Faced with a choice between the Wisconsin and Illinois river routes, he picked the latter, and set out for the lower tip of the lake and the portage path to the headwaters of the Illinois.

Despite fear of attack, the portage was safely accomplished. Coursing down the Illinois, Charlevoix was enthusiastic in praise of the country through which it flows, describing it as "beautiful, consisting of unbounded meadows where buffaloes are to be seen grazing in herds of two or three hundred. . . ." Further downstream they came to landmarks of the heroic struggles of those earlier French emissaries to this wilderness, LaSalle and Tonti, the Rock and Fort Crèvecoeur where they had established posts, the remains of freshly destroyed Indian villages, and the half-burned bodies of two Indians still espaliered in their execution frames, grim reminders of the bloody war in progress over this lovely country. An entry for October 5, 1721, notes sighting parrots[35] for the first time; four days later came a far more significant entry: "We found ourselves in this river, which makes at present so great a noise in France. . . ." A short distance farther downstream at the confluence of the Mississippi and the Missouri Charlevoix recorded his conviction that "here is the finest confluence of two rivers that, I believe, is to be met with in the whole world, each of them about a half a league in breadth. . . ." Using the frontiersman's guide to fertile land, the presence of "canes" (the native bamboo of the Mississippi Valley and the South), he pronounced the land exceedingly rich and easily prepared for cultivation by simply cutting the canes and firing the area desired. In fact, Charlevoix's was a sustained paean of enthusiasm for this Mississippi wilderness. At the mouth of the Ohio he expresses the belief that "there is not . . . a place in all Louisiana more proper for a settlement than this, nor where it is of greater importance," being the confluence of great rivers leading north, south, east, and west.[36]

The Arkansas country, a few days further downstream, inspired more superlatives: "As to the forests which almost entirely cover

[35]Charlevoix, *Journal*, vol. 2, p. 189; "parrots" were the now extinct Carolina parakeets.
[36]Charlevoix, *Journal*, vol. 2, p. 228.

this immense country, there is nothing, perhaps, in nature comparable to them, whether we consider the size and height of the trees,
or their variety," giant cypresses, pecans, sweetgums, and magnolias among them. This, Charlevoix noted, was the region Hernando de Soto had explored almost two centuries earlier, where
death had ended his wilderness treasure hunt—an association with
the past rarely if ever noted by Mississippi travelers before Charlevoix.

By mid-December he had reached the Yazoo country where, despite the season, he reports "a great many alligators"; undeterred,
"our people . . . bathe in this river as freely as in the Seine." Further
downstream, like other travelers, he was greatly impressed by the
beauty, fertility, and good air of the Natchez region, and regretted
that its selection as the site of Louisiana's metropolis had been
abandoned. Charlevoix's observations of the natives there echo du
Pratz's much more full and intimate account.[37]

Below Natchez, Charlevoix's long-sustained enthusiasm evapo-
rates. The monotonous flat low country evoked as little praise as did
the new capital, still scarcely more than a crude camp on the riverbank. There Charlevoix concluded his account of Louisiana with
these words to the duchess: "Such, Madam, is the country which has
been so much talked of for some years past, and of which so few
entertain a just idea."[38]

Charlevoix never returned to his quest for a waterway to the
Western Sea; but for another half century the wishful conviction
persisted that there was in the heart of the continent an easy way
to the mythical Straits of Anian and thence to the Pacific. Among
those who dreamed of discovering it were Major Robert Rogers, the
famous Ranger, and a fellow veteran of the French and Indian
campaigns, Captain Jonathan Carver, both of Massachusetts. For
the better part of two decades after the close of that conflict, they
struggled to realize the dream they shared. Out of that struggle
would come one of the most significant and revealing books of
eighteenth-century America: *Jonathan Carver's Travels Through the In-*

[37] *Ibid.*, p. 234.

[38] Charlevoix sailed from Biloxi early in 1722 hoping to reach Quebec in time to
attempt again an expedition west beyond Lake Superior; however, after being shipwrecked on the Florida Keys, he was forced to return to Biloxi in a small boat, skirting
the coast all the way. There he took ship again, this time for France. Apparently with
his return to France his projected search for a waterway to the Western Sea died—
vol. 2, pp. 283ff.

terior Parts of North America in the Years 1766, 1767, and 1768.[39]

Carver, although born in Massachusetts, had grown up and married in Connecticut. In 1756, then in his mid-forties,[40] he enlisted in the local company, served as a sergeant at the siege of Fort William Henry in 1757, and eventually rose to captain, thanks partly to his mapmaking talents. Doubtless during the long evenings of talk around campfires Carver and Rogers heard many a tale of the mystery-shrouded regions beyond the Mississippi, and speculations as to where lay the more likely approaches to the legendary Straits of Anian (then believed to extend far into the continent behind the "island" of California), tales that whetted their interest in seeking for themselves the adventure and glory of making their way overland from the Great Lakes to the Strait and thence to the Pacific. Following the defeat of the French their stubbornly held dream was given a substantial boost by the appointment of Rogers as governor at Mackinac. From that trade center at the junction of lakes Huron, Michigan, and Superior he could direct the arrangements for the expedition and forward the necessary supplies to the Mississippi posts.[41] By late spring 1760, with plans made and official support arranged, Carver set out from Boston for Mackinac. In midsummer, their plans completed, he departed that post on the first exploratory leg of their western expedition. Approaching an Ottawa village on Green Bay, he describes his reception: "The Indians began a *feu-de-joi;* in which they fired their pieces loaded with balls . . . in such manner as to fly a few yards above our heads: during this they ran from one tree or stump to another, shouting and behaving as if they were in the heat of battle." Carver was assured by his men that this was their customary welcome.

A few days later, with the blessing of the chief, who hoped that

[39](London, 1778). Carver's *Travels* was an immediate and widespread success. It went into more than thirty editions, including German, French, Dutch, Scottish, and American—John Parker, *The Great Lakes and the Great Rivers: Jonathan Carver's Dream of Empire* (East Lansing, Mich., 1965); Timothy Severin, *Explorers of the Mississippi* (New York, 1968), Chap. 9; W. P. Cumming, S. Hillier, D. B. Quinn, and G. Williams, *The Exploration of North America, 1630–1776* (New York, 1974), pp. 68–69, 79–80.
Carver's travel diary, which had rested unpublished in the British Museum, has been lately published by the Minnesota Historical Society under the editorship of John Parker, who has included in the volume a biographical sketch of Carver with much new material: *The Journals of Jonathan Carver and Related Documents, 1766–1770* (Minneapolis, 1976).
[40]There is wide disparity over the dates given for Carver's birth. The introduction to his *Travels* gave it as 1732, the *DAB* as 1710.
[41]DeVoto, *Course of Empire*, pp. 245ff., 591–592.

the Great Spirit would favor him "with unclouded sky, and smooth waters by day," a beaver blanket and pleasant dreams by night, and "continued protection under the great pipe of peace," Carver left the Ottawa village to follow Joliet and Marquette's Fox-Wisconsin River route of a century ago. It was a beautiful and bountiful one, where Indians raised quantities of corn, beans, pumpkins, squash, and watermelons, and the lakes along the way abounded with fish, while myriads of geese and ducks were fattening themselves on the wild rice, which grew so thick in the shallows that in many places it impeded the passage of the canoes. Carver reports waterfowl so numerous that "frequently the sun would be obscured by them for some minutes together," and that "deer and bears are very numerous."[42]

At the point where the Wisconsin joins the Mississippi, the river is about a mile wide and studded with islands of extraordinarily rich soil, but thinly wooded. At an Indian village on the west bank Carver bought a dugout canoe, his bark canoes being ill adapted to travel on the big stream; "and with two servants, one a French Canadian and the other a Mohawk . . . proceeded up the Mississippi." By the end of October he had reached that widening of the river known as Lake Pepin, 100 miles or more above the mouth of the Wisconsin, where along the shore "large droves of deer are frequently seen feeding . . . and a great plenty of turkeys and partridges. On the plains are the largest buffaloes of any in America."[43]

From time to time, as he made his way upstream, he was a guest at native villages, always meeting with "most hospitable and courteous treatment," which convinced him that "till they are contaminated by the example of their more refined neighbors they retain this friendly and inoffensive conduct"; but he acknowledged their cruelty to their enemies to be a hereditary failing—a cruelty he was later to witness and describe in revolting detail.[44] While he was a guest at a village of the Naudowessie (Sioux), native couriers came in with an alarming report of an imminent attack by a band of Chippewa, powerful enough "to swallow them all up." Invited by his hosts to lead them in the expected battle, Carver undertook instead to serve as mediator, and met with such success that he became a most acceptable guest in Naudowessie villages throughout their country.

[42]Carver, *Travels*, pp. 37–39.
[43]*Ibid.*, pp. 54–56.
[44]*Ibid.*, pp. 25, 338–340, 60–62.

At a place above Lake Pepin, about 30 miles below the Falls of St. Anthony, Carver visited a remarkable cave, called by the Indians *"Wakon-Teebe,"* the Dwelling of the Great Spirit. Approached through a narrow entrance, the interior walls were covered with Indian pictographs cut into the stone, but half concealed by encroaching growths of moss. From far and wide the bones of deceased Sioux were brought for burial near this hallowed place.

Shortly after he left the sacred cave, as winter approached, ice formed on the river and Carver was forced to abandon his canoe, continuing on foot toward the Falls of St. Anthony. Along the way he met a young Winnebago "prince" traveling with his family on an intertribal mission. Having heard much of those falls, the young chief arranged to leave his family behind and join Carver on the path leading upriver. In the wintry silence the roar of the cataract could be heard 15 miles away. As soon as they reached the falls, the chief "began with an audible voice to address the Great Spirit, one of whose places of residence he imagined this . . . wonderful cascade" to be. The falls, which had been named by LaSalle's errant companion, Father Louis Hennepin, after his rescue from the Sioux in 1680, were described by Carver as being "250 yards over" and about 30 feet in height. These measurements and the sketches Carver prepared provided the basis for the frequently reproduced engraving that was to appear in his *Travels.* Although his was a wintry view of the falls, "a more pleasing and picturesque view cannot, I believe, be found throughout the universe." In the rapids below was a small island, "on which grow a great number of oak trees, every branch of which, able to support the weight, was full of eagle's nests," for there "they find a constant supply of food . . . from the animals and fish which are dashed to pieces by the falls."[45]

After pushing yet another 60 miles above the falls to the mouth of the Rum River, which he called the St. Francis, Carver and his companion were forced by bitter weather to turn back and seek winter quarters under shelter. At the mouth of the St. Pierre (the Minnesoto on modern maps), which comes into the Mississippi from the west a short distance below the falls, Carver bade his companion farewell and set out up that river. Following its course westward, by mid-December he was in the heart of "the country of

[45]*Ibid.,* pp. 70, 71.

the Naudowessies of the Plains," a people who in later years became well known as the Dakota or Plains Sioux.[46] When he met the party with whom he would live for the next seven months, he approached them with confidence, "satisfied that the pipe of peace which was fixed at the head of my canoe, and the English colours which were flying at the stern, would be my security." At their village, made up of "a great number of tents, and more than a thousand Indians . . . two of the chiefs presented their hands to me, amidst the astonished multitude, who had most of them never seen a white man before. . . . We began to smoke the pipe of peace."[47]

Captain Carver spent the winter of 1766–67 with these people, living in the cramped intimacy of a Naudowessie tepee. In the spring he left the Indian camp in the company of nearly 300 Indians on their annual pilgrimage to the sacred cave to carry with them their dead for interment, each body bound up in a buffalo skin. Along the way he had found his hosts the most cheerful and happy travel companions he had ever had.[48] At the ceremonies at the cave Carver reports that he was formally installed as an adopted chief, an honor to which he responded with a long speech, rich in hyperbole in the Indian style and delivered in their tongue, which by then he had mastered. Such elation as this new honor may have brought him was soon more than offset by a bitter disappointment. From traders on the Mississippi he learned that his arrangements for the trade goods and supplies he would need to continue his expedition to the Western Sea had gone awry. This left him with no alternative but to return to Mackinac and attempt to remedy things. The route he selected lay far north of that he had taken to reach the Sioux country. He ascended the Chippewa, crossed over to the Upper St. Croix, continued eastward to Lake Superior, thence along its north shore down the rapids of Sault Ste. Marie, and on to Mackinac, where he spent the winter of 1767–68. His observations along the way are revealing: bountiful copper deposits, water in Superior so clear that rocks on the bottom could be clearly seen through 6 fathoms of water, at the Falls of Ste. Marie "one of the most pleasing prospects in the world," where in certain seasons fantastic quantities of fish can be easily caught and, when the lakes froze, fishing

[46]Robert H. Lowie, *Indians of the Plains* (New York, 1954; American Museum of Natural History edn., 1963) pp. 212–213.
[47]Carver, *Travels*, p. 75.
[48]*Ibid.*, pp. 82–86.

through holes in the ice was so successful that "we frequently caught two [trout] at a time of forty pounds each." But for Carver, far more exciting than any of these were the tales he heard of what one might expect to find far to the west in the land of his dreams. There were stories of light-skinned people who farmed the country of the Shining Mountains beyond the prairies and whose common utensils were made of gold. His long-harbored dreams made him quite ready to believe that in those Shining Mountains—so called because of the infinite crystals of which they were composed—could be found "more riches in their bowels, than those of Indostan and Malabar, or those produced on the Golden Coast of Guinea; nor will I except the Peruvian Mines."[49]

Inspired by these convictions, the restless captain left Mackinac for Boston as soon as the lakes became open for travel, in the hope of getting an account of his travels published there and of rebuilding his frustrated plans for the transcontinental expedition. But he met with little encouragement in Boston, and decided to sail for England. In London he renewed his dual efforts to secure a publisher for his *Travels* and to find support for the expedition he hoped to lead. The projected expedition apparently went ahead faster than the publication of his *Travels,* for in its Appendix he says that in 1774 plans had been laid for an expedition under the leadership of Richard Whitworth (a member of Parliament with extensive knowledge of geography), Colonel Rogers, and himself. It was to be manned by fifty or sixty men, including a sufficient number of mariners and artificers "for building forts and vessels." But in the final sentence of the *Travels* he reports its fate: "The grants and other requisites for this purpose were even nearly completed when the present troubles in America began, which put a stop to an enterprize that promised to be of inconceivable advantage to the British dominions."[50] Carver died in 1780, and the torch he had so long carried passed from his hands to others, some of whom will appear in later pages of this work.

In the early decades of this century, long after Carver's *Travels* had faded into obscurity, several historians undertook critical studies of Carver and his book. They made charges of plagiarism, and less substantial charges of want of veracity. It was shown that Carver had borrowed freely from Hennepin, Charlevoix (who had himself

[49]*Ibid.,* pp. 132, 139, 147–148, 122.
[50]*Ibid.,* pp. 541–543.

borrowed from the *Jesuit Relations* much more than Carver borrowed from him), and others.[51] In preparing this chapter I too found additional borrowings, from James Adair's *The History of the American Indians* and from du Pratz's *History*. Such borrowings were mostly confined to the latter parts of Carver's work where, after concluding the account of his travels, he undertakes a description of the American natives, and to its final 100 pages dealing with the natural history, where most of the passages derived from du Pratz appear.

The fact remains that few if any eighteenth-century works had a more widespread impact than Carver's *Travels*. Through other writers the circles of its influence spread far and wide. The *Travels* became a source of inspiration and material for Victor Hugo and Chateaubriand in France, for the poet Schiller in Germany, for Bulwer-Lytton in England, and James Fenimore Cooper in America, to mention some who thus augmented Carver's influence in the revealing of America.[52]

[51]E. G. Bourne, "The Travels of Jonathan Carver," *The American Historical Review,* XI (1906), 287–302; W. Browning, "The Early History of Jonathan Carver," *Wisconsin Magazine of History,* III (1920), 291–305; Louise Phelps Kellogg, "The Mission of Jonathan Carver," *Wisconsin Magazine of History,* XII (1928), 127–145. Much of criticism leveled at Carver in the past will likely be quieted by the 1976 publication of Carver's *Journals,* cited above.

[52]Bourne, "Travels of Jonathan Carver"; J. M. Gautier, "Un Inspirateur Anglais de Chateaubriand et de Schiller: Jonathan Carver," *Revue de Littérature Comparée,* XXIII (1949), 416–422; J. M. Gautier, "Une Source de Victor Hugo," *ibid.,* XXIV (1950), 446–447; Thomas Philbrick, "Source of J. Fenimore Cooper," *American Literature,* XXXVI (1964), 109–214.

CHAPTER 4

The Eighteenth-Century Natural History Circle

THE scientific discovery and description of the thousands upon thousands of plant species that graced America's wide and varied terrain, and the rich animal life that this plant life supported, presented quite different problems from those that challenged the explorers in search of geographical knowledge. Mountains and passes through them, rivers and lakes, forests and prairies and the ways over and across them beckoned the traditional explorer of the American wilderness. A rapid cross-country passage might serve to embellish the maps of vast regions with geographical features, while the botanist or zoologist accompanying the geographical explorer could hope to accomplish little more than a superficial discovery of the flora and fauna of the region, and that only along the traveled path. Since many plants are highly specialized in their environmental requirements, the plant collector cannot hope to discover the plant life of a region without exploring all the topographical variations of the entire area. The same is true to a somewhat lesser degree of fauna supported by the region's flora. Consequently, the discovery of the natural history of America required the contributions of numerous explorer-naturalists, and a high degree of cooperation among them, exchange of knowledge and specimens, publication of findings, and the support of personal or institutional patrons. In short, it called for vast and informal concert of effort.[1] With the exaltation of scientific interest in the Age of Enlighten-

[1]A striking illustration of this aspect of scientific exploration is displayed in Elsa Guerdrum Allen, "The History of American Ornithology Before Audubon," *Transactions of the American Philosophical Society,* new series, XLI, Pt. 3 (1951), in which she

ment, that concert of effort stimulated the evolution of natural history circles among those dedicated to the advancement of scientific knowledge.

Such a circle came into being in England in the latter years of the seventeenth century and the early decades of the eighteenth with James Petiver, for whom John Lawson was collecting at the time of his death, as one of its central figures. Another was Sir Hans Sloane, whose extensive natural history collections were to become the nucleus of the British Museum. Samuel Dale and William Sherard were two more of this group who often gathered at the Temple Coffee House. Their joint and several efforts played an important role in disclosing American natural history. Like the Royal Society, of which most of the circle were members, the group initiated expeditions, contributed financial support to collectors and naturalists in the field, and maintained a worldwide correspondence with like-minded people: Petiver was said to have had some eighty correspondents in the New World alone.[2]

In 1719 Dale proposed that the group sponsor a young acquaintance, Mark Catesby, recently returned from visiting relatives in Virginia, "with paintings of Birds, etc., which he hath done [who] may be very useful for the perfecting of Natural History," as "he intends againe to returne. . . ." As it turned out, this was a proposal of great moment in the story of the natural history of Britain's American colonies. As a lad in his native Essex, Mark Catesby had been possessed by an inclination "to search after Plant and other Productions of Nature," an inclination that had persisted through the years to April 1712, when, at the age of twenty-nine, he landed in that "Earthly Paradise," Virginia, to satisfy his "passionate Desire of viewing . . . the Animal and Vegetable productions in their native countries; which are strangers to England."[3]

---

treats some forty naturalists who made significant contributions to the knowledge of American birds prior to Audubon.

[2]George Frederick Frick and Raymond Phineas Stearns, *Mark Catesby, The Colonial Naturalist* (Urbana, Ill., 1961), pp. 17–18; Raymond Phineas Stearns, *Science in the British Colonies of America* (Urbana, Ill., 1970).

[3]Mark Catesby, *The Natural History of Carolina, Florida, and the Bahama Islands; Containing the Figures of Birds, Beasts, Fishes, Serpents, Insects, and Plants: Particularly the Forest-Trees, Shrubs, and Other Plants, Not Hitherto Described, or Very Incorrectly Figured by Authors. Together with Their Descriptions in English and French. To Which, Are Added Observations on the Air, Soil and, Waters; with Remarks upon Agriculture, Grain, Pulse, Roots, Etc. To the Whole Is Prefixed a New and Correct Map of the Countries Treated of* (2 vols., London, 1729–47), vol. 1, p. 1. The biographical data on Catesby is based largely on the Frick

Catesby remained in Virginia for seven years, roaming widely from Williamsburg, even venturing into the little known backcountry as far as the Blue Ridge. He became a frequent guest at Westover, the palatial plantation home of the cultivated but eccentric and flamboyant William Byrd II, member of the Royal Society and brother-in-law to Robert Beverley. In his *Secret Diary,* Byrd provides beguiling glimpses of the young naturalist hunting for hummingbird nests, sighting a bear cub in a tree, advising his host on his gardens, and even singing merrily of a June morning.[4] But, as Catesby later "was ashamed to own," except for "sending from thence some dried specimens of plants and some of the most specious of them in tubs of earth at the request of some curious friends," amongst whom was Mr. Dale, those Virginia years were mostly given over to gratifying his "inclination in observing and admiring the various productions of those Countries."[5]

More than two years passed before Dale's proposal that the Temple Coffee House group should sponsor Catesby's return to America was realized. It was 1722 before the naturalist sailed again for America, this time not for Virginia but Carolina, a change in destination prompted perhaps by the wide attention then directed toward Britain's southernmost Atlantic coastal colony, and the power of suggestion of Lawson's popular work on the natural history of that region. Thanks to his Virginia apprenticeship, Catesby, during a stay of less than three years in Carolina, more than fulfilled his exacting obligations to his sponsors. He developed and perfected his skill as an artist, and gathered the specimens, notes, sketches, watercolors, and other material for the magnificent work to which he was to devote the remainder of his long life. The *Natural History* occupied Catesby's talent, industry, and zeal for more than twenty years; completed in 1743, it remains the most valuable contribution to the natural history of colonial America.

During Catesby's first year, his expeditions in the environs of Charleston revealed a region that had an "even greater variety" of flora and fauna than Virginia. Exploring along the Savannah, 150 miles above its mouth, Catesby "was delighted to see Nature differ

and Stearns biography cited above. See also Henry Savage, Jr., *Lost Heritage* (New York, 1970), pp. 57–92.

[4]Louis B. Wright and Marion Tinling (eds.), *The Secret Diary of William Byrd of Westover. 1709–1712* (Richmond, Va., 1941), pp. 523, 534–544, 585–592.

[5]*Natural History*, vol. 1, p. 1.

in the Parts and to find [t]here an abundance of things not to be seen in the lower parts," while the red hill country beyond afforded not only a

succession of new vegetable appearances, but the most delightful Prospects imaginable, besides the diversions of hunting Buffaloes, Bears, Panthers, and other wild Beasts. In these excursions I employ'd an Indian to carry my Box, in which, besides Paper and Materials for Painting, I put dry'd Specimens of Plants, Seeds, etc. as I gather'd them. To the Hospitality and Assistance of these friendly Indians I am much indebted, for I not only subsisted on what they shot, but their First Care was to erect a Bark Hut, at the Approach of Rain to keep me and my Cargo from Wet.[6]

That statement in his Preface gives little suggestion of the ordeal and struggle of those busy years in a raw and turbulent colony, beset during his stay by hurricane, earthquake, yellow fever, and other virulent epidemics, as well as attacks by pirates on the sea and Indians in the interior. Of one of these vicissitudes Catesby reports:

about the middle of September here fell the greatest floud attended with a Hurricane that has been known since the country was settled. Great numbers of Cattle, Horses, Hogs, and some people were drowned. The Deer were found frequently lodged on high trees. The wind was so violent that it tore up by the roots great numbers of Trees, and disrobed most others of their leaves, Cones, and seed. . . .[7]

Catesby, however, was more fascinated than fearful of that terror of most newly arrived Europeans, the rattlesnake, reporting cheerfully enough that a "monster" of 8 or 9 pounds "was gliding into the house of Colonel Blake of Carolina and had certainly taken his Abode there undiscovered had not the domestick Animals alarmed the Family with their repeated Outcries [and in] Wrath and Indignation, surrounded him, but carefully kept their distance . . . while he, regardless of their threats, glided slowly along." He adds that rattlesnakes are "never the Aggressors except in what they prey upon; for unless they are disturbed they will not bite and when provoked they give Warning by shaking their Rattles. They are commonly believed to be the most deadly venomous Serpent of any of these parts of America."[8]

In portraying his wilderness creatures, Catesby often pictured

[6]*Ibid.*, pp. viii–ix.
[7]Frick and Stearns, *Catesby*, p. 24.
[8]*Natural History*, vol. 2, p. 41.

them in company with botanical or other scientific subjects, sometimes for artistic effect but more often because of environmental associations. In so doing, he anticipated the popular scientific illustrations of the next century, most notably Audubon's great works. Catesby employed this device most often in his bird paintings: the "Parrot of Carolina" with the "Cypress of America," the mast of which was the favorite fare of the now extinct Carolina parakeet; the hummingbird and its favorite, the red-flowering trumpet vine; and the Baltimore oriole with the striking tulip tree, a combination Audubon would emulate a century later.

Although the dominant interest of Catesby's patrons was botany, the most popular science of the day, in America Catesby's interest veered increasingly toward ornithology, so that, when his great work was done, he had set a mark in American ornithology that would stand until the publication years later of Alexander Wilson's *American Ornithology,* [9] and by the end of his years in the Carolinas he could truly say that "very few Birds have escaped my Knowledge except some Water Fowl."[10] Among the birds he illustrated and described, Catesby's favorite was the mockingbird, which he depicted beautifully on a spray of flowering dogwood. "The Indians," he reported, "by way of Eminence or Admiration, call it Concontlatolly, or four hundred Tongues; and we call it . . . the Mock-Bird, from its . . . imitating the Notes of all Birds from the Hummingbird to the Eagle. . . . They may be said not only to sing but to dance" in a formal ritualistic way, with "many pretty antic gesticulations with their Melody."[11]

One of Catesby's favorite collecting areas near Charleston was the dense subtropical forest bordering the Ashley River, in which Colonel Blake and his neighboring planters had hewn openings for cultivation. There, easily available, were the models for his colorful parakeet and cypress painting; there also the habitat of the spectacular great ivory-billed woodpecker, with its 3-inch beak, "as white as ivory." "The bills of these Birds," he wrote, "are much valued by the Canada Indians, who make Coronets of them . . . fixing them . . . in a Wreath, with their points outward. The Northern Indians having none of the Birds in their cold Country, purchase them from

[9]Philadelphia, 1808–14.
[10]*Natural History,* vol. 1, p. ix.
[11]*Ibid.,* p. 27. Catesby is credited with describing and illustrating 109 species—Allen, *History of American Ornithology,* pp. 465–467.

the Southern People at the price of two, sometimes three Buckskins a Bill."[12] In the pine flats beyond the Ashley he readily found the subjects for his paintings of the pitcher plant and its related species, the hooded trumpet and the golden trumpet, which he depicted with the frogs of the area. Catesby's illustrations were the first known depictions of these decorative and interesting *Sarracenia,* an exclusively American genus of carnivorous plants, most species of which are restricted to the Southeast.[13]

Catesby does not locate his observations of the passenger pigeons, but doubtless he witnessed their incredible flights in the oak-rich hill country along the Upper Savannah. These now extinct birds came "in Winter to Virginia and Carolina, from the North, in incredible numbers; in so much that in some Places where they roost which they do on one another's Backs, they often break down the Limbs of Oak with their weight; and leave their Dung some inches thick under the Trees." They stripped the woods of acorns and other masts. He described a flight in Virginia as lasting three days, "with not the least interval in losing sight of them."[14]

With these few tastes of Mark Catesby's monumental work in America we must follow him back to London, where for the next twenty years he dedicated himself to completing the task he had set. His field drawings received high praise from his patrons and others of the natural history circle, but financial backing for his projected work was more elusive. Undaunted, he taught himself to engrave as he had taught himself to be an artist, albeit with emphasis upon accurate depiction, without the "niceties" of perspective. His drawings of plants were always done with specimens "just gathered," and his animals, particularly the birds, were painted while alive; and "where it could be admitted I have adapted the Birds to those Plants on which they fed or have any relation to. . . ."[15]

Beset by financial troubles, Catesby sought a loan from a friend and fellow enthusiast, Peter Collinson, a Quaker wool merchant, who had assumed the role left vacant by the death of Petiver, that of nucleus of the natural history circle with its ever-widening circumference. This remarkable man—whose trade involved him with numerous correspondents in the colonies and countries all over the

[12]*Natural History,* vol. 1, p. 16.
[13]John K. Small, *Manual of the Southeastern Flora* (New York, 1933), pp. 580–583.
[14]*Natural History,* vol. 1, p. 23.
[15]*Ibid.,* p. vi. Catesby's mentor in the art of engraving was the painter, Joseph Groupy.

world, and whose scientific correspondents included such figures as Linnaeus, Johann Gronovius, and Johann Dillenius—served for many years as clearinghouse for communications and specimens from naturalists from the far corners of the earth.[16] Not long after the first volume of Catesby's *Natural History* was completed, Collinson, with Sir Hans Sloane, successfully proposed him for membership in the Royal Society.[17]

Catesby's great work in its completed form consisted of two magnificently illustrated folio volumes depicting and describing the flora and fauna of those parts of America he had visited, with emphasis on botany and ornithology, but with mammals, fish, reptiles, insects, and shells also included; descriptive texts in both English and French appear on the page opposite each plate. Into those volumes had gone almost half his life, that of arduous journeys into the wilderness areas of Virginia and Carolina with all their incidental hardships and hazards; but above all they represented years of tedious solitary toil. The initial 100 copies of the first volume alone entailed laboriously getting 10,000 engravings from his painstakingly prepared copper plates, then separately water-coloring every leaf, flower, and feather on each of these engravings. It is difficult to overestimate the importance of Catesby's extraordinary achievement and the resulting stimulation of interest in the fauna and flora of America. Unique in its day, his impressive and highly regarded work did much to acquaint Europeans with the natural productions of America in a way that more scientific but nonpictorial works could not do. Unquestionably his *Natural History*, with its two later English editions and several pirated editions on the continent, played a significant role in Europe's continuing discovery of America.[18]

A most fascinating aspect of that continuing discovery was the evolution during the eighteenth century of a natural history circle in America itself, a delightful brotherhood. It was a diffuse circle, with circumference elastic enough to stretch across a wide geography and embrace kindred spirits however remote; without formal organization, but sufficiently tight-knit to permit its members to enjoy an intellectual intimacy and nourishing climate for the seeking

[16]Norman G. Brett-James, *The Life of Peter Collinson* (London, n.d.); Brooke Hindle, *The Pursuit of Science in Revolutionary America, 1735–1789* (Chapel Hill, N.C., 1956), pp. 11ff.

[17]Frick and Stearns, *Catesby*, pp. 38–39.

[18]*Ibid.*, pp. 99–108, 109–110. In Allen, *History of American Ornithology*, pp. 463–478, the author calls Catesby the "Founder of American Ornithology."

and dissemination of new knowledge. The tireless pen and purposeful drive of Peter Collinson in his dockside office on the Thames fostered the creation of the circle. He it was who stimulated fraternal bonds almost to the point of giving it substance, enabling it, without semblance of formal organization, to remain viable well into the nineteenth century.

From its earliest days the circle's center was in Philadelphia, or, more specifically, at Kingsessing, 4 miles from the city on the lush farm of John Bartram. There, on a hillside running down to the Schuylkill, the Quaker Bartram, born in 1699, was developing the first botanical garden in the colonies. In the environs of Philadelphia, then the intellectual capital of Britain's American colonies, lived a sizable group of men with scientific interests, many of whose botanical interests are immortalized in plant names: James Logan, the two Bartrams, Benjamin Franklin, Benjamin Smith Barton, Humphry Marshall, Benjamin Rush, David Hamilton, and other lesser lights. Thanks largely to Peter Collinson, who often arranged by letter the introduction of Americans to fellow colonials with similar interests, the circle reached out to embrace botanical enthusiast Cadwallader Colden of New York, already widely known for his book *The History of the Five Nations;* [19] John Clayton, Isham Randolph, and Dr. John Mitchell in Virginia; and Dr. Alexander Garden of Charleston.

At least in its earlier years, John Bartram's farm was the nucleus of the circle, while Bartram himself, on his wide-ranging botanical quests, augmented Collinson's correspondence by facilitating much of the interchange among its members.[20] Honest, independent, energetic, and insatiably curious, Bartram gradually built up his own knowledge and the first real botanical garden in America, a project that led to his recognition as America's first notable native botanist.[21]

[19]London, 1727, 1747.

[20]Hindle, *Pursuit of Science,* pp. 11–58, provides a scholarly account of the evolution of the natural history circle.

[21]William Darlington, *Memorials of John Bartram and Humphrey Marshall with Notices of their Botanical Contemporaries* (Philadelphia, 1849), pp. 37–44. Subsequent citations to this work are to the 1967 edition, edited by Joseph Ewan (New York and London, 1967). Most of the biographical material on John Bartram can be found in Darlington. For other sources, see Savage, *Lost Heritage,* Chap. 4; John Bartram, "Diary of a Journey Through the Carolinas, Georgia, and Florida, From July 1, 1765, to April 10, 1766," annotated by Francis Harper, *Transactions of the American Philosophical Society,* new series, XXXIII, Pt. 1 (Philadelphia, 1942), introduction; Josephine

The relationship between Peter Collinson and John Bartram, one of the fortunate chances of history, is an example of symbiosis at its most felicitous. When their fruitful association began, Collinson, tied to his wool business in Gracechurch Street, sought in the colonial farmer a means to satisfy his own insatiable hunger for American plants; while the farmer Bartram, with a growing family to support, saw in the London merchant's patronage an opportunity for financial support of his longed-for botanical explorations. Their relationship soon developed into a professional arrangement by which Bartram traveled ever wider afield for an expanding group of wealthy, mostly titled patrons. So the merchant became the catalyst in the transformation of an almost unlettered farmer into such a respected figure in international natural history circles that Linnaeus himself would describe him as the greatest natural botanist in the world.[22]

During their more than thirty-year correspondence—a rich exchange of scientific information, philosophical ideas, and personal anecdotes—letters from Bartram were often read to the Royal Society. The journals kept faithfully by Bartram of every expedition were likewise shared and often passed on by Collinson to other correspondents, and in several instances published in London.

The comfortably settled auditors of the Society could little appreciate the hazards and hardships behind those simple letters and journals. In 1738 Bartram reported having gone south

as far as Williamsburgh, so up the James River to the mountains in many very crooked turnings and windings, in which, according to the nearest computation I can make. . . . I travelled 1100 miles in five weeks time; having rested but one day in all that time . . . I gathered abundance of seeds. . . . Indeed, beyond the mountains in Virginia and Pennsylvania, there is a great variety, that I saw; and the inhabitants say the ground is covered with delicate beautiful flowers in the spring. . . .[23]

Herbst, *New Green World* (New York, 1954); and Helen Gere Cruickshank (ed.), *John and William Bartram's Trails* (New York, 1957). There are many descriptions of John Bartram by his contemporaries; see, for example, J. Hector St. John de Crèvecoeur, *Letters from an American Farmer* (New York, 1963), pp. 181–193; and E. G. Swem (ed.), *Brothers of the Spade, Correspondence of Peter Collinson of London and John Custis of Williamsburg, Virginia* (Barre, Mass., 1957), p. 50.

[22]Donald Culross Peattie, *John Bartram* in *Dictionary of American Biography* (New York, 1929), II, p. 26.

[23]Darlington, *Memorials*, pp. 120–121.

Frequently, he traveled north. In one instance he went in company with Lewis Evans, surgeon, surveyor, and cartographer, and Conrad Weiser, an Indian interpreter, on an official mission to the Five Nations. Their route took them through St. Anthony's Wilderness and a great pine and spruce swamp, "full of roots and abundance of old trees lying on the ground or leaning against live ones. They stood so thick we concluded it almost impossible to shoot a man at 100 yards. . . ."[24] The map prepared by Evans based partly on that expedition was published in 1755 as the *General Map of the Middle British Colonies in America*, with a valuable geographical essay that suggests in its Bunyanesque place names the hazards and hardships of a journey through a vast wilderness of "Endless Mountains," "Dismall Vales," and "Impenetrable Mountains."[25]

Usually, however, Bartram traveled without company on long, lonely journeys, occasionally brightened by visits with other naturalists, most of whom had been introduced to him by Collinson. Among his hosts on Virginia excursions was John Clayton, Clerk of Court at Gloucester, Virginia, for whom the delicate spring beauty *Claytonia* is named. Gronovius, famed botanist of Leyden, had based his *Flora Virginica* upon Clayton's herbarium.[26] Another Virginian of Bartram's acquaintance was Dr. John Mitchell—of Urbana on the Rappahannock but educated in Edinburgh—for whom is named the charming little evergreen herb we call the partridgeberry and the Canadians *pain de perdrix, Mitchella repens.*[27] Mitchell's

[24]John Bartram, *Observations on the inhabitants, climate, soil, rivers, productions, animals, and other maters worthy of notice. Made by Mr. John Bartram, in his travells from Pensilvania to Onondago, Oswego and the Lake Ontario, in Canada. To which is annex'd, a curious account of the cataracts at Niagara. By Mr. Peter Kalm, a Swedish gentleman who travelled there* (London, 1751); Hindle, *Pursuit of Science*, p. 32.

[25]Lewis Evans, *A General Map of the British Colonies in America* (Philadelphia, 1755). For a comparative account of the ten different editions of this map published between 1755–1807, see Henry N. Stevens, *Lewis Evans, His Map of the Middle British Colonies in America* (London, 1905); see also Lawrence H. Gipson, *Lewis Evans* (Philadelphia, 1939).

[26]Leyden, 1739, 1741. For biographical information on Clayton, see Edmund and Dorothy Smith Berkeley, *John Clayton, Pioneer of American Botany* (Chapel Hill, N.C., 1963).

[27]Mitchell's *Nova Genera Plantarum* (Nuremburg, 1748) was dedicated to Peter Collinson. For biographical information on John Mitchell, see Edmund and Dorothy Smith Berkeley, *Dr. John Mitchell, The Man Who Made the Map of North America* (Chapel Hill, N.C., 1974).

famous *Map of the British and French Dominions in North America* had gone through at least nineteen editions by 1792.[28]

Two other Edinburgh-educated physicians who hosted the wide-ranging Bartram were Cadwallader Colden of New York and Alexander Garden of South Carolina, upon both of whom Linnaeus had conferred a measure of immortality in the naming of *Coldenia* and *Gardenia*. With a letter of introduction from Collinson, Bartram stopped at Colden's estate near the Catskills in 1742 and was delighted to find the doctor "one of the most facetious, agreeable gentleman" he had ever met with.[29] That agreeable gentleman was also New York's surveyor-general and lieutenant-governor, member of its council, a scholar and botanist, and one of the first colonials to master the Linnaean system of plant classification. His *History of the Five Nations,* the earliest chronological account of the historically immensely important Iroquois, was highly esteemed in America and abroad.[30] Colden agreed with John Lawson that for the injustices imposed on the American natives, "we have reason to be ashamed. . . . Instead of Vertues we have taught them Vices." And he warned that the harvest of that treatment would turn those potential friends into "faithless, Thieves and Robbers," who would join with every enemy of the colonists.[31]

It was while visiting at "Coldengham" that John Bartram met the urbane Scot Dr. Garden, who had traveled north to escape the climate of South Carolina, which he deplored as a "horrid country where there is not a living soul who knows the least *iota* of Natural History." Garden was fascinated by the simple plant man, in whom he saw one "distinguished by genius, acuteness and liberality, as well as by eminent botanical learning and experience." Bartram was equally impressed by the doctor. Although most of Garden's considerable work on American fishes, reptiles, insects, and plants was simply assimilated into the *Systema Naturae* of Linnaeus, he nevertheless gained wide enough recognition as a scientist to be elected to

[28]London, 1755; Hindle, *Pursuit of Science,* p. 58. For a detailed discussion of the importance of Mitchell's map, see Berkeley, *Dr. John Mitchell,* pp. 175–211.

[29]Darlington, *Memorials,* pp. 142–161.

[30]See Hindle, *Pursuit of Science,* pp. 38–48.

[31]Cadwallader Colden, *The History of the Five Indian Nations* (Ithaca, 1958; reprint of 1747 edn.), p. vi. For biographical data on Colden, see Alice Mapelsden Keys, *Cadwallader Colden* (New York, 1906), and *The Letters and Papers of Cadwallader Colden, 1711–1775* (New York, 1918–37).

fellowship in the Royal Societies of Uppsala, Edinburgh, and London.[32]

Alexander Garden, brilliant and talented in many fields, was a man of emphatic opinions. He often deplored the fact that there were so few naturalists among the English colonists, whom he considered on the whole ignorant and careless of their wealth of flora and fauna, thus leaving the field open to more enterprising foreigners. One such was a tall young Swede named Peter Kalm, sent to America by the Swedish Academy to seek out plants suitable to Sweden's soil and climate. "The learned Dr. Kalm," Garden complained, "went home to Sweden laden with the spoils of our northern colonies [. . . it] looks as if we must be obliged to strangers to point out our own richness. . . ."[33]

Kalm's mission was a reflection of the passion, indeed almost obsession, for natural science and particularly botany that swept eighteenth-century Europe like a religion. One of its high priests, Carl Linné or Linnaeus, whose system of classification brought order and coherence to the study, attracted to his classroom at Uppsala an ardent group of young disciples who then, like the knights of Camelot in search of the Holy Grail, scattered over the face of the globe in search of nature's treasures.[34] Many of these eager crusaders disappeared into the jungles of Africa or South America never to emerge. Kalm, a favorite of Linnaeus's—who honored his disciple by assigning his name to one of America's most beautiful flowering shrub families, the mountain laurels or *Kalmia* —was more fortunate.

This young gleaner of American riches left Sweden for America "in the name of the Lord right after dinner, on October 5, 1747." He stopped in England long enough to secure Peter Collinson's official blessing in the form of letters of introduction to Franklin, Colden, and Bartram. "I found that I had come to a new world," he wrote soon after his arrival in Pennsylvania the following September;

[32]Darlington, *Memorials*, p. 327; Hindle, *Pursuit of Science*, p. 53; also on Garden, Edmund and Dorothy Smith Berkeley, *Dr. Alexander Garden of Charles Town* (Chapel Hill, N.C., 1969). Carolus Linnaeus, *Systema Naturae* (Stockholm, 1767).

[33]Berkeley, *Dr. Alexander Garden*, pp. 41–42.

[34]For a biography of Linnaeus, see Wilfrid Blunt, with the assistance of William T. Stearn, *The Complete Naturalist, a Life of Linnaeus* (London, 1971); also Donald Culross Peattie, *Green Laurels* (New York, 1938), pp. 78–141; and Sir James Edward Smith (ed.), *A Selection of the Correspondence of Linnaeus and Other Naturalists* (2 vols., London, 1821).

everywhere such plants as I had never seen before. All the trees were yet as green and the ground still as much covered with flowers as in our summer. Thousands of frogs croaked all night long in the marshes and brooks. The locusts and grasshoppers made likewise such a great noise that it was hardly possible for one person when speaking to understand another. The trees, too, were full of birds, which by the variety of their fine plumage delighted the eye, while the infinite variety of their tunes was continually re-echoed.[35]

Kalm lost no time in seeking the guidance of John Bartram, whom he recognized as one who has "acquired a great knowledge of natural philosophy and history . . . and many rare plants which he first found," and who possessed "that great quality of communicating everything he knew." In all, Kalm spent three and a half years traveling in New York, Pennsylvania, New Jersey, and Canada, observing, questioning, and collecting material for his journal, entitled *Travels in North America*. [36]

Kalm's industrious pen, "like the parson's barn, rejects nothing" —as Collinson once said of his own curiosity. Descriptions of birds, animals, plants, medicinal herbs, minerals, and geography rub elbows with religious attitudes, longevity, marriage customs, Indians, their marvelous bark canoes, snakebite, and dysentery—a rich potpourri, simply and directly served up with no pretentions of style. Although phlegmatic in temperament, the Swedish naturalist was moved by the beauty and charm of the landscape he encountered in America, where in late May the sweet bay filled the air with a sweet and pleasant scent, "making it agreeable beyond description to travel in the woods," and where could be found the hummingbird, "the most admirable of all the rare birds of America . . . its plumage most beautifully colored," the mockingbirds, "the best singing birds in the world," and the whippoorwill, "a nocturnal bird whose voice is heard in North America throughout the whole night."[37]

[35]Peter Kalm, *Travels into North America, Containing its Natural History and a Circumstantial Account of Its Plantations and Agriculture in General, with the Civil Ecclesiastical and Commercial State of the Country, the manners of the Inhabitants, and Several Curious and Important Remarks on Various Subjects* (English trans., 2 vols., London, 1770); original edn., Stockholm, 1753). This and subsequent citations are to the Dover edition, edited by Adolph B. Benson (2 vols., New York, 1937), vol. 1, pp. x, 17, 39–40. See also imprint of 1772 London edition, illustrated, with an introduction by Ralph Sargent (Barre, Mass., 1975).

[36]Kalm's *Travels* were published in Sweden (1753–61), and soon translated into German, English, Dutch, and several French versions—*Travels*, pp. xiii–xv; see the introduction for biographical material on Kalm.

[37]Kalm, *Travels*, vol. 1, pp. 109, 112, 116, 288.

Before he left to return to Sweden, Kalm visited Niagara Falls. His description of the great cataract, which appeared in the *Pennsylvania Gazette* for September 1750, was the first eyewitness report of that natural wonder to be published in English. Kalm described the falls from where he sat with pen and ink, "on the brink of them, at hardly a fathom's distance from the place where an enormous mass of water hurls itself perpendicularly down from a height of 135 French feet or, about 34⅔ fathoms." He noted the great number of dead birds commonly observed at the foot of the falls, a phenomenon he attributed to the heavy fogs and mists that obscure the hazard, so that the birds are engulfed in the downsweep. Even to the stolid Kalm these falls, from his aerie, were an enormously impressive sight, on which "one could not gaze and contemplate without feelings of awe and astonishment."[38]

On his homeward voyage Kalm stopped in London and again visited Collinson, just then preparing for publication John Bartram's journal of his 1743 mission to the Lake Ontario Indians. The manuscript, given up for lost when the ship it traveled on was captured by the French, had arrived safely in London on the person of the ransomed ship captain.[39] Kalm was dismayed by Bartram's plain, unadorned account, in such marked contrast to his fascinating speech.[40] To enhance the impact of Bartram's narrative, he and Collinson arranged to publish with it Kalm's *Curious Account of Niagara*, which had already appeared in America.

Meanwhile, through the years the mutually profitable relationships between Bartram and Collinson had ripened into a deep and warm friendship, with each partner tireless in his efforts to please the other. Bartram, it is true, often complained, with justification, of inadequate financial compensation for the time and energy expended in the service of his English patrons. It was a truly delighted Collinson who, in 1765, wrote his friend across the sea: "This day I received certain intelligence from our gracious king, that he had appointed thee his botanist with a salary of fifty pounds a year. . . . Now, my dear John, thy wishes are in some degree accomplished, to range over Georgia, and the Floridas."[41]

The journey that followed in 1765–66, described by Bartram in

[38]*Ibid.*, vol. 2, pp. 693–703.
[39]See Darlington, *Memorials*, p. 172, and Herbst, *New Green World*, p. 46.
[40]Kalm, *Travels*, vol. 1, p. 61.
[41]Darlington, *Memorials*, p. 268.

his *Diary of a Journey Through the Carolinas, Georgia, and Florida,* was the last and greatest expedition of the now aging botanist.[42] His companion in adventure on that Southern expedition was his son, William, heir to his father's role as explorer and naturalist, and destined to give enduring expression to their common passion in his book, best known as Bartram's *Travels,* one of the great classics of natural history literature.

At this time William was twenty-six, a dreamy, talented youth seemingly afloat without a rudder, often helplessly awash in the wake of his purposeful father. Unlike his father, he had been formally educated and was gifted as an artist. Since the age of fifteen he had been producing accurate and beautiful paintings of natural history subjects, which had brought him favorable attention from his father's scientific friends and patrons in England. "Botany and drawing are his darling delight," wrote the elder Bartram to Collinson; "he can't settle to any business else." John Bartram had anxiously sought advice and help in directing William's future from both Collinson and that mentor of the natural history circle and old friend of the Bartram household, Benjamin Franklin. Over the years these able and practical men had busied themselves with patterns for the precious fabric of William's life, while the boy was shifted, willy-nilly, from one false start to another in the alien world of business, for which he had neither taste nor talent. It was from one such venture, as keeper of a country store on the Cape Fear River in North Carolina, that John rescued his son in 1765 to join him in his Southern pilgrimage.[43]

After two months exploring in the Carolinas they continued southward, crossing Georgia along a wilderness trail across the low pine flats through open stands of virgin longleaf pines, some so tall the trunks rose 90 feet to the bottommost branch. Near the Altamaha River they missed their way and came by chance on "several very curious shrubs, one bearing beautiful good fruite," as John reported in his diary, thereby recording the discovery of two of America's rarest and most beautiful shrubs, the *Franklinia* and the *Pinckneya.* The former, which John named for his friend Benjamin,

---

[42]Francis Harper (ed.), John Bartram's "Diary of a Journey Through the Carolinas, Georgia, and Florida, From July, 1765, to April 10, 1766," in *Transactions of the American Philosophical Society,* new series (Philadelphia, 1942), XXXIII, Pt. 1, pp. 6ff. Cited hereafter as Bartram, *Diary.*

[43]Darlington, *Memorials,* p. 200.

has been found nowhere else growing in the wild and is now exclusively a cultivated plant, while the latter remains among the rarest of American wild shrubs.[44]

It was not easy going: "Travailed 30 miles over many bay and cypress swamps . . . this day's rideing was very bad thro bay swamps, tupelos . . . and cypress in deep water . . . dined by a swamp on bread and pomgranite," and later, "lodged in ye woods under a pine amongst ye palmetoes and near a pond and musketoes." John suffered from a virulent malaria and dysentery. But Florida, with its slow-flowing waters bordered by lush growth and exotic blossoms, its great springs and abundant wildlife, was sufficient compensation; a botanical paradise, in which they lingered through the winter, making a river trip in search of the source of the St. Johns, and collecting specimens for John's royal patron.[45]

In the spring the elder Bartram returned north, reluctantly leaving William on the St. Johns determined to become a planter—a brief and well-nigh disastrous experiment for which he was ill equipped and ill adapted. Through the intercession of Henry Laurens he was rescued to return to the farm on the Schuylkill, where at last he found a means of escape from years of vain floundering. It came in the form of the patronage of Dr. John Fothergill, an eminent and wealthy English physician and avid collector of rare plants from all corners of the earth. Seizing upon this opportunity to turn his beloved avocation into a practical vocation, William lost no time in setting out again for Florida.[46]

Soon he was back on the St. Johns, no longer bound to a hopeless farm but free, gliding down the peaceful river between flower-bedecked banks, lush forests, and deep mysterious swamps from whose still waters the majestic columns of cypresses rose 80 or 90 feet to umbrella-like tops with streaming tresses of somber green moss, where storks, cranes, and eagles had their nests. Seeking his rest at evening in groves fragrant with the incense of magnolia, sweet illicium, and juniper, or beneath the widely spreading branches of a liveoak, William would spread his bed of skins and, after a supper of fish and fruit, fall asleep to the song of the melodious mockingbird or the mournful cries of the whippoorwill, to awaken at dawn to the flutter and chattering of the parakeets seek-

[44]Bartram, *Diary*, p. 31.
[45]*Ibid.*, pp. 31–33.
[46]Darlington, *Memorials*, pp. 438–442, 333–334.

ing their favorite fare in the lofty cypresses. Over and over his exuberant prose is interrupted by a *Te Deum* of praise: "O thou creator supreme, almighty: how infinite and incomprehensible thy works: Most perfect, and every way astonishing."[47]

Among the most astonishing of the Creator's works in this botanical paradise was the "subtle, greedy alligator," subject of one of William Bartram's most famous passages: "Behold him rushing forth from the flags and reeds. His enormous body swells. His plaited tail brandished high, floats upon the lake, the waters like a cataract descend from his opening jaws. Clouds of smoke issue from his dilated nostrils. The earth trembles with his thunder." With florid detail Bartram recounts a battle between two rival alligators in all its bloody turbulence, ending with the victor king of the waters, "whose shores and forests resound with his dreadful roar, together with the triumphant shouts of the plaited tribes around, witness of the horrid combat." He relates his own hazardous encounter with these frightful monsters, when he found himself hemmed in by a close assembly of them cutting off his retreat. Fortunately the beasts were there to feast on great schools of fish making their way through a narrow pass; the shaken naturalist managed to escape a terrifying reptile banquet in which "the horrid noise of their closing jaws, their plunging amidst the broken banks of fish and rising with their prey above the water" struck him as "truly frightful."[48]

The informed, careful scientist blended in Bartram's nature so harmoniously with the sensitive and poetic artist that his narrative abounds in fascinating description that is at once factually accurate and aesthetically beautiful. Such a medley is his well-known prose poem to a queen of the southern lowlands, *Gordonia lasianthus*—tall and straight as a spire, with long, slender, deep green lancelike leaves, large, perfectly white, extremely fragrant flowers, renewed every morning in such incredible profusion that the tree appears

[47]William Bartram, *Travels through North and South Carolina, Georgia, East and West Florida, the Cherokee Country, the Extensive Territories of the Muscogulges, or Creek Confederacy and the Country of the Choctaws, Containing an Account of the Soil and Natural Productions of those Regions, Together with Observations on the Manners of the Indians* (Philadelphia, 1791). This and all subsequent citations are to the Naturalist's edition, edited by Francis Harper (New Haven, 1958), pp. 5–6, 54–59, 38. For biographical data, see Harper's introduction, pp. xvii–xxxv; also Joseph Ewan, *William Bartram, Botanical and Zoological Drawings, 1756–1788* (Philadelphia, 1968); and my *Lost Heritage*, Chap. 5.
[48]Bartram, *Travels*, pp. 75–78.

silvered over with them—which is followed by a practical, scientific analysis of the tree's relation to its environment, its needs and growth patterns, and commercial value. Nowhere is that harmony of artist and naturalist more effective than in his magical description of the great springs of Florida. Seated on a green knoll at the head of the crystal basin, surrounded by fragrant groves and charmed by the many melodies of birds, Bartram gazes in awe at the

inchanting and amazing crystal fountain, which incessantly threw up, from dark, rocky caverns below, tons of water every minute, forming a basin, capacious enough for large shallops to ride in, and a creek of four or five feet depth of water, and near twenty yards over, which meanders six miles through green meadows, pouring its liquid waters into the great Lake George.[49]

Bartram's eager response to all the creatures of the wilderness embraced the Indian with particular sympathy. In the eyes of this gentle and romantic Quaker, the "generous and true sons of Liberty" were indeed the noble savages of legend. He traveled freely among them, visiting their villages so frequently that he began to be saluted as "Puc Puggy," the flower hunter, and as such was accorded hospitality and protection. This was among the Seminoles of central Florida, a people who, in Bartram's eyes, seemed "free from want or desires" and "as blithe and free as the birds of the air and like them as volatile and active, tuneful and vociferous."[50]

Tearing himself from Florida's bounties, Bartram moved northward with the birds to the mountains of the Cherokees, noting, as he approached their villages, the flame azalea blossoming in such profusion and radiance that he was alarmed "with the apprehension of the hills being set on fire." It was there among the splendid Cherokees, in a beautiful mountain vale, that he and a trader companion had their idyllic encounter with a group of Cherokee maidens gathering wild strawberries on the hillsides and sporting among themselves in gay and innocent play—a scene of which he left one of his most famous descriptions, as idyllic as a Greek pastoral.[51]

From the domain of the Cherokee Bartram traveled southward across Georgia to Pensacola, Mobile, and eventually on to the banks of the Mississippi, a place old John had long yearned to reach. "O:

49*Ibid.*, pp. 102, 104–105.
50*Ibid.*, pp. 118, 134.
51*Ibid.*, pp. 204–205, 225–226.

what a noble discovery I could have made on the banks of the Ohio and Mississippi," he had lamented to Collinson, adding that William, too, wanted to go as draughtsman. Now William at last had reached the Father of Waters; "fascinated by the great sire of rivers," he lingered beside it for some weeks, studying the plants and geology revealed in its banks and especially the rich birdlife displayed along its waters. At Pointe Coupee he noted "great numbers of wild fowl wading in the shoal waters"; here too were "geese, brant, gannet and the great and beautiful whooping crane *(Grus alber).*"[52]

That was the westward reach of William Bartram's travels. From there he turned homeward, stopping long enough in Mobile to despatch his collections to Dr. Fothergill before joining a caravan of traders headed for Carolina through regions where the Choctaw and Creeks were on the warpath. Also at war were his own people, all up and down the coast across which lay his homeward route;[53] but in the *Travels* there is not the slightest reference to the Revolution, already two years in progress. He reached the family farm early in 1777, several months before his father's death. After four years of solitary roaming William had come home for good. Quietly, gently, he moved into his father's vacated seat; the garden on the Schuylkill remained the hub of the botanical world as William easily and comfortably assumed John's mantle as sage of natural history and central figure of the American natural history circle.[54]

It took a dozen years for the unhurried William to transform his journals into Bartram's *Travels,* partly because as the work progressed he kept expanding its scope. To his account of his travels he added a catalogue of 215 birds of America, twice as many as Catesby had included in his work, and an essay embracing his observations on bird migration, nesting, and other facets of ornithology.[55] He also prepared a still highly regarded report on the Indian tribes he had visited in his travels, Seminole, Creek, Cherokee, and Choctaw. With charity and justice reminiscent of John Lawson, he defended those people of the forest whose hospitality he had often enjoyed during his wilderness years. His image of them gave great encouragement to the concept of the Noble Savage,

[52]Bartram, *Travels,* p. 271.
[53]*Ibid.,* pp. 310–312.
[54]*Ibid.,* pp. xxviiff.
[55]*Ibid.,* pp. 181–191.

agreeable to his view that "as moral men they certainly stand in no need of European civilization."[56]

Bartram's *Travels* (published in Philadelphia in 1791 and in London the next year), certainly one of the most delightful journals in any language, holds a select place in the revealing of America. Its reception in America was disappointing; but in Britain and on the continent, where the Romantic movement was coming into full flower, the *Travels* found an audience eager for all it had to offer: tropical paradises inhabited by primitive people of Rousseauan virtue; dangerous adventures in exotic wonderlands teeming with strange plants and animals; the whole marvelous feast served up in vivid, poetic prose.[57]

Embraced by Romantic prose writers and poets and enhanced by their power of creative imagination, the material of Bartram's chronicle took on new life. The most striking examples of his influence are to be found in the works of Coleridge and Wordsworth in England, whose *Lyrical Ballads*, in 1798, challenged the literary establishment. Touched with the lyric magic of Coleridge's genius, the rivers of Bartram's Florida meander forever through the Xanadu of *Kubla Khan*, where the mighty fountains ceaselessly erupt amid ancient forests and aromatic trees; the sparkling brilliance of Bartram's snakebirds and fishes flicker and glow in the water snakes of the *Ancient Mariner*. For Wordsworth, too, Bartram was a rich source of poetic invention. He is believed to have carried a copy of the book on his journey to Germany where he wrote the melancholy and melodious *Ruth*, the story of an English maiden betrayed by a youth from Georgia, who, fresh from life among the Cherokee, beguiled her with tales of a wilderness straight out of Bartram: green savannas, magnolia, gordonia and cypress trees, Indian maidens gaily gathering strawberries, and flame azalea:

> He told of girls—a happy rout!
> Who quit their fold with dance and shout,
> Their pleasant Indian town,
> To gather strawberries all day long;
> Returning with a choral song
> When daylight is gone down.

[56] *Ibid.*, pp. 305–332.

[57] *Ibid.*, pp. xxii–xxvii, 670–671. There were at least nine other editions, mostly pirated, in Ireland and on the continent, during the decade after the *Travels* were first published in Philadelphia.

> He told of the magnolia spread
> High as a cloud, high over head!
> The cypress and her spire;
> —Of flowers that with one scarlet gleam
> Cover a hundred leagues, and seem
> To set the hills on fire.[58]

Not only Bartram's natural history descriptions, but his underlying philosophy appealed enormously to the Romantics, who shared his faith in the innate nobility of man, unspoiled by the artificialities of civilization, his emphasis on living in harmony with nature, and his idealization of life in forest and field.[59]

In France, the embodiment of the Romantic spirit, François René de Chateaubriand, borrowed here and there from du Pratz, Charlevoix, Imlay, and Carver, but especially from Bartram, and enhanced his borrowings with the ardor and passion of his genius to spread before his readers exhilarating and beautiful depictions of the American wilderness in all its strange, savage beauty. The basis for his American writings was his own brief voyage to America in 1791, as a very young man in love with the idea of freedom, solitude, and the joys of unspoiled nature. In his five-month visit he certainly did not go to all the places he professed to have seen. No matter. With the eyes of the poet he looked upon great forests, floated on the waters of magnificent rivers, talked with Indians, and felt the freedom and solitude of the wilderness.[60]

Few have ever written more enchantingly of that wilderness than Chateaubriand, especially in *René*, a romantic *cri de coeur* and partial self-portrait of the author as a young Frenchman adopted by the Indians; and in *Atala*,[61] a haunting prose poem of star-crossed Indian lovers. These tales, both set in the American South, are reminiscent of Bartram in setting, imagery, and in the concept of the Noble Savage embodied in the blind Natchez chief, Choctas. Trans-

[58]"Ruth," from *The Poetical Works of William Wordsworth* (London, 1964), p. 153.

[59]John Livingston Lowes, *The Road to Xanadu* (Cambridge, 1927), *passim;* E. H. Coleridge (ed.), *Poems of Samuel Taylor Coleridge* (London, 1935), pp. 187, 287; Wordsworth: *Poetical Works*, p. 152.

[60]Morris Bishop, *A Survey of French Literature* (New York, 1955), pp. 5–6.

[61]*Atala* (Paris, 1801); *René* (Paris, 1802); both were originally designed as parts of Chateaubriand's prose epic of the Red Indians, *The Natchez*, which was finally published in his *Oeuvres Complètes* (Paris, 1826–31). See Gilbert Chinard, *Exotisme Américain dans l'Oeuvre de Chateaubriand* (Paris, 1918), pp. 98–99.

lated into many languages and enormously popular, Chateaubriand's romanticized picture of America contributed greatly to the
European image of the continent.

It appears very doubtful that William Bartram was ever aware of
his reception by European literati. For many years after the first
appearance of his *Travels* the gentle author of this unique book,
called by Thomas Carlyle "a kind of Biblical article," lived his quiet
life beside the Schuylkill, where, as the sage of Kingsessing, he
delighted to welcome to the famous garden an ever-growing number of pilgrims. There Thomas Jefferson, George Washington, and
Alexander Hamilton visited him; more congenial, perhaps, were the
visits of fellow naturalists, many from across the sea, seeking advice
and assistance. Among those who found hospitality at the Bartram
farm was the French scientist André Michaux, the first trained botanist to travel extensively in this country and one of the most glamorous figures in the long, adventure-filled saga of botanical discovery.[62]

Born in 1746 in the splendid shadow of Versailles, on the royal
domain of Satory entrusted for generations to his farmer forebears,
Michaux seemed destined to a farmer's life. In 1770, however, after
the death of his wife at the birth of their son, François André,
Michaux sought solace in the study of botany in the nearby gardens
of Marie Antoinette's Trianon, under the tutelage of those botanical
masters, Bernard and Antoine Jussieu. A dozen years devoted to his
botanical education and apprenticeship in France and England prepared him superbly for a botanical odyssey that would lead him
from France to the fragrant gardens of Persia, to the virgin wilderness of America, and on to his death in tropical Madagascar.[63]

With a royal commission to travel the fabled lands of Alexander's
conquests, Michaux set out in 1782 for Aleppo and Baghdad. For
three years he wandered those enchanted lands, exploring the little
known regions between the Caspian Sea and the Indian Ocean, as
well as those of the Tigris and Euphrates. In the course of these
wanderings he is said to have suffered capture at the hands of
marauding nomads, who seized and stripped him and were prevented from killing him only by the timely arrival of the British

[62]Bartram, *Travels*, pp. xxvii, xxix.
[63]Factual data on Michaux's pre-American years is mostly derived from M. De-
Leuze, "A Brief Narrative of the life and Travels of André Michaux," *City Gazette*
(Charleston, S.C., July 20–27, 1804). See also Savage, *Lost Heritage*, Chap. 6.

consul; on another occasion he was reported to have used his medicinal plant lore to cure a hostile sheik in exchange for his release from captivity.

In 1785 he returned triumphantly to France with a large collection of seeds and an extensive herbarium. Scarcely had he shaken the sands of Eastern deserts from his shoes when he was despatched on another royal mission, this time westward to the New World in search of useful plants, particularly forest trees, shrubs, and game birds, to be sent back for the royal forests, primarily that at Rambouillet.

Accompanied by his son François, who was then fifteen, and a nurseryman, Paul Saulnier, Michaux arrived in New York in October 1785. With characteristic competence and industry he soon established a nursery or way station for his collections across the Hudson at Hackensack. In his first season, despite winter weather and his unfamiliarity with the country, he managed to make frequent forays into the surrounding areas and send back to France no less than 5,000 seedling trees, along with 12 boxes of seeds and a number of live partridges. That typified the pace Michaux would maintain for eleven incredibly active years during which he journeyed, often alone, seldom with more than one or two companions, over most of the regions east of the Mississippi. From Florida northward almost to Hudson's Bay and westward to the great river itself, he followed the wilderness trails or broke his own through dense forests and snake-infested swamps, or floated the broad waters of the Mississippi, Ohio, and Tennessee on his tireless quest.

Michaux established a second nursery, near Charleston, that was soon flourishing with rare and choice American seedlings awaiting shipment to France, side by side with Old World plants introduced to America by him. Among those Michaux is credited with introducing are the camellia, the "mimosa" *(Albizzia julebrissin),* the ginkgo, the tea bush, and the tallow tree *(Sapium sebiferum);* also the sweet olive and Grecian laurel *(Laurus nobilis).*

A meticulous scientist, Michaux kept a day-by-day record of his journeying, noting distances, traveling conditions, and listing plants observed along the way and personal encounters, all with a minimum of personal comment. These journals, often prepared by the flicker of a campfire or moonlight, remain a precious legacy for lovers of the plant kingdom. There, in sparse, economical prose, is recorded the lost wild beauty of Eastern America. There too is revealed the amazing courage, dedication, and zeal of the man.[64]

Some of Michaux's most significant discoveries were made "dans les hautes montagnes de Caroline," to which he returned time and again, lured by the fabulous botanical riches of that wilderness Eden where from almost any peak one may look out over forests made up of far more species than are native to all the forests of Europe from the conifers of the far north to the sun-drenched shores of Attica.[65] In December 1788, on a journey to the headwaters of the Savannah River, his journal records an arduous struggle through all but impenetrable thickets of rhododendron and living walls of poison-thorned smilax, along towering cliffs where one false step could be fatal, across gorges, torrents, and ravines where dense growth and frowning mountains shut out the sunlight and bewildered the traveler. It was in that region, on a single journey, that Michaux was rewarded by the discovery of the lovely and elusive Oconee bells (Shortia galacifolia) and by Rhododendron minus, that most delicately beautiful of native rhododendrons, two of a multitude of plants to which, as discoverer, his name is attached.[66]

Week by week, as the years passed, from swamp and mountain, valley and riverbank, the wagonloads of plants and seedboxes were despatched to Charleston en route to the royal forests of France. Still the horizon-bewitched botanist dreamed of species undiscovered beyond the western skyline, across the Mississippi and the mountains beyond. With fire in his heels, he conceived a plan to undertake a discreet voyage, with but a companion or two, across the continent to the Pacific. To effect this plan, in 1793 he sought and secured the sponsorship of the American Philosophical Society and the financial assistance of a group of its members, including his friends Secretary of State Jefferson and President Washington. With that august patronage he set out westward across Pennsylvania and down the Ohio, where, owing to his activity as courier for the bold schemings against Spanish Louisiana, led by Citizen Genet, the new ambassador from the Revolutionary French régime, his mission was peremptorily canceled by President Washington. But the seed of

[64]C. S. Sargent (ed.), "Journal of André Michaux," *Proceedings of the Philosophical Society*, XXVI (1889), 1–145. Portions of Michaux's *Journal* in English translation are contained in Reuben Gold Thwaites (ed.), *Early Western Travels, 1748–1846* (32 vols., Cleveland, 1904–7) vol. 3 (1904), pp. 25–104.

[65]Edwin Way Teale, *North with the Spring* (New York, 1951), p. 188.

[66]Michaux, *Journal*, pp. 43–47.

Michaux's plan would later flower into the expedition of Lewis and Clark.[67]

In other ways, too, Michaux was a victim of the cataclysmic upheavals in his native land. He had been unpaid by the bankrupt monarchy for several years of his American mission, and in order to carry on had been forced to sacrifice his and his son's patrimony. Now, even more distressing, he learned with dismay through reports filtering out of his crisis-ridden country that of the more than 60,000 trees he had laboriously gathered and shipped to France, only a fragment had survived the storms of Revolution. In hope of salvaging some part of those losses, he set sail for France in 1796 but was shipwrecked on the shore of Holland with the loss of some of his American journals, serious damage to his herbarium, and the near loss of his life. When he finally reached Paris, despite the parlous conditions there, recognition and honors were accorded him. Characteristically, he plunged immediately into the task of preparing publications on his American botanical researches. When that work was substantially completed, although he continued to harbor a desire to return to America to explore the West, he was attached to a party setting out for the East Indies. Put ashore on Madagascar for botanical research, he died there of fever in 1802.[68]

Michaux's American botanical discoveries were published in his book on American oaks, *Histoire des Chênes de l'Amérique,*[69] beautifully illustrated, mainly by that master of botanical illustration, Pierre Joseph Rédouté, and in a two-volume *Flora Boreali-Americana,*[70] also illustrated by him, the first comprehensive and systematic work on the North American flora—giant steps in revealing the amazing wealth of American plant life.

"Not one among the self-sacrificing explorers and collectors of this continent," wrote a notable successor in the field, "better deserves the gratitude and appreciation of the world of science. No one of them has ever seen more clearly, or has endured more willingly and uncomplainingly the perils and hardships of the frontier and wilderness."[71]

[67] *Ibid.,* pp. 89–98.
[68] *Ibid.,* pp. 140–145.
[69] Paris, 1801.
[70] Paris, 1820.
[71] *Ibid.,* Sargent, introduction, p. 7.

CHAPTER 5

The Discovery of the Old Northwest

A FTER the publication of Carver's *Travels* and Bartram's *Travels* there was sufficient material available to provide Americans and Europeans alike with a good general idea of not only the thirteen original colonies and Florida, but also the country contiguous to the Mississippi and a considerable distance into the prairies beyond. But there was still little knowledge of the country between the Appalachians and the Mississippi excepting those relatively limited areas of the Old Northwest where British troops had campaigned against the French and Indians and established a sprinkling of fortifications. It fell to the lot of a farm boy, John Filson, sometime schoolteacher and surveyor from Chester County, Pennsylvania, to play a major role in lifting the curtain of obscurity that had so long hidden that transmontane realm. And he did so by means of one slim volume and a map, both published in 1784.[1]

Enticed by glowing word-of-mouth reports of the excellence of the region known as Kentucky, Filson had joined the early wave of emigrants headed for greener pastures beyond the gentle Blue Ridge, the more rugged Alleghenies, and the widespread ridges of the Cumberlands. Fabulous country it was, according to the reports of the leather-stockinged long hunters, incredibly fertile, a place of

[1] John Filson, *The Discovery, Settlement, and present State of Kentucke: and An Essay towards the Topography, and Natural History of that important Country: To which is added, An Appendix* (Wilmington, Del., 1784; the map was published in Philadelphia, 1784). My citations are to the edition in the March of America Facsimile series: John Filson, *The Discovery and Settlement of Kentucke* (Ann Arbor, Mich., 1966).

mysterious caves and mineral springs, and wildlife beyond belief—
and yet a country all but uninhabited. It was probably during the
summer of 1783 that the thirty-year-old Filson arrived at the region
of Big Bone Lick in the great bend of the Ohio; a few days later he
filed legal claims to tracts of land aggregating more than 12,000
acres of land, one of 5,000 acres on the Ohio only 10 miles from
the famous Lick. His overflowing enthusiasm for the Kentucky
country and, doubtless, for potential profits from his land claims,
prompted Filson to broadcast word of this new-found Eden. Barely
a year later he was back at home arranging with a printer in nearby
Wilmington for the publication of a book he had written, and with
a Philadelphia engraver to prepare the plate for a map of Kentucky
he had drawn to accompany it. Before the close of 1784, both book
and map were being advertised for sale in Philadelphia. With a title
wider than its content, *The Discovery, Settlement and present State of
Kentucke* was destined to have impact far exceeding its size, preten-
sions, or even the most roseate expectation of its author, primarily
for its Appendix, "The Adventures of Col. Daniel Boon; containing
a Narrative of the Wars of Kentucke." Those thirty-three pages
ensured the success of the book and provided the foundation upon
which the Boone legend was built. In a single package it provided
immortality for Boone himself and a prototype for the American
frontier hero—model for scores of later fictional heroes, most notably James Fenimore Cooper's Leatherstocking.[2]

Extravagant descriptions of the Kentucky country provided Filson's hero with an ideal setting for Boone's action-packed Narrative
—a marvelous land of unsurpassed climate, without the heat of
Virginia and Carolina or the winters of the territories to the north.
It was a land of crystal waters flowing between limestone walls of
spectacular grandeur, fordable only on roads that myriads of buffalo
had discovered and developed through the ages by their passing
and repassing; whose waters teemed with catfish weighing as much
as 100 pounds and salmon up to 40, where "geese and ducks are
amazingly numerous"; of grasslands of incredible fertility, ready for
the plow, while other areas were well timbered with an unmatched
variety of desirable trees. Turkeys and partridges were common, as
were also parakeets and ivory-billed woodpeckers. Deer, elk, bears,
beavers, muskrats, otters, and mink as well as panthers, wildcats,

[2]John Walton, *John Filson of Kentucke* (Lexington, Ky., 1956), pp. 45, 51.

and wolves were still numerous, and herds of buffalo, which "by their size and number, fill the traveller with amazement and terror, especially when he beholds the prodigious roads they have made from all quarters, as if leading to some populous city." There were springs from which salt could be easily gotten, and others producing "bitumen" that would serve to supply one's lamps; still others where quantities of great bones and teeth of unknown giant beasts could be found, and enormous caves, with rivers flowing in them— truly a land matchless elsewhere on earth. The map of Kentucky that Filson prepared to accompany the book was superior to any previous delineation of the region. It served to augment his flowing descriptions, with accurate notations of soils, terrain, natural wonders, and other attributes of the land.[3]

It was against such a backdrop that Boone told his story, albeit couched in the flowery verbiage of Filson rather than the talk of an unlettered backwoodsman. His account covered fifteen years, from the time Boone left his Yadkin River home in North Carolina in 1769 as one of the first whites to explore the region the Indians called Kentucky, "the dark and bloody land," up to his establishment at his new home on the Kentucky. What a story he had to tell! It was a Spartan narrative of hardship and daring, of endless battles with Indians, of captivity and escape, frustration and defeat, but ultimate victory. It told of the death of two of his sons, a brother, and numerous friends at the hands of the Indians; of his own captivity and his daughter's; and of thrilling rescues. During one of Boone's captivities he was taken all the way to Detroit, where his captors rejected an offer by the British commandant to redeem and parole him. It lasted long enough for Boone to accommodate himself so well to Shawnee ways that he was formally adopted into the tribe, a citizenship he readily abandoned when he learned of a planned attack upon his white kinsmen. To warn his people at Boonsborough required a 160-mile, four-day dash through the wilderness and a crossing of the wide Ohio River. All in all, Boone's

[3]Filson, *Kentucke,* pp. 12–36. Filson reported also the story of the Welsh prince Madoc who, according to Welsh historians, sailed west from Wales with a shipload of his countrymen, in 1170, in search of new lands to settle, and discovered a fertile country where he founded a colony. After returning to Wales for supplies and reinforcements, he set sail with ten ships to the West, and was never heard of again. Tales of blue-eyed Indians, speaking Welsh, descendants of the lost colony, persisted as a part of the mythology of the American West. Filson recounts rumors of a Welsh-speaking Indian tribe living far up the Missouri—Filson, *Kentucke,* pp. 95–96.

story was one designed to appeal to the heroic imagination innate in most of its readers.[4]

The obscurity of Filson's own life has been matched by his post-mortem obscurity,[5] for the impact of his work upon posterity came mainly from the energy of those who purloined it. The single edition of which he was the beneficiary soon found itself competing with a succession of pirated editions.[6]

Chief among those who appropriated Filson's work to their own use was Gilbert Imlay, an unsavory character who is now mainly remembered as the faithless lover of the famous champion of women's rights, Mary Wollstonecraft. While Imlay can be credited with a major role in revealing the transmontane country, his own pen contributed less than did his use of the productions of other less aggressive reporters. He not only appropriated to his own use Filson's work but is often credited with the "discovery" of Daniel Boone.

After serving in the American army during the Revolution, Imlay left his native New Jersey and crossed the mountains into Kentucky, where it is thought he stayed less than three years before departing for England in 1785. There, in 1791, he wrote his best known work, *A Topographical Description of the Western Territory of North America*, which was published in London the following year, and included excellent new maps. Like Charlevoix, Imlay employed the device of a series of letters, purportedly from Kentucky to a friend in England. His descriptions of the Ohio River country often were so enthusiastic that he concluded his account with an apology for what he feared sounded like a rhapsody, but was in truth entirely factual. Although much of what Imlay offered his readers as his own writing was derived (frequently literally and without attribution) from earlier travelers in the Old West, a common practice in those days, his book met with a success so far exceeding the original circulation of those borrowings that, ironically enough, he secured for himself an

[4]*Ibid.*, pp. 49–82.

[5]Filson died at the hands of Indian claimants of the area where as co-founder he was laying out a town that would later become the city of Cincinnati—Walton, *Filson*, p. xiii.

[6]Before a year had passed, unauthorized translations of Filson's book appeared in France and Germany, a process that continued for a full century—*ibid.*, pp. 43–44. His Dan Boone story spawned even more publishing ventures, among which bibliographers list more than fifty biographies of the homespun hero Filson introduced to the world of letters—*ibid.*, p. 51.

important place in the history of the revealing of America. The maps accompanying Imlay's volume greatly enhanced its contribution, particularly a splendid one of Kentucky prepared by Elihu Barker.[7]

When the time came for a third edition of his book, Imlay revised and expanded his text and added, with full credit to their authors, several works that had been earlier published as separate books. In addition to Filson's *Discovery* with the Appendix on the Boone story, he included two books written by Thomas Hutchins, an American engineer who served throughout most of the Revolution as a British officer but had switched his allegiance to the American cause late in the conflict. One dealt with the Lower Mississippi and Gulf regions, and the other with North Carolina and the colonies to the north and territory to the west.[8]

However spare and selective it may be, no account of the revealing of America during the eighteenth century can neglect the great and lasting impact of the New World's most eminent intellectual. Thomas Jefferson, in addition to being one of the leading stimulators of the young nation's natural history circle, was one of the prime movers in revealing the tangible physical aspects of the country, and, even more importantly, its evolving democratic ideals, institutions, and freedoms. Moreover, those who read what he wrote were mostly of the scientific and political elect. Jefferson's modestly titled book, *Notes on the State of Virginia,* which appeared in print in France in 1785,[9] was destined to become the most influential of the many voices on America during the closing decades of the century. Now, tested in the crucible of time, Jefferson's *Notes* is recognized as an enduring classic of American literature and history.

The origin of Jefferson's book is a story in itself. In the summer of 1780 the secretary of the French legation in Philadelphia, François Marbois, seeking more detailed knowledge of his country's new ally, sent a series of questions to the governors of each of the thirteen states. When Virginia's delegates to the Continental Con-

[7]See *Dictionary of American Biography,* vol. 19, for more on Imlay.

[8]Thomas Hutchins, *Topographical Description of Virginia, Pennsylvania, Maryland, and North Carolina* (London, 1778), and *An Historical Narrative and Topographical Description of Louisiana, and West Florida* (Philadelphia, 1789). For biographical data on Hutchins, see introduction by Joseph G. Tregle, Jr., in the 1968 reprint of the latter (Gainsville, Fla., 1968). For more on Imlay's book, see Thomas D. Clark, *A History of Kentucky* (Lexington, Ky., 1960), p. 268, and Willard R. Jillson, *Filson's Kentucke* (Louisville, Ky., 1930), p. 155.

[9]Thomas Jefferson, *Notes on the State of Virginia* (Paris, 1782; rev., 1785).

gress received their copy of the questionnaire, they forwarded it to Jefferson, then the state's governor. The Marbois queries reached Jefferson in the summer of 1780. It was a time of mounting crisis for the wartime governor, now thirty-seven and at probably the most trying period of his entire long and eventful life. In the fall the British had succeeded in driving the state government from Richmond and then from its refuge in Charlottesville, where the governor, after narrowly missing capture, was forced to flee Monticello in disguise. His official catastrophes had their full complement of personal disasters: the death of a little daughter, the declining health of his wife, his own injury in a fall from a horse. It is a source of wonder that anyone under such circumstances could produce a carefully prepared and learned manuscript, couched in language of literary excellence, by way of response to the French diplomat's queries.[10]

When Jefferson began the preparation of those responses, his Virginia was an enormous domain, embracing about half the nation. Before the first, strictly limited, 1785 French edition of the *Notes* appeared, Virginia had, through voluntary cession to the Congress, diminished its bounds to the area now embraced in the Virginias and Kentucky—a diminution that left vestigial passages in the *Notes,* such as descriptions of the Wabash and Illinois rivers, reports of mineral deposits in Ohio and Illinois and of the Indians of the Old Northwest and the Great Lakes. The *Notes* was far more than merely a series of descriptive and factual responses to cut-and-dried queries. Often the presentation of his facts provided Jefferson with a springboard for a wide gamut of philosophical or scientific discussions, some directly to the point, some by way of intriguing digressions. It was those qualities that transformed Jefferson's catalogue of facts into a historical and literary classic that left its mark deeply engraved on America and on Europeans' view of America.[11] Of less lasting importance, but greatly valued during the earlier years of the book, was the map carefully prepared by Jefferson himself from the famous 1751 map, which had been the work of his father Peter, and his neighbor and partner Joshua Fry.[12]

For his description of the parts of Virginia to the west, beyond

[10]Henry Steele Commager, *Jefferson, Nationalism and the Enlightenment* (New York, 1975), pp. 33ff.; Brooke Hindle, *The Pursuit of Science in Revolutionary America, 1735–1789* (Chapel Hill, N.C., 1956), pp. 319–332; William Peden, introduction to Jefferson's *Notes* (New York, 1954), pp. xii–xix. My note references are to that edition.
[11]Jefferson, *Notes,* p. xxiv.
[12]*Ibid.,* p. 261, note 1 to Query II.

his personal knowledge of the country, Jefferson sought facts from all available sources: correspondence, travel diaries, word-of-mouth inquiry, and such published material as Thomas Hutchins's *Topographical Description,* carefully crediting his sources. Together these sources enabled him to provide descriptions of the rivers, terrain, resources, and natives of the whole vast region. The first few pages are devoted to a general description of Virginia, the only mundane part of the work. From there on one finds facts inviting speculation, evoking poetic enthusiasm, summoning scientific corollaries, suggesting economic possibilities, and sparking excursions into sociological or political discussion. Jefferson rose to each in turn.

Every river of consequence merits detailed information: "The Illinois is a fine river, clear, gentle, and without rapids; insomuch that it is navigable for batteaux to its source . . . (and) 10 miles above its mouth, is 300 yards wide." "The Wabash is a very beautiful river, 400 yards wide at its mouth . . . is interrupted with frequent rapids and shoals . . . [but] overflows periodically in correspondence with the Ohio, and in some places two leagues from its banks." "The Ohio is the most beautiful river on earth. Its current gentle, waters clear, and bosom smooth and unbroken by rocks and rapids, a single instance only excepted."[13] The Ohio's widths, distances, high and low waters, and navigation follow in careful detail. His description of the water gap of the Potomac at Harper's Ferry evokes our emotions:

The passage of the Potowmac through the Blue Ridge is perhaps one of the most stupendous scenes in nature. You stand on a very high point of land. On your right comes up the Shenandoah, having ranged along the foot of the mountain a hundred miles to seek a vent. On your left approaches the Potowmac, in quest of a passage also. In the moment of their junction they rush together against the mountain, rend it asunder, and pass off to the sea. . . . But the distant finishing which nature has given to the picture is of a very different character. It is in true contrast to the foreground. It is as placid and delightful, as that is wild and tremendous. For the mountain being cloven asunder, she presents to your eye, through the cleft, a small catch of blue horizon, at an infinite distance in the plain country, inviting you, as it were, from the riot and tumult roaring around, to pass through the breach. . . . This scene is worth a voyage across the Atlantic.

[13] *Ibid.,* pp. 9–12, answer to Query II.

For Jefferson, it invites scientific speculations as to how it came to be.[14]

A like mood of patriotic pride and intellectual speculation introduces the reader to the Natural Bridge of Virginia, "the most sublime of Nature's works." "It is on the ascent of a hill which seems to have been cloven through its length by some great convulsion. . . . It is impossible for the emotions, arising from the sublime, to be felt beyond what they are here: so beautiful an arch, so elevated, so light, and springing, as it were, up to heaven, the rapture of the spectator is really indescribable!" And in the gorge 270 feet below, the waters of Cedar Creek flowing toward the James are "sufficient in the driest seasons to turn a grist mill. . . ."[15]

Jefferson's report on Virginia's marble and limestone leads to conjectures on the metamorphoses of rocks and inconclusive discussions of how fossil seashells came to be in mountaintop stones. He dismisses out of hand both Voltaire's view that they grew there in the stone and the then commonly accepted view that they were proofs of the biblical Deluge, refuting the latter by calculations showing that, even if all the air were water and it were all precipitated onto the earth, it would add only 52½ feet to the sea level. So, he concludes, shell-bearing stones must have originated on the bottoms of lakes or seas. But wonder remained. Could there have been convulsions of such awesome magnitude as would be required to hurl "to the height of 15,000 feet, such masses as the Andes?" Uncharacteristically, Jefferson leaves another mystery undiscussed when he tells of the niter deposits found in at least fifty Virginia caves—apparently never suspecting the lowly bat as creator of that natural resource.[16]

After a catalogue of the more important plants of Virginia, identified by both popular and Linnaean names, and due homage to "our great botanist Dr. [John] Clayton and his *Flora Virginica,*"[17] Jefferson turns to the query relating to the animals native to Virginia. Here he launches a memorable polemic, at once dispassionate scientific report and passionate argument in refutation of the aspersions upon life, human and animal, in the New World. In Paris the comte de Buffon ruled as the supreme arbiter in the realm of natural

[14]*Ibid.*, p. 19, answer to Query IV.
[15]*Ibid.*, pp. 24, 25, answer to Query V.
[16]*Ibid.*, pp. 30–34, answer to Query VI.
[17]Leyden, 1739.

history. With chagrin Jefferson had read in Buffon's renowned *Histoire Naturelle* its author's persuasion of the degeneration of animal life in the New World. Buffon believed that between like species in America and Europe, when compared, the American was inferior; and that inferiority, he claimed, extended also to people living in America. Buffon used the Indian as proof, declaring him inferior in size, strength, intelligence, and potency to Europeans. He had gone so far as to extend his "principle" of degeneracy to Europeans removing to America. Other continental scientists, philosophers, and historians hastened to accept Buffon's assumptions as established fact. Fervently, Jefferson seized upon the opportunity afforded by the query dealing with the animals of Virginia to refute Buffon's claims with a devastating array of factual documentation that showed the exact opposite to be true: the American animals more often than not were larger than their European counterparts, and the American Indians the physical equal of any Old World men.

To launch his attack on Buffon's views and similar views espoused by Abbé Raynal,[18] Jefferson marshaled at the outset his heaviest artillery—the fossil bones of mammoths with five or six times the bulk of an elephant, dug from the environs of Kentucky's Big Bone Lick. If one could accept the Indian tales that these creatures still inhabited remote regions to the northwest, they alone might be sufficient refutation of Buffon's pronouncement of American animal degeneracy. But Jefferson was unwilling to stand on that unsubstantial ground. He assembled long lists of American and European species, tabulated *vis-à-vis* their respective weights, which demonstrated that the American were generally the larger.[19] When he prepared a revision for his first English edition in 1785, Jefferson piled Pelion on Ossa by importing, from New Hampshire, the skin, bones, and antlers of a bull moose and the antlers of an elk and a caribou, to serve as empirical proof that in size the deer kind of America far exceed their largest European counterparts.[20] So impressive was the evidence marshaled by Jefferson that Buffon issued a supplemental volume to his *Histoire Naturelle* correcting most of his aspersions on life, both animal and human, in America, and Abbé

[18]Guillaume Thomas Raynal, *A Philosophical and Political History of the Settlements and Trade of the Europeans in the East and West Indies* (4 vols., London, 1776; Henry Steele Commager, *Was America a Mistake?* (Columbia, S.C., 1968), pp. 49–74, 122–138.

[19]Jefferson, *Notes*, pp. 50–58, answer to Query VI.

[20]Edwin T. Martin, *Thomas Jefferson: Scientist* (New York, 1952), p. 121; Bernard Mayo (ed.), *Jefferson Himself* (Boston, 1942), pp. 38–41.

Raynal retracted most of his in respect to British North America.[21]

There was another sequel to the Buffon-Jefferson controversy that involved and widely publicized a bit of cherished American literature. It was Jefferson's belief that, given education and civilized environment, the American Indian would prove himself quite the white man's equal. In the oratorical arts, for example, Indians often displayed superior luster, as exemplified by the now famous speech of Logan, a Mingo chief, after the murder of his whole family by a band of uncontrolled frontier vigilantes. Let Logan's colorful oratory, quoted by Jefferson, speak for itself:

I appeal to any white man to say, if ever he entered Logan's cabin hungry, and he gave him not meat; if ever he came cold and naked, and he clothed him not. During the course of the last long and bloody war, Logan remained idle in his cabin, an advocate for peace. Such was my love for the whites, that my countrymen pointed as they passed, and said, "Logan is the friend of white men." I had even thought to have lived with you, but for the injuries of one man. Col. Cresap, the last spring, in cold blood, and unprovoked, murdered all the relations of Logan, not sparing even my women and children. There runs not a drop of my blood in the veins of any living creature. This called on me for revenge. I have sought it: I have killed many: I have fully glutted my vengeance. For my country, I rejoice at the beams of peace. But do not harbour a thought that mine is the joy of fear. Logan never felt fear. He will not turn on his heel to save his life. Who is there to mourn for Logan?—Not one.[22]

Jefferson's response to the query concerning Virginia's aborigines is perhaps as revealing of Jefferson himself as of the Indians, although he painstakingly provides full tabulations of the tribal names and numbers at various times past of all known tribes in the middle latitudes from the Atlantic to the Mississippi. When he elaborates his Indian catalogue with an account of the Indians' ways, and says of them that, lacking laws, their only controls are "their manners, and the moral sense of right and wrong, which like the sense of tasting and feeling, in every man make a part of his nature," he reveals himself as the idealist and political philosopher:

An offense against these is punished by contempt, or by exclusion from society . . . [so that] crimes are very rare among them: insomuch that were it made a question, whether no law, as among the savage Americans, or too

---

[21]Commager, *Was America a Mistake?*, p. 32; Commager, *Jefferson, Nationalism, and the Enlightenment*, pp. 39–45.

[22]Jefferson, *Notes*, p. 63, answer to Query VI.

much law, as among the civilized Europeans, submits man to the greatest evil, one who has seen both conditions of existence would pronounce it to be the last: and that the sheep are happier of themselves, than under the care of the wolves.[23]

In expressing such sentiments, Jefferson was giving voice to the mounting enlightenment of his century—a century of intense and unflagging interest in the American Indian. The changes this spelled in Europeans' attitudes toward the American aborigines are clearly reflected in accounts of the receptions given to those native Americans who from time to time were brought to London to be properly awed by the power the city represented. In earlier days such visitors had often been received as curiosities, on the order of circus exhibits rather than guests of the realm. However, as early as 1710 a change of attitude appeared. In that year the visit of four Iroquois chiefs created a great stir in the city. Provided with comfortable lodgings and European attire, they were escorted on tours of the city and formally presented at the court of Queen Anne. Much was made of their picturesque but simple eloquence. They inspired poems and articles in the *Tatler* and the *Spectator* by Steele and Addison.[24] In the more Romantic circles a tendency to ennoble the savage continued to increase. A half century after the visit of the four Iroquois, a deputation of Cherokee "kings" was brought over for a visit designed to offset French blandishments during the French and Indian War. Jefferson, then a student at William and Mary, was much impressed when he interviewed them as they were preparing to take ship for London in the spring of 1762, under the guidance of Lieutenant Henry Timberlake. On their arrival, they too evoked great popular interest and the full panoply of elegance of official recognition: visits to Westminster Abbey and the Tower of London, presentation at the court of George III, sittings for portraits by Sir Joshua Reynolds, while the magazines of the day broadcast accounts of the progress of their reception.[25]

Although in recording his generous views of those native Americans Jefferson was reflecting to some degree the belief in the superi-

[23]*Ibid.*, p. 93, answer to Query XI.

[24]Benjamin Bissell, *The American Indian in English Literature of the Eighteenth Century* (New Haven, 1925), pp. 57–63.

[25]Chapman, J. Milling, *Red Carolinians* (Chapel Hill, N.C., 1940), pp. 307–308; Henry Timberlake, *The Memoirs of Lieut. Henry Timberlake* (London, 1765; reprinted, Johnson City, Tenn., 1927), pp. 133–147. Timberlake and Thomas Sumter escorted the Cherokee "kings" from their Tennessee mountain homes to London.

ority of the Noble Savage to civilized man as revealed in the writings of Jean Jacques Rousseau in France, and such American contemporaries as William Bartram, Philip Freneau, Jonathan Carver, and James Adair, a belief unquestionably not shared by most of his fellow countrymen, he was voicing convictions developed from his own studies of those people—studies extending back over several decades. He had known many of them personally. He was an assiduous collector of Indian vocabularies and himself made archeological excavations in an Indian mound on the Rivanna River near Monticello. In fact, Jefferson can be credited with founding American ethnology. He spoke of the American natives with considerable authority, particularly in the field of Indian linguistics.[26] It was Thomas Jefferson the scientist speaking when he proposed a philological approach to the problems of Indian history and origins:

A knowledge of their several languages would be the most certain evidence of their derivation which could be produced. . . . Were vocabularies formed of all the languages . . . it would furnish opportunities to those skilled in languages of the old world to compare them with these, now or at a future time, and hence to construct the best evidence of the derivation of this part of the human race.[27]

Jefferson's responses to the final queries relating to laws, government, and religion gave the Virginian savant an opportunity to espouse his heartfelt convictions touching on religious freedom, the ideal government for an ideal individualistic agrarian society, and his portentous fear of the institution of slavery. His responses to those subjects were to become a major factor in inculcating in the minds of men at home and abroad an image of a "democracy" that only partially and ephemerally existed in fact, yet lingered in the minds of many as a cherished political illusion. But these discussions were destined to involve him in the most bitter and vitriolic political controversies in the nation's history when, in later years, in the heat of political campaigns, excerpts from what he had written in the *Notes* would be dredged up out of context and employed by his opponents to prove their author "a howling atheist" and "confirmed infidel," bent on undermining the Bible, a traitor to his class, possessed of all manner of iniquitous attributes. The charges would lead him to lament bitterly: "Oh! that mine enemy would

[26]Jefferson, *Notes,* pp. 98, 282, answer to Query XI.
[27]*Ibid.,* p. 101, answer to Query XI.

write a book! . . . I had written a book, and it has furnished matter of abuse for want of something better!" Numerous assaulters and defenders alike read the book, thereby enhancing its impact. To meet the demand, the year 1801 alone saw five separate American editions of *Notes on the State of Virginia,* accelerating its mounting influence.[28]

Shortly after the new century dawned, Jefferson moved into the as yet unfinished White House. Its East Room, like Monticello, soon became a veritable museum of fossil bones, animal specimens, and Indian artifacts. Even in the face of dissension at home and the parlous state of foreign affairs, the restless, ever-inquiring President might often be found on solitary botanizing expeditions along the towpath of the Potomac Canal, where, he states, "there is not a sprig of grass that shoots uninteresting to me," even as his curious, exploring mind reached out to remote horizons, far beyond the Virginia he had described, and pondered ways and means to satisfy that curiosity.[29]

Although more than two centuries had passed since the British laid claim to North America's Atlantic coast, few had much firm information as to the nature of the regions beyond the western prairies. The few whites who had penetrated the region were mostly either French voyageurs, notoriously secretive as a necessity, or Spaniards, confined within the intellectual bastions of a fearful and suspicious imperial Spain. There were only the scantiest leaks to provide a minimum of factual data for the curious, such as Jefferson, or for those seeking to portray the western regions on maps with some semblance of reliable interior detail, such as Jedidiah Morse, the man history would describe as the father of American geography.

It is not too surprising therefore that Jefferson had recorded in his *Notes* a belief that the hills from which the cold, muddy Missouri issued were but a single ridge of "Stony Mountains," inferior in stature above their base to the peaks of Virginia's Blue Ridge or Alleghenies[30]—a belief that Gilbert Imlay had more recently sustained when he maintained that "the hills which divide the waters of the Pacific ocean from the waters of the Mississippi . . . generally

[28]Abernathy, introduction to Jefferson, *Notes* (New York, 1964), p. xvi.
[29]Martin, *Jefferson: Scientist,* pp. 7–20, and *passim.*
[30]Jefferson, *Notes,* p. 20, answer to Query IV.

called the Shining Mountains" were neither "so high or so rugged as the Allegany mountains."[31]

Nor is it at all surprising that in 1797 the latest map of North America, that of Jedidiah Morse published in *The American Gazeteer,* [32] was all but devoid of interior detail throughout the whole area known today as the American West. The only suggestion of the Rocky Mountains shown on that map was an abbreviated chain in the latitude of southern Alaska, designated the "Stoney Mts." Morse, born in Connecticut and educated at Yale, had been for a dozen years a Congregationalist clergyman in Charlestown, Massachusetts, when this latest of his works appeared. By then his geographies were already well on the way to the long-standing monopoly of the field they were to hold during their author's lifetime.[33] His 1797 map,[34] expanding westward the area covered by earlier cartographers, revealed the outline of the entire future nation, with a 1,500-mile vacuum beyond the Mississippi—a challenge to explorers, inviting the daring to seek out the features poorly glossed over by a few random Indian names and imaginary river courses. Soon Jefferson would become the mover, the manipulator, and vicarious explorer in search of those missing features, as bands of adventurers set out to see for themselves what was actually in those vast, mysterious expanses.

[31]Imlay, *Topographical Description,* pp. 74–76.
[32]Boston, 1797.
[33]*Geography Made Easy* (New Haven, 1784), the first geography published in the United States, went through twenty-five editions. *The American Geography* (Elizabethtown, 1789), known in its later editions as *The American Universal Geography* (11th edn., Boston, 1807), went through seven editions in America and almost as many in Europe—Hindle, *The Pursuit of Science,* p. 317, note 55.
[34]Reproduced among the illustrations to this volume.

CHAPTER 6

The Expedition of Lewis and Clark

A T Fort Mandan, 1,600 miles up the Missouri River from its confluence with the Mississippi, the morning of April 7, 1805, dawned clear and cold. A freezing wind was blowing out of the north. From bank to bank, across the wide expanse of the river, huge ice floes were drifting downstream, harbingers of spring in the region now known as North Dakota. In this rolling prairie country the "Great Muddy" winds its way between banks clothed with cottonwoods growing beneath protecting high bluffs on either side of a relatively narrow alluvial valley. In a lush grove of yet leafless cottonwoods, under the lee of the bluff on the north side of the river, stood the crude log structure fashioned the previous November by the two score adventurers of the Corps of Discovery, under the command of Meriwether Lewis and William Clark, to serve as their winter quarters, and named by them Fort Mandan because of its proximity to a village of Mandan Indians.[1] Simple and crude as it was, it had proved its worth, adequately protecting the party from the rigors of winter even when temperatures dropped as low as 40 below zero. At the same time, it had served effectively in deterring

[1]Elliott Coues, *History of the Expedition under the command of Lewis and Clark to the Sources of the Missouri River, thence across the Rocky Mountains and down the Columbia River to the Pacific Ocean, Performed during the Years 1804–5–6, by Order of the Government of the United States* (4 vols., New York, 1893); reprinted, 3 vols., New York, 1963; Dover edn., 1965), p. 196; also, *History of the Expedition under the command of Captains Lewis and Clark* (as above, prepared for the press by Paul Allen, 2 vols., Philadelphia, 1814), p. 128. The latter is the work of Nicholas Biddle, the original official editor of the Lewis and Clark journals. My citations of the Coues work are to the 1965 Dover edition; citations to Biddle are to the 1814 edition.

the attacks they feared might be launched against them by the disaffected and dangerous Sioux, with whom they had had unpleasant
encounters on their way up from St. Louis during the previous
summer. Now the whole place was alive with activity—in the fort,
along the path leading to the riverbank, and by the water's edge
where a varied array of river craft was being readied for departure.

Despite the finger-numbing cold and the bustle about him, Captain Lewis had brought out his portable desk and settled down to
write a long letter to President Jefferson, his hero, friend, mentor,
and the instigator of the voyage of discovery that had brought them
to this austere wilderness. That the young officer (he was then but
thirty) could write undistracted by the activity about him was
unquestionably due to the absolute confidence he placed in the
Corps' co-commander, Captain William Clark, thirty-four, friend
and fellow Virginian, under whom Lewis had seen service in Indian
campaigns in the Ohio country. The year and a half they had now
shared the command of the Corps of Discovery had amply proved
the worth of the rugged Clark. Now, while Lewis wrote, Clark was
exercising one of his special skills, the fine art of loading riverboats
to ensure as far as possible their stability and, through judicious
dispersal of essential equipment, to minimize the consequences of
disaster. Free of distraction, Lewis could compose a cover letter to
accompany the largest of the expedition's boats, returning to St.
Louis with a wide variety of natural history specimens: plants, skins,
skeletons, antlers, even live prairie dogs, magpies, and prairie hens,
as well as Captain Clark's journal of the voyage thus far, his geographical notes, and Lewis's own report on the Indians he had
encountered.[2]

In his account for that day Lewis noted the departure of the barge
to return with despatch to St. Louis, and then reported:

At the same moment that the Barge departed from Fort Mandan Capt.
Clark embarked with our party and proceeded up the River. As I had used
no exercise for several weeks, I determined to walk on shore as far as our
encampment of this evening.

Our vessels consisted of six small canoes and two large perogues. This
little fleet altho' not quite so respectable as those of Columbus or Capt.
Cook, were still viewed by us with as much pleasure as those deservedly

[2]Reuben Gold Thwaites (ed.), *Original Journals of the Lewis and Clark Expedition* (8
vols., New York, 1904–5), vol. 7, pp. 318–323; Bernard DeVoto (ed.), *The Journals of
Lewis and Clark* (Boston, 1953), Appendix III, pp. 493–494.

famed adventurers ever beheld theirs; and I dare say with quite as much anxiety for their safety and preservation. We were now about to penetrate a country at least two thousand miles in width, on which the foot of civilized man had never trodden; the good or evil it had in store for us was for experiment yet to determine, and these little vessells contained every article by which we were to expect to subsist or defend ourselves. however as the state of mind in which we are, generally gives the colouring to events when the immagination is suffered to wander into futurity, the picture which now presented itself to me was a most pleasing one. entertain[in]g as I do, the most confident hope of succeeding in a voyage which had formed a darling project of mine for the last ten years, I could but esteem this moment of my departure as among the most happy of my life.[3]

President Jefferson was well aware of Lewis's long-standing interest in this "darling project."[4] As early as 1792, when Jefferson was Secretary of State, Lewis, then barely eighteen, had unsuccessfully sought an appointment as companion to the French botanist, André Michaux, in his proposed Western journey.[5] Jefferson had prepared detailed instructions for Michaux to follow, some of which he now adapted as guidelines for Lewis and Clark, including the intriguing suggestion that birch bark should be used for important records along the way, "it being little liable to injury from wet and other accidents."[6]

Long before the Michaux proposal, however, Jefferson had recognized the necessity for Western exploration. From France ten years earlier he had written George Rogers Clark, the "Conqueror of the Old Northwest," and older brother of William, suggesting that the unemployed conqueror should lead an expedition cross-country to California.[7] Though nothing came of that suggestion, three years later, while still in Paris, he gave encouragement to the tireless adventurer, John Ledyard, in his plans to cross Russia to the Pacific, cross the Pacific with Russian fur traders to northern California, and thence travel back across the continent to the Atlantic. Ledyard carried through the first part of that heroic project, but in eastern

[3]DeVoto, *Journals*, p. 92.

[4]Biddle, *History*, vol. 1, p. vii; Coues, *History*, pp. xix–xx.

[5]See above, Chapter 4. For a more detailed account of Michaux's transcontinental project, see Henry Savage, Jr., *Lost Heritage* (New York, 1970), pp. 179–223.

[6]Thwaites, *Original Journals*, vol. 7, pp. 202–204; P. L. Ford (ed.), *The Writings of Thomas Jefferson* (10 vols., New York, 1892–99), vol. 1, pp. 158–161.

[7]Thwaites, *Original Journals*, vol. 7, p. 193.

Siberia Catherine the Great had him arrested, brought back, and expelled from the country.[8]

One can readily imagine, then, the satisfaction with which President Jefferson must have welcomed the specimens and reports sent back to him from Fort Mandan. It would not be surprising to learn that affairs of state stood neglected while the rapt philosopher-President gleaned all that this wilderness cargo had to tell him: the specimens competently prepared, classified, and labeled in accordance with instruction by the savants of the Philosophical Society;[9] Clark's journals and preliminary report, showing his flair for geography; and perhaps most interesting of all, Lewis's report of the customs and vocabulary of the Indians of the Missouri country.

Particularly impressive were the reports on the Missouri River, which even at the Mandan villages had measured almost 1.5 miles in width. Equally impressive was the fertile and teeming land through which it flowed. Clark's journal, written in colorful style, abounding in imaginative phonetic spelling, recorded in full detail his observations of the river, its environs, and the men and animals encountered along the way. Seven miles below the village of St. Charles, he noted "a remarkable coal hill" composed of "a great quantity of coal," and 200 miles upstream, "Curious paintings on the projecting rock of Lime stone inlade with white red and blue flint, of a verry good quallity, the Indians have taken of this flint great quantities." Clark described their examination of a bluff, above the present Sioux City, Nebraska, which appeared to contain "Alum, Copperas, Cobalt Pyrites; a Alum Rock Soft & Sand Stone," all of which Captain Lewis tasted and "was Near poisoning himself by the fumes & tast of the Cobalt." Near this bluff the first and only casualty of the expedition was buried, Sergeant Floyd, a victim of "Biliose Chorlick."[10]

The ferocious heat was interrupted only by sudden and violent storms, and the "ticks and musquiters" were "verry troublesome."

[8]While still communicating with Jefferson about another attempt, Ledyard died on a voyage up the Nile—*ibid.*, vol. 7, pp. 195–197; John B. Brebner, *The Explorers of North America* (New York, 1933), pp. 381–386; Van Wyck Brooks, *The World of Washington Irving* (Philadelphia, 1945), p. 145.

[9]The Philosophical Society had given Lewis preparatory cram courses in botany, medicine, navigation, and other fields of natural history before his departure, in order to supplement the President's instructions.

[10]The site of Floyd's grave was impressively depicted by George Catlin some thirty years later—George Catlin, *Letters and Notes on the Manners, Customs, and Conditions of the North American Indians* (London, 1841; New York, 1973), plate 118.

However, the journal reports (from Sioux City on) incredibly bountiful game in "a most butiful landscape" with "numerous herds of buffalo." Giant catfish were caught without difficulty; "Fields brought in five deer"; another of the party "killed an Elk Buck." They collected the skin and sent back a description of an animal new to them (a badger), which preyed on the myriads of prairie dogs, or "barking squirrels," as they called these heavy-bodied relatives of the chipmunk. As they toiled their way across the Dakota prairies, antelope and deer were added to the ubiquitous buffalo and elk.[11]

Meeting Pierre Dorian, an old French trader on his way back to his base in St. Louis, they persuaded him to turn back upstream and help them to enlist some Sioux chiefs to be escorted to Washington to meet the President. The journal noted the company's encounters with Indians of this dangerous and powerful tribe who, in spite of their reputation for ferocity, cried out in sympathy for a member of the Corps being punished by flogging, with the explanation that they "never whipped even their Children."

By November 1804 the Corps of Discovery had reached the country of the Mandans and Minnetarees, the former already famous to the outside world for their relatively light skins, unique customs, and the villages they built of closely crowded, large round domed houses, covered with sod.[12] The brisk northwest winds, with more than a touch of winter, had now regularly added their force to the river's adverse current, making progress painfully slow. The decision was made to construct a makeshift fort and living quarters under the protection of the high north bluff a few miles below the villages of those friendly people. Throughout the winter a remarkable rapport developed between the natives and their new neighbors, a rapport only occasionally tarnished, by the freedom of the men of the expedition with the Indian women. Of all the party Clark's giant Negro slave, York, proved most popular with the native girls. Clark himself had been honor guest of the Mandans at their three-day "Buffalo Dance," a weird and lewd spectacle designed to encourage "the buffalow to come near So that they mey Kill them."[13]

[11]Quotations from DeVoto, *Journals,* pp. 4–52.
[12]To many travelers the Mandans were the "Welsh Indians," descendants of the party of the twelfth-century Welsh prince Madoc: a belief of remarkable persistence —Charles Michael Boland, *They All Discovered America* (New York, 1961), pp. 283–300; Bernard DeVoto, *The Course of Empire* (Boston, 1952), pp. 68–73, 373–379; also Catlin, *Letters and Notes,* vol. 1, pp. 206–207.
[13]Biddle, *History,* vol. 1, pp. 150–152.

Frequently during the winter the Corps had reciprocated these hospitalities by providing their own special brand of entertainment, which would be repeated over and over all the way to the Pacific and back. The highlights were Peter Cruzatte with his fiddle and York with his dancing antics. While the whole Corps usually joined in the roistering all-male dancing exhibitions, it was the French riverman's charmed fiddle (which magically survived all the terrible storms, river, and packhorse catastrophes) and the black giant's performances that enraptured their appreciative guests.

All this and much more was there in Clark's journal for the President's edification. There, too, were a variety of reports and information gleaned from the natives and from white fur traders met with in the village. The enlistment of one of those traders, Touissant Charbonneau, a Frenchman who had been ten years living among the Prairie Indians and had become conversant with their language, was to prove one of the most fortunate strokes of luck of a remarkably lucky expedition. Not only was he a valuable interpreter; even more importantly, he had a young Indian wife, Sacajawea. A Shoshone Indian of the Rocky Mountains who had been kidnapped by a war party and sold to Charbonneau, Sacajawea was destined to prove immensely helpful to the expedition as guide and interpreter for communication with the mountain people, and above all as interpreter of the wilderness itself to these white interlopers in a strange and often hostile land.

Thirty-one people, under the prideful eye of Captain Lewis, had launched their boats among the ice floes that April afternoon of 1805, and set out up the great muddy stream. They included twenty-five of the original carefully selected members of the Corps, mostly from the army; two later recruited on the Mississippi; Captain Clark and his man York; the interpreter Charbonneau (who, like several others, could not swim), his Shoshone girl-wife, and their two-month-old baby Baptiste. Although it was then the third week of spring, the scenes about them were still wintry. Clark recorded seeing a mosquito and "great numbers of Brant flying up the river. . . . Great numbers of gees feedin in the prairies," and maple and elm in bud.[14] Sacajawea provided their first spring produce, roots she discovered while searching for wild artichokes, which Lewis described as resembling the root of the Jerusalem artichoke in flavor.

[14]Coues, *History*, pp. 253ff.

From now on, with increasing frequency, there were exciting and dangerous encounters with grizzly bears. The expedition generally called them white bear, as the breed was then without scientific name; later, on the basis of Lewis's description, it was appropriately named *Ursus horribilis.* [15] The grizzly is America's largest and most dangerous carnivore, weighing up to 1,000 pounds, swift, fearless of man, and incredibly hard to kill, even with the superior rifles of the Corps. Their tracks were commonly observed along the riverbanks where they fed on the carcases of buffalo who had fallen through the ice and were now drifting downstream. From the Indians, Lewis had

a very formidable account of the strength and ferocity of this animal, which they never dare to attack but in parties of six, eight or ten persons; and are even then frequently defeated with the loss of one or more of their party. . . . When the Indians are about to go in quest of the white bear, previous to their departure, they paint themselves and perform all those superstitious rights commonly observed when they are about to make war upon a neighbouring nation.[16]

Near the present North Dakota-Montana line, which the expedition reached a fortnight after leaving the Mandans, game was more bountiful than ever before. It was there that Clark discovered and examined a recently constructed native bier. The body of the deceased lay on an elevated platform, "raised about 6 feet, enclosed in Several robes tightly laced around her with her dog Slays [travois poles], her bag of different coloured earths near her." While absorbed in inspecting those mute symbols of native beliefs, Clark was joined by Captain Lewis, on his way back to camp from a short foray in search of game. He had "in his walk killed 2 Deer & wounded an Elk & a Deer, our party shot in the river four beaver & cought two, which were verry fat and much admired by the men, after we landed they killed 3 Elk 4 Gees & 2 Deer. . . . Saw several buffalow lodged in the drift wood which had been drouned in the winter in passing the river."

A few days later, at the mouth of the Yellowstone, Lewis reported that

the whol face of the country was covered with herds of Buffaloe, Elk and Antelope; deer are also abundant but keep themselves more concealed in

[15]*Ibid.,* p. 288n.
[16]DeVoto, *Journals,* p. 95.

the woodland. the buffaloe Elk and Antelope are so gentle that we pass near them while feeding, without appearing to excite any alarm among them; and when we attract their attention, they frequently approach us more nearly to discover what we are, and in some instances pursue us a considerable distance apparently with that view.[17]

So it went, day after day, as they pushed their way another several hundred miles upstream, through the violent storms, sudden freezes, and searing heats of the capricious spring and early summer of that big sky country. From the Yellowstone to the Great Falls of the Missouri there were frequent encounters with grizzlies; discovery of the elegant bighorn sheep (*Ovis canadensis*) and later its surefooted fellow denizen of crags and precipices, the mountain goat (*Oreamnos americanus*); and the excitement and false encouragement of sighting the shining snow-capped peaks of the isolated Little Rocky Mountains, a good 300 miles short of the Rockies themselves.[18] They saw "the remains of a vast many mangled carcases of Buffalow which had been driven over" a precipice by the Indians, and landscapes weird and improbable outside of dreams: cliffs

woarn into a thousand grotesque figures, which with the help of a little immagination and an oblique view, at a distance are made to represent eligant ranges of lofty freestone buildings, having their parapets well stocked with statuary; collumns of various sculpture both groved and plain . . . supporting long galleries in front of these buildings . . . some deprived by time or accident of their capitals; some lying prostrate . . . it seemed as if these seens of visionary inchantment would never have any end. . . .[19]

When in early June the Corps reached twin forks of the river, one flowing out of the northwest that Lewis named Maria's, the other flowing from the southwest, they were faced with a dilemma as to which to follow. As usual the captains agreed with each other—in this case in the face of almost total disapproval expressed by their men—that the southwest fork was the one they should follow, believing it to be the one advised by their Mandan friends far down the river. On their return east, they were to divide forces to permit exploration of the one they had named Maria's,[20] and with that in mind they chose a spot near its mouth for a cache of such essential supplies as would be required on their return.

[17]*Ibid.*, pp. 97, 99.
[18]Biddle, *History*, vol. I, p. 230.
[19]DeVoto, *Journals*, pp. 120, 123.
[20]In later use the Maria's would lose its apostrophe.

The captains had not long to wait for vindication of their choice at the perplexing forks. Five days later, on June 13, Lewis, walking with three companions across the rolling country bordering the river, arrived at an eminence that "overlooked a most beautifull and level plain of great extent . . . [where] there were infinitely more buffaloe than I had ever before witnessed at a view." A little further on, his "ears were saluted with the agreable sound of a fall of water and advancing a little further . . . [he] saw the spray arise above the plain like a column of smoke. . . ." Here at long last were the great falls of the Missouri of which the Mandans had told them so much. Seated high above the falls the awe-struck Lewis entered in his journal a description of the "majestically grand" scene below. He estimated the falls to be about 300 yards wide overall, of which 100 yards on the further side formed

a smoth even sheet of water falling over a precipice of at least eighty feet, the remaining part of about 200 yards on my right formes the grandest sight I ever beheld, the . . . projecting rocks below receives the water in it's passage down and brakes it into a perfect white foam which assumes a thousand forms in a moment sometimes flying up jets of sparkling foam to a hight of fifteen or twenty feet. . . . [I]n short the rocks seem to be most happily fixed to present of the whitest beaten froath for 200 yards in length and about 80 feet perpendicular.[21]

They had now been gone nine weeks and covered almost 1,000 miles since leaving the Mandans without seeing even a single Indian. They had come across some abandoned shelters below the falls, a discarded moccasin to be identified by tribe by Sacajawea, a dropped, worn travois pole, masses of dead buffalo beneath a cliff, even an occasional footprint, but no Indians. This was increasingly disturbing; if they were to cross the mountains before another winter, horses were essential, and these were obtainable only through trade with Indians.

Next day reconnaissance along the river for a dozen miles above the falls clearly revealed the awesome challenge now confronting the expedition. Although in coming this far the men had endured, sometimes for days on end, hardships in icy water up to their waists, towlines cutting into their shoulders, sharp rocks mangling feet already riven by cactus spines, sieges of boils, and venereal infections picked up from acquiescent squaws, they had as yet faced

[21]DeVoto, *Journals*, pp. 136–139.

nothing comparable to what now awaited them. For 15 miles the river, closely confined between steep banks and cliffs up to 100 feet high, plunged over that long series of falls and rapids, which reached a spectacular climax in the Great Falls themselves. The country back from the river, over which the portage mandated by the falls would have to pass, was equally inhospitable—prairie country covered with a vicious spiny cactus and deeply cut at intervals by steep-sided ravines. Even the beasts hereabouts seemed to display unprovoked animosity. On making his reconnaissance Lewis was chased by a furious grizzly that had charged him without provocation or warning, forcing him to take refuge in the icy waters of the swift-flowing river. And the buffalo acted in macabre ways, crowding each other into the rapids. Lewis saw "ten or a dozen disappear over the falls in a few minutes." Later, as night approached, three bull buffalo gave him a fright by advancing menacingly toward him. Soon after he came upon a creature he described as a "tyger cat," crouching in readiness for attack. Such uncommon dangers led him to retreat hastily to the protection of the camp. The menacing events persisted: at dawn next day Lewis awoke to find a very large rattlesnake sharing the cover of the tree under which he slept.

Meanwhile Clark, on the river with the boats, was having his trials too, directing the weary crews in dragging the boats as near to the falls as possible, while at the same time trying desperately, with the limited medical skills at his command, to cure Sacajawea, who was critically ill and of whom he had obviously become very fond. All his medications seemed useless. It was only after Lewis returned and dosed her with the sulphur waters of a convenient spring that a cure was effected.[22]

During the days that followed, while Captain Clark surveyed and mapped the falls and rapids and marked out an 18-mile portage leading cross-country to the gentle reaches above, Lewis supervised the construction of four sets of wheels from sections cut from the one large tree they were able to find. For axles they used the boat masts. Making the wheels, hauling the baggage from Portage Camp below to White Bear Island Camp above the rapids, and carrying the heavy dugout canoes from one to the other, required ten days of unremitting toil. Violent storms swept down upon them, one with hailstones 7 inches around that "sorely mawled" the men. A flash

[22]Biddle, *History,* vol. 1, p. 271.

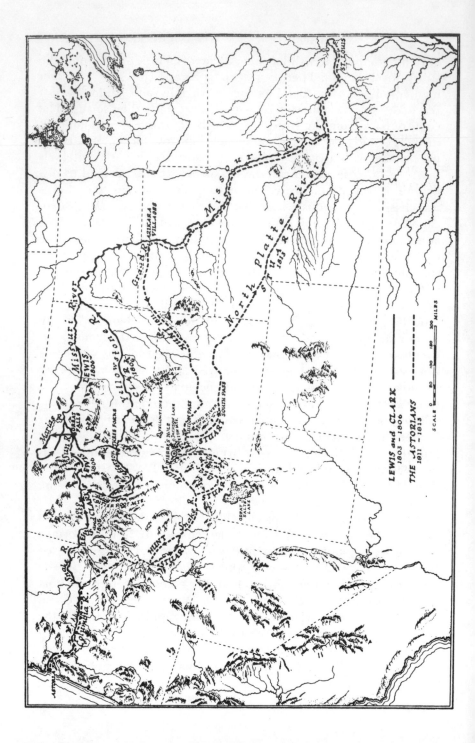

LEWIS and CLARK
1803 - 1806

THE ASTORIANS
1811 - 1813

SCALE 0   50   100   150   200   300
        MILES

flood caught Clark, Charbonneau, Sacajawea, and the baby in one of the ravines, from which they escaped drowning only through Clark's heroic efforts and cool presence of mind. The occasional icy winds sweeping down from the white-robed "Shining Mountains" to the south provided the sole relief from tormenting myriads of mosquitos that followed them everywhere as they struggled and strained across the portage. Grizzly attacks became so frequent that the men were required to go at least in pairs whenever they left the protection of the group.

The ordeal of the portage had thoroughly tried the men, and not one had been found wanting. Clark reported proudly:

the men has to haul with all their strength, wate & art, maney times every man all catching the grass & knobes & stones with their hands to give them more force in drawing the Canoes & Loads, and notwithstanding the cool-ness of the air in high presperation and every halt, those not employed in reparing the course, are asleep in a moment, maney limping from the soreness of their feet some become fant for a fiew moments, but no man complains all go chearfully on. . . .[23]

By mid-July the whole arduous operation was complete. Another cache below the falls had taken care of Lewis's desk, natural history specimens, and books. New dugouts had been made to take the place of the pirogue left below, an unanticipated delay made neces-sary when a folding boat designed by Lewis proved a dismal failure. As they set out upstream again, Indian signs increased: the frame of a very big lodge, more than 200 feet in circumference, sur-rounded by traces of tepee sites, Indian paths along the river, smoke signals seen in the distance, but still no sight of a living Indian.

As the river became shallower and the current more swift, their progress grew more slow. Painfully they made their way through the striking Gates of the Mountains and southward to the Three Forks, up the Jefferson fork and the Beaverhead, and on past a place recognized by Sacajawea as the campsite of the Shoshones where, five years earlier, they had been attacked by Plains Indians and she was carried off by the victors. The river was fast becoming almost too shallow for navigation as the mountains, now rising into the sky in every direction, encroached ever closer upon the narrowing val-ley. Game was alarmingly scarce, a few pronghorns and sometimes a small group of bighorns, but both these species commonly proved

[23]DeVoto, *Journals*, pp. 147–148.

adept at avoiding the hunters. Obviously the time was drawing close when a negotiable portage to westward-flowing waters would have to be found. As Captain Clark was badly disabled by a tumor on his ankle, Captain Lewis and three men set out to try to find a portage along the river and to locate the Snake Indians, Sacajawea's Shoshones.[24]

Two days out on that reconnaissance to search for recently traveled Indian paths, Lewis deployed two of his men, one far to his left and the other far to his right, to parallel his own route up a branch of the aptly named Beaverhead. They had progressed about 5 miles when Lewis saw, "with the greatest delight, a man on horseback ... coming down the plain toward them." But despite Lewis's resort to the sign language and symbolism of friendship garnered from Sacajawea—laying his gun on the ground and walking forward unarmed, holding up a blanket and then ostentatiously spreading it on the ground, repeatedly calling out the words for "white man," displaying mirrors, beads, and other baubles—the suspicions of the Indian increased with every narrowing of the distance between them. Suddenly, suspicion overcoming curiosity, the Indian turned about, gave his horse the whip, and was soon out of sight.[25]

Next day, however, fate proved more kindly. August 12, 1805, was destined to be one of the most propitious and significant days in the annals of the expedition. Soon after setting out to follow the hoofprints of the mounted Indian encountered the afternoon before, Lewis was encouraged by the discovery of fresh temporary shelters and recent root digging. These signs so revived their spirits that by mid-morning one of the men, seeing how diminished the stream they were following had become, "in a fit of enthusiasm, with one foot on each side of the river, thanked God that he had lived to bestride the Missouri."[26] The reconnaissance party soon reached "a handsome bold running Creek of cold clear water. here I first tasted the water of the Columbia river." That evening Lewis's men

[24]Biddle, *History,* vol. 1, p. 350.

[25]Coues, *History,* vol. 2, pp. 476–481.

[26]Actually the branch of the river here bestridden is far short of the most remote source of the Missouri. Not far south of the "hole" up which Lewis and his companions were traveling toward the continental divide at Lemhi Pass, the Beaverhead River turns back eastward and becomes the Lima. This has its source in Red Rock Lake very near the western boundary of Yellowstone Park, a good 100 miles further off than where Lewis's companion thought the mighty Missouri was flowing between his legs.

prepared their last reserve of food, a piece of cured pork brought all the way from St. Louis, to be consumed at their first repast beside Pacific waters.[27]

The following day was only a little less significant, for they at last made contact with Sacajawea's people. Coming upon three squaws busily engaged in root gathering, Lewis and his companions, by means of a skillful blend of sign language and alluring gifts, had just succeeded in allaying their fear when, as Lewis tells it, "we met a party of about 60 warriors mounted on excellent horses who came in nearly full speed, when they arrived I advanced towards them with the flag. . . ." They advanced, and

embraced me very affectionately in ther way which is by puting their left arm over your wright sholder clasping your back, while they apply their left cheek to yours . . . we wer all carressed and besmeared with their grease and paint till I was heartily tired of the national hug. I now had the pipe lit and gave them smoke; they seated themselves in a circle around us and pulled of their mockersons before they would receive or smoke the pipe.[28]

After that relations ripened speedily, particularly when they all went together a few days later to meet the main body of the Corps at the fork of the Jefferson.

There beside the river, after the boats had come up and preliminary greetings were under way, as Sacajawea was "renewing among the women the friendships of her former days, Captain Clarke went on, and was received by Captain Lewis and the chief," Cameahwait, whom Sacajawea later recognized as her brother.[29] Now with the language barrier bridged and the bond of Sacajawea's dual citizenship established, negotiations for horses proceeded apace. Although this half-starved band of some 400 Indians possessed little in the way of material wealth, being armed only with bows and arrows and a short leather whiplike device tipped with a round 2-pound stone, which made a formidable weapon, they were rich in

[27]Biddle, *History*, vol. 1, p. 360; Coues, *History*, vol. 2, pp. 484–485. To reach the Columbia River the Corps crossed the continental divide through Lemhi Pass, on the border between Beaverdam County, Montana, and Lemhi County, Idaho. Across the divide the Lemhi River flows, by a circuitous route, through the Salmon and Snake rivers to reach the Columbia. On the advice of native guides, the Corps followed a more direct route by crossing over to the *Kooskooskee* River, now known as the Clearwater; this carried them directly to the Snake River, which it joins at the Idaho-Washington border.

[28]DeVoto, *Journals*, p. 191.

[29]Biddle, *History*, vol. 1, p. 382.

horses, many of which "would make a fine figure on the South side of the James River or the land of fine horses."[30]

With horses secured to cross the mountain barrier, the Corps began at once to prepare for departure. In great secrecy yet another cache was organized to receive articles not susceptible to land transport, ammunition, and other essentials that would be needed on their return journey. The dugouts were weighted with rocks and sunk to preserve them until their return. Harness was fabricated from rawhide, pack saddles from rawhide and the flanges of oars; equipment was dried and repacked in saddlebags and back packs. But then we read in Lewis's journal that "Captain Clark and myself now . . . agreed that he sould set out tomorrow morning with eleven men furnished with axes and other necessary tools for making canoes . . . to proceede . . . down the Columbia. . . . In the meantime I was to bring the party and baggage to the Shoshone Camp," just across the divide on the Lemhi River. Clearly this is yet another residue of that wishful conviction, inherited from Carver and Imlay, that the Shining Mountains probably petered out in these northern latitudes, or in any event were so diminished that but a short portage would carry one to the "Oragon" River. It also reflects Jefferson's belief that these Western mountains were inferior to those of the East and posed no great obstacle to passage.

Although such geographical misconceptions as the Straits of Anian and a great River of the West leading to it from the heart of the continent had gradually lost strength since Carver's day, only now was the immensity of the Western mountain barrier being discovered by the Corps.

It soon became apparent that neither the Columbia waters Lewis's band had found beyond the pass nor the Salmon River into which they flowed were possible for navigation. With that knowledge, the Corps set out under native guidance along a trail leading northward from the Lemhi to cross the incredibly difficult terrain separating it from the headwaters of the Kooskooskee, a river known today as the Clearwater.

No mere catalogue of the geographical sequences of the expedition's transit of the Rockies can even suggest the extent of the ordeal it spelled for the weary and embattled Corps. Once again game was scarce. The fine Shoshone horses began to falter and

[30]DeVoto, *Journals*, p. 195.

break down under the weight of their loads. The whole party, including both captains, was stricken with violent dysentery. Even when they reached salmon waters and were able to barter dried salmon from the natives, their stomachs, so long accustomed to a diet entirely of meat, revolted, and the journals degenerate into chronicles of illness interspersed with other difficulties and disasters.[31]

On October 6, on the bank of the Clearwater itself, with new canoes shaped (in the Indian manner) using fire and axes, and water-tested, with their saddles and other supplies cached (likewise in the Indian manner), and their thirty-eight surviving horses all branded and delivered into the care of a reliable Nez Percé chief, the Corps was ready to become waterborne again, aided by the current for the first time in two years. Before the first day's navigation of the Clearwater was done, it had emerged from the mountain forest and entered a wide open country devoid of trees except for fringes along its banks, the sort of landscape that would continue monotonously for the next 300 miles down the Snake and then the Columbia all the way to where it breaches the verdant Cascades. There was, however, no monotony of navigation. On that first day on the Clearwater they shot ten dangerous rapids. Day after day navigation of these swift Western rivers presented challenge after challenge, and a corresponding series of accidents to men and canoes.[32] No longer, though, was there danger of starvation. Since the natives' diet of dried salmon and wild roots continued to be revolting to most of the men, they chose instead a regular diet of roasted dog, despite the undisguised disgust of the natives of the dog-ridden (and flea-ridden) villages from whom, despite their disapproval, such fare was readily obtained at cheap barter rates.

Of all the Indians encountered beyond the Missouri, the Nez Percés, with whom they had become well acquainted in the Clearwater region, made the most favorable impression. Clark described these "Cho-pun-nish," as he called them, as

Stout likely men, handsom women, and verry dressy in their way, the dress of the men are a White Buffalow robe or Elk Skin dressed with Beeds which are generally white, Sea Shells & the Mother of Pirl hung to ther hair & on a piece of otter skin about their necks hair Ceewed in two parsels hanging

31 *Ibid.*, pp. 239–240.
32 Biddle, *History*, vol. 1, pp. 460–465.

forward over their Sholders. . . . Some fiew were a Shirt of Dressed Skins and long legins & Mockersons Painted. . . . The women dress in a Shirt of Ibex or Goat Skins which reach quite down to their anckles with a girdle . . . their Shirts are ornemented with . . . Beeds, Shells & curious bones. . . .[33]

On October 16 the crude little flotilla entered the Columbia itself. A week of rapid progress carried them down its crystal waters where fish could be seen 15 or 20 feet below, while along its edges floated incredible masses of dead and decaying salmon, their life purpose fulfilled with their upstream spawning run. The native villages along the banks were occupied by friendly people of the same linguistic stock as the Nez Percés. Mats covered their dwellings—roofs, sides, and flea-infested floors—and served as platters for their food. For cooking, water contained in baskets so closely woven as to be water-tight was brought to a boil by immersing in it heated stones. Even after death, mats played important roles, covering the sheds under which lay the bones of the deceased, spread out on yet other mats. The attire of the squaws of these villages was markedly different from that of earlier Indians. Instead of the long garments of the Nez Percés, the women of the Columbia, according to Clark, "only ware a truss or pece of leather tied around them at their hips and drawn between their legs and fastened before. . . ." To the men of the expedition, most of whom had spent many a laborious hour making dugout canoes, the crowning achievement of these Lower Columbia natives was their light and beautiful high prowed dugouts—graceful craft and amazingly seaworthy in both rapids and surf.[34]

As the Corps approached the cascades of the Lower Columbia, the natives gathered in crowds to see what these white men would do when confronted with such stupendous obstacles. At Celilo Falls, in sight of the snow-capped peaks rising from the Cascades, they were forced to drag their heavy dugouts and carry their supplies across the rocks for more than a quarter of a mile, and then employ ropes plaited of strips of elk skin to let the boats down another short but precipitous fall. Next below Celilo Falls was the Short Narrows (the Dallas), then the Long Narrows, and finally the notorious Cascades of the Columbia.[35] At the Short Narrows a deep, fast-flowing

[33]DeVoto, *Journals,* pp. 246–248.
[34]Biddle, *History,* vol. 2, pp. 12–17, 35–36.
[35]Now flooded by Bonneville Dam.

river, almost a quarter of a mile wide, was funneled into a steep-sided rock gorge only 45 yards in width. After sending their guns and other valuables and those who could not swim down by the path along the cliff, the boats were navigated down the boiling torrent two at a time. By much the same procedure the Long Narrows were passed, again without serious loss or injury.[36]

Now with the cold and drizzly winter weather of the Northwest Coast upon them, the Corps learned with relief from their native audience that only the ferocious rapids of the Cascades lay between them and Pacific tidewaters. Clark with two of his men examined the challenge presented by these most formidable of the falls of the Lower Columbia, where the river breaks through the densely forested Cascade Mountains that crowd in upon it on either side. Clark reported that this

Great Shute . . . continued with great rapidity and force thro a narrow channel much compressed and interspersed with large rocks for ½ a mile, at a mile lower is a verry considerable rapid at which place the waves are remarkably high . . . with the water of this great river compressed within the space of 150 paces in which there is great numbers of both large and Small rocks, water passing with great velocity forming & boiling in a most horriable manner, with a fall of about 20 feet. . . .

Emulating the Indians, who "took their Canoes on their Sholders carried them below the Great Shute," they set about taking their small canoe and all the baggage by land, "940 yards of bad slippery and rockey way . . . after which we got the 4 large canoes over by slipping them over the rocks on poles . . . in passing . . . three of them recved injuries which obliged us to delay to have them repared."[37]

While the Corps rested before venturing the last of the Cascades' white water, many of the natives who had followed along the river to see how these strangers coped joined the Corps for a friendly smoke. They were a dirty and an unprepossessing lot, small in stature and with flat heads. Except for their friendliness, their beautiful canoes, and their large and sturdy wooden houses built of boards riven by elk horn axes, the explorers had little favorable to report of them. Moreover, they would soon prove themselves invet-

[36]Coues, *History,* pp. 664–668.
[37]DeVoto, *Journals,* pp. 269–271.

erate thieves and a constant nuisance in their persistent efforts to sell their women's favors.[38]

A remarkable landmark on the north side of the river, a "detached rock 800 feet high and 400 paces around," which they named Beacon Rock, marked the last of the Cascades of the Columbia. Finally, 100 miles short of the river's mouth, they reached Pacific tidal waters. And they were bountiful waters. "Great numbers of sea otters [*Lutra canadensis pacifica*] in the river below the falls." These richly furred creatures, 5 or 6 feet long, were soon to become the heart of the fortune-building triangular trade with China that would rapidly drive that beautiful mammal to the brink of extinction. Along the riverbanks skunks abounded; elk and deer again made their appearance. On the river itself the explorers were greeted by "great numbers of waterfowl of Different kinds, such as Swan, Geese, white & grey brants, ducks of various kinds, Guls & Pleover." Below the Cascades, where the river left the mountains, the country on both sides was thickly covered by an amazing forest of pine trees, some more than 200 feet high and from 8 to 10 feet through at the stump. It was, however, a region of fog, rain, and chilling winds.

In the estuary near the mouth of the Columbia, the Corps became virtually prisoners of the weather for more than three weeks while rain, wind, and waves bound them to the exposed north shore, the surf rolling in from the Pacific against their helpless craft. Relief finally came on a day mild enough to permit their escape across the rough waters of the estuary to the protection of the south shore. There, some 3 miles back from the Columbia, on the bank of a tidal creek, they set to work preparing their long-overdue winter quarters. Before embarking to cross over to the south side, Clark took time to carve on a large pine this famous legend: "William Clark December 3rd 1805. By land from U. States in 1804 & 1805."[39]

By the end of December the weather-weary men, many of whom were ill, the captains, Sacajawea, and the baby, Baptiste, now nicknamed Pompey, were all under roof in a structure they dignified by the title of "Fort Clatsop." In fact it was merely a double row of adjacent cabins, joined at either end by palisades of logs, the construction greatly simplified by the facility with which the surround-

[38] *Ibid.*, p. 272.
[39] *Ibid.*, p. 294.

ing Douglas spruce could be split into boards more than 2 feet in width.[40]

By mid-March 1806, after a dreary winter broken only by visits to the coast, preparations for departure were nearing completion. Lists of the men of the expedition, with statements of its accomplishments, were posted in the fort and entrusted to a friendly native chief for safekeeping in the hope that, if disaster overtook them on the return journey, the world might still be apprised of their success in reaching the Pacific by land.[41] On March 23, when the rain let up and the sun came out, they left Fort Clatsop, homeward bound.

Their return journey must here be condensed into a few sentences. From Fort Clatsop, all the way to Lolo Pass over the Bitterroot range, the Corps remained intact retracing generally its route west.

Forced by a tardy spring to linger for weeks in the Nez Percé country, it was not until the end of June that they were able to make it through Lolo Pass to Traveler's Rest on the Bitterroot River.

At Traveler's Rest, as agreed during the winter, the captains divided their command and took divergent routes. Lewis with nine of the most able men continued almost due east up the Hellgate and Blackfoot rivers, across the continental divide, and down the Sun River to the Great Falls of the Missouri. Leaving three of his party to retrieve and condition the contents of the caches left there on their way west, Lewis and the others continued northward to explore the Marias River, a side trip which, but for his skill at bluffing, would probably have cost him and his six companions their lives at the hands of a band of Blackfeet, two of whom were killed in the encounter.

Meanwhile Clark, with the bulk of the Corps, was retracing very nearly the same circuitous route of the previous year: southward up the Bitterroot, thence across the divide, but through a different pass, from which Sacajawea easily pointed out the way to the place where the boats had been submerged in the Beaverhead. After retrieving the boats and the supplies cached nearby, Clark assigned

---

[40]Biddle, *History*, vol. 2, p. 96. The Douglas spruce or Douglas fir *(Pseudotsuga taxifolia)* was named in honor of David Douglas, a Scottish botanist who made a botanical expedition to the Pacific Northwest in 1825—Susan D. McKelvey, *Botanical Exploration of the Trans-Mississippi West, 1790–1850* (Arnold Arboretum, Jamaica Plain, Mass., 1955), pp. 299–341.

[41]Biddle, *History*, vol. 2, p. 204.

eight of his men to take them down the Jefferson and Missouri to the portage at the falls where they would join the three men detailed there by Lewis. Together those eleven would complete the portage, recover the pirogue left below the falls, and continue downriver to rendezvous with Lewis at the mouth of the Marias. From there they were to move on downstream to the mouth of the Yellowstone to await the arrival of Clark's contingent.

Clark, with Sacajawea, Pompey, and the remaining ten men of the Corps, all well mounted, left the Missouri at Three Forks. Again under the guidance of Sacajawea, they struck out eastward along the Gallatin River and thence, along a buffalo path, crossed over to the Yellowstone River at a point immediately north of what is today Yellowstone Park. After following the Yellowstone for several days, they found a grove of trees, two of which were suitable for making two large dugouts. For stability the two canoes were lashed together and all but four of the party taken aboard to course swiftly toward the Missouri and their appointed rendezvous. According to Clark's plan, the remaining four men were to drive the horses along the river to the mouth of the Yellowstone, where they would be used for barter with the natives. However, the four were soon robbed of all their horses by a roving band of Crows, and were forced to take to the river in two hastily fashioned bullboats in which they floated down to their meeting with Clark.

Four days later, on August 12, 1806, Lewis's reunited command came surging down the river, shouting as they paddled, joyously completing that almost incredible wilderness rendezvous. Despite the fact that Lewis had been shot through both thighs in a hunting accident and now lay flat on his back in the bottom of the pirogue, it was an ebullient reunited Corps of Discovery that set out for St. Louis, some 1,800 miles down the muddy waterway, early the next morning. At noon on September 23 they beached their travel-battered fleet on the bank of the Mississippi in front of the fort at St. Louis, to the accompaniment of official salutes and "the heartiest and most hospitable welcome from the whole village."[42]

As Lewis and Clark made their way east from St. Louis with a retinue consisting of York, a Mandan chief and his family, and a band of Osages—all headed for Washington to pay their respects to

[42]Coues, *History,* pp. 1, 213.

the President—the press was breaking the great news all across the country. It was exciting on many counts, but for the moment the survival of the expedition made the news sensational. Then, as soon as the highlights of the journey became known, Americans began thinking of their burgeoning nation as spanning the whole wide continent from sea to shining sea. The captains and their indomitable followers had revealed to the country its manifest imperial destiny.

Although news of the expedition swiftly swept America and Europe and promptly stimulated new expeditions into the Great West, the whole story as related in the captain's journals and the scientific data they had collected was surprisingly slow in becoming available.[43] But eventually, in the months and years that followed, Lewis and Clark would reveal in great depth and detail the nature of the northwest prairie country, the Northern Rockies, and the Pacific Northwest, the rigors of climates, the spectacular terrains, and the fascinating variety of plant, animal, and human life claiming

[43]Although within a year after the return of the Corps a ghost-written version of Sergeant Patrick Gass's journal had appeared in print, the real story of this crowning epic of American exploration did not appear for another seven years. Delays resulting from Lewis's death in 1809, difficulties in getting a suitable editor and securing a commitment from a publisher, and, finally, the arduous task of editing the voluminous journals and the mass of ancillary material into a coherent narrative, consumed years. It was Nicholas Biddle, an erudite Philadelphia attorney, who eventually undertook the editing task, a three-year stint as it turned out. Before Biddle could get his manuscript of the history of the expedition ready for the printer, three more editions of Gass's account had appeared, while in England a volume based on Gass was enjoying a good reception. Then came the War of 1812, business in distress and the country distracted. Nevertheless in February 1814, "the History that was to make so much history" finally appeared. Although it would become an American classic, ironically Biddle's fine work for many years saw but a single edition in America. Even before it appeared, the publisher of the *History of the Expedition under the command of Captains Lewis and Clark* had failed, a casualty of the wartime economy, an event that greatly dampened proper launching of the work. Competition from repeated editions of Gass's briefer account, and spurious reports pretending to be by Lewis and Clark, curtailed demand for the lengthy authentic work. To all that must be added the formidable competition from numerous authentic but unauthorized issues of the *History* itself. The first of these appeared in London in the same year that Biddle's work appeared in Philadelphia; German, Dutch, and Irish editions followed in rapid succession. In fact, the Lewis and Clark expedition had such a powerful popular appeal that more than forty imprints, representing about twenty distinct editions of books purporting to report it, appeared before the next authorized, unabridged edition of Biddle's *History* in 1893—evidence enough of the major contribution of the doughty captains to the revealing of America.

For Lewis's brief later career and mystery-shrouded death, see John Bakeless, *Lewis and Clark, Partners in Discovery* (New York, 1947), pp. 408–428; and for Clark's long and valuable later career, *ibid.*, pp. 429–450. See also Coues, *History,* pp. cvii–cxxxii.

those varied lands as home.[44] Here was a vast store of new information and some (but remarkably little) misinformation, most notably their continued espousal of Jonathan Carver's belief that the great waterways of the West had closely proximate sources—which Carver thought lay in the vicinity of Lake Winnepeg. The captains moved this placenta of Western waters 1,000 miles southward to a region near the "Spanish Settlements," where in their view would be found the sources of the Platte, the Yellowstone, the Snake, the Willamette, the Colorado, the Rio Grande, and the Arkansas. But this was conjecture. All that they saw with their own eyes they revealed with remarkable accuracy and intelligence.[45]

[44]The collections of plants, animal skins, minerals, and artifacts served to illustrate their accounts, particularly after they became featured exhibits in Peale's Museum —Brooks, *World of Washington Irving,* p. 18; Coues, *History,* pp. 250, 821–900; McKelvey, *Botanical Exploration,* pp. 67–85.

[45]DeVoto, *Journals,* p. 322; William H. Goetzmann, *Exploration and Empire* (New York, 1967), p. 25; Bernard DeVoto, *The Course of Empire* (Boston, 1952), p. 519.

CHAPTER 7

Zebulon Montgomery Pike

PIKE'S Peak in central Colorado and dozens of other place names in the Mississippi Valley serve as enduring memorials to the impact of young Zebulon Montgomery Pike on the young American republic, almost his twin in years. There is fortuitous but marked symbolism in the most notable of those memorials, the mountain that bears his name. It is one of the most famous in the world, but that fame rests on its appearance of height, the remarkable road constructed to its summit in later years, and no doubt also on the alliteration of its name, rather than on its actual stature, for there are at least twenty-seven more lofty peaks in Colorado alone. It is even unlikely that Pike was the first Anglo-American to lay eyes on its famous snowcap, which appeared to him on November 15, 1806, when he first saw it 150 miles away, as a "small blue Cloud" floating in the western sky; and certainly he never set foot on it.[1] The fame and stature of the peak and the fame and stature of the man are both wrapped round with exaggerations, errors, and deceptions—yet both remain durably significant.

Zebulon Pike's early childhood was spent in his native New Jersey, where he was born on January 5, 1779. By 1793 his father, Captain Zebulon Pike, had brought his family to his military post, at the raw frontier village of Cincinnati, where the seeds of the career of the younger Pike were sown. There he enlisted in the army at fifteen and met the nefarious General James Wilkinson who, for more than a

[1]W. Eugene Hollon, *The Lost Pathfinder, Zebulon Montgomery Pike* (Norman, Okla., 1949), pp. 129, 124.

decade, was to be a major influence in his career and would later all but destroy that career.[2]

Before the handsome young soldier had attained his majority, he had advanced to a first lieutenancy. Through the report of a companion at their station, Fort Allegheny, we see him as a zealous, efficient, strong-willed, but courteous young officer, stoic in the face of hardship and unremitting in driving himself to acquire knowledge in every field he thought might aid his career.[3] At twenty-two he eloped with Clarissa, daughter of a prosperous Kentucky farmer, his maternal uncle Captain James Brown, and thereby permanently estranged himself from that part of his family. He held various commands in the Ohio River region and developed friendships with many who would touch his destiny, among them future President William Henry Harrison, and the "rival" explorer Meriwether Lewis, who came to Pike's frontier post at Kaskaskia to recruit volunteers for his impending expedition to the Pacific. It was to Kaskaskia that General Wilkinson directed a letter to Pike in the early summer of 1805, ordering him to proceed to St. Louis. There he was to prepare for an expedition the lieutenant himself would lead to seek the source of the Mississippi, and along the way to negotiate peace among the Indian tribes of the Upper Mississippi, to acquire appropriate sites for future military posts, and to deal with Canadian fur traders operating within that newly acquired part of Louisiana.[4]

Since much of the territory through which Pike was to lead his Mississippi expedition had been earlier and better described by Jonathan Carver, we can ignore Pike's account in his prosaic journal. After hasty and inadequate preparations Pike and twenty companions set out on August 9, 1805, to find the source of the Mississippi, accomplish his several missions, and "return before the waters are frozen up," obviously an impossible assignment.[5] In the determined attempt they made to fulfill their mission, the party—and especially Pike himself and the few companions who undertook a midwinter search for the river's source—met with such incredible hardships that the wonder is they came back alive. The fruits of the

[2]*Ibid.*, pp. 18–20.
[3]Elliott Coues (ed.), *The Expeditions of Zebulon Montgomery Pike to the Headwaters of the Mississippi River, through Louisiana Territory, and in New Spain, During the Years 1805–6–7* (2 vols., New York, 1895), pp. xxiv–xxvi.
[4]Hollon, *Lost Pathfinder*, pp. 52–53.
[5]Coues, *Expeditions*, vol. 2, p. 843.

expedition were few. Pike deluded himself that in reaching Lake Leech he had discovered the source of the Father of Waters (an error that remained unrevealed until after his death), and he did secure from the Indians land cessions for military installations, most notably one at St. Anthony's Falls. But the successes he claimed in establishing a firm peace among the warring natives and bringing the Canadian fur traders to heel soon proved transitory. His maps of the river and descriptions of the country through which it flowed were misleading. And it was long after the river had become "frozen up" and thawed again under the suns of spring, when the travel-worn band returned to St. Louis, on April 30, 1806, without the native chiefs Pike had been instructed to bring down for parleys in the territorial capital.[6] Nevertheless, his exploits were considered of sufficient importance to receive the praise of President Jefferson in a message to Congress as "very useful additions . . . to our knowledge of the Mississippi . . . by Lieutenant Pike, who has ascended to its source and whose journal will shortly be made ready" for Congress.[7]

Even as Pike was busy getting his family settled at Belle Fontaine, a military post near St. Louis, and deep in attempts to give order and shape to the notes and journal of his Mississippi expedition, he heard from General Wilkinson that plans were in the making for him to lead another, more challenging, expedition into the southern plains and the Rockies to seek out the headwaters of the Arkansas and Red rivers not far from the Spanish provincial capital of Santa Fe. Unlike the Lewis and Clark expedition to the Northwest, this southwestern reconnaissance of newly acquired Louisiana Territory was not undertaken at the behest of the President. Instead, like Pike's Mississippi expedition, it originated with General Wilkinson and thus, *ipso facto,* would become tainted by the suspicions aroused by the Burr Conspiracy and other Wilkinson schemes described later in this chapter.

Such suspicions we now know were without foundation. When Jefferson initiated the Lewis and Clark expedition, Louisiana was Spanish territory. By the time Wilkinson initiated Pike's, Louisiana

---

[6]Coues, *Expeditions,* p. 827; Donald Jackson (ed.), *The Journals of Zebulon Montgomery Pike* (2 vols., Norman, Okla., 1966), vol. 2, p. 229.

[7]Hallon, *Lost Pathfinder,* p. 53; Jaines D. Richardson (ed.), *Messages and Papers of the Presidents, 1789–1897* (10 vols., Washington, D.C., 1907), vol. 1, p. 408; Timothy Severin, *Explorers of the Mississippi* (New York, 1968), Chap. 10, provides a more detailed account of Pike's Mississippi expedition.

had become American territory and he was both its governor and military commander. Moreover, it was widely known that the President desired to dispatch a number of exploring parties into the new territory to take inventory, so to speak. In accordance with those general plans, Pike's expeditions were regularly reported to the Secretary of War and through him to the President.[8] There is little room for doubt that Pike's southwestern expedition was an intelligence-gathering undertaking, designed to secure commercial, political, military, and geographical information. What is pertinent here is that it greatly expanded American geographical and conceptual horizons to include immense strange regions heretofore known only to the Spanish.

Wilkinson's orders enumerated the objectives of the expedition: to convey some fifty Osage Indians back to their Osage River towns, from which they had been captured several months earlier; to arrange a lasting peace between the Osage towns and their Kansas neighbors; to establish good relations with the Pawnee and Comanche nations; to explore the headwaters of the Arkansas and Red rivers; to avoid alarm or offense to the Spaniards of the New Mexico settlements; to remark particularly the geography, geology, and natural history features of interest along the way; to keep these observations in notebooks together with directions, distances, and periodical celestial observations; and finally, to dispatch part of his party down the Arkansas River to make a survey of it and determine its navigability, while the remainder were to continue on to the Red River and descend it to the Mississippi.[9] Later there were supplemental instructions dealing with Indian trade and interpreters, and this announcement: "Doctor Robinson will accompany you as a volunteer. He will be furnished with medicines, and for the accommodations which you give him, he is bound to attend your sick."[10] Much mystery surrounds this able and daring young doctor, John Hamilton Robinson, who would become Pike's most reliable companion. Wilkinson made him one of the party although he was not under his command or even in the army. Apparently he was on a special secret spying mission for Wilkinson, and intended to leave Pike's party when it reached the Upper Arkansas.[11] In addition to

[8]Jackson, *Journals*, vol. 1, pp. ix–x.
[9]Coues, *Expeditions*, vol. 2, pp. 562–565.
[10]Jackson, *Journals*, vol. 1, p. 289.
[11]*Ibid.*, vol. 2, pp. 376.

the exploring group, Pike's command included nineteen noncommissioned officers and privates, most of whom had been with him on his Mississippi expedition.[12] From his journals the impression is unavoidable that the rapport between Pike and this group left much to be desired—an impression supported by his later description of them as a "dam'd set of rascels."[13]

It was not until July 15 that Pike's motley command embarked to ascend the Missouri and its tributary Osage. Disaster was inherent even in this tardy beginning. As in the case of his Mississippi mission, it was utterly impossible for Pike to perform this one without wintering en route. Obviously Wilkinson had little concept of the distances, difficulties of travel, and rigors of climate when he ordered his young protégé and his own son, Lieutenant James B. Wilkinson (who was not very strong), to cross more than 1,200 miles of uncharted wilderness, penetrate the Rocky Mountains in search of the sources of two rivers, and return by an even less known route before winter.

Five weeks after they started out, Pike's entourage was still toiling up the Osage to the villages of their Indian charges, by the meandering river 500 miles from St. Louis. Every dawn they could hear the wailing chants of Indians mourning the loss of their dear ones, killed or carried off in raids. Upstream, beautiful cliffs edged the river while the splendid forests of the Lower Missouri gave way to prairies. Frequently giant cedars hid from view the rolling grasslands extending to the horizon on either side, where Pike envisioned "future seats of husbandry," supporting "numerous herds of domestic animals," "to crown with joy those happy plains."[14]

On their arrival at the Osage towns, Pike's party was witness to the wildly emotional reunion of the redeemed captives and their families. However, the gratitude of the Osage proved shortlived, despite (or perhaps because of) the two weeks that Pike's party remained camped nearby. When they first arrived, the Americans had been given a flattering reception and later were accorded the honor of witnessing the great medicine dance of the Osage. For their part the Americans had distributed the usual Indian presents, bestowed medals on the chief men, and presented an American flag to the nation. As they had reached the head of practical navigation,

[12]*Ibid.*, pp. 358–360.
[13]Jackson, *Journals*, vol. 1, p. ix.
[14]Coues, *Expeditions*, vol. 2, pp. 514, 381ff.

it became essential that mounts should be obtained if the expedition was to proceed. But when Pike began to bargain for horses, of which the Osage had many, the cordiality quickly evaporated. Days of bargaining produced but fifteen animals, some very poor—hardly sufficient to transport the heavy baggage.

Nevertheless, on September 3 the file of twenty-three Americans, fifteen packhorses, and fifteen Indians set out from the Osage towns as a cross-country expedition, the first by Americans to venture across western plains.[15] They trudged their weary way southward down the Osage Trace for several days, thence west and northwest toward the Pawnee towns on the Republican River,[16] which they reached three weeks later, considerably depleted in both native companions and pack animals. A week after departing the Osage towns, Pike records complaints of feet "blistered and very sore" from the 56 miles over rough, flinty hills covered during the previous three days. Fortunately, game continued bountiful. "I stood on a hill," he reports, "and in one view below me saw buffalo, elk, deer, cabrie [pronghorn] and panthers." The expedition's Indian companions killed six of the buffalo, explaining this excessive take by the fact that they were crossing the hunting ground of enemies, so "they would destroy all the game they possibly could." Two days later Pike tried to restrain such wanton slaughter, "not merely because of the scarcity of ammunition, but," as he conceived, "the laws of morality forbid it also."[17]

As they drew near the close-packed aggregation of circular, grass-thatched houses of the Pawnee town, the men, most of whom were "wrapped in buffalo robes, otherwise quite naked," advanced to within a mile of them, then halted, divided into two troops, and "came on each flank at full charge, making all the gestures and performing all the maneuvers of a real war charge," before "the chief advanced in the center and gave us his hand. . . ." With that preliminary the calumet was passed round and eight fine horses were delivered to Pike's Osage companions as gifts to bind their declaration of peace.[18]

From their Pawnee hosts they learned that a large Spanish expedition of 100 dragoons and 500 mounted militia had been ranging the

[15]Hollon, *Lost Pathfinder*, pp. 110–111.
[16]About where it crosses the boundary between Nebraska and Kansas.
[17]Coues, *Expeditions*, vol. 2, pp. 401–402.
[18]*Ibid.*, pp. 409–410.

western plains all the way from the Red River to the Platte, searching for Pike's party and any other American trespassers that might be found, in order to turn them back or arrest them. In any attempt to counter the Spanish influence, the unmounted and bedraggled band of Americans was thus at a great disadvantage. Efforts to obtain more horses produced few results, and Pike's attempts to secure the allegiance of the Pawnee fared little better, though he did manage to persuade the chief, who presided at the grand council of 400 warriors, to surrender their Spanish standard and replace it with an American flag.[19]

On October 6, when the Americans set out toward their next objective, the headwaters of the Arkansas, the mounting disaffection of their red-skinned hosts turned into a dangerous confrontation between 400 Pawnee horsemen and Pike's tiny command. A determined show of force permitted the expedition to depart unharmed and follow the fresh trail southward left by the Spanish troop on its way to New Mexico. However, three days later a band of more than 100 Pawnee warriors overtook and quickly surrounded Pike's plodding party. To invite a breach of peace, the Indians began to plunder the Americans' supplies. Only the combination of a firm show of resistance and the fortuitous appearance of a distracting herd of elk saved the day; Pike's journal could report, instead of a bloody battle, the dramatic spectacle of fifty or sixty mounted Indians sinking their arrows "up to the plume" into the fleeing animals.[20]

The Arkansas, which they reached in mid-October, seemed a strange and unseemly river. Lieutenant Wilkinson reported that when his detachment had arrived there four days earlier, it was a stream only 20 feet wide and 6 inches deep; but now, after two rainy days, it was a raging torrent covering the whole 450-yard expanse between its 4-foot-high cottonwood-fringed banks, beyond which "on the north side is a low swampy prairie; on the south, a sandy sterile desert. . . ."[21]

Preparations were launched to provide Lieutenant Wilkinson with the means for navigation down the capricious Arkansas. Mean-

[19]*Ibid.*, pp. 414–416. The ill-concealed dissatisfaction of the natives after surrendering the Spanish flag induced Pike to return it, with the admonition that it should not be raised when the Americans were among them.

[20]*Ibid.*, p. 421.

[21]*Ibid.*, pp. 427–428, 546.

while Pike and Dr. Robinson made repeated expeditions into the surrounding country in fruitless attempts to find the path followed by the Spanish troops. On one of these they came upon a very large prairie dog village and in the course of passing it killed several of these "prairie-squirrels," as Pike, with more biological accuracy, called them, and "nine large rattlesnakes which frequent their villages."[22] His observation of these creatures inspired what turned out to be the most extensive dissertation on natural history in his journal and one of the earliest known descriptions of the prairie dog: "The sites of their towns are generally on the brow of a hill near some creek or pond. . . . Their holes descend in a spiral form; therefore I could never ascertain their depth; but I once had 140 kettles of water poured into one of them . . . without effect. . . . Their villages sometimes extend over two or three miles square . . . [and] there is generally a burrow every ten steps," but they never extended their excursions in search of food "more than half a mile from their burrows."

We killed great numbers of them [Pike continues] . . . and found them excellent meat after they were exposed a night or two to the frost. . . . It is extremely dangerous to pass through their towns, as they abound with rattlesnakes . . . and strange as it may appear, I have seen the wishtonwish [prairie dog], the rattlesnake, the horn frog [horned toad], with which the prairie abounds . . . and a land-tortoise take refuge in the same hole.[23]

Apparently Pike did not see and report on yet another sharer of prairie dog towns, the burrowing owl, common to most such villages.[24]

On October 28, after a night of heavy snow and a freezing morning, Pike and Wilkinson said their farewells. Pike resumed the march westward by land toward the river's source; Wilkinson, with five soldiers and two Osage Indians, embarked for the voyage downstream in two makeshift craft, a small dugout, and a large bullboat fashioned from cottonwood saplings, four buffalo hides, and two elk skins.[25] To make any progress at all the men had to take to the icy water and haul the boats along. Two days later the river froze over

[22]*Ibid.*, p. 429.

[23]*Ibid.*, pp. 430–431.

[24]Later observers have established that Pike is in error in his belief that these several creatures live together in harmony, and that the prairie dogs' burrows spiral downward.

[25]*Ibid.*, p. 432.

1. This British map, circa 1700, indicates the prevailing geographical knowledge of North America at the dawn of the eighteenth century.

(Kendall Collection, South Caroliniana Library, University of South Carolina.)

2. Simon Gribelin's adaptation (with osprey and eagle added), for Robert Beverley's *History and Present State of Virginia*, of Theodore de Bry's engraving of John White's painting showing the Indians' methods of fishing.

(Alderman Library, University of Virginia.)

3. Isaac Basire's engraving of Cherokee embassy to England in 1730, under the guidance of Sir Alexander Cuming. Depicted here in British attire, the figure on the right is Onaconoa (Attakullakulla), later better known as the "Little Carpenter," famous Cherokee leader.

(South Caroliniana Library, University of South Carolina.)

4. John Lawson's illustrations for the natural history section of his *New Voyage to Carolina*, depicting buffalo, blacksnake attacking a rattlesnake, opossum, bobcat attacking deer, fishing bear, and raccoon using its tail to fish for crabs.

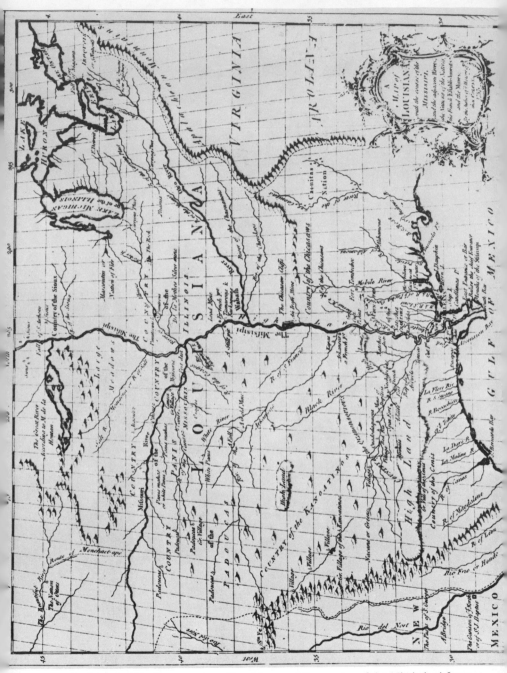

5.   Le Page du Pratz's 1757 map of Louisiana and the course of the Mississippi from his *History of Louisiana*.

6. The Falls of St. Anthony on the Mississippi, depicted by Jonathan Carver, in his *Travels*.

7. William Bartram (1739–1823), from a portrait by Charles Willson Peale.

(Independence National Historical Park Collection.)

8. Alexander Wilson (1766–1813), from a portrait by Rembrandt Peale.

(American Philosophical Society.)

9. François-André Michaux (1770–1855),
from a portrait by Rembrandt Peale.

(American Philosophical Society.)

10. Thomas Nuttall (1786–1859), from an
engraving published in London in 1825.

11. William Clark (1770–1838), from a portrait by Charles Willson Peale.

(Independence National Historical Park Collection.)

12. Meriwether Lewis (1774–1809), from a portrait by Charles Willson Peale.

(Independence National Historical Park Collection.)

13. Zebulon Montgomery Pike (1779–1813), from a portrait by Charles Willson Peale.

(Independence National Historical Park Collection.)

14. John Charles Frémont (1813–1890), from a portrait by Bass Otis.

(National Portrait Gallery, Smithsonian Institution.)

15. Mark Catesby's painting of the "crested jay" (blue jay) and smilax, from his *Natural History*.

(South Caroliniana Library, University of South Carolina.)

16. Catesby's painting of the leopard frog and pitcher plant, from his *Natural History*.

(South Caroliniana Library, University of South Carolina.)

17. William Bartram's painting of the *Franklinia alatamaha*.

(Courtesy of the Trustees of the British Museum, Natural History.)

18. William Bartram's watercolor painting of the American lotus or water chinquapin, the Venus's flytrap *(lower left)*, and the great blue heron.

(Courtesy of the Trustees of the British Museum, Natural History.)

19.   The geographical knowledge of North America on the eve of the Lewis and Clark Expedition. This 1797 map accompanied *The American Gazetteer* of geographer Jedidiah Morse.

(South Caroliniana Library, University of South Carolina.)

20. New Harmony, Indiana, about 1830, during the Owen occupation.

(Reproduced, by permission, from George B. Lockwood, *The New Harmony Movement*, Dover Edition [New York: Dover Publications, Inc., 1971].)

. An illustration, from François-
dré Michaux's *North American Sylva*, of
e black walnut, the work of botanical
ist P. J. Redouté.

homas Cooper Library, University of
uth Carolina.)

22. The ivory-billed woodpecker, pileated woodpecker, and red-headed woodpecker, drawn to scale and colored by Alexander Wilson, for his *American Ornithology*.

(Courtesy Rare Book and Manuscript Library, Columbia University.)

23. J. J. Audubon's Carolina parrots, feeding on cockleburs, engraved and colored for his *Birds of America*.

(University of South Carolina Information Services photograph.)

24. Virginia opossums feeding on persimmon fruit, from *The Viviparous Quadrupeds of North America,* by J. J. Audubon and John Bachman.

(Thomas Cooper Library, University of South Carolina.)

25. John James Audubon, painted by his sons, Victor and John Audubon.
(Courtesy, American Museum of Natural History.)

and the boats had to be abandoned. What with the men being clad only in summer clothing, the bitter cold weather, a barren saline countryside, a severe shortage of ammunition, and an even greater scarcity of game, the very survival of Wilkinson's little party was in question until the miserable band found temporary refuge at a hospitable Arkansas Osage town. Having made new dugouts and encountered "every hardship to which a voyage is subject at so inclement a season of the year,"[26] Wilkinson's group finally reached Arkansas Post, a short distance up from the Mississippi—seventy-three days after first embarking—to become the first American expedition to cross the region between the Kansas and the mouth of the Arkansas.[27]

Meanwhile the main party under Pike had been enduring hardships and dangers even worse than those suffered by Wilkinson's detachment. On the same day, January 9, 1807, that Wilkinson reached Arkansas Post, Pike's men were still on the banks of the Arkansas, but 750 miles to the west, desperately raising a makeshift shelter against the violent storms and wintry cold of the Colorado Rockies. General Wilkinson had gravely underestimated the assignment he had given Pike, for according to his plan, Pike was already long overdue at Natchitoches, at least 800 miles down the Red River, far to the south beyond both the Cimmaron and Canadian rivers.

After seeing Wilkinson set out downstream, Pike's remaining command had marched west along the river, from time to time picking up the elusive trail of the Spanish troop and following it in the hope that it might reveal the route customarily used by travelers to Santa Fe. For three weeks the weather was propitious, game plentiful, and life easy. As they moved further west, both the wild horses sighted in increasing numbers and the pronghorn displayed an unrealistic lack of fear of man. These creatures often allowed their curiosity to overcome fear, although not quite completely enough to permit Pike's men, despite many efforts, to rope even one of the beautiful, fleet steeds. Immense herds of buffalo, all females and calves, were almost constantly in view. Pike was intrigued by the riddle of this display of sex segregation among the buffalo. Watching a herd that he said contained at least 3,000 cows and calves, he thought it "worthy of remark that in all the extent of the country yet

[26]*Ibid.,* p. 556.
[27]Hollon, *Lost Pathfinder,* p. 122.

crossed, we never saw one cow, and that now the face of the earth appeared to be covered with them." It was a "terrestrial paradise." "I believe," Pike added, "that there are buffalo, elk, and deer sufficient on the banks of the Arkansaw alone, if used without waste, to feed all the savages in the United States territory for one century."

Yet these southwestern plains, in Pike's view, held little utility for his country beyond serving as a buffer region between its people and those of the Spanish dominions:

a barren soil, parched and dried up for eight months in the year [which] presents neither moisture nor nutrition sufficient to nourish timber. These vast plains of the western hemisphere, may become in time equally celebrated as the sandy deserts of Africa; for I saw in my route, in various places, tracts of many leagues, where the wind had thrown up the sand, in all the fanciful forms of the ocean's rolling wave, and on which not a speck of vegetable matter existed.[28]

He predicted that "our citizens being so prone to rambling and extending themselves on the frontiers will through necessity, be constrained to limit their extent on the west to the borders of the Missouri and Mississippi, while they leave the prairies incapable of cultivation to the wandering and uncivilized aborigines of the country." Those remarks were the first from which grew the myth of the Great American Desert—a myth that would persist and spread for more than half a century.[29]

Pike's party had taken two and a half weeks crossing the heart of this "desert," which he deemed so suitable to the uncivilized and so unsuitable to the civilized, when he descried a snow-capped peak floating "like a small blue Cloud" in the rarefied air above the western horizon. Before long this spectacular mountain known today as Pike's Peak was in full view, and soon, too, the towering ramparts of the Sangre de Cristo range running southward across the whole western horizon. It was a stirring sight. When they mounted a hill the better to view the grand panorama, the men "with one accord gave three cheers to the Mexican mountains," which "appear to present a natural boundary between the province of Louisiana and New Mexico." Deceived by the effects of the clear, dry air of the region and season, they were baffled by the fact that

[28]Coues, *Expeditions,* vol. 2, pp. 438, 522, 525.

[29]Jackson, *Journals,* vol. 2, pp. 27–28n. Later Stephen Long would expand the misconception of the Great American Desert and more firmly entrench it in the public mind—see below, p. 277.

it required ten more days travel through this spectacular game-rich country before they could reach a point from which an assault might be made on the magnificent peak. Along the way one day they killed seventeen buffalo, more than one for each of the party; and next day, while occupied with drying meat, they enjoyed "a general feast of marrow-bones, 136 of them furnishing the repast."[30]

It was on a cold, clear late November day, while the men and their few remaining horses were taking a greatly needed rest stop near what is now Pueblo, Colorado, that the tireless Pike decided he had reached a place from which he might undertake to scale his Grand Peak. Pike, Dr. Robinson, and two of the men set out for the mountain, which loomed magnificent against the northwest sky, with the expectation of reaching its base in the course of a few hours walk across the prairie. However, it was two days before they reached it and then set out for the summit, which now appeared so near that they left their supplies and blankets behind and began their climb, expecting to return the same evening. Instead, after climbing all day, nightfall forced them to take refuge in a cave where, dressed only in light cotton clothes and without blankets, they huddled together against the cruel alpine cold. Next day another hour of climbing and plowing through waist-deep snow brought them to the summit. To their surprise and chagrin the grand peak rose before them some 15 miles beyond, "entirely bare of vegetation and covered with snow," and as high again as that they had already ascended, enough to convince them that "no human being could have ascended to its pinical."[31] That was Pike's nearest approach to Pike's Peak. On his return to the camp by the river a few days later, he took instrument readings to determine its altitude. He gave the peak an altitude of 18,581 feet—about 4,500 feet more than its actual height.

On the last day of November 1806, as the whole party resumed its way upstream in search of the river's source somewhere among the rugged peaks to the west, the thermometer dropped to 20 below zero; nevertheless, Pike pushed on deeper into the mountains until the men reached spectacular Royal Gorge, the Grand Canyon of the Arkansas. Faced with this formidable impediment to further progress up the main stream of the Arkansas, they explored a tributary coming in from the north, and there discovered the saddle between

[30]Coues, *Expeditions,* vol. 2, pp. 444–447.
[31]*Ibid.,* pp. 457–458.

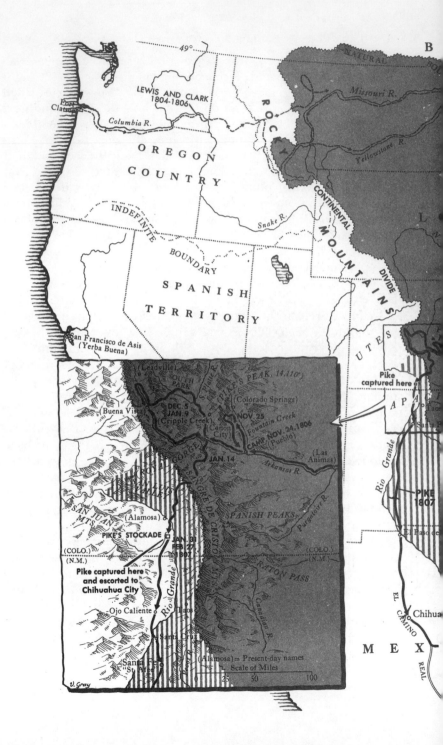

49°

LEWIS AND CLARK
1804-1806

Fort
Clatsop

Columbia R.

ROCKY

NATURAL

Missouri R.

Yellowstone R.

B

LO

OREGON

COUNTRY

Snake R.

INDEFINITE

BOUNDARY

SPANISH

TERRITORY

M
O
U
N
T
A
I
N
S

CONTINENTAL DIVIDE

San Francisco de Asis
(Yerba Buena)

UTES

Pike
captured here

APA

(Leadville)

SOUTH
PARK

S. Platte R.

PIKE'S PEAK, 14,110°

(Buena Vista)

DEC. 5
JAN. 9
Cripple Creek

(Colorado Springs)

NOV 25

Cañon
City

Fountain Creek

CAMP NOV. 24, 1806
(Pueblo)

NOV. 24, 1806

(Las
Animas)

JAN. 14

Arkansas R.

SAN JUAN
MTS.

ROYAL GORGE

(Alamosa)

SANGRE DE CRISTO MTS.

SPANISH PEAKS

Purgatoire R.

PIKE'S STOCKADE

JAN. 31
FEB. 27
1807

(COLO.)
(N.M.)

Pike captured here
and escorted to
Chihuahua City

Rio Grande

RATON PASS

Canadian R.

(COLO.)
(N.M.)

Ojo Caliente

Taos

Santa Cruz

Santa Fe
St. Aug

(Alamosa) = Present-day names
Scale of Miles

Rio Grande

PIKE
1807

El Paso de

EL

CAMINO

Chihua

M E X

REAL

25   50   100

V. Gray

JOURNEYS OF
ZEBULON PIKE
1805-1807

---- Present-day boundaries

Scale of Miles

0   100   200   300

Pike's Peak and the main body of the mountains to the west that leads to South Park, a mountain-girt tableland area that in later years was to become a refuge famous among explorers and mountain men. Descending into South Park, they found a river "40 yards wide, frozen over . . . the occasion of much surprise. . . ." With that comment Pike recorded his discovery of the headwaters of the South Platte. Later, in his "Dissertation on Louisiana," Pike would expand what he thought he had found here to include not merely the sources of the Arkansas and South Platte, but also those of the Colorado, Rio Grande, and Yellowstone, all coming "from that grand reservoir of snows and fountains." Thus he reiterated the supposed existence of Jonathan Carver's common source of Western America's great rivers, but locating it yet further south in central Colorado. From a position in those mountains he boasted: "I can visit the source of any of those rivers in one day."

From South Park, Pike's party aimed "southwest for the head of Red River." Obviously Pike had convinced himself that the Arkansas extended only a little way beyond its Grand Gorge, where they had left it two weeks before. Therefore the substantial stream they found flowing southward along the west flank of Park Range must be the Red, the commonly held belief being that that was the next river south of the Arkansas. The sight of the new stream instilled the hope that at last they were headed for home—a conviction that made Christmas Eve 1806 one of contentment there by the frozen stream, although they could only "celebrate that day with . . . buffalo meat without salt," and all were ill-clothed for winter—"many without blankets, having been obliged to cut them up for socks, etc., and now lying down at night on the snow. . . ."[32]

The most harrowing part of the expedition was still ahead. Soon their catalogue of woes was replete: near starvation, frostbite, horses failing and falling to destruction, leaving their burdens to be carried on the backs of the men or drawn along on crude improvised sleds. To top the bitter cup came Pike's embarrassing discovery that his "Red River," which they had been hopefully following downstream, was actually their long-standing companion, the Arkansas. This became apparent when they arrived back at Royal Gorge, which they had left four weeks before.

Suffering "great mortification" in confessing his error, Pike was

[32]*Ibid.*, pp. 464–466, 523–524, 473.

briefly at a loss as to which way to move. However, the quandary soon gave way to bold and precipitate action. He abandoned the few remaining horses, intending to back-pack and sled their essential equipment and supplies across the mountain barrier rising southwest of them and descend to the Red River waters he was certain would be found there. Preparations for this most perilous, and in truth, most foolhardy leg in the entire course of the expedition immediately got under way. The men constructed a small block house to shelter two of their number, who were to be left in charge of the horses and equipment that fourteen men setting out on the midwinter dash across the mountains to the Red River could not manage. Those left behind were to be sent back for when an "eligible route was discovered." On January 14, 1807, the fourteen set out to the south toward what appeared to be a pass between the Wet Mountains and the unbroken western barrier of the Sangre de Cristo Mountains. Two weeks later they were still fighting their way up the rugged terrain, struggling through snowdrifts 4 feet deep in search of a way through the mountains. Nine of the men had suffered frozen feet, two so severely that they had to be left behind in a makeshift shelter with a supply of meat, ammunition, assurances of rescue—and tears. Later, another with frozen feet was again left behind before a negotiable pass was finally found. At last over the pass, the remaining eleven found a path down which they limped, encouraged by the sight of many trees adorned with pictographs, and a mountain brook, "hailed with fervency as the waters of Red river." Their way down into San Luis Valley (for that was where they were) led southward between the western flank of the mountain range and an amazing expanse of sand dunes, which extended along the foot of the range for 15 miles. Of those spectacular dunes, now known as Great Sand Dunes National Monument, Pike commented that "their appearance was exactly that of the sea in a storm, except as to color, not the least sign of vegetation existing thereon."[33]

Two days later, after skirting the southern edge of the dunes and heading down the valley, they came upon a bold young river flowing southeast. As it was devoid of timber for shelter and boats, they pushed on for a dozen miles to a tributary coming in from the west through a sparsely wooded area. Ascending it about 5 miles, they settled on a site that could provide "timber in order to make tran-

[33] *Ibid.*, pp. 473–493.

sports to descend the river with," and a post defensible for four or five men, to be occupied "while the others returned to assist the poor fellows who had been left behind. . . ." While the men were engaged in its construction, Pike and Robinson, in search of game,

ascended a high hill south of our camp, whence we had a view of all the prairies and rivers to the north of us. It was . . . the most sublime and beautiful inland prospects ever presented to the eyes of man. . . . The main river . . . proceeds down the prairie, making many large and beautiful islands . . . all meadow ground, covered with innumerable herds of deer. The great and lofty mountains covered with eternal snows, seemed to surround the luxuriant vale crowned with perennial flowers, like a terrestial paradise shut out from the view of man.[34]

At this point (February 5) the doctor, "having some pecuniary demands in the province of New Mexico," prepared to leave the party as it continued preparations "to descend to Nachitoches." At this point also, it became quite apparent that Robinson was a secret agent for General Wilkinson; but whether for the general in the performance of his military duties or in his capacity as an Indian trader seeking to expand his personal business to include trade with New Mexico, we shall doubtless never know. Robinson's departure reduced the number in the camp to four, five others having set out to recross the Sangre de Cristo Mountains to rescue those left behind and bring in the equipment.

A week later, while Pike and a companion were out hunting, they met and circumspectly made the acquaintance of two mounted Spanish soldiers, who reported that they were four days travel from Santa Fe. Obviously Robinson's arrival had informed the authorities there, regardless of what he may have told them, that the expedition they had tried to turn back the previous fall must now be close at hand. Hence this two-man scouting party, which spent the night with the Americans before returning to Santa Fe. Obviously, too, there would soon be other Spanish visitors. Meanwhile part of the rescue party returned with two of the other men, and from those left in the mountains and still unable to travel, several bones from their frozen feet and a plea not to leave them to perish in the snowbound wilds.[35]

[34] *Ibid.*, pp. 494, 496–497. This area is south of Antonito, Colorado, near the New Mexico boundary.
[35] *Ibid.*, pp. 497–499, 503–505.

Ten days after the departure of the Spanish guests, the little band at the stockade was surprised by the sight of an approaching Spanish troop—not so much by the visit itself, but rather its impressive array: fifty dragoons and fifty mounted militia, all armed with lances, rifles, and pistols. After formal greetings had been exchanged and breakfast shared together, Pike was told that he was twelve days travel from the nearest point where the Red River is sometimes navigable. When he expressed surprise that it was not navigable from where they were then sitting, he was told that he was on the "Rio del Norte," the Rio Grande. Many who have written of Pike and his expedition have concluded that his surprise was not genuine, but rather a deliberate pretense, which in later years he studiedly defended as sincere when his reputation was under attack because of his continued friendship and admiration for General Wilkinson.[36] Be that as it may, Pike and his men, except for two left at the stockade to await the return of the second rescue party, were taken into custody by the Spanish troop and escorted down to Santa Fe.

After being questioned and having his papers examined by the governor there, Pike was sent on south under escort to Chihuahua for further inquisition, albeit gentle and gentlemanly, with gracious hospitality throughout. Nevertheless, in Chihuahua his papers were confiscated and he was sent under guard by a long roundabout route, to avoid roads and places of military significance, back northeast across Texas to the American border post at Natchitoches on the long-sought Red River—the very place his orders had called for him to have reached the previous year, by a very different route. Pike arrived at the post at the end of June 1807. Eventually all but two of his men (one, having killed the other, was imprisoned in Mexico) were permitted to return to the United States.[37]

During the four months of his 1,500-mile escorted tour of Mexico, from the Colorado stockade through Santa Fe, El Paso, Chihua-

[36]Most notable among those who were convinced that Pike was quite aware of where he was and that he had gone there purposely to spy for the general, or on some sinister mission to the Spanish command at Santa Fé, was Elliott Coues, biographer and editor of the 1895 edition of *Pike's Expeditions.* The still unresolved debate as to whether Pike was genuinely physically lost or only morally lost in a web of plots has no place here. But this author is forced to the conclusion reached by Donald Jackson, the most recent editor of Pike's *Journals,* that the evidence will not support charges that Pike knowingly engaged in any subversive or disloyal activity against his country.

[37]Jackson, *Journals,* vol. 2, pp. 351–354.

hua, Monclova, San Antonio, and Nagadoches, to Natchitoches, Pike accumulated a surprising mass of information—geographical, commercial, political, and military—a feat aided no doubt by the warm personal friendship that developed between quasi-prisoner Lieutenant Pike and his Spanish counterpart, Lieutenant Facundo Melgares. He easily observed and remembered such things as the pervading fear of the completely uncivilized Apache and Comanche war parties, even in long-settled regions where most of the residents were themselves Indians, but with more sedentary traditions. Much of what Pike gleaned along the way would later be employed by him in a section of his report entitled "Observations on New Spain." Since at least 1,000 miles of his excursion through New Spain were across areas destined to become part of the United States, that product of his expedition was also pertinent to the revealing of America.

Captain Pike (for he had been promoted in his absence) had no sooner arrived in Natchitoches than he found himself relentlessly swept into the swirling controversy and scandal known to history as the Burr Conspiracy (or sometimes as the Wilkinson-Burr Conspiracy). Inevitably Captain Pike was involved as friend, protégé, and favored junior officer of General Wilkinson. Although Wilkinson served as principal accuser of Aaron Burr at the treason trial of the former Vice President then in progress at Richmond, he was actually, so many came to believe (and later evidence supports their belief), the principal villain of the piece—a double-dealing traitor, long in the employ of both the United States and Spain. Pike's expedition to the Southwest on Wilkinson's orders, with Wilkinson's son, his "captivity" in Mexico, and his open and unswerving belief in and devotion to his general, all fitted nicely into the suspicions emanating more strongly from Richmond with each fresh sensational development in the trial.

Consequently, for the next four years the young officer who had arrived in Natchitoches in the summer of 1807 expecting the sort of accolade and gratitude given to Lewis and Clark and their men found it necessary to devote most of his time and effort to attaining for himself and his men some recognition. Since honors and rewards had not been spontaneously forthcoming, he set himself to evoke them by various means. Forthwith, he undertook to advance their cause through the publication of full accounts of both his expeditions. But the distraction of the controversies and scandals that constantly threatened his reputation, combined with an ineptitude of expression and literary composition, and the loss of papers in Mexico so that he had to reconstruct most of his journal entries from memory, all conspired to justify Pike's publisher's introductory note to Pike's *Expeditions,* professing his doubt that "any book ever went to press under so many disadvantages."[38]

Despite those difficulties, Pike's long-suffering editor, John Conrad, had stayed with the frustrating task, and in 1810 Pike's account of both his expeditions was published in Philadelphia. Since curiosity concerning the country's vast new Western territories, aroused at the time of the Louisiana Purchase and further stimulated by both the Lewis and Clark and the Pike expeditions, had had little satisfaction up to the time of the release of Pike's account, his book was received with great interest in America and abroad.[39] Despite its many defects, it played a major role in establishing the fame of its author and principal character.

On April 5, 1813, word reached him at his camp on Lake Ontario that he had been promoted to brigadier general. Little more than two weeks later, on the eve of an attack on the British across the Lake at York, Pike, in a dramatic letter to his father, said: "If success attends my steps, honor and glory await my name. . . ." Success did indeed attend him, but while resting after the assault, he was caught in the blast of an exploding British magazine and mortally wounded. For one who so frequently professed his thralldom to heroism and often confessed dreams of glory, such dénouement was in accord with his concept of a soldier's reward. In his last words he asked that

[38]*Ibid.,* vol. 1, pp. xxv–xxvi.

[39]*An Account of Expeditions to the Sources of the Mississippi, and Through the Western Parts of Louisiana to the Sources of the Arkansaw, Kans, La Platte, and Pierre Jaun, Rivers; Performed by Order of the Government of the United States During the Years 1805, 1806, and 1807. And a Tour Through the Interior Parts of New Spain . . . in the Year 1807* (Philadelphia, 1810). Europe's long-standing and continued interest in Louisiana paved the way for a modified and improved London edition in 1811, and French and Dutch editions the following year. The American and English editions had insert maps of the Upper Mississippi, of the Missouri and Arkansas region between St. Louis and Santa Fe, and of New Spain and Mexico, which added greatly to the volume's reception. But the last two maps were omitted from the French edition, for it had come to the attention of the Parisian editor that those two maps had been reproduced from the work of Alexander von Humboldt without the great geographer's consent and without credit. In consequence Pike became involved in yet another controversy, this one reaching up in intellectual circles to correspondence on the subject between Humboldt and Jefferson—Coues, *Expeditions,* vol. 1, pp. xxxv–xliv; Jackson, *Journals,* vol. 2, pp. 377, 387–388. Pike's *Account* appeared more than three years before Biddle's Lewis and Clark work.

the surrendered British flag should be placed beneath his head.[40] So ended the life of Zebulon Montgomery Pike, the brave, sometimes even reckless young leader who played a part second only to that of Lewis and Clark in the continuing discovery of the American West.[41]

[40]Hollon, *Lost Pathfinder,* pp. 210–214.
[41]Jackson, *Journals,* vol. 1, p. x.

CHAPTER 8

The Astorians and the Oregon Trail

LEWIS and Clark had made their triumphant return from the Columbia River in 1806. Four years later John Jacob Astor launched his own expedition to the Pacific—a commercial enterprise financed by the fortune he had built in the fur trade during the quarter century since his arrival from Germany as a peddler of musical instruments.

The successful Lewis and Clark expedition had revealed the fur riches of the West and inspired Astor's plan for a global effort to establish an international fur trade, with its central depot at the mouth of the Columbia River. It would be augmented by a protected transcontinental trade route along the Lewis and Clark Trail, up the Missouri and down the Columbia, to the projected headquarters post.[1] To this end, in 1810 Astor had added the Pacific Fur Company to the American Fur Company he had organized in 1808 to operate in the trans-Mississippi West. The Pacific Company was designed to take advantage of the high-risk, high-profit China fur trade already being ventured by American merchants, and, additionally, to serve as supplier to Russia's Alaskan fur posts. This imperial plan, based on trade agreements arranged in Montreal, St. Louis, and St. Petersburg, the fur trade centers of the day, was to be launched by two simultaneous expeditions—one by land, the

[1]The Columbia River had been first entered in 1792 by the American ship *Columbia,* under the command of Captain Robert Gray of Boston, thereby giving a new name to the river, which until then had been known as the Oregon.

other by sea—both focused on the mouth of the Columbia.[2]

Though the scope and audacity of Astor's conception deserved a better fate than the commercial disaster that awaited it, the ultimate débâcle in no way diminishes the significance of the Astorians, as those involved soon came to be known, to the history of the West. Their story was immortalized by Washington Irving in *Astoria, or Anecdotes of an Enterprise Beyond the Rocky Mountains*[3]—a dramatic tale of a magnificent failure that, at the cost of more than sixty lives lost and a fortune eroded, nevertheless became the nation's gain.[4]

Astor's plans began to materialize in July 1810, with the departure westward from Montreal of a party of voyageurs, recruited there by Wilson Price Hunt, an experienced Indian trader, chief partner in the grand enterprise. Second in command was Donald McKenzie, a native Scot, with ten years experience in the fur trade with Astor's main competitor, the North West Company. A clerk, John Reed, and fourteen crewmen rounded out the party that set out along the traditional water route west, via the Ottawa and across Lakes Huron and Michigan to Green Bay, thence up the Fox and down the Wisconsin and Mississippi to St. Louis, where they arrived in Septem-

[2]Bernard DeVoto, *The Course of Empire* (Boston, 1952), pp. 538–540.

[3]2 vols., Philadelphia, 1836. Other editions appeared in 1836 in London and Paris, soon to be followed by Dutch, German, French, Russian, and Swedish translations —*Astoria*, p. xxiv.

Astoria was enthusiastically received in both America and Europe, the *Spectator* regarding it as Irving's *chef d'oeuvre*—*Spectator* (Oct. 22, 1836), 1,016–1,017, and Edgar Allan Poe in *The Southern Literary Messenger* for January, 1837, terming it masterly. This and my subsequent references to *Astoria* are to the University of Oklahoma Press edition of 1964, edited by Edgeley W. Todd.

In his preparation of *Astoria*, Irving had access to Astor's records of the enterprise as well as several already published reports of participants. Gabriel Franchère, a young French Canadian, had recounted the voyage to Astoria on the *Tonquin* in his *Relation d'un Voyage à la Côte du Nord-ouest de l'Amérique Septentrionale, dans les Années 1810, 11, 12, 13, et 14* (Montreal, 1820); redactions in French of Wilson Price Hunt's diary of his overland journey to the Columbia River, and of Robert Stuart's narrative of the returning Astorians in 1812–13, as well as an account of the *Tonquin*'s voyage from New York to Astoria's site in 1811–12, had appeared in *Nouvelles annales des voyages de la géographie et l'histoire* (vols. 10 and 11, Paris, 1821). Also Ross Cox published his *Adventures on the Columbia River* (2 vols., London, 1831).

Although Irving's fame is based on his skill as a man of letters, historians have judged him a competent and accurate historian as well. See, for example, DeVoto, *Across the Wide Missouri* pp. 401–402, and Hiram M. Chittenden, *A History of the American Fur Trade of the Far West* (3 vols., New York, 1902), vol. 1, Chap. 14, reprinted in Andrew B. Myers (ed.), *A Century of Commentary on the Works of Washington Irving* (Tarrytown, N.Y., 1976), pp. 103–110.

[4]Gabriel Franchère, *Adventures at Astoria, 1810–1814*, edited and translated by Hoyt C. Franchère (Norman, Okla., 1967), pp. xxxi–xxxii.

ber. Along the way, at Mackinac Island, they were joined by another Scot, Ramsay Crooks. After a delay of seven weeks they set out up the Missouri, only to be forced into winter camp on its banks a mere 450 miles above its mouth. There they were joined by another Astor partner, Robert McClellan.

Meanwhile, soon after Hunt's party had arrived in St. Louis, its ocean counterpart had sailed from New York in the *Tonquin,* a 300-ton well-armed vessel with a crew of twenty-one, under the command of Captain Jonathan Thorn, on special leave from the U.S. navy. His passengers included four other partners, Scotsmen David and Robert Stuart, Alexander McKay, and Duncan McDougall, the last named as Astor's proxy, having command of the expedition except at sea, when Captain Thorn took precedence. Also of the supercargo were a dozen clerks,[5] several artisans, and thirteen Canadian voyageurs—an overwhelmingly alien group, many with backgrounds that immutably stamped them with divided loyalties. Despite steadily mounting tension between the willful and independent partners, hungering to assert themselves, and Captain Thorn, a brutal and rigid martinet, the *Tonquin* successfully rounded Cape Horn on Christmas Day 1810, and reached the Sandwich (Hawaiian) Islands in mid-February.[6]

After a period of rest and recuperation on those idyllic isles they resumed their voyage to the mouth of the Columbia. Before sailing Captain Thorn recruited a dozen Sandwich Islanders, who had demonstrated remarkable skill in managing their light craft and the ability to "swim and dive like waterfowl," thereby adding to the diversity of the Astorians' already diverse assembly of Americans, Canadians, Scots, and French. It was late in March 1811 when the *Tonquin* reached the mouth of the Columbia, where

the aspect of the river and the adjacent coast was wild and dangerous. The mouth . . . is upward of four miles wide with a peninsula and promontory

[5]One of them was Alexander Ross, who in later years published his own account of the Astoria venture, in *Adventures of the First Settlers on the Oregon or Columbia River, etc.* (London, 1849).

[6]*Astoria,* pp. 49–61. Among mariners it had become customary, after the ordeal of rounding the Horn, to make for that island paradise to recover, refit, resupply, and give the men a spell of relaxation before continuing on their missions. An annotated English translation of the *Nouvelles Annales* account of the Astorian venture, including a brief account of the voyage of the *Tonquin,* appears as Appendix A in Philip Ashton Rollins (ed.), *The Discovery of the Oregon Trail: Robert Stuart's Narratives* (New York, 1935), pp. 267–328. Rollins's work will be cited hereafter as *Robert Stuart's Narratives.*

on one side, and a long low spit of land on the other; between which a sand bar and chain of breakers almost block up the entrance. The interior of the country rises into successive ranges of mountains, which at the time of the arrival of the *Tonquin,* were covered with snow.

A whaleboat with a crew of four under the command of the chief mate, which was sent in the face of a wild sea to sound the bar and locate a channel, was never seen again. After two more efforts and the loss of another boat and all but two of its crew, the *Tonquin* finally found a way into the river and took refuge behind the northern promontory, Cape Disappointment.[7]

Three weeks later a site on the south bank of the estuary, not far from decaying Fort Clatsop, was selected for the location of the combined trading post and fort they named Astoria. During April and May the men cleared the site of its heavy forest cover and from the logs hewed the materials for their log-walled, bark-roofed quarters, warehouse, and magazine, and the palisades to make their post defensible. They assembled and launched a small schooner, for which prefabricated parts had been brought out from New York.[8] Early in June the *Tonquin* sailed away on her planned trading expedition up the Pacific coast. She was to call again at Astoria on her homeward voyage, at which time partner Alexander McKay, who was going with the ship to manage the initial trading with the Russians, planned to return to the Columbia post. A few days later in Nootka Sound, Vancouver Island, where the *Tonquin* had dropped anchor to trade with the Nootka Indians, trouble erupted between the crew and the Indians who had crowded on deck. As the fight against hopeless odds raged and death of all hands appeared certain, a wounded officer succeeded in reaching the magazine and, by exploding it, killed all aboard, except an Indian interpreter who swam to safety and eventually carried news of the disaster back to the forlorn establishment at Astoria.[9]

While the men who had gone out on the *Tonquin* were erecting their trading post at Astoria, Hunt's cross-country contingent was still in winter camp on the banks of the Missouri. Leaving his men camped there, Hunt returned to St. Louis, mainly to enlist an interpreter capable of communicating with the dreaded Sioux. With

[7]*Astoria,* pp. 76–81; Ross, *Adventures,* p. 76.
[8]*Astoria,* pp. 90–92. The present Astoria, Oregon, is on the site of Fort Astoria—see *Robert Stuart's Narratives,* pp. 270–271.
[9]*Astoria,* pp. 107–114; *Robert Stuart's Narratives,* pp. 271–272.

great difficulty he secured the services of Pierre Dorian, half-breed son of Old (Pierre) Dorian, who had been an interpreter with the Lewis and Clark expedition. On Hunt's return journey to the camp, two more notable persons accompanied him: the Scottish botanist John Bradbury, who was later to publish an account of his travels,[10] and the eccentric and restless English naturalist Thomas Nuttall, then on his first major expedition in America. Along the way they visited with and received the counsel of old Daniel Boone, already a legendary figure, and John Colter, one of the stalwarts of the Lewis and Clark outfit, now a trapper and solitary roamer of the wilderness who related great tales of his adventures, doubtless including his tallest tales of a region in northwest Wyoming—a place already known as "Colter's Hell."[11]

Long after Hunt and his companions rejoined the party and spring had arrived, rain and high water kept the travelers immobile on the bank of the swollen, muddy Missouri. Passenger pigeons came and went on their way to their Northern breeding grounds, "wheeling and shifting suddenly as if with one mind and one impulse; the flashing changes of color they present, as their backs, their breasts, or the underparts of their wings are turned to the spectator, are singularly pleasing. If suddenly startled while feeding in the midst of a forest, the noise they make in getting on the wing is like the roar of a cataract. . . ."[12]

At length the foul weather passed, permitting the Astorians to leave their winter quarters on April 21, 1811. Taking to the boats again were about sixty people, including five partners, the two naturalists, forty Canadian voyageurs, interpreter Dorian, his squaw and children, and several hunters.

As the Missouri River portion of Hunt's route to the Rockies had already been explored by Lewis and Clark and had become a familiar way, only a few highlights and new discoveries of this part of the Astorians' journey have a place in this account. Mid-July found them camped near the Arikara[13] village at the mouth of a small Missouri tributary misnamed the Grand. They had been delayed there for a

[10]John Bradbury, *Travels in the Interior of America* (Liverpool, 1817). According to Bernard DeVoto, Bradbury and Nuttall were the first trained scientists ever to enter the Far West—DeVoto, *Across the Wide Missouri*, p. 183.
[11]Now Yellowstone National Park; *Astoria*, pp. 146–156; William H. Goetzmann, *Exploration and Empire* (New York, 1966), pp. 20–22.
[12]*Astoria*, pp. 154–155.
[13]Also known as the Ricarees or simply Rees.

month while Hunt pursued difficult and frustrating negotiations to secure sufficient horses to move his party overland directly west, which he elected to do rather than continue the slow and circuitous river route Lewis and Clark had followed. For the naturalists, Nuttall and Bradbury, any delay was a delight. On the way upriver they had chafed at the restrictions boat travel imposed on their scientific rambles. Nevertheless, they had been making exciting finds of "immense beds of coal," "great veins of iron," "soils strongly impregnated with sulphur, copperas, alum, and glauber salts," and a wide variety of plants new to them.[14]

Camped nearby for part of their Arikara halt was another party of Americans. One of these was Manuel Lisa, notoriously aggressive personification of Astor's bitter rival the Missouri Fur Company.[15] At one point it required all the diplomatic skills of Bradbury and an adventuring young writer, Henry Marie Brackenridge, who had come up with Lisa's outfit, to arrange a truce between the rival parties just as violence seemed inevitable. Thereafter Brackenridge was much in the company of his learned associates in Hunt's camp until he and Bradbury turned back downriver to St. Louis, and Nuttall joined Lisa to continue upstream as far as the Mandans. Brackenridge was yet another who recorded at least part of the cross-country Astorians' experiences.[16]

Meanwhile, as the overland Astorians were impatiently enduring the second interruption in their westward progress, Astor's waterborne party on the Columbia estuary was enduring its own difficulties. Tidings of the loss of the *Tonquin* and Alexander McKay had cast gloom over the infant settlement. The onset of the winter rains and the all-pervading damp chill, plus a shortage of provisions, further eroded their spirits. But their greatest concern, as the winter

[14]*Astoria*, pp. 178–179. For the naturalists' botanical accomplishments, see S. D. McKelvey, *Botanical Exploration of the Trans-Mississippi West, 1790–1850* (Arnold Arboretum, Jamaica Plain, Mass., 1955), pp. 107–150.

[15]The dramatic story of the rise and fall of the Western fur trade and the colorful characters involved in it is the subject of Washington Irving's *Adventures of Captain Bonneville, U.S.A. in the Rocky Mountains and the Far West,* edited by Edgeley W. Todd (Norman, Okla., 1964; originally published in 2 vols., Philadelphia, 1837). It is also the subject of DeVoto's *Across the Wide Missouri* and of Alexander Ross's *The Fur Hunters of the Far West,* edited by Kenneth Spaulding (Norman, Okla., 1956).

[16]Henry Marie Brackenridge, *Views of Louisiana with a Journal of a Voyage up the Missouri River, in 1811* (Pittsburgh, 1814); *Journal of a Voyage up the River Missouri* (Baltimore, 1815). Henry Marie should not be confused with his famous father, Pennsylvania Judge Hugh Henry Brackenridge, author of the satire *Modern Chivalry.*

wore on, was for the fate of Hunt's long-overdue party. There was a measure of relief from that anxiety when in mid-January, eleven of the overland Astorians, in "fluttering rags," including McClellan, Donald McKenzie, and Reed, came paddling down the river. Another month passed before Hunt and his miserable band arrived for a joyous reunion with the earlier party, from whom they had separated some 400 miles back in the wilderness on the austere banks of the treacherous Snake River.[17]

Now with most of those who had endured the 2,073-mile journey from the Arikara village on the Missouri reunited at Astoria, there were tales aplenty to be recounted—the adventures and discoveries, suffering and trials encountered in making their way across that immense unexplored wilderness, much of it through regions of awesome terrain and rigorous climate.[18] In composite, what a story it turned out to be! To sample it, we must return to their departure from the Missouri the previous July.

It will be recalled that Hunt's month-long halt at the Arikara village had been to secure horses to provide overland transport for his party. In deciding to leave the Missouri at the mouth of the Grand, he had followed the advice of three newly recruited members of his entourage. The three were all Kentucky "hunters of the 'dreadnaught' stamp," who were on their way back east from beyond the mountains, where they had been with trapper Andrew Henry at his fort on Henry's Fork of the Snake River, when they met the Astorians. Fear for continued survival under conditions there had prompted them to head back to the safety of their Kentucky homes, an aim abandoned when the opportunity to join the well-equipped and comparatively large Astorian group presented itself. As they turned back westward with Hunt they were to become, in effect, the Sacajawea of Hunt's party, all the way from the Missouri to their erstwhile station southwest of Yellowstone Park. They assured Hunt that the route they had traveled on their way from Fort Henry would be bountifully supplied with game and far more easily

[17]*Astoria*, pp. 323–324; Ross, *Adventures*, p. 185.

[18]*Astoria*, p. 321n. The 2,073-mile estimate was Hunt's calculation. All but 250 miles of it was across regions accounted unexplored. All the overland Astorians were now reassembled save a group left at Henry's Fort to trap, several of the voyageurs who had deserted to take up life with the Indians, and two who had drowned in the Snake—Wilson Price Hunt, *Journey of Mr. Hunt and His Companions from St. Louis to the Mouth of the Columbia by a New Route Across the Rocky Mountains*, in Robert Stuart, *Discovery of the Oregon Trail*, edited by Philip Ashton Rollins (New York, 1935), p. 308.

traveled than the Great Falls-Three Forks route of Lewis and Clark, which would have taken them 300 or 400 miles further north before reaching the mountains. The Kentuckians' route led almost due west to the Big Horn, thence up the Wind River, and across the continental divide through Union Pass.[19]

The month the Astorians devoted to the ritualized circumspect process of trading for horses netted them only eighty-three animals, barely more than required for baggage. Nevertheless, on July 18, with but two months of summer left and half the continent before it, the caravan filed out from the Arikara village and headed west along the left bank of the Grand. Their way led across "immense prairies bounded only by the horizon and destitute of trees," although all about were the remains of forests long gone, memorialized by the petrified trunks of trees, some still erect. On those naked plains their only fuel was buffalo chips, "as the Arabs of the desert use [the droppings] of the camel," a hardship ameliorated by the plentiful supply, for immense herds of buffalo literally covered the landscape. As it was the rutting season the bulls were uncommonly fierce and pugnacious, causing a "universal restlessness and commotion throughout the plain," the "low bellowings" resounding "like distant thunder," the bulls "butting their huge shagged fronts together, gouging each other with their short black horns, and tearing up the earth with their feet in perfect fury." On these rich hunting grounds they came upon a band of friendly Cheyennes, from whom, by devoting another precious fortnight to bargaining, Hunt secured thirty-six more horses, enabling everyone to ride for half of each travel day.[20]

Across the country drained by the Little Missouri, the Powder, and the Bighorn, through the weird formations of the Black Hills, across the rugged passes of the snow-capped Big Horns, from the realm of the buffalo to that of the black-tailed deer, the bighorn sheep, pronghorn, and terrifying grizzly bear, the Astorians made their tortuous way under the guidance of the three Kentuckians. It was now September and they were entering the haunts of the notorious Crow Indians, master equestrians and reputedly the most adept horse thieves of the Northwest. When the Astorians encountered a band of them, however, they found them agreeable enough to negotiate with for more horses and dressed buffalo

[19] *Astoria*, pp. 175–177.
[20] *Ibid.*, pp. 217, 226; Hunt, *Journey*, p. 282.

robes. Another band traveling their way along the Big Horn proved so friendly that

the two cavalcades of white and red men . . . pushed on together, and presented a wild and picturesque spectacle, as, equipped with various weapons and in various garbs, with trains of packhorses, they wound in long lines through the rugged defiles, and up and down the crags and steeps of the mountains . . . The children were perfect imps on horseback. Among them was one so young that he could not yet speak.

The two cavalcades parted where the Wind River joins the Big Horn.[21]

Hunt's column followed a path up the Wind River, where the wintry blasts sweep down its narrow valley with such persistence that snow is prevented from accumulating. Along a tributary that came down from the Wind River range to the west, a path led up toward a mountain saddle, known today as Union Pass, in western Wyoming. Up this path the caravan toiled to that cleft in the backbone of the continent, the culmination of the long ascent begun 1,500 miles away in St. Louis, to which they had devoted almost a year. Seven or eight hundred miles yet lay between this pass and the mouth of the Columbia, most of it through the tremendous and inhospitable ranges of the Northern Rockies at their widest extent, mountains regarded by the Indians of the region with awe, and clothed by them in mystery and superstition. In their minds,

this immense range of mountains, which divides all they know of the world, and gives birth to such mighty rivers, is still more an object of awe and veneration. They call it the "crest of the world," and think that Wacondah, or the master of life, as they designate the Supreme Being, has his residence among these aerial heights. . . . Here also is the "Land of Souls," in which are the "towns of the free and generous spirits," where those who have pleased the master of life while living, enjoy after death all manner of delights.[22]

With fear and misgiving the cold and hungry Astorians toiled on toward the crest of Union Pass. At the crest, however, when the grand panorama of the Gros Ventre range and the Grand Tetons appeared before them, joy and exuberance quickly replaced their apprehensions. In breathtaking grandeur rose the Three Tetons, which, they were told, would guide them far through the confusing

[21] *Astoria*, pp. 249, 254.
[22] *Ibid.*, pp. 242–243.

maze of the ranges and subranges, often running in unexpected directions, that characterize the Northern Rockies. In anticipation of that service, Hunt gave the Three Tetons their enduring alternate appellation of Pilot Knobs. Ironically, in the first test of their guidance, the Pilot Knobs failed. On their descent from the pass the Astorians picked up a path running along a stream that led southward into a beautiful valley with excellent pasturage and game in great plenty, only to discover that instead of being on Columbia River waters, they were following down the Green River Valley of the Upper Colorado. Turning back, they sought out the Hoback, whose waters eventually fall into the Columbia, and followed it as it meandered among rocks and precipices. When obliged to ford it, the men were often in danger of being swept away. At length they emerged from its stupendous defiles into a stern mountain valley where the Hoback joins the Snake, which sweeps off through the valley in such turbulence that they named it Mad River. A few miles away they could see again the snowy peaks of the Tetons, the Pilot Knobs, great "landmarks of the Columbia."[23]

Now having reached the westward limit of the Kentuckians' experience, Hunt was in a quandary as to whether to try to navigate this mad river or continue by land, despite the rough terrain and the advancing season. Almost all the party were in favor of taking to the river, although it looked dangerous and trees suitable for making canoes were scarce. As the defiles began to echo to the sounds of axes, Hunt, as a precaution, sent a party forward to reconnoiter the river for some distance below. Before it had returned with its alarming report, two passing Snake Indians, seeing the men at work on the boats, shook their heads and by signs gave a like report. This discouraging information brought about a decision to abandon the unfinished canoes and move north across a spur range to the shelter of Henry's Fort on Henry's Fork of the Snake. There they could secure the game their guides assured them would be found, pending a decision as to the most advisable course to follow in view of the mounting hazards of the winter sweeping down upon them.

The abandoned fort appeared to Hunt to be an advantageous spot, with a readymade facility for one of the several planned satellite trading posts where the Astorians were to collect furs to be forwarded down to the main establishment at the mouth of the

[23] *Ibid.*, p. 262. The valley through which the river sweeps is Jackson Hole in southwestern Wyoming.

Columbia. The river it was seated upon was such a beautiful stream, so navigable, and bordered by such splendid trees suitable for canoes, that decisions practically made themselves. In a matter of days the Company had in operation a strategically located mountain trading post. The decision to proceed west by water reinstated, trees were being fashioned into dugouts while trappers, equipped with horses, ammunition, and traps, were moving out in pairs to launch their business.

On October 18, in fifteen heavily laden canoes, those who were to continue west pushed off from the fort into the deceptively smooth, broad-breasted river. Spirits were high as they shouted their farewells to two caretaker Snake Indians to whom they had entrusted the new post and their seventy-seven remaining horses, pending the return next season of those who would manage the post. At first navigation was easy, progress swift, and esprit high, as they coursed down nearly 250 miles of Henry's Fork and the Snake itself without seeing a human being in all that wild desert solitude, almost destitute of animal life, through which the river carried them.[24] When at last they did come upon a band of wandering Snake Indians digging roots to sustain themselves through the approaching winter, the poor Indians fled in terror, leaving behind all their pitifully meager possessions.

But suddenly the river turned wild and boisterous. Long stretches of tremendous rapids were interspersed with high falls around which portages were difficult and dangerous. The men persisted, even when the river rushed through canyon walls and tumbled wildly over precipitous falls. In one portage they carried four of the heavy boats 6 miles over treacherous terrain, only to lose them all and much equipment in an attempt to let them down by ropes through the next bad place. A little further down one of the boats smashed sideways on a rock, spilling its contents and crew into the tempestuous current, with the loss of one man, the boat, and its entire precious cargo.[25]

These accidents, and the recollection of the incredulity with which the Indians had viewed their preparation of boats, discouraged any further attempt to navigate the unruly Snake—a river

[24] *Ibid.,* pp. 268–274. The series of falls and rapids encountered here by the Astorians include Shoshone Falls (212 ft.) and Twin Falls.

[25] *Ibid.,* pp. 274–279. This disaster occurred at Clappine's Rapids, a mile and a half below the Milner Dam in southern Idaho—*Robert Stuart's Narratives,* p. 122, note 65.

now known as perhaps the least susceptible to navigation of any river of consequence in America. A mile below the site of that last disaster, at a place where the river entered a turbulent gorge only 40 feet wide that they named "Cauldron Linn," they decided to abandon the boats, cache all but the most essential equipment, and continue on foot along the river's course until horses might be secured. Now, in the barren wilderness in which they found themselves with only a five-day supply of food, famine stared them in the face. To facilitate foraging, Hunt divided his men into five groups, each to set out a different way.[26]

Of all the separate parties that set out from the Devil's Scuttle Hole, as the men soon dubbed Cauldron Linn, to make their way by diverse routes to the fort at Astoria, only that under Hunt made discoveries sufficiently important for this account to detail: except for his short-lived effort to continue northward along the course of the Snake beyond the mouth of the Boise River, from which he was forced to retreat after reaching Hell's Canyon, Hunt's route was to become substantially the route of the Oregon Trail. To ensure a supply of water at every stop through this desert country, Hunt at first deemed it advisable to stay close by the river; but it soon became obvious that this was a mistake, for the Snake cut ever deeper into the rugged plateau as it rushed toward the mile-and-a-half-deep Hell's Canyon, where a man might die of thirst in full view of its waters, beyond reach in the canyon below.[27]

By early December, four weeks after leaving Cauldron Linn, he estimated that they had covered 472 miles, almost every mile an ordeal. But they were now stalled. One day the snow was so deep, the north wind so wild, the surface so rocky and broken, and the men so weak from hunger that they could make but 4 miles. Three more days netted them only 19. From an eminence they got a wide view of the country into which they had penetrated:

In every direction they beheld snowy mountains, partially sprinkled with pines and other evergreens, and spreading a desert and toilsome world around them. The wind howled over the bleak and wintry landscape, and seemed to penetrate to the marrow of their bones. They waded on through the snow, which at every step was more than knee deep.[28]

[26]*Astoria*, pp. 282–284. The party was now where the Snake reaches furthest south in its great 180-degree sweep across southern Idaho.
[27]The Grand Canyon of the Snake River, the deepest gorge on earth.
[28]*Astoria*, p. 293; Hunt, *Journey*, pp. 293–297.

Although the snow alleviated their thirst, which a few days earlier had driven some of the party to resort to drinking urine, their hunger was still extreme, only partially appeased by a little dried salmon, and the meat of two dogs and one of three horses acquired along the way from Indians who were themselves near starvation and so terrified at the approach of the white men, the first they had ever seen, that they often fled, concealing their few animals, but abandoning their small children, left hiding in the bedstraw.

The endless array of snow-covered mountains looming up in every direction at length drove the Company, in despair, to seek shelter in the canyon. Down its wall they slipped and slid to the bottom where, to their relief, it was warmer and the snow was only ankle deep. Hunt determined, as the only way out of their desperate situation, to lead his woebegone band back upriver along the edge of the canyon to some Indian villages he had seen on the Weiser and Payette, tributary streams of the Snake he had crossed a few days before. This return journey was survived only through the capture by Hunt's men of a few horses at a Shoshone village along the way. When they reached the Weiser, Hunt was informed by the natives of a more feasible path to the Columbia. He was told they should cross to the west side of the Snake and follow a trail northwestward across the Blue Mountains to the Umatilla River, and down it to its confluence with the Columbia. However, their informants warned against attempting this journey in winter, and indicated the sincerity of their warning by their reluctance to supply a guide. Eventually one was secured, but only after much cajoling and the promise of a princely reward.

Ignoring the Shoshones' warnings, Hunt's band effected a perilous crossing of the Snake by bullboat ferry, and on Christmas Eve 1811 left the disastrous banks of "La maudite rivière enragée," as the voyageurs termed it, which had already taken two of their number.[29]

Although the weather was bitterly cold, they pushed forward with renewed spirit, particularly after they came on a Shoshone village of six lodges where they managed to acquire a good supply of horses and dogs. As they crossed over the summit of the Blue Mountains and saw, spreading out below them, a snowless plain, they hailed it "as the poor Israelites hailed the first glimpse of the

[29]"The accursed mad river"—*Astoria*, pp. 301–305.

promised land, feeling at last that their painful pilgrimage might be drawing to a close." Heading down toward it they saw among the rocks and precipices "gangs of that mountain-loving animal, the blacktailed deer." Soon they reached the Umatilla River, flowing down from the Blue Mountains on its way northwest to the Columbia. It was there that the overland Astorians met their first Pacific Indians, Sciatogas, meaning "eaters of camass roots."[30] By Indian standards these people were well off, dressed in leather hunting shirts and leggings and robes of buffalo or deer skins. At the town, which consisted of thirty-four mat-covered lodges, about 2,000 horses ranged the nearby pastures. Hunt pronounced the Sciatogas "a proud and spirited race, uncommonly cleanly," who never ate horse or dog flesh and who hunted deer on horseback, using the circling procedure of the Plains horse hunters. Although they had axes, brass kettles, and other trade goods, secured from itinerent trading vessels on the lower Columbia, they preferred many of their primitive ways, employing bows and arrows, and bottle-shaped stone mallets and wedges of elk horn to split logs. They continued to cook in bowls of wood or tightly woven basketry in which hot stones were immersed in the contents. Before they departed from these friendly people, Hunt secured a commitment that they would "use all diligence in collecting quantities of beaver skins"; no doubt they "proceeded to make deadly war upon that sagacious, but ill fated animal, who, in general, lived in peaceful insignificance among his Indian neighbors, before the intrusion of the white trader."[31]

Next day was the great day when the way-worn travelers at last beheld the long-sought waters of the Columbia itself. "The sight was hailed with as much transport as if they had already reached the end of their pilgrimage," although in fact some 250 miles of difficult way yet lay between them and their objective. Having carried Lewis and Clark along that route, past the Celilo Falls, the Dallas, and the Long Narrows to the stormy estuary of the Columbia, we shall not here travel it again with Hunt and his woebegone band. They reached Astoria without further disasters on February 15, 1812, after eleven months of unbroken wilderness travel. "A shout of joy burst from each canoe at the long-wished-for sight." Among those

[30]A people of confused distinctiveness and relationships—*Robert Stuart's Narratives*, Appendix B, pp. 354–355.

[31]*Astoria*, pp. 310–313.

who rushed down to greet them at the water's edge were some of their old comrades and fellow sufferers, Reed, McClellan, and McKenzie, whom they had last seen three months before as they set out separately from the Devil's Scuttle Hole.

During the celebration that ensued, replete with fish, venison, and a generous issue of grog, Hunt heard the accounts of their experiences. Although, when they set out, each had aimed for a different route, amazingly enough their three parties had found each other in the Snake River Mountains, and in company managed to get through them before the onset of the heavy snows that had forced Hunt to retreat from the same region. Nevertheless, it was only by sheer good fortune that they had survived to tell their story. They too suffered days of terrible thirst as they followed down the east rim of Hell's Canyon where its almost sheer walls rose as much as 8,000 feet from the river below, with rarely a "place where the travellers could get down to drink of its waters. Frequently they suffered the torments of Tantalus; water continually within sight, yet fevered with the most parching thirst [so that] some of the men had recourse to the last expedient to avoid perishing." Their escape from starvation was equally narrow. However, at the time of their most critical distress they reached the Columbia Valley, where food secured from the natives sustained them down to Astoria.[32]

Spring came to the lush and dripping forest surrounding Astoria's palisaded cabins and with it the arrival of the *Beaver,* the first of the annual supply ships sent out from New York.[33] The winter had passed tranquilly. Despite the almost daily rains the Astorians had learned much of this coastal region, its climate, the productions of its incredibly magnificent forests, its teeming waters, and its inhabitants. With the arrival of spring there was much to be done to forward the enterprise. Most urgent was the necessity of dispatching reports to Astor informing him of the present state of his Pacific enterprise.

Soon after the arrival of the *Beaver* and the last of the overland

[32]*Ibid.,* pp. 314, 320–321, 322–324.

[33]*Ibid.,* pp. 351–353. The *Beaver* was to continue northward along the coast (as the *Tonquin* had set out to do), to supply the Russian fur stations and pick up furs from them for barter in Canton, at fabulous rates in Chinese goods, before setting sail for the Horn and home. For discussion of the *Beaver* voyage from New York, see Ross Cox, *The Columbia River,* edited by Edgar I. Stewart and Jane R. Stewart (Norman, Okla., 1957). Cox was a passenger on the *Beaver* from New York to Astoria as a member of the Astoria company.

Astorians, plans were laid for a select band to become the Company's transcontinental couriers. As its leader the reliable twenty-seven-year-old Scot, Robert Stuart, who had originally come out by sea, was selected.[34] To provide the overland experience he lacked, several trusty, well-tried men who had come across with Hunt were to accompany him, along with two of the partners, Robert McClellan and Ramsay Crooks, both now weary of the enterprise. They departed Astoria on June 29, 1812, traveling for protection past the robber-infested portages in the company of a larger group headed upriver on other missions to the interior. Beyond the Walla Walla village, the tiny courier band would be on its own. The greatest hazard they met on this first leg of their journey east was the numerous rattlesnakes, "on which the men were in danger of treading. They were often found, too, in quantities about the encampments. In one place, a nest of them lay coiled together, basking in the sun." They killed or wounded thirty-seven at that place.[35]

As the Walla Walla were equestrian people, Stuart, with replenished stores of trade goods, was able to purchase twenty horses— enough to permit his band to become a mounted expedition, an essential in view of their very late start. Then the

little band mounted their steeds and took a farewell of their fellow-travellers, who gave them three hearty cheers as they set out on their dangerous journey. The course they took was to the southeast, towards the fated region of the Snake River. At an immense distance rose a chain of craggy mountains, which . . . from their azure tints, when seen at a distance, had received the name of Blue Mountains.[36]

It was the season of the great spawning runs of the salmon, so as they followed up the west bank of the Snake they often came upon places the Indians frequented to replenish their stores of that staple food. At one such place, which they named Salmon Falls, they reported a

perpendicular fall of twenty feet on the north side of the river, while on the south side there is a succession of rapids. The salmon are taken here in incredible quantities, as they attempt to shoot the falls. It was now a favorable season, and there were about a hundred lodges of Shoshones busily

[34] *Robert Stuart's Narratives*, pp. xxxv–xlvi; Robert Stuart, *On the Oregon Trail: Robert Stuart's Journey of Discovery*, edited by Kenneth A. Spaulding (Norman, Okla., 1953), pp. 9–11.
[35] *Astoria*, pp. 356–360.
[36] *Ibid.*, pp. 361–362.

engaged in killing and drying fish. The salmon begin to leap the centre of the falls, where some station themselves on rocks, and others stand to their waists in water, all armed with spears, with which they assail the salmon as they attempt to leap, or fall back exhausted. It is incessant slaughter, so great is the throng of fish.

Some of those magnificent fish, according to one observer, had been seen to leap 30 feet from the commencement of the foam at the foot of the fall completely to the top.[37]

A little beyond Salmon Falls was that memorable place where the river had finally defeated the persistence and daring of the overland Astorians and cowed them into abandoning their hope of riding its treacherous waters to the sea. Here Stuart and his band expected to draw from the caches they had left there to augment their meager supplies. To their dismay, they found that six of the nine caches had been opened and rifled of everything useful (the three remaining caches supplied dry goods, ammunition, and beaver traps).

On arrival at the mouth of the Portneuf River in southeast Idaho, Stuart had to make a decision. Several weeks earlier an Indian they met on the trail, who had served Hunt well as guide on his westward journey, had told Stuart that there was a far safer and easier way across the Rockies than that Hunt had followed between the Missouri and Cauldron Linn. As Stuart would soon discover, and reveal for others to follow, the route the Indian recommended crossed the continental divide in the neighborhood of South Pass, and from there followed the North Platte River to the Missouri. This was the route that would soon become famous as a critical section of the Oregon Trail, the main highway to the great Northwest, particularly during the thirties and forties when, summer after summer, successions of wagon trains crawled its 2,000 miles to the promised lands of the century, California and Oregon.[38]

Up the Portneuf and thence over to Bear River, which feeds into Great Salt Lake, Stuart led his band on a direct course toward South Pass, the one easy pass across the Rockies. He might well have made it to St. Louis before winter froze all travel had it not been his bad luck to encounter a band of Crows while camped on the Bear—an

---

[37] *Ibid.*, p. 373; *Robert Stuart's Narratives*, pp. 108–118; Stuart, *On the Oregon Trail*, pp. 84–85. This fishery is at Lower Salmon Falls, Idaho.

[38] *Astoria*, pp. 377–378; Goetzmann, *Exploration and Empire*, pp. 33, 168, 170, 179; *Robert Stuart's Narratives*, p. 84.

encounter that was serious enough to deflect them from their appointed route toward South Pass.[39]

In the hope of losing the harassing band of Crows and quitting their country as quickly as possible, Stuart turned sharply north toward the Grand Tetons and the headwaters of the Snake. It proved a disastrous maneuver. They lost not only all their horses but themselves as well in that confusing wilderness of mountains and rivers that run in surprising directions. While they were breaking camp on September 19, a mounted Crow

galloped past the camp, bearing a red flag. He reined his steed on the summit of a neighboring knoll and waved his flaring banner. A diabolical yell now broke forth on the opposite side of the camp, beyond where the horses were grazing, and a small troop of savages came galloping up, whooping and making a terrific clamor. The horses took fright and dashed across the camp in the direction of the standardbearer, attracted by his waving flag. He instantly put spurs to his steed and scoured off followed by the panic-stricken herd, their fright being increased by the yells of the savages in the rear.[40]

Thoroughly shaken, the courier band, now on foot, continued its northward flight along the infant Snake. Numerous beaver ponds impeded the men's progress while also providing salvation, for in that region almost devoid of game they were reduced to complete dependence on the yield of a single beaver trap. Finding travel along the river nearly impossible, they left it to strike eastward across the mountains through Teton Pass. The crossing of the Tetons into beautiful Jackson Hole left the wanderers exhausted and near starvation, from which they were providentially saved by coming upon a lone, decrepit buffalo bull. Employing every skill and precaution they could muster, they managed to secure it.[41]

Snow and bitter cold increased the men's misery as they moved southward from Jackson Hole down the western flank of the Wind River Mountains, across "a level plain about ten miles in circumference, and encrusted to the depth of a foot or eighteen inches with salt as white as snow," and through the icy waters of tributary

[39] *Robert Stuart's Narratives*, pp. 129–130.

[40] *Ibid.*, pp. 131–135; *Astoria*, p. 383. Here Irving embellishes Stuart's account to make a good story—see Stuart, *On the Oregon Trail*, pp. 20, 97–103.

[41] In the course of their northward detour Stuart's band was in such dire straits that one of his Canadian hunters attempted to force a casting of lots at gunpoint for one of their number to be slaughtered to feed the others—Stuart, *On the Oregon Trail*, p. 98n.; *Robert Stuart's Narratives*, pp. 157–158.

streams of the "Spanish River,"[42] as they resumed their way toward their Indian friend's "easy" route over the divide. On October 22 they crossed the wide saddle of South Pass, but in descending its eastern slope, instead of veering left to the headwaters of the Sweetwater (as later, better-informed travelers along the Oregon Trail would do), they proceeded along the south flank of the Antelope Hills and Green Mountains, effectively walling themselves off from the river, until they found a way across the Green Mountains through the "savage grandeur" of the narrow and treacherous gorge of Muddy Gap to the Sweetwater and an easier trail.[43] By the end of October, enduring increasing foretastes of winter's bitter cold and realizing that it would be impossible to make it down to St. Louis before ice closed the river, Stuart decided to find a suitable campsite where the party might await in safety the coming of spring.

The place selected was a cottonwood grove on the south bank of the wide North Platte, about two days travel below its confluence with the Sweetwater. The forested mountains rising from the edge of the valley

were broken and precipitous, with huge bluffs protruding from among the forests. Their rock recesses, and beetling cliffs, afforded retreats to innumerable flocks of bighorn, while the woody summits and ravines abounded with bears and black-tailed deer. These, with the numerous herds of buffalo that ranged the lower grounds along the river, promised the travellers abundant cheer in their winter quarters.

To add to that prospect, so pleasant for men long subjected to hardship and want, they raised a comfortable cabin of logs and buffalo hides, which they soon had well stocked with game.[44]

One morning about daybreak, while the men were at work in the cabin preparing garments against the deepening winter, a series of savage yells signaled the end of their peaceful existence. Outside, surrounding the cabin, was a party of twenty-three Arapaho warriors in full battle dress. With punctilious formal hospitality but extreme wariness, Stuart and his men surrendered most of their store of food to the hungry guests. Although the war party departed in

---

[42]Green River.

[43]*Astoria,* pp. 405–410. For Stuart's diary entries and his later additions redacted in the *Nouvelles Annales* text covering this historically important part of the route of the returning Astorians, and the editor's enlightening notes, see *Robert Stuart's Narratives,* pp. 159–186; Stuart, *On the Oregon Trail,* p. 122n.

[44]*Astoria,* p. 412.

peace, their hosts had little doubt that they would soon return in a less docile mood, and no sooner were the Indians out of sight than preparations were under way to quit the comfortable riverside abode.[45] New Year's Day 1813 found them 150 miles further down the North Platte, hard at work on a new shelter in a riverside grove of cottonwoods, where, unmolested, they stayed the winter out.

Early in March the ice on the Platte broke up, permitting Stuart's men to launch two canoes they had made from hollow cottonwood logs, only to learn what would soon be known as the hallmark of that unique river, that even in the fullness of its spring flow it is never navigable, even by a dugout. Characteristically the Platte is phenomenally wide but very shallow, and full of shifting sandbars and sinuous channels. By dint of wading in the icy water and dragging their craft along they managed to advance one of the boats a few miles down before they became convinced of the futility of the effort and resumed travel on foot. Near the end of March they had reached the region of central Nebraska where the merged waters of the North and South Platte make a stream "nearly a mile in width, but too shallow to float even an empty canoe." The country spread out into a vast level plain, like "the bosom of the ocean." The dreary sameness of the prairie began to grow extremely irksome despite the signs of spring: wild geese, prairie hens, swans, wild horses, and buffalo covering the country. In picking up driftwood for fuel, they found some with marks of an ax, which caused "much speculation as to the time when and the person by whom the trees had been felled. Thus they went on, like sailors at sea, who perceive in every floating weed and wandering bird, harbingers of the wished-for land."[46]

Somewhat further along they observed another unique feature of the strange stream they were following—its amazing long islands; one, Grand Island, Stuart estimated to be 75 miles long and 24 wide. Here at last they began to meet other whites, and from them heard the news of the calamitous war with the British that had been in progress since before they had left Astoria, and which even then was spelling the doom of the whole Astorian enterprise. As the water in the river had now become much deeper, Stuart stopped at an Oto village long enough to have Indian craftsmen construct a large canoe of poles, willows, and elk and buffalo skins. In this craft,

[45] *Ibid.*, pp. 414–418; *Robert Stuart's Narratives*, pp. 191–193.
[46] *Astoria*, p. 423.

20 feet long and 4 wide, his entire party embarked and shortly afterward emerged "into the broad turbid current of the Missouri," which swiftly carried them down to St. Louis. They arrived on April 30, 1813, "having been ten months in performing this perilous expedition from Astoria."[47]

Despite the distractions of a nation deeply involved in a divisive and frustrating war, the arrival of Stuart's little band was important news. The St. Louis paper carried an account of their voyage, which, in the manner of the day, became source material for other papers. In due course the account of Stuart's arrival reached New York and Astor's study in his East River mansion.[48] It was wonderfully cheering news. Now, despite the loss of the *Tonquin* and all the lives and treasure thus far expended on his Astoria venture, it appeared quite possible that his imperial enterprise had been successfully launched. But Stuart's news was a year old. Even as the old merchant was garnering encouragement from Stuart's dispatches, the evil star that seemed to plague the enterprise from its inception was contriving its end.

Soon after Stuart had left Astoria in June 1812, the *Beaver* set sail for the Russians' Alaska posts, with Hunt aboard to open the trade there. In the fall she was to return him to Astoria and continue on to Canton to dispose of the Russian furs. But sundry delays, adverse weather, and rotting rigging had compelled the *Beaver* to sail directly from the fur seal stations to China. There the captain learned of the war and, fearing for the safety of his vessel, refused to leave. Consequently, it was not until November of the following year, 1813, that Hunt managed to get back to Astoria. As the summer of 1813 ripened, discouragement at that lonely post had deepened. There had been no word from the long-overdue *Beaver*, or from Hunt, and to make matters worse the expected annual boat from New York was also long overdue. By July, morale had plummeted to such a low level that the partners remaining at Astoria had prepared, signed, and dispatched to Astor, through the good offices of their competitor the North West Company, a statement of their determination to abandon the enterprise unless their situation had

[47] *Ibid.*, pp. 424–427.

[48] For the spread and impact of the account of the expedition of the returning Astorians, see Rollins's foreword to *Robert Stuart's Narratives*, pp. lxvi–lxx. Rollins ranks Stuart's overland diaries second only to the chronicles of the Lewis and Clark expedition.

greatly improved by the next summer. It was ill fortune that doomed
the enterprise, rather than any fault inherent in the planning or
implementation by Astor. He had sent yet another boat out in
March 1813, which was badly mauled by a terrible storm south of
the Hawaiian Islands, and soon afterward completely destroyed in
the surf when a landing was attempted.

The sense of isolation created by the war and the rumors of the
impending arrival of British warships accelerated negotiations by
the partners with the officials of the North West Company, the
former employer of many of them, to sell out and surrender their
post. Before the end of the year such a deal had been made. That
and the arrival of a British warship effectively sealed the fate of
Astor's Western dream.[49] In the spring of 1814, those Astorians
unwilling to alter their loyalties left the Columbia to return across
the continent—the final dramatic act of the Astorian adventure,
which, while failing in its commercial purpose, had pioneered the
Oregon Trail, focused popular attention on the fertile Northwest
regions, and contributed greatly to the discovering of America.

[49]Ross, *Fur Hunters*, pp. 3–9.

CHAPTER 9

Bearers of the Natural History Torch: Nineteenth Century

THE role of the field naturalists in nineteenth-century America inevitably reflected the explosive expansion and development of the nation. The Louisiana Purchase and the trail-blazing expedition of Lewis and Clark dramatically expanded the scope and complexity of their role on a stage of new and awesome dimension. Eventually, to meet the challenge of the immense and little known West, government expeditions and institutional specialists took over the functions performed in the eighteenth century by the informal association of naturalists known as the natural history circle, which, international as was its scope, was based primarily on individual enterprise, with relatively limited terrain of discovery.[1] That eighteenth-century pattern lingered on side by side with the developing new order of official science for several decades into the new century, with frequent examples of personal continuity, the passing of the torch from master to disciple, or father to son, as in the case of the Bartrams, and later, of the French botanists André and François André Michaux.

Less than two years after André Michaux, frustrated in his hopes of returning to America, had departed on his fatal expedition to the East, his son, François, then thirty years of age, was commissioned by the French government to proceed to the United States, there to study agricultural methods and find trees suitable for French forests —an assignment no less urgent in 1801 than his father's similar

[1]See above, Chapter 4, "The Eighteenth-Century Natural History Circle."

undertaking for the monarchy in 1785. The long rivalry with England for mastery of the seas, with its demand for timber suitable for shipbuilding, the loss of her American dominions, and the impoverished state of her domestic forests had left France with a desperate need for massive reforestation. Michaux, *fils,* whose early years as his father's traveling companion in the American wilderness had been followed by a formal scientific education in Paris, was an ideal choice for such a mission.

Landing in South Carolina in October 1801, Michaux spent the next six months collecting seeds in the area, using as his base his father's old botanical garden, which he found almost totally neglected. From Charleston he took ship for New York, where he was happy to find his father's Jersey garden still thriving under the devoted care of his father's gardener, Paul Saulnier. After a stopover in Philadelphia with the famous William Bartram, Michaux set out in June 1802 for Pittsburgh and the Ohio River country, on a journey that would take him, in less than four months, nearly 1,800 miles: down the Ohio to Mayesville, overland across Kentucky to Nashville, thence eastward across the Great Smokies and Blue Ridge, and back to Charleston, which he reached in time for another seed harvest before sailing for France in the spring. His account of this journey, published the next year under the title *Voyage á l'ouest des Monts Alléghanys dans les États de l'Ohio, et du Kentucky, et du Tennessée, et retour á Charleston par les Hautes-Carolines,*[2] was an immediate success.

Whereas the inimitable notebook journals of Michaux, *père,* the day-to-day observations of a gifted naturalist in the field, focused primarily on the plant world, his son's report is a discursive narrative, an entertaining, revealing, unvarnished look at frontier America, rough and raw as it appeared to the cultivated young scientist. For those whose interests lie in the ways of the frontier in the early years of the nineteenth century, Michaux's *Travels* is a rich cache, replete with descriptive passages dealing with the carousing and

---

[2]Paris, 1804. A translation published in London in 1805 under the title of *Travels to the West of the Alleghany Mountains, in the States of Ohio, Kentucky, and Tennessea, and Back to Charleston by the Upper Carolines,* appears in Reuben Gold Thwaites (ed.), *Early Western Travels, 1748–1846* (vol. 3, Cleveland, 1904), pp. 105–306. My citations are to Thwaites. Another French edition, three English translations, and a German version followed within the decade. For a fuller discussion of Michaux's career, see Henry Savage, Jr., *Lost Heritage* (New York, 1970), Chap. 6. See also the introduction by Thwaites to edition above.

fighting propensities of the inhabitants, their costumes and folk cures, the flea-infested log cabins—two men could build one in four or five days, complete with fireplace and chimney of clay and sticks —which still provided the housing for a third of the non-Indian population beyond the Alleghenies, the execrable inns with their common bedrooms and dirty sheets and their limited fare of salt beef, ham, and fowl, the prices of commodities, transportation by covered wagons, river barges, and the seagoing vessels he saw under construction on the Ohio, 2,000 miles of river from the open sea.

To Michaux, scion of generations of farmers wedded to a single farm, the most enigmatic trait of many of those frontier folk was their resistance to permanence. Many chose to supply their tables and satisfy their hunger by hunting, rather than by cultivating the rich soils at their cabin doors. For an inordinate number the temptation to keep moving on seemed irresistible: hundreds of flat boats and barges floating down the Ohio, laden with "families . . . their horses, cows, poultry, waggons, ploughs, harness, beds . . . abandoning themselves to the mercy of the stream, without knowing the place where they should stop, to exercise their industry, and enjoy peaceably the fruit of their labour under one of the best governments that exists in the world."[3]

The records of these frontier ways, illuminating, entertaining, and sometimes distressing, were however only incidental to the botanist's mission and dominant interest, the American forest. Near Marietta he measured a sycamore, *Platanus occidentalis,* 47 feet in circumference. He judged that, after the sycamore, the largest trees of Eastern America were the tulip trees, *Liriodendron tulipifera,* whose tall, straight trunks provided the raw material for canoes commonly in use on the river, one of which was 24 feet long, 18 inches wide, and as many deep: a similar craft provided his own transport part the way down the Ohio. In the shipyards along the bank he noted the special uses to which the white oaks, red oaks, hickories, and pines of the region were put in boat building, and was fascinated by the ropewalks, where the cordage for the rigging was being produced. Further down the river, his attention was focused on the sugar maples and the operations for the extraction of maple sugar. Gliding down the *Belle Rivière* of his ancestral kinsmen, Michaux

[3] F. Michaux, *Travels,* p. 166.

noted with poetic rapture, near the mouth of the great Kanawha, its forested banks,

sloping, and elevated from twenty-five to forty feet . . . planted, at their base, with willows from fifteen to eighteen feet in height, the drooping branches and foliage of which form a pleasing contrast to the sugar maples, red maples, and ash trees, situated immediately above. The latter, in return, are overlooked by palms [sycamores], poplars, beeches, magnolias of the highest elevation, the enormous branches of which . . . extend toward the borders, overshadowing the river, at the same time completely covering the trees situated under them. This natural display, which reigns upon the two banks, affords on each side a regular arch, the shadow of which, reflected by the crystal stream, embellishes, in an extraordinary degree, this magnificent coup d'oeil.[4]

The path Michaux followed on foot from Lexington to Nashville led him some 70 miles across the Kentucky Barrens, a rolling, treeless prairie region, which, to his surprise, was actually beautiful meadow country covered with grass 2 or 3 feet high, displaying such an amazing variety of wildflowers that he was able to gather "about ninety different species of them." He reported that every spring terrifying prairie fires swept across that entire region, devouring its plant cover, endangering its inhabitants and their domestic stock, and effectively preventing the establishment of forest cover.[5] Back again in tree country, on his way across eastern Tennessee, he noted with delight the beautiful yellowwood, *Cladrastis lutea*, discovered in 1796 by his father, who had suggested its potential as a source of yellow dye, and gathered seed and wood samples to take back to France for study.

Then eastward through the Cherokee country and over the mountains. Struggling, as had his father, through tangled forests of rhododendron, across deep ravines and mountain torrents, Michaux arrived in September at the charming plantation of Davenport, his father's friend and guide on his many expeditions into that mountain country. Eight years had passed since André Michaux and Davenport, on the summit of Grandfather Mountain, had sung the *Marseillaise* together, and shouted: "Vive l'Amérique et la République Française, Vive la Liberté!"[6] There in the house on a moun-

[4]*Ibid.*, pp. 173, 160, 163, 181–182.
[5]*Ibid.*, p. 218.
[6]A. Michaux, *Journal*, in *Proceedings of the American Philosophical Society*, XXVI (1889), 112.

tain stream in "les hautes Montagnes de Caroline" so beloved by André, François spent a week studying plants and collecting seeds, "far from thinking," as he later wrote, "that at the same time this worthy man was entertaining me about his old travelling companion, I lost a beloved father who died a victim of his zeal for the progress of natural history upon the coast of the island of Madagascar."[7]

This was the climax of François Michaux's mission to the great American forest. From the mountains to Charleston there was little to please the traveler. After a few months devoted to gathering seeds and putting collections in order, he sailed home to France in the spring of 1803.

The success of his American mission, the popularity of his *Travels*, and his valuable report on the naturalization of American trees to France, with a tabulation of those he deemed useful and adaptable to France, established his reputation.[8] His official duty done, he plunged into the preparation of his great pioneer work on American trees.

In 1806, while that work was still in progress, Michaux made yet another visit to America. While in New York he traveled up the Hudson River as one of the two passengers on Robert Fulton's steamboat *Clermont* on her maiden voyage in August 1807. At Philadelphia, Michaux was warmly received by the nation's scientific élite and elected to membership in the American Philosophical Society. While a guest at the Bartram place, he met a friend and protégé of William Bartram, the Romantic poet and ornithologist Alexander Wilson, destined to become the father of American ornithology. Michaux, in the minds of many, was regarded as holding the same role for American forestry, primarily owing to the great stimulus given that embryonic science by the splendid work he was preparing for publication, the *Histoire des arbres forestiers de l'Amérique Septentrionale*. The first scientific manual of American trees east of the Mississippi, this work, magnificently illustrated with color plates, the majority of which were by the incomparable P. J. and H. J. Redouté, would appear in Paris between 1810 and 1813, and in 1817 be followed by English versions under the title of *North American Sylva*.[9] One of the important books on the New World, Michaux's *Sylva* for

[7]F. Michaux, *Travels*, p. 285.

[8]François André Michaux, *Mémoire sur la naturalisation des arbres de l'Amérique Septentrionale . . . Comparées avec ceux que produit la France* (Paris, 1805).

[9]The first American edition was published in Philadelphia in 1817.

the first time revealed the variety and wealth of the great forest cover of Eastern America. Michaux not only precisely identified and accurately described each species of tree, but enlivened many of his accounts with anecdotes and personal comments. No doubt his knowledge of his own country's depleted forests intensified his appreciation of the richness of America's woodlands and sharpened his awareness of the need for conservation. Repeatedly in the *Sylva* he warned against the wasteful practices of Americans in their forests: for instance, he deplored the waste of wood in supplying tanbark—magnificent trunks of oak and hemlock left to rot after removal of the bark—and he suggested alternate, more economical measures; in his account of the palmetto or cabbage palm, he sharply criticized the common practice of destroying a century-old tree in order to obtain a few ounces of the heart to eat, a practice he considered "pardonable only in a desert destined to remain uninhabited for ages," and which he compared in prodigality with the custom common among the early settlers of Kentucky of killing and discarding the carcass of a 1,200- or 1,500-pound buffalo, only for the pleasure of eating the tongue. Michaux foresaw the days of tree culture and forest management; with select tree farming in mind, he suggested that areas occupied by red maple could be better utilized by oaks, ashes, and sugar maples. In his enlightened approach to arbor culture and his recognition of the relations between trees and the environment, Michaux anticipated the science of ecology.

By coincidence, in 1808, the year of François Michaux's return to France, the man who was to continue his work on American trees and cover the forests beyond the Mississippi arrived in Philadelphia from his native England. Thomas Nuttall, then but twenty-three, was destined to play major roles in several fields of American natural history.[10] During his thirty-four years in North America, this many-faceted scientist would explore its territories from coast to coast and from Florida to the St. Lawrence, and would become a major contributor to the advancement of American botany, ornithology, and minerology.

Thomas Nuttall was born in 1785 in a Yorkshire village in the Pennines. Educated in country schools, trained as a printer, he early

[10]The source of most of my biographical material on Thomas Nuttall is the definitive biography by Jeannette E. Graustein, *Thomas Nuttall, Naturalist: Explorations in America, 1808–1841* (Cambridge, Mass., 1967).

developed a passion for natural history, seizing every opportunity to explore the English countryside and to enrich his education by study. Drawn by the lure of the undiscovered flora and fauna of the New World, he sailed for the United States in the spring of 1808, fully determined to devote his life to the natural history of America.

Nuttall's first two American years were spent in and about Philadelphia, where, supporting himself by sporadic jobs as a journeyman printer, he soon found a haven in Bartram's garden and a congenial friend and mentor in William. In Philadelphia was Peale's Museum, "a world in miniature," where the eager young naturalist could study at leisure the natural history of the country he had come to explore. There, under the supervision of Charles Willson Peale and his son, Rembrandt, were displayed in orderly fashion specimens of mounted mammals and birds, many in habitat groups, reptiles, fishes, insects, and shells. There too were minerals, fossils, and Indian artifacts, and more than a mild Western lure in the recently acquired Lewis and Clark exhibits, brooded over by a wax figure of Meriwether Lewis clad in an ermine robe given him by the Shoshone chief, Sacajawea's brother, and holding in his hand a calumet.[11]

One of the most prestigious men in America at this time in the field of natural history was Benjamin Smith Barton, professor of medicine, botany, and natural history at the University of Pennsylvania, and author of *Elements of Botany*. In need of a field collector, Barton, in 1809, sponsored Nuttall on collecting trips to parts of Pennsylvania, Delaware, and New York, and on one occasion as far as the St. Lawrence; in 1810, apparently pleased with his protégé's performance, Barton proposed to Nuttall a journey of two years duration to the Great Plains of the West for the purpose of collecting "animals, vegetables, minerals, Indian curiosities, etc."[12]

Nuttall, for whom the opportunity for Western exploration seemed a dream come true, set out from Philadelphia with high hopes on April 12, 1810. Unfortunately, neither he nor his patron had the slightest conception of the true nature of wilderness travel. Barton's directions as to routes and means of travel proved so fanciful and unrealistic that Nuttall was soon forced to make his own

[11]Graustein, *Nuttall*, p. 21; see also Charles C. Sellers, *Charles Willson Peale* (2 vols., Philadelphia, 1947).

[12]For an analysis of the relationship between Barton and Nuttall, see Graustein, *Nuttall*, pp. 38–41, 49–53.

decisions. At the old Jesuit settlement of MacKinac Island, at the confluence of the three great western lakes, he was fortunately able to join Wilson Price Hunt, leader of the overland Astoria expedition, who was even then equipping his brigade to follow the Lewis and Clark route west from St. Louis to the mouth of the Columbia River.[13]

After wintering in St. Louis, the expedition, in the spring of 1811, set out up the Missouri, heading for the Mandan villages. Once the boats had passed the mouth of the Platte, 600 miles above St. Louis, Nuttall, who had been conscientiously collecting whenever possible along the way, realized with delight that a thrilling challenge of unfamiliar trees, flowers, and animals lay before him. Every day brought new discoveries. Nuttall's total absorption in his quests often resulted in his loss of all sense of danger; on one occasion he wandered more than 100 miles from the post before being discovered in a state of collapse from hunger and exhaustion, and brought in by an Indian who had chanced upon him.

In the autumn of 1811 Nuttall left the Mandans, returned to St. Louis with a party of fur traders, continued on down the Mississippi to New Orleans, and sailed for England. The next three years he spent in England, a visit prolonged by the War of 1812. It was a fruitful period; he consulted libraries and botanical herbariums, preparing his collections for future publication, arranged with a nursery to sell his seeds and plants, and formed useful professional associations with the scientific community, particularly the members of the Linnaean Society to which he was elected in 1812.[14]

In December of the following year a German botanist, Frederick Pursh, presented to the Linnaean Society his new work on the flora of North America, *Flora Americae Septentrionalis*, including descriptions of plants brought back by the Lewis and Clark expedition, but marred by errors, inaccuracies, and false claims to discoveries by the author.[15] Eager to publish his own botanical work and present his own discoveries, Nuttall returned to the United States in the spring of 1815. His next three years were devoted to field studies and collecting in the South, where he wandered widely over the Caroli-

[13]See above, Chapter 8.
[14]The Linnean Society of London was founded in 1788—see Graustein, *Nuttall*, p. 84.
[15] 2 vols., London, 1814. Frederick Pursh (1774–1820) of Saxony served as head gardener at Woodlands, the famous garden of William Hamilton, near Philadelphia. For a critical discussion of Pursh's *Flora*, see Graustein, *Nuttall*, pp. 85–93.

nas, Georgia, and across the mountains through the Cherokee country to Tennessee and Kentucky. His classic work on the taxonomy of American flora, *Genera of North American Plants,* published in 1818, was unique in its scope, containing descriptions of no less than 834 genera, including many Nuttall had discovered. It quickly became a landmark in American botany, and won for Nuttall international recognition.[16]

Nuttall had been recognized in scientific circles in North America even before the completion of his *Genera,* and had been elected, in 1817, a member of both the American Philosophical Society and the Academy of Natural Sciences.

The Academy of Natural Sciences was founded in Philadelphia in 1812 by a small group devoted to the science of natural history. Notable among its early members was William Maclure, Scottish-born geologist and wealthy patron of science and education. His geological map of the United States, published in 1817 with explanatory notes, was the first map of its scope in geological history. A generous patron of the young Academy of Natural Sciences, Maclure served as its president for twenty-two years.

One of the founders of the Academy and a close friend of both Maclure and Nuttall was Thomas Say, as wide-ranging in his scientific interests as Nuttall. The tall, slender Say—whose portrait in 1812 by Charles Willson Peale shows him as a handsome youth, with dark, wide-awake eyes and resolute chin—has been credited variously with establishing the fields of conchology, entomology, and zoology in America.[17] A great-grandson of John Bartram, he had from early youth, encouraged by his uncle William Bartram, pursued the muse of natural history with single-minded ardor, living and working in the tight quarters of the fledgling Academy of Natural Sciences, where he is reported to have slept beneath the Academy's mastodon skeleton, an example followed by Nuttall when he was toiling to produce his *Genera.*[18]

In 1817 Say set out with William Maclure, George Ord, and Titian Peale, to explore the romantic Georgia sea islands, where moss-

[16]*Genera of North American Plants with a Catalogue of the Species through 1817* (Philadelphia, 1818). In contrast to the elder Michaux, Pursh, and other predecessors, Nuttall made his work more widely accessible by presenting his botanical descriptions in English rather than the traditional Latin—Graustein, *Nuttall,* pp. 121–122.

[17]Harry B. Weiss and Grace M. Ziegler, *Thomas Say, Early American Naturalist* (Springfield, Ill., 1931). This biography is the principal source of my material on Say.

[18]Weiss and Ziegler, *Say,* p. 35; Graustein, *Nuttall,* p. 120.

draped oaks, groves of orange trees, and houses built of sea shells were features of the scene; then on into Florida, still a Spanish colony, and up the St. Johns, following the Bartrams' trails with Kinsman William's *Travels* as their guide.[19] Upon their return both Say and Nuttall were recommended to Thomas Jefferson by the brilliant but controversial Dr. Thomas Cooper, as naturalists qualified for employment on government-sponsored expeditions.[20] Although Nuttall failed to get an appointment, Say was invited to join the scientific group accompanying Major Stephen H. Long's trans-Mississippi expeditions of 1819 and 1823. The most valuable results of those expeditions were the discoveries of Say and his fellow naturalists, published later in the scientific reports of Edwin James and William Keating that accompanied Long's official reports.[21]

Failing to get a berth on a government expedition to the West as he had hoped, Nuttall set out alone in the fall of 1818 for the Arkansas country, which despite Pike's and Wilkinson's reports of its inhospitality, attracted him irresistibly as a garden of unknown species. For a year and a half, under the sponsorship of fellow members of the American Philosophical Society, he explored regions now embraced in Louisiana, Arkansas, and Oklahoma. This journey, described in his *Travels into the Arkansas Territory*, was fraught with hardships, and a devastating fever that brought him near death. Although it was richly rewarding in new plant species, its extreme difficulties convinced him that alone he could not cope with the myriad adversities incidental to explorations in such regions, and could fulfill his dreams of Western exploration only with an organized expedition. For that opportunity he would wait well over a decade.[22]

In 1823 Nuttall accepted appointments as professor of natural history and botany and curator of the Botanical Garden at Harvard

[19]Weiss and Zeigler, *Say*, pp. 54–60.

[20]*Jefferson Papers*, Coolidge Collection, Massachusetts Historical Society, Boston, Mass. *The Jefferson Papers* of the University of Virginia (Charlottesville, Va., University of Virginia Library, 1950), nos. 1702 and 1716. Nuttall's English nationality seems to have been a barrier to his appointment—Graustein, *Nuttall*, pp. 130–131, p. 420, note 45.

[21]S. H. Long and Edwin James, *Account of an Expedition from Pittsburgh to the Rocky Mountains* (2 vols., Philadelphia, 1823); S. H. Long and W. H. Keating, *Narrative of an Expedition to the Lake of the Woods* (2 vols., Philadelphia, 1824).

[22]Thomas Nuttall, *A Journal of Travels into the Arkansas Territory, During the Year 1819* (Philadelphia, 1821). See also S.D. McKelvey, *Botanical Exploration of the Trans-Mississippi West, 1790–1850* (Arnold Arboretum, Jamaica Plain, Mass., 1955), pp. 164–188.

University. Utilizing the scientific resources available to him at Harvard, and field work on numerous less ambitious expeditions more and more oriented toward ornithology, Nuttall prepared his *Manual of Ornithology of the United States and Canada,*[23] the first general handbook of American birds, systematically arranged and fully described in fine literary style. The first volume, published in 1832, was warmly welcomed both in America and abroad. Ralph Waldo Emerson advised a young relative that this "beautiful book on American birds" was one that "everyone who lives in this country ought to read."[24]

During Nuttall's sojourn in Cambridge, Thomas Say and many of his scientific associates were becoming committed to the planned Utopian experiment in living at New Harmony, on the Indiana bank of the Wabash. Of the dozens of backwoods Utopias reflecting the spirit of the Enlightenment that struggled hopefully to take root on American soil in the nineteenth century, none would be more significant than New Harmony. Founded in 1826 under the sponsorship of Robert Owen, reformer and philanthropist, and his fellow Scot William Maclure, versatile patron of science and education, its peaceful and idyllic site on the Wabash had been developed by an industrious group of German dissenters under George Rapp. The Rappites, finding the stimulus of pioneering essential to the success of Rapp's doctrines, had moved on to a newer frontier. The Wabash settlement, which Owen and Maclure purchased, comprised nearly 30,000 acres, 3,000 already under cultivation in farms, orchards, and vineyards; substantial homes; well-equipped factories; and an imposing church at its center. Here Owen hoped to establish a community ruled by reason and brotherly love, with equality for all, universal education, and cooperative enterprises, devoid of the tensions of competition and free from religious differences.[25]

Lecturing before large and distinguished audiences in the East, Owen attracted to his cause, in addition to the predictable quota of

[23]2 vols., Boston, 1832, 1834. The first volume (1832) covered land birds, the second volume (1834) water birds, with an appendix of land birds discovered since the publication of the first volume. Nuttall prepared a second edition in 1840; three more editions, slightly revised, appeared near the turn of the century—Graustein, *Nuttall*, pp. 249–253.

[24]*Journals of Ralph Waldo Emerson* (Boston, 1909), Feb. 1, 1832, p. 457—quoted in Graustein, *Nuttall*, p. 250.

[25]A. E. Beston, Jr., *Backwoods Utopias* (Philadelphia, 1950); George B. Lockwood, *The New Harmony Movement* (New York, 1905; Dover edition, New York, 1971). Subsequent citations are to the Dover edition.

Dickensian eccentrics, a nucleus of intellectual and enlightened people, European and American. In the winter of 1825 Owen and Maclure, in the company of some thirty-five ladies and gentlemen, embarked at Pittsburgh in a keelboat christened *The Philanthropist,* to course down the Ohio to New Harmony.[26]

Among this "boatload of knowledge," as the keelboat's passengers came to be called, in addition to Say, were Charles Lesueur, the French artist and naturalist, and a bevy of young ladies, chaperoned by the formidable Marie Frétagoet, a capable French pedagogue. Among her charges was the beautiful and talented Lucy Sistaire, soon to become the wife of Thomas Say. An engaging picture of the society established on the Wabash is provided for us by the touring duke of Saxe-Weimar, who visited New Harmony in April 1826. The duke was charmed to find the "Harmonists" in their costumes—short jackets and white pantaloons for the men, and knee-length coats for the women—engaged in plain living and high thinking, busy with their communal enterprises by day, followed by lively evening gatherings for music and dancing, where polished manners and cultivated customs prevailed. However, the Harmonists' noble dreams of the perfectability of human nature were short-lived. After barely two years, overwhelmed by difficulties and frustrations, Owen confessed the failure of his socialistic experiment and withdrew from the increasingly fragmented project.[27]

There remained at New Harmony, nevertheless, an intellectual residue of rare incandescence, an oasis of genius in the wilderness, centered upon Maclure's educational foundation[28] and the activities of the resident scientists and artists. It attracted scholarly visitors from near and far, to whom it offered not only a haven for intellectual exchanges and scientific research in its excellent libraries and laboratories, but a flourishing printing press as well. Among the notable books published at New Harmony was a new edition of Michaux's *Sylva,* complete with its Redouté illustrations, the plates for which Maclure had brought from Paris.[29]

For several years outstanding scientific work continued to be

[26]Lockwood, *New Harmony,* pp. 80–81.

[27]*Ibid.,* pp. 79–81, 123–133, 174.

[28]Anthony Trollope's brother Henry was for a time a student in Maclure's school at New Harmony. For Mrs. Trollope's description of Maclure and his school, see Frances Trollope's *Domestic Manners of the Americans,* quoted in Weiss and Ziegler, *Say,* p. 132.

[29]Graustein, *Nuttall,* p. 353.

done at New Harmony, mostly by Say and Lesueur, the most productive zoologists in the country during the first half of the century. Say, forced by Owen's withdrawal and Maclure's departure for Mexico to assume multiple duties in the community, was prodigiously busy, contributing to scientific journals and advancing the work on his monumental *Entomology*, of which the first of three volumes had appeared before he came to New Harmony.[30] At the same time he was preparing his *American Conchology*, illustrated in color by his wife Lucy, and published at New Harmony.[31] Charles Lesueur was almost equally active and productive. Lesueur, a gaunt and weather-worn gentleman, but with the elegant bearing and the manners of his native France, was involved in the study and painting of American fishes, in works on reptiles and marine invertebrates, and the preparation of an account of the Indian mounds of Indiana.[32]

One of the most interesting and colorful visitors attracted to New Harmony was the Prussian prince Maximilian of Wied-Neuwied, a veteran of the Napoleonic wars and a dedicated naturalist of Humboldtian versatility. He had previously spent two years exploring in Brazil and had embodied his discoveries in a scholarly work that had won him distinction in scientific circles. On his way to make a similar and comparative study of the American West, the prince, at fifty thin and travel-worn but still dynamic, arrived at the colony in the early fall of 1832. With him was a gifted young Swiss artist, Karl Bodmer, whose accurate and beautiful paintings would enhance the work of the prince's eloquent pen.[33] While wintering at New Harmony before continuing westward, the prince, with Say and Lesueur, roamed the dense forests of the region. He was greatly impressed by the fine tulip trees, "with thick and high trunks as straight as a ship's mast,"[34] by maples so large that three men could not span them, and by the giant sycamores, some over 40 feet in circumference; sometimes the naturalists, on their winter excursions, took shelter in the hollow trunks to warm themselves with a cosy fire. In spring,

[30]The other volumes were still in preparation when Say came to New Harmony, as were their illustrations—the work of his friends Titian Peale and Charles Lesueur. For a description of Say's *Entomology*, see Weiss and Ziegler, *Say*, pp. 190–191.

[31]Weiss and Ziegler, *Say*, p. 192.

[32]Lockwood, *New Harmony*, p. 318; Weiss and Ziegler, *Say*, pp. 167–169.

[33]Bernard DeVoto, *Across the Wide Missouri* (Boston, 1947), p. 17.

[34]Maximilian, Prince of Wied, *Travels in the Interior of North America, 1832–1834*, in Reuben Gold Thwaites (ed.), *Early Western Travels, 1748–1846* (vol. 22, Cleveland, 1906), pp. 165–166, 193.

the prince and Bodmer set off downstream for St. Louis, gateway to the West.

Another interesting visitor to New Harmony was Constantine Samuel Rafinesque, a brilliant, picturesque, and eccentric naturalist.[35] Born in Constantinople and educated in France, Rafinesque traveled over most of Europe and western North America, avidly collecting plants, minerals, and fishes.[36] A man of prodigious energy, he served briefly as professor of natural history at Transylvania University in Kentucky, composed, edited, and published a scientific journal, wrote his autobiography,[37] and is said to have produced in all some 900 books and pamphlets. In spite of his intelligence and industry, however, Rafinesque was a tragic figure, too erratic, undisciplined, and unreliable in his scientific work to be fully accepted by the scientific community of his day. The recognition accorded him for his pioneer work in natural history, particularly in ichthyology, came too late: he died in a Philadelphia garret in 1840, in poverty and neglect.[38]

New Harmony lost one of its greatest luminaries with the death, in the fall of 1834, of the gentle Say, commemorated by his fellow workers in the name of many a plant and animal species. In 1837, David Dale Owen, appointed United States geologist to take charge of a survey of the Northwest, established the headquarters of the United States Geology Department at New Harmony, and for a few years more the community remained a center for scientific enterprise before declining to the status of historical site.[39]

In 1834, the year of Say's death and Maximilian's departure for home, came Thomas Nuttall's long-awaited opportunity to realize his cherished dream of exploring the Far West. A Cambridge friend, Nathaniel Jarvis Wyeth, had developed a prospering West Indian trade in ice cut from Cambridge ponds, and it was he who provided Professor Nuttall with his opportunity. Wyeth, too, confessed a persistent enthrallment with the West. Several years previously, undaunted by Astor's magnificent failure, he had planned to launch an attempt to establish an international fur and fish trading business centered on a major trading station at the

[35]Lockwood, *New Harmony*, pp. 77–79.

[36]T. J. Fitzpatrick, *Rafinesque: A Sketch of His Life with Bibliography* (Des Moines, 1911).

[37]C. S. Rafinesque, *A Life of Travels and Researches in North America and Southern Europe* (Philadelphia, 1836).

[38]Donald Culross Peattie, *Green Laurels* (New York, 1938), pp. 261–267.

[39]Lockwood, *New Harmony*, Chap. 23.

mouth of the Columbia River.[40] In 1832, at the age of twenty-nine, he had led an expedition all the way to Fort Vancouver; but inadequate planning, misfortunes, and the entrenched position of the British fur monopoly on the Columbia had defeated his attempt.[41] Even as he was returning across the Rockies, however, he committed himself to another attempt by agreeing with Milton Sublette of the Rocky Mountain Fur Company to bring out its trade goods the next spring in time for the annual rendezvous of its trappers in the Green River Valley.[42]

In his second effort, Wyeth planned to field a far more ambitious expedition. His bold plans included Nuttall, who would serve as naturalist of the overland arm of this rerun of the Astorian adventure. In recruiting Nuttall he was emulating the make-up of government expeditions such as those of Stephen Long, but he added a new dimension by including the Protestant missionaries Jason and Daniel Lee. Professor Nuttall provided a numerical balance between the men of God and the men of science by recruiting a promising young Philadelphia ornithologist, John Kirk Townsend. As it turned out, Townsend was an important addition, for it was he who would provide the best contemporary account of the second Wyeth expedition in his *Narrative of a Journey across the Rocky Mountains*, [43] a classic among early Western travel accounts.

To Townsend their setting out from Independence, which they had reached in late April by steamboat, "was altogether so exciting I could scarcely contain myself. Every man in the company seemed to feel the same kind of enthusiasm," as the caravan of 70 men and 250 horses began their march. "Captain Wyeth and Milton Sublette took the lead, Mr. N. and myself rode beside them; then the men in double file, each leading, with a line, two horses heavily laden. . . . The band of missionaries with their horned cattle, rode along the flanks."[44] From the outset the naturalists were continually delighted with the abundance of bird life: orioles, western tanagers, western kingbirds, Say's phoebes, mountain bluebirds, sharp-tailed

[40]DeVoto, *Across the Wide Missouri*, pp. 61–66.

[41]*Ibid.*, pp. 65–66. One of Wyeth's company on his first Oregon expedition had been his young cousin John B. Wyeth, who upon his return to Cambridge wrote a critical and malicious account of his cousin's enterprise—John B. Wyeth, *Oregon* (Cambridge, Mass., 1833).

[42]DeVoto, *Across the Wide Missouri*, pp. 181–191.

[43]John Kirk Townsend, *Narrative of a Journey across the Rocky Mountains to the Columbia River and a Visit to the Sandwich Islands* (Philadelphia, 1839); also in Thwaites (ed.), *Early Western Travels*, vol. 21, to which my subsequent citations of Townsend refer.

[44]*Ibid.*, p. 171; the missionaries had now grown to five.

grouse, red-shafted flickers—on and on in bewildering variety of species, both known and unknown. Spring migration was at its peak when they reached the North Platte, presenting the greatest variety of species Townsend had ever seen, while Nuttall was finding dozens of new plant species every day. Bemoaning the haste with which the column pushed westward, as they approached those harbingers of the Rockies, the Laramie Mountains,[45] Townsend commented: "none but a naturalist can appreciate a naturalist's feelings . . . his delight amounting to ecstacy . . . when a specimen such as he has never before seen, meets his eye, and the sorrow and grief which he feels when he is compelled to tear himself from a spot abounding with all that he has . . . sought for."[46] There was certainly no chance of lingering as they pressed on in early June through the Laramie Mountains, dreary and forbidding, with deep gorges, frowning precipices, and craggy rocks, where the air became so chill that the men, wrapped in their blanket capes, huddled shivering in their saddles.

Crossing the North Platte, they arrived a few days later at South Pass. Beyond the pass, over the divide on the banks of Green River still sometimes known as the Siskadee but called by Nuttall the Colorado of the West, they were to deliver the trade goods they had hauled all the long way for the Rocky Mountain Fur Company; but they found that William Sublette had brought out enough to supply the Company—a serious financial blow to Wyeth's plans.

After two weeks rest at the rendezvous on Ham's Fork, a pleasant valley with good pasturage on the Siskadee, Wyeth, hoping to dispose of his goods, led his brigade northwest toward the Bear River, a tributary of the Great Salt Lake. They arrived on July 8 at Beer Springs, beside the Bear River, where they stopped for a day or two to pasture the horses. Nuttall described the springs, strongly impregnated with carbonic acid, as delicious, sparkling like champagne, a refreshing treat.[47]

Continuing northwest, they reached by mid-July the junction of the Portneuf and the Snake, on the latter's great south arc, where Wyeth erected a fortified post he called Fort Hall, the first perma-

[45]At that time known as the "Black Hills."
[46]Townsend, *Narrative,* pp. 140–141.
[47]Thomas Nuttall, *The North American Sylva; or a Description of the Forest Trees of the United States, Canada and Nova Scotia, Not Described in the Work of F. Andrew Michaux* (3 vols., Philadelphia, 1842–49), vol. 1 (1842–43), pp. 69–70.

nent American outpost beyond the divide.[48] For the naturalists it provided a welcome interim of relative rest and rehabilitation before setting out across the often cruel Snake River country that lay between Fort Hall and Walla Walla, outpost of the teeming regions of the Lower Columbia. When at last they gazed on that majestic stream, the discomforts, hardships, and dangers of their long journey were quickly forgotten. Nuttall and Townsend were ready enough, after a brief rest as guests of the Hudson Bay Company's trading post at Fort Vancouver, 100 miles up from the sea, to join Wyeth in his exploration of the Willamette River that runs into the Columbia from the south opposite Fort Vancouver.[49] Townsend described the Willamette as a clear and beautiful stream, half the width of the Columbia, dotted with verdant islands; the snow-capped peaks of the Cascades, rising to the sky, provided a magnificent backdrop. At Willamette Falls the river itself became an awesome sight, beautiful at a distance, and "grand and almost sublime" at closer approach. There, "although the roar of the cataract was almost deafening, and the rays of the sun reflected from the white and glittering foam" were blinding, Townsend "became so absorbed in the contemplation of the scene" as to forget everything else.[50] Everywhere in this strange new region, so richly endowed by nature, the naturalists were filling their bags and notebooks. But "the botanist in all this array," wrote Nuttall with a touch of nostalgia, "fails to recognize one solitary acquaintance of his former scenes; he is emphatically in a strange land; a new creation, even of the forest trees, is spread around him."[51] One of his more notable discoveries in that strange "new creation" was the exquisite western dogwood *(Cornus nuttalli)*, from the seeds of which each spring one of the fairest displays in London's Kew Gardens now blossoms.

The *May Dacre*, sent around the Horn with the heavy equipment needed for settlement, sailed up the river shortly after Wyeth's arrival, and was soon off for the Sandwich (Hawaiian) Islands with a cargo of lumber and Nuttall and Townsend as passengers.[52]

[48]DeVoto, *Across the Wide Missouri*, pp. 191–192, 198–199, 204–205; Graustein, *Nuttall*, pp. 301–302; Ray Allen Billington, *The Far Western Frontier, 1830–1860* (New York, 1956), pp. 63–65. Wyeth sold Fort Hall to Hudson's Bay Company in 1837.

[49]Townsend, *Narrative*, p. 278.

[50]*Ibid.*, p. 302.

[51]Nuttall, *Sylva*, vol. 1, p. vii.

[52]William H. Goetzmann, *Exploration and Empire* (New York, 1967), pp. 164–168; Graustein, *Nuttall*, pp. 304–309.

It became apparent that, as a business enterprise, Wyeth's second bold attempt, like his first, had suffered defeat. But although this second fur-trading and fishing venture failed to survive the competition of the powerfully entrenched Hudson's Bay establishment, it nevertheless left its mark in the disclosing and initial settlement of the Willamette Valley, and in the discoveries of the naturalists, the first to cross the continent.

Nuttall and Townsend returned from the islands to Oregon in time for the 1835 spring salmon run, the northward bird migration, and the early flowers of the Northeast Coast. The following spring, homeward bound, Nuttall stopped in California. Near Monterey, the little Spanish capital of upper California, he observed magpies much like those of Europe in the branches of an oak with holly-like leaves, and a thorny gooseberry "with pendulous flowers as brilliant as those of a Fuchsia." There too one could hear the mockingbird rapturously imitating the songs of neighboring birds, while the "wolves" (coyotes) as tame as dogs yelled every night through the villages. Even more novel were the cacti as large as small trees and "the rare blooming aloes [that] grew without care in the garden hedgerows."[53]

Returning in late spring to Boston on the *Alert*, Nuttall met a Harvard student, Richard Henry Dana, another American whose name looms large in revealing the California of that day. Almost two years had passed since Dana had sought health by shipping as a seaman on the brig *Pilgrim* bound for the California coast. *Two Years Before the Mast*, his account of that voyage and his return to Boston on the *Alert*, was destined to become the classic account of life on a nineteenth-century American merchantman. But in addition to descriptions of life at sea, Dana's book, more significantly here, revealed to a host of readers the little known California coast—from the dreary, desolate, windswept shores of San Pedro (Los Angeles) to the "extremely well wooded" harbor at Monterey, where "everything was as green as nature could make it" and the trees full of birds; and the vast solitude of San Francisco Bay, where there was no sign of life except hundreds of red deer, "on the high and beautifully sloping hill," and a few Indians around the ruined mission.[54] *Two Years Before the Mast* was popular in the Eastern United

[53]Graustein, *Nuttall*, pp. 313–315; Nuttall, *Sylva*, vol. 1, pp. xi–xii.
[54]Richard Henry Dana, *Two Years Before the Mast* (Boston, 1840), pp. 106–107, 78, 270, 433.

States and in Europe from the first; 2,000 copies were sold in a single day in Liverpool, England, alone.

The *Alert* reached Boston in September 1836. That same month John James Audubon returned to the United States after two years in Europe where the elephant folio plates for his *Birds of America* were being prepared. Audubon was greatly in need of specimens from the West. To his delight he learned of the return of "our learned friend . . . Thomas Nuttall," who promised to obtain for him duplicates of all the species he had brought to the Academy at Philadelphia. The very next day Nuttall brought him specimens of five species. With the cooperation of the Academy of Natural Sciences, most of the specimens collected by Nuttall and Townsend were made available to Audubon; some seventy-five eventually made their appearance in *Birds of America.* In his *Ornithological Biography* Audubon acknowledges his debt to Nuttall, "who generously gave me of his ornithological treasures all that was new and inscribed in my journal the observations which he had made respecting the habits and distribution of all the new and rare species. . . ."[55]

The collections brought home by Nuttall and Townsend were varied and miscellaneous.[56] There were thousands of original specimens to be sorted, classified, and described, a task that absorbed them for many months. In 1837 Nuttall arranged for hundreds of new botanical species, discovered and described by him, to appear in a new manual of American flora, being prepared by John Torrey and Asa Gray, to which Nuttall's discoveries were a major contribution.[57] During that same period the tireless naturalist was managing to find time for public lectures, field trips, and preparation of a new edition of his *Ornithology,* expanded to include his Western discoveries.[58]

Nuttall also provided his valuable supplemental volumes to François Michaux's *North American Sylva.* Since its publication in 1819,

[55]Graustein, *Nuttall,* pp. 319–322; John James Audubon, *Ornithological Biography* (5 vols., Edinburgh, 1831–39), vol. IV, introduction, as quoted by Graustein. Francis H. Herrick, *Audubon the Naturalist* (2d edn., 2 vols., New York, 1938), vol. 2, pp. 150–151, 154.

[56]McKelvey, *Botanical Exploration,* pp. 586–627.

[57]John Torrey and Asa Gray, *Flora of North America* (New York, 1838–40). For full discussion of Nuttall's major contributions to the *Flora* of Torrey and Gray, a subject too detailed for inclusion here, see Jeannette E. Graustein, *Nuttall,* pp. 326–351.

[58]It was published in Boston in 1840.

new species that had escaped Michaux's attention, mostly Florida species, had been discovered, and Nuttall now had his Western collection to add to the catalogue. By the beginning of 1841 he was deep in the exacting task of composing the text of the new volumes, supervising the drawings for the plates, and arranging for the coloring, all as in the original Michaux volumes. His descriptive texts, written in an easy conversational style, were enlivened by remarks on the utility, mythology, and regional folklore of a species, sometimes with comments from earlier botanists such as the Bartrams and Catesby. The *Sylva* supplement was a distinguished achievement and a fitting swan song for Nuttall's American career.

Even before that final contribution to American natural history was completed, he had been summoned back to England to take up residence on an ancestral estate in his native land. After thirty-four years of single-minded devotion to the natural history of his adopted country, it was a repatriation that seemed "almost an exile."[59]

[59]Nuttall, *Sylva*, vol. 1 of Supplement, p. xii.

CHAPTER 10

Alexander Wilson and
John James Audubon, Ornithologists

IN the spring of 1810, as the Astorians were launching their pioneer commercial journey westward from St. Louis, in the Kentucky village of Louisville a dramatic meeting took place between two men, strangers to each other but both destined to play major roles in revealing the beauty and variety of American birds. Louisville, named for Louis XVI, and still dominated by old French families, had recently taken to its heart the glamorous young Frenchman, John James Audubon, and his bride Lucy, who had come down the Ohio on a flatboat two years before and were now living with their infant son at the Indian Queen Hotel. Though Audubon seemed to spend more of his time in forest and field than in the trading store he shared with his partner, he was present in their emporium that fateful March morning when a tall, gaunt, and weary Scot, carrying under his arm two folio volumes, entered the store. Alexander Wilson, newly arrived in Louisville, was in search of subscribers for a projected ten-volume work on the birds of America, of which two volumes, already completed, were submitted for inspection to the amazed Frenchman.

"How well do I remember him as he walked up to me," recalled Audubon, years later, "his long, rather hooked nose, the keenness of his eyes, and his prominent cheekbones; stamped his countenance with a peculiar character." He recalled his pleasure in Wilson's paintings, to which he was only prevented from subscribing by his partner, Rozier, who, aware that Audubon could ill afford the subscription price of $120 for the series, pointed out the superiority of Audubon's own drawings. When, at his visitor's request, Audubon displayed a portfolio of his bird sketches, the surprised Wilson told him he was quite unaware that anyone else was so engaged except himself. "He asked me if it was my intention to publish, and when I truly answered in the negative, his surprise seemed to increase."[1]

Save for their common gift for painting and their common passion for birds, Audubon and Wilson could hardly have offered greater contrast. The thin, worn face and dark, melancholy eyes of the Scot, who had been by turns weaver, peddler, poet, and teacher, bore witness to the toil, discouragement, and despair that had so often marked his forty-four years, from his hard childhood and youth in Scotland to this March morning in 1810, when he spread out on the counter before the astonished gaze of the one man who could surpass him the vivid glory of his bird paintings.

From Wilson we have only the most reticent report of his Louisville experience, a reference to a shooting trip with Mr. A. and an examination of Mr. A's "very good" crayon drawings. Yet just as it seems obvious that Wilson's visit was one of the seminal influences in determining Audubon's future work, so it seems evident that the totally unexpected discovery of the existence of such a potential rival as Audubon raised the intensity of Wilson's efforts to fever pitch. He had been at his task for seven years; he had barely three more left to live.[2]

It is difficult to overestimate the achievement of this lone Scot in revealing to the world the birds of America. The son of a weaver and part-time smuggler, Wilson was born in Paisley, Scotland, in 1766. Though destined for the ministry by his mother, he spent his early childhood years as a herd boy in the rugged country southeast of his home, where the long lonely days in the misty Scottish hills nourished his innately poetic temperament and encouraged his love of nature; his adolescent years were spent in the harsh discipline of weaver's apprentice, which implanted in him a capacity for hard work. Until his twenty-seventh year his time was divided among

[1]Francis H. Herrick, *Audubon, The Naturalist* (2d edn., 2 vols., New York, 1938), vol. 1, pp. 220–222; J. J. Audubon, *Ornithological Biography* (5 vols., Edinburgh, 1831–39), vol. 1, p. 437.

[2]Herrick, *Audubon*, vol. 1, pp. 224–225; Elsa G. Allen, "The History of American Ornithology Before Audubon," *Transactions of the American Philosophical Society*, IV, Pt. 3 (Philadelphia, 1951), p. 562; Robert Cantwell, *Alexander Wilson, Naturalist and Pioneer* (Philadelphia, 1961), pp. 200–201.

weaving, peddling, and poetry, traveling, as he said, "beneath a load of silks and sorrows" from village to village, attempting with small success to gain subscriptions along the way for his book of poems. A brief triumph with a comic dramatic ballad, published anonymously in 1792 and attributed by some to Robert Burns, was followed the next year by arrest and imprisonment for a poem attacking an oppressive mill owner, an attack that, in the climate of fear and suspicion following the French Revolution, smacked of sedition. Broken in spirit by a long trial, public humiliation, and three months incarceration,[3] the young poet contrived, after a dogged stint at the loom, to pay for deck passage aboard the *Swift* bound for America. After a fifty-three-day voyage, he landed in Newcastle, Delaware, in the scorching mid-July of 1794.[4]

During the long walk through woods and fields from Newcastle to Philadelphia, Wilson, who had nothing but his flute, the clothes on his back, and his hopes, marveled at all he saw, but especially at the wonder and variety of American birds. He recalled later that the red-headed woodpecker seemed to him then the most beautiful bird he had ever seen.

There followed eight years of struggle—miserably paid teaching jobs here and there, which Wilson described as "the most spirit-sinking, laborious work," alternating with weaving and peddling. Throughout these years of drudgery, he assuaged his loneliness with books in a passionate dedication to learning, later to be reflected in the ease and grace of his prose. He taught for five years in the German community of Milestown, Pennsylvania, and spent a wretched winter in a log cabin school in northern New Jersey. After failing to find work in Philadelphia, in the spring of 1802 he accepted an appointment as schoolmaster at Gray's Ferry, between Bartram's Kingsessing and Philadelphia. In a mood of deep dejection, he resumed his teaching "with the sullen resignation with which a prisoner enters his dungeon or a malefactor mounts the scaffold."[5] Fortune, however, at long last began to smile upon him. The lovely rural setting and comfortable living quarters, together with a sympathetic and friendly family, were balm to his harassed

[3]See Cantwell, *Wilson*, Appendix, pp. 265–276, for text of poem and record of Wilson's court trial.

[4]My factual data on Wilson's life is derived from James Southall Wilson, *Alexander Wilson, Poet Naturalist: A Study of His Life, with Selected Poems* (New York, 1906), and Elsa Allen's and Robert Cantwell's books cited above.

[5]Cantwell, *Wilson*, p. 114.

spirit. Once more he began to write poems, one of which, "The Solitary Tutor," gives an idyllic picture of his new life: the neat stone schoolhouse on the sloping green above the winding Schuyl-kill, the trees full of singing birds, the cosy yellow cottage shaded by poplars and white-flowered catalpas:

> Here many a tour the lonely tutor takes,
> Long known to Solitude, his partner dear,
> For rustling woods his empty school forsakes,
> At morn, still noon, and silent evening clear.
> Wild Nature's scenes amuse his wand'rings here;
> The old gray rocks that overhang the stream,
> The nodding flow'rs, that on their peaks appear,
> Plants, birds, and insects are a feast to him,
> Howe'er obscure, deform'd, minute, or huge they seem.[6]

Whatever of his leisure was not given to poetry was spent watch-ing and studying the birds of the area with increasing fascination. Even in his rooms Wilson kept the healing company of wild crea-tures: opossums, snakes, squirrels, birds, and lizards. His place re-minded him, he said, of Noah's Ark. Dreams of fame through poetry began to revive. He felt, he said, "like a harp re-strung." With new confidence, he reached out for friendship. In Philadelphia a fellow Scot, Alexander Lawson, engraver, not only drew the younger man into a stimulating group of scientists and artists, but suggested that he try his hand at drawing and painting. By the spring of 1804, Wilson was confessing that he had become so absorbed in this new pursuit he had hardly time to swallow his meals.

Perhaps the most potent factor in the metamorphosis of the coun-try schoolmaster into an accomplished ornithologist was the friend-ship of William Bartram. The famous Bartram garden, only a mile from Gray's Ferry, became a Mecca for Wilson, between whom and the gentle William, artist, author, and Romantic naturalist, a deep and abiding friendship developed. Now in the autumn of his life, the elder naturalist recognized in the younger man a kindred soul and well understood the frustrations of his search for focus. Bartram welcomed him to the peaceful home and garden (within whose 8 acres Wilson discovered fifty-one pairs of nesting birds), shared his knowledge of bird life, and encouraged and instructed him in draw-ing and painting. Totally dedicated to his new passion for the bird

[6]Wilson, *Alexander Wilson*, pp. 170–171.

kingdom, Wilson spent every leisure moment in the study and drawing of birds, collecting specimens living and dead, and keeping
varieties of birds in cages while raising others from fledglings. His
rooms became aviary and museum so that, waking and sleeping, he
was surrounded and absorbed by birds, and he regularly carried
paintings of them to Bartram for criticism. By late winter 1804 he
dared confess to the skeptical Lawson: "Quixotic as it may appear
. . . I am most earnestly bent on pursuing my plan of making a
collection of all the birds in this part of North America."[7]

About this time, three of Wilson's poems appeared in *The Literary
Messenger and the American Register,* then edited by Charles Brokden
Brown, an encouragement that temporarily tore him between two
muses. In thrall to both, he undertook in October 1804 a 600-mile
walk to Niagara Falls, a journey he described in an illustrated verse
chronicle, *The Foresters.*[8] With two companions, Wilson set forth
early one "soft, meek-eyed Indian summer" day, all three bravely
accoutered in white breeches, short coats, and high-crowned beaver
hats. A fowling piece, powderhorn, shot, a dirk in his belt, and a
knapsack stuffed with drawing and writing materials and victuals
rounded out Wilson's equipment.

Much of the way was through uncharted wilderness. What they
met with in the settled parts of their route was disagreeable enough
to make the wilderness a relief: "Black wet bread, with rancid butter
spread," and "beastly drunkards who beside us fed." Far better to
lie wrapped in a blanket, beneath a stormy sky, than in "beds with
fleas and bugs accursed . . . where every seam its tens of thousands
poured."

But from the beginning the birds more than compensated for
hardships of settlement or wilderness: a pair of grouse they shot for
food, and that tiny feathered jewel, the ruby-crowned kinglet; the
great slit-eyed owl, as adept as the osprey in snatching fish from the
river; and the blue and white Canadian jay. To collect specimens of
the great variety of waterfowl on Lake Cayuga, Wilson rented a skiff
and over-burdened himself with plovers, herons, and ducks. Crossing over to Lake Oneida, the three men descended the Oswego
River to Lake Ontario, where they and their skiff were taken on
board a lake sloop for the journey 200 miles westward along the
south shore of the inland sea to Niagara.

[7]Cantwell, *Wilson,* p. 125.
[8]Published in Philadelphia, 1809–10.

The magnitude and power, the beauty and wonder of the great Falls, was an overwhelming experience for the poet and artist in Wilson. In the gorge below the Falls he watched the bald eagles, attracted there by the carcasses of squirrels, deer, bears, and other animals that, in trying to cross the river above, had been "dragged into the current and precipitated down . . . among the rocks . . . below." Years later, when Wilson painted the great eagle for his *Ornithology,* although he used as model a specimen taken on the Jersey shore, he gave the bird a Niagara background.

At a time when many American writers still looked to Europe for their inspiration, *The Foresters*—2,219 lines of rhymed couplets in which it sometimes seems as though the poet is determined to put into verse every squirrel, bird, and stone encountered along the way —was one of the first American poems to describe the American wilderness directly from life:

> No scene nor character, to bring to view
> Save what fair truth from living Nature drew.[9]

Alexander Wilson had become an American citizen on June 9, 1804, a proud and happy day for the freedom-loving Scot. When, the following March, President Jefferson, whom Wilson did not know but fervently admired, began his second term in office, Wilson, as a mark of his respect, sent him paintings of birds he had shot on his Niagara journey. Jefferson, always deeply interested in ornithology, responded with a friendly letter of thanks, commenting on his unfamiliarity with the Canadian jay, and asking Wilson to look out for a certain bird the President had often seen and heard but could not identify. From his description of the bird and its song, similar to that of a nightingale, Wilson suspected the bird was the wood thrush, a species that would be included in the first volume of his ornithology, on which he now worked with increasing ardor.

In 1806, release from the toil and drudgery of teaching came to Wilson fortuitously through an offer from Bradford & Inskeep, a leading Philadelphia publishing firm, of the editorship of *Rees's Cyclopaedia.* Soon the young Bradford was so impressed by Wilson's ornithological work that he committed his firm to publication of Wilson's now famous *American Ornithology,* [10] provided that, after 200

[9]Wilson, *The Foresters,* lines 95–96, *The Portfolio,* no. 6, June 1809; Robert Plate, *Alexander Wilson—Wanderer in the Wilderness* (New York, 1966), pp. 81–82.

[10]Alexander Wilson, *American Ornithology* (9 vols., Philadelphia, 1809–14).

copies of the first volume had been produced, subscriptions could be obtained to finance the remainder of the project. Alexander Lawson, impressed by Bradford's commitment, undertook to do the engraving of the illustrations and to supervise their coloring. This left Wilson, in addition to his job as editor of the *Cyclopaedia,* the demanding roles of collector, observer, artist, author—and book salesman too, when it became apparent, as it soon did, that subscriptions could be obtained only through personal solicitation.

For this purpose an illustrated prospectus was issued, describing the planned ten-volume, folio-sized work, to be published over five years; every volume would contain ten plates, portraying in color from one to six different birds each, together with full textual coverage of each species. When one considers that this was the first attempt to prepare an illustrated, comprehensive ornithology covering the birds of America "from the shores of the St. Lawrence, to the mouth of the Mississippi, and from the Atlantic to the interior of Louisiana," and that this attempt was to be made by a self-educated schoolteacher and poet who had spent only a dozen years in America, the progress of Alexander Wilson toward that achievement during the remaining seven years of his life was remarkable —even heroic.

Throughout the undertaking Wilson had continually to add to his knowledge, spend long hours collecting, studying, and drawing each species, feed the results in a steady stream to Lawson for engraving and coloring, and the text to the printers as needed: all this when the science of American ornithology was still in a fluid state, subject to change from day to day with new discoveries and classifications. Before Wilson, American ornithology was still largely an uncharted wilderness; he sought to become its most productive cartographer.

Not surprisingly, Wilson began with the birds of his neighborhood, which he knew well and loved, and of which he could write with authority and warmth. He often enhanced his accounts, written with the grace and charm of style that would assure his work a special place in bird literature, with poems of his own, lyrical descriptions of his subjects and their habits, accounts of first-hand observations or those of friends, such as Bartram's telling of the courtship of the bluebirds. Propinquity governed Wilson's order of presentation: Volume 1 included the jay, wood thrush, wren, and other familiar denizens of the woods and fields around Gray's Ferry, closing with the red-headed woodpecker, the bird he had so admired his first day in America. Volume 2 included such favorites as the inimitable mockingbird, the cardinal, and that ornithological jewel the hummingbird, all lovingly described.

To obtain the essential subscriptions, Wilson set out again and again on exhausting journeys, eventually covering most of the cities and countryside east of the Mississippi. After suffering bitter disappointment from his lukewarm reception in New York and New England, he was encouraged by success beyond his hopes in the South, where he also found rich sources of bird specimens. A subscription mailed from President Jefferson, long a hero to the liberty-loving Scot, was especially cheering.

In late February 1810, Wilson set out with his two completed volumes in search of specimens and subscribers. It was a strenuous journey westward that took him, via Pittsburgh, down the Ohio in a little skiff (he named it *The Ornithologist*) to Louisville and his memorable meeting with Audubon. Crossing Kentucky and Tennessee, and thence down the wild and dangerous Natchez Trace, he eventually reached New Orleans; from there he returned to Philadelphia by boat. On the long journey, rich in both bird harvests and subscriptions, he solaced his loneliness with old Scottish melodies played on the flute, and the company of a pet Carolina parakeet he had caught near Kentucky's Big Bone Lick, where he experienced the thrilling sight of the arrival of a great flight of those pigeon-sized, bright green birds with heads of gold and red. "They came screaming through the woods in the morning about an hour after sunrise," he wrote, and "when they alighted on the ground it appeared at a distance as if covered with a carpet of the richest green, orange, and yellow."[11]

When, in August of 1810, he returned to Philadelphia, Wilson embarked with single-minded devotion on the task of completing the *Ornithology,* working with a steady concentration and an almost desperate energy as if aware of how little time he had left. Sketching and writing with the mastery and devotion to his subjects that would make his work a classic, Wilson completed the seventh volume of the projected ten before he died in 1813, at the age of forty-seven. Scientific recognition in the form of election to membership in the Academy of Natural Sciences and the American Philosophical Soci-

[11]*Ibid.,* vol. 3, p. 92.

ety was accorded him a few weeks before his death.

Wilson's arduous undertaking had been made easier by the constant friendship and sympathy of the Bartram family, with whom he made his home at intervals for months at a time, and by the loyal support of his scientific friends, notably George Ord, who assumed the task of completing the eighth volume and preparing a ninth, including in the latter a biographical sketch of Wilson, with this tribute: "When we reflect that a single individual 'without patron, fortune, or recompense,' had accomplished in the short space of seven years, as much as the combined body of European naturalists have taken a century to achieve, we feel almost inclined to doubt the evidence of our senses."[12]

In after years in Wilson's native town of Paisley, the Scots people put up a memorial statue to their famous son, attired as a wilderness traveler, with a gun slung at his back, a dead bird in his right hand, a pencil in his left, his parakeet and sketchbook at his feet. Only his flute and a book of lyrics are missing. Alexander Wilson's real memorial, however, in addition to the many species of birds named for him, is his *Ornithology*, the contribution to his adopted country of which he had said: "Few Americans have seen more of their country than I have done, and none love her more."[13]

In contrast to the concentrated span of barely ten years from the beginning of Wilson's study of bird drawing until the completion of his *Ornithology*, the apprenticeship to their common muse served by his more famous successor was a long and rich one.

Born in Les Cayes, Santo Domingo (now Haiti), on April 26, 1785, Jean Jacques Audubon was brought to France as a lad and legally adopted there by his natural father, sea captain Jean Audubon, and his wife Anne.[14] A much-indulged youth, with little formal schooling save in natural history, music, and drawing, he was free to roam the fields and forest around his family home in Brittany, where he developed an early love for nature, especially birds. According to his account, he had completed nearly 200 drawings of

---

[12]George Ord in *ibid.*, vol. 9, p. xliv.

[13]Letter to Thomas Crichton, Paisley friend and first biographer of Alexander Wilson—quoted in Cantwell, *Wilson*, p. 247. See also Henry Savage, Jr., *Lost Heritage* (New York, 1970), p. 282.

[14]My biographical data on Audubon is drawn from Herrick's *Audubon, The Naturalist*, and Alice Ford, *John James Audubon* (Norman, Okla., 1964). Alice Ford's excellent and scholarly biography presents much new material.

French birds, "all bad . . . yet representations of birds,"[15] before his father sent him to America in 1803 to learn English and, what seemed perhaps more important, to escape conscription into Napoleon's army.

During his year at Mill Grove, his father's beautifully situated Pennsylvania estate on a tributary of the Schuylkill[16] only 25 miles from the country schoolhouse at Gray's Ferry, young Audubon embraced the pleasant carefree life of a charming and talented sportsman, enthralled by the beauty of the countryside and the wealth of its animal and bird life. "Hunting, fishing, drawing and music occupied my every moment; cares I knew not, and cared naught about them."[17]

In 1804, however, impelled by his engagement to Lucy Bakewell, the sixteen-year-old daughter of a prosperous English-born neighbor, Audubon faced the necessity of earning a living. Seeking his father's advice and assistance, the young artist returned to France, where he lingered for a year absorbed in painting French birds, while his father arranged and set up for him a trading partnership with another young Frenchman, Ferdinand Rozier, with whom Audubon once more sailed for America.

To reassure Lucy's father, still doubtful of his future son-in-law's practical abilities, Audubon spent several months in New York dutifully studying the rudiments of business methods and trade. But he was a creature of the outdoors, not the office, and he often stole away from the countinghouse to haunt the glorious shores and forests of the Hudson. Here he garnered rich harvests of birds for models. Somehow too he managed to establish a friendly association with Dr. Samuel Mitchill, the city's most eminent naturalist. Who can doubt that he showed Mitchill his early portrayals of goldeneye, canvasback, widgeon, and wood ducks?[18]

When the apprenticeship was over, the partners, lured by the frontier, set out in 1808 with Lucy and all their stock of merchandise, to float down the Ohio to Louisville. Once the store was estab-

[15]Maria R. Audubon, *Audubon and His Journals,* edited by Elliott Coues (2 vols., New York, 1960), vol. 1, p. 15.

[16]Captain Jean Audubon, father of the artist, visited Philadelphia in 1789 and purchased the Mill Grove property. He never lived there, but almost immediately leased it to the former owner. The young Audubon, during his stay at Mill Grove (1804–5), boarded with the Quaker tenant William Thomas and his family—Herrick, *Audubon,* vol. 1, pp. 100–105.

[17]Audubon, *Audubon and His Journals,* p. 17.

[18]Herrick, *Audubon,* vol. 2, p. 376.

lished, Audubon, drawn by the still teeming wilderness beyond the raw village, often played truant, roaming the Kentucky countryside with gun and sketchbook, leaving Rozier to mind the store and the practical Lucy to attend to mundane affairs—a pattern that would persist throughout their relationship.

Soon after Wilson's visit the partners, disappointed in Louisville, moved their trading post down the river to Henderson. Here Lucy and the baby remained, while Audubon and Rozier explored on down the Ohio. Wintering at the Great Bend of the Mississippi opened up an exciting world for the young artist-naturalist, a world of Indians, wolves, bears, deer, and above all, endless varieties of birds. In the spring of 1811 the ill-assorted business associates dissolved their partnership, freeing Audubon to rejoin his family at Henderson.

During the next nine years, Audubon engaged fitfully and for the most part disastrously in a variety of business ventures, while with unabated ardor pursuing his avocation. Relentlessly the stack of bird paintings in his portfolio grew in number, and in excellence too. Throughout these years of wandering and hit-or-miss, hand-to-mouth existence, it was the gallant Lucy who kept the family, which now included two sons, Victor and John, afloat.[19] Working as governess in the households of wealthy frontier families, tutoring and teaching, she maintained her faith in her husband's genius, sure of his devotion and yielding with good grace to the demands of his only other passion. "I have," she once said, "a rival in every bird."[20]

In 1820 Audubon, with Lucy's support, resolved to attempt to publish his ornithology. It proved an irrevocable decision. Greatly daring, he set out in October 1820, accompanied by a lad of thirteen —the greatly talented Joseph Mason, who would do the flower paintings—on a quest that was to become a lifelong effort to reveal through brush and pen all the birds, and, eventually, all the mammals of America.

They left Cincinnati on Columbus Day on a flat-bottom cargo ark bound for New Orleans. Below the mouth of the Ohio ivory-billed woodpeckers were plentiful, while quantities of geese were seen feeding on wild grapes. As Audubon and Mason progressed southward, the numbers and varieties of birds increased. When they passed Chickasaw Bluffs on November 30, the trees bordering the

[19]Victor Gifford Audubon, born in Louisville, Kentucky, in 1809; John Woodhouse Audubon, born at Henderson, Kentucky, in 1812.
[20]Constance Rourke, *Audubon* (New York, 1936), p. 51.

river were full of parakeets; flocks of teal were flying up the river and sandhill cranes southward. Next day they observed hundreds of gulls, four bald eagles feeding on a deer carcass, and astonishing swarms of grackles and of purple finches heading south in great flocks. As they neared the mouth of the Arkansas, they came on large black birds of the cormorant kind, which were new and exciting to Audubon, and swans and V's of geese in "travelling order," the young in the center of the lines and a large old gander in the lead. They captured a wounded bald eagle, despite its vigorous defense, to serve as a live model.[21]

In the ornithological paradise where the beautiful, transparent Yazoo entered the Mississippi, they observed ducks and geese by the thousands and millions of cormorants.[22] Audubon and his protégé, when not scouring the woods or shooting from the boat for specimens, devoted their time to sketching and painting. So skillful was young Mason that his mentor declared him superior to any painter of flowers in America.[23] Below Natchez they traveled in greater speed and comfort in a keelboat. There were now marked changes in the river and its borders. The great stream, as if weary from its long course, became lethargic, while the banks seemed to reflect its mood in somnolent forests of moss-curtained cypresses, liveoaks, and pines. The change of habitat brought new bird life. Audubon and Mason were kept busy collecting and sketching all the way to New Orleans, where they arrived in early January 1821.

For the next ten months the two artists spent their time in and around the old French city, dividing their days between painting and tutoring, and forays into the country for models for their collection of lifesize bird portraits. In February Audubon was able to send his wife twenty completed paintings, eight of which, he noted, had not been included in Wilson's work. Among them were some of his best known plates, the White-headed Eagle, the Great-Footed Hawk, and one of his masterpieces, a striding turkey hen with brood.[24] From this period too were the beautiful painting of sum-

[21] Audubon's journal of his 1820–21 journey down the Ohio and Mississippi, in Donald Culross Peattie (ed.), *Audubon's America* (Boston, 1940), pp. 144–145.
[22] *Ibid.*, pp. 148–150.
[23] Ford, *Audubon*, p. 125. Mason's best work has been compared to that of the famed P. J. Redouté—see Peattie (ed.), *Audubon's America*, p. 135.
[24] Ford, *Audubon*, pp. 165–166; Herrick, *Audubon*, vol. 1, p. 311. Audubon had access to a copy of Wilson's *American Ornithology*, belonging to James Wilkins—Peattie (ed.), *Audubon's America*, p. 153.

mer tanagers, feeding on Mason's incredibly realistic muscadines, and that of a pair of redstarts raiding an equally realistic wasp nest.

In late summer 1822 Joseph Mason set out for Philadelphia. After nearly two years of constant companionship, it was a painful parting for both artists. Happily for Audubon, Lucy and their two sons joined him in New Orleans in December. For over three years the Audubons remained in Louisiana and Mississippi. Audubon gave lessons in drawing, dancing, and the flute; Lucy served as governess, and as teacher in a plantation school.

In the spring of 1826 Audubon resolved to try his luck and his fortune in England. With Lucy's accumulated savings, a hefty packet of letters of introduction, and his great portfolio of bird paintings, he boarded the schooner *Delos* bound for Liverpool. The route across the Gulf, and up the Atlantic coast as far as the Grand Banks, was rich in waterfowl and shore birds, fish and porpoises. The leisurely two-month voyage provided Audubon with the opportunity to study these subjects in more detail than had been his wont, as well as time for dissections to study the basic structures and to discover the diet proclivities of each creature.[25]

Making good use of his letters of introduction, the picturesque "American woodsman," with flowing locks and charming mien, was enthusiastically embraced by the social and scientific circles of Liverpool. Within a week of his arrival he was invited to exhibit his drawings at the city's Royal Institution. Soon crowds were paying the admission price and proclaiming the delighted ornithologist a new-found genius. Manchester responded only somewhat less rapturously. The end of October found him in Edinburgh, captivating that capital's scientific, literary, and social aristocracy, including the idolized Walter Scott who, Audubon hoped, might be induced to celebrate the beauty of the American wilderness before it passed. Audubon's Edinburgh exhibit too was a great success. He was elected to the Wernerian Society and the Royal Society of Edinburgh. The unrestrained Audubon, so long accustomed to failure, gloried in his burgeoning success and hastened to share it all with Lucy: "My Dearest Friend, wilt thou not think it wonderful; to me it is like a dream. . . ."[26] Amid such wining and dining, one wonders

[25]Alice Ford (ed.), *The 1826 Journal of John James Audubon* (Norman, Okla., 1967), pp. 3–44.

[26]Letter from Audubon to his wife, March 12, 1827, in Herrick, *Audubon,* vol. 1, p. 370.

how there was time for anything else. Responsive and grateful, Audubon made sketches and paintings for his hostesses, a wild turkey gobbler in oil for the Royal Society, and later, when he got around to writing of the birds he had so long delineated, he attached the names of his new-found friends to many species: Bewick's wren, for example, Harlan's Hawk, Henslow's bunting, and Traill's flycatcher.[27]

Within a month of his arrival he had made arrangements with an able engraver, William Home Lizars, to prepare the first series of plates that was to accompany his prospectus. In early April 1827 the prospectus and Lizars's first aquatinted plates were ready, and Audubon set out for London to enlist subscribers for *The Birds of America*.[28]

Armed with an impressive array of letters to the élite of London, Audubon was well received in the capital. One of the first to welcome him was Sir Thomas Lawrence, the portrait painter, who thought Audubon's birds "very clever indeed" and who helped him to find a market for his "potboilers," in oils, of American mammals.[29] About a month after Audubon arrived, he received the disturbing news from his Edinburgh engraver, Lizars, that all his colorists had walked off the job, forcing cancelation of the work. Fortunately Audubon was able to persuade Robert Havell and his son, master engravers in London, to take over the task. This monumental undertaking, which would not be completed until the final folio volume was delivered to its subscribers in the summer of 1838, involved the reproduction of some 100,000 large plates, each to be laboriously hand-colored, and called for the employment by Havell of up to fifty artisans and colorists.[30]

Audubon made a visit to France in the fall of 1828, where he met Pierre Joseph Redouté, and won the approval of Baron Georges Cuvier, then France's most prestigious naturalist.

Back in London, Audubon made his plans to return to America. The need for more field collecting, to fulfill his promise that the

[27] *Ibid.*, vol. 1, p. 354.

[28] *Ibid.*, p. 374. The project anticipated three double-elephant folio volumes, each to contain 133 plates. The plates were to be engraved on copper and printed on the finest quality paper, all birds and flowers to be lifesize and colored by hand; the work was to appear in parts of five plates each, and the subscription price for the whole was $1,000.

[29] Ford, *Audubon*, pp. 212–213.

[30] Ford, *Audubon*, p. 446; Herrick, *Audubon*, vol. 1, pp. 382–384, vol. 2, pp. 192–197.

Birds of America would display all the birds of America, and the longing to see his family impelled him to take ship for New York in the spring of 1829. But instead of the triumphal return he might have expected, his reception in scientific circles in New York was rather cool. His fellow members of the Lyceum of Natural History had resented his efforts to change the name of Cooper's Hawk (which honored a member of their society) to Stanley's Hawk, to compliment Lord Stanley who had been his host at Liverpool. Furthermore, current malicious attacks claimed that Audubon's famous rattlesnake and mockingbirds painting, as well as the supposedly scientific paper he had presented to Edinburgh's Wernerian Society describing the habits of the rattlesnake, smacked much of science fiction.[31]

Rebuffed, Audubon lingered only long enough for an exhibit of his drawings, then withdrew from the scene. After three weeks of hunting and painting in Camden, New Jersey, he set out on collecting expeditions to Great Egg Harbor on the Jersey shore, long the favorite collecting place of Wilson and his friend, George Ord. Then he continued on up the Lehigh River into the neglected Pocono Mountains. Not until November did he finally join poor Lucy, whom he had left three years earlier.[32]

In a few months the Audubons were off again for England. Debarking in late April, he was greeted by the exhilarating news of his election to the Royal Society. By fall, work on the text to accompany his great picture book was once again well under way, thanks in part to a happy association with the talented Scottish naturalist William MacGillivray. The first volume of this work, entitled *Ornithological Biography,* appeared in Edinburgh in 1831; the fifth and last not until 1839. These books happily combined MacGillivray's technical description of each species with bits of Audubon's rich store of bird lore, enriched by personal incidents. Interspersed as separate chapters in the first three volumes were some sixty of these "Episodes," described as "delineations of American scenery and manners." Although some were exaggerated or dramatized personal experiences, they were charmingly and vividly written and provided entertaining reading.[33]

One of the "Episodes," "The Eccentric Naturalist," described a

[31]Ford, *Audubon,* p. 251.
[32]*Ibid.,* p. 258.
[33]Herrick, *Audubon,* vol. 1, pp. 273–284.

visitor to the Audubon home in Henderson in 1818, identified only as "M. de T.," but easily recognized as the naturalist Constantine Rafinesque. This picturesque figure, with lank, black hair and long beard, arrived at the Audubons' dressed in a long yellow coat stained all over with plant juices, a waistcoat of the same, and tight pantaloons, bearing a letter from a friend of Audubon's saying that he was sending him "an odd fish," which might "prove to be undescribed." "M. de T" captivated his host with his good nature, his enthusiasm for natural history, and his scientific erudition, although such erudition did not prevent Rafinesque from becoming a victim of Audubon's practical jokes. He unsuspectingly accepted, and later published as rare finds, drawings and descriptions of wholly mythical fishes and birds concocted by Audubon. In spite of this hoax and the mocking tone in which he described his strange visitor, Audubon was not blind to Rafinesque's genuine ability, and "The Eccentric Naturalist" is, on the whole, a sympathetic portrait.[34]

Work on the volumes of the *Biography* was spurred by the threat of renewed competition from Wilson's work. As Audubon and MacGillivray toiled away on their text, three new editions of Wilson's *Ornithology* were being prepared for British publication, one of them embellished with appropriate botanical commentary and illustration, largely drawn from Michaux's *Sylva*.[35] Charles Lucien Bonaparte, also, was bringing out his four-volume ornithology, virtually a supplement to Wilson.[36]

Toward the end of summer 1831, as Havell's engraving and coloring in London and MacGillivray's editing in Edinburgh moved ahead, the need for yet more field work in America became urgent. Once again the Audubons sailed for America. In the hope of securing government assistance in his quest, Audubon hastened to Washington. There, in October 1831, he solicited cabinet members and Colonel James Abert, chief of the Topographical Engineers, to provide transport for an ornithological scouring of the shores of Florida and the Gulf. Colonel Abert, who was to be the central

[34]"The Eccentric Naturalist," *Ornithological Biography*, vol. 1, p. 455; see also Herrick, *Audubon*, vol. 1, pp. 285–300; Ford, *Audubon*, pp. 98–99; and Peattie (ed.), *Audubon's America*, pp. 49–57. For earlier discussion of Rafinesque, see above, Chapter 9.

[35]Herrick, *Audubon*, vol. 1, p. 439.

[36]Charles Lucien Bonaparte, *The American Ornithology, or the Natural History of Birds Inhabiting the U.S. not given by Wilson* (4 vols., Philadelphia, 1825–33). It was published in parts—see Allen, *History of American Ornithology*, p. 566.

figure behind the scenes of American exploration for the next thirty years, readily acceded.[37] And with two young assistants Audubon sailed on to Charleston to collect there, while awaiting the arrival of the government boat placed at their disposal.

On a Charleston street, soon after their arrival, an encounter occurred that was to prove one of the outstanding events of Audubon's life. He met the Reverend John Bachman, Lutheran minister and ardent naturalist, who persuaded the artist and his party to make their headquarters in his home. This hospitable household, where Audubon remained for nearly a month, included Bachman's sister-in-law, Maria Martin, who later contributed some of the most exquisite botanical accompaniments to Audubon's bird paintings. A deep and abiding friendship, based on their common passion for natural history, developed between the enthusiastic, gifted Audubon and the studious, unassuming minister. Under Bachman's expert guidance, Audubon and his party collected and prepared 300 specimens, including 60 land and water birds. Only the fear of missing the early spring breeding season in south Florida impelled them to leave Charleston and set off down the coast.[38]

On St. Anastasia Island, off St. Augustine, they collected a rich variety of water birds. Audubon worked at fever pitch to portray accurately the colors and texture of the feathers before they faded, and in the evenings he labored to set down in his notes all he had observed of flight patterns and nesting habits of each species. Recalling Bartram's ecstatic account of the St. John's River, he seized an opportunity to ascend that fabled stream in a naval boat; but the paucity of birds and the monotonous nature of the country through which the river flowed made it a disappointing journey.[39]

At last, in April 1832, the long-awaited revenue cutter *Marion* picked up the bird seekers and sailed south with them for the Florida Keys and the Dry Tortugas. Let Audubon supply a sample of their bird collecting there:

The flocks of birds that covered the shelly beaches of Sandy Island and those hovering overhead, so astonished us that we would for awhile scarcely

[37]Herrick, *Audubon*, vol. 2, p. 5.

[38]Ford, *Audubon*, pp. 283–286; Herrick, *Audubon*, vol. 2, p. 7. For biographical data on John Bachman, see C. L. Bachman, *John Bachman* (Charleston, S.C., 1888). See also Claude Henry Neuffer (ed.), *The Christopher Happoldt Journal* (Charleston, S.C., 1960).

[39]Ford, *Audubon*, pp. 286–291.

believe our eyes. . . . Our first fire among a crowd of Great Godwits laid prostrate sixty-five of those birds. . . . Rose colored Curlews stalked gracefully beneath the mangroves. Purple Herons rose at almost every step we took, and each cactus supported the nest of a White Ibis. The air was darkened by whistling wings, while on the waters, floated Gallinules and other interesting birds.[40]

On his return north, Audubon stopped to present Bachman with four live eaglets captured in Florida; while in turn Bachman added new specimens from the Charleston area to Audubon's Florida collection of 1,000 bird skins.[41]

Eager to study and collect bird specimens in the summer habitats of the migratory birds, Audubon planned an expedition to the North Atlantic coastal regions. Meantime, he was needed in London, so his eldest son Victor hurried over to serve as his father's surrogate, handling mounting publication problems with Havell. Audubon resumed the collecting begun in Maine and New Hampshire the previous season.

In June 1833, in a chartered vessel manned by a group of young volunteers, Audubon, with his second son John, sailed from Eastport for the Gulf of St. Lawrence and the coast of Labrador to observe and sketch the ducks, geese, auks, cormorants, gulls, and shearwaters that abounded in those teeming waters. But weighed against the cost and the twelve weeks consumed, the expedition fell short of their expectations, netting only seventy-three bird skins and twenty-three drawings.[42]

Next spring Audubon was back in England with his collection of specimens from almost three years in America, 100 of his older drawings reexecuted, and, not least, many new ones portraying new species, as well as sixty-two new patrons for the *Birds of America*.[43] He hurried to Edinburgh to work with MacGillivray on the second volume of the *Ornithological Biography*, which came out in December. That task held the Audubons in Scotland for over a year, from 1835 to mid-1836, when it became clear that more field work was urgent.

When finally they sailed for New York in the late summer of 1836, the end of the great project was in sight: 350 plates were completed, only 85 to be done. There was still one serious gap—Far Western

[40]Audubon, *Audubon and His Journals*, vol. 2, p. 264; Peattie (ed.), *Audubon's America*, p. 184.
[41]Ford, *Audubon*, p. 292.
[42]Herrick, *Audubon*, vol. 2, pp. 48–50.
[43]*Ibid.*, p. 66.

species, unnumbered and as yet unseen. As if in answer to prayer, a letter awaited Audubon in New York announcing that the skins of about 100 species of Western birds, collected by John Kirk Townsend and Thomas Nuttall, had been received by the Academy of Natural Sciences in Philadelphia. Unhesitatingly, Audubon deferred a subscription-seeking trip to Boston in favor of a bird-seeking trip to Philadelphia. Alas, the Society refused to make the collection available to him without the permission of its collectors. Then, by great good luck, the *Alert* arrived in port with Richard Dana, Nuttall, and barrels of "truck," including an additional collection of Western birds. To Audubon's delight, Nuttall proved characteristically generous and cooperative.[44] It was an enormous relief to the weary Audubon who, although but fifty-five, was aging so rapidly that the possibility of an expedition to the Far West was fading.

Now with his long-suffered thirst for Western species alleviated, and a successful subscription campaign in the East completed, he set out with John to scour the Gulf Coast. Thanks again to Colonel Abert and to President Jackson himself, who had shown sufficient interest to entertain the Audubons at the White House, Audubon once again had the advantage of a coastguard cutter. As it turned out, the expedition along the Gulf Coast and into Texas was one of the most disappointing of Audubon's career. They came back to Charleston, where young John Audubon and Maria, daughter of John Bachman, were married. Then Audubon, John, and Maria left for England, where they joined Lucy and Victor.

Work on *The Birds of America* had now been in progress for nearly twelve years. Determined to carry out his original purpose of portraying every bird yet discovered in the United States, Audubon worked unremittingly. Finally, on June 20, 1838, the last plate was completed. It was a magnificent production. Each bird, of the 489 species represented, was portrayed lifesize, with amazing verisimilitude of color and posture and appropriate botanical accompaniment, accurately depicted.[45] Hailed by Cuvier as "the greatest monument erected by man to Nature,"[46] *The Birds of America* holds a unique permanent place as a landmark of Ameri-

[44]Graustein, *Nuttall*, pp. 318–319.

[45]There were finally four volumes in all. These contained 87 numbers of 5 hand-colored, copper plate engravings each—a total of 435 double-elephant aquatints, covering 489 species of birds. Ford, *Audubon*, p. 446; Herrick, *Audubon*, vol. 2, p. 177.

[46]Dean Amadon's introduction to John James Audubon, *The Birds of America* (Dover edn., 7 vols., New York, 1967). Though Audubon was widely praised in his lifetime, his fame has grown immeasurably with the years—Herrick, *Audubon*, vol. 1, pp. 4–5.

can natural history and a glorious work of American art.

Although his greatest work was now triumphantly completed, Audubon continued to carry on. The last volume of the *Ornithological Biography* appeared in May 1839, and the *Synopsis of Birds*, a catalogue of North American birds, in July of the same year, both prepared in collaboration with MacGillivray.

That autumn Audubon, his work in England done, sailed with his family for his final return to America. Compelled by a continuing need for income and wishing to reach a larger public than was possible with the costly folio edition, Audubon made plans with Victor and John to issue a miniature combination of the *Birds of America* and the *Ornithological Biography*. By the close of the year work on this octavo edition was well under way. A visit from John Bachman brought a definite determination to proceed with the proposed work on the quadrupeds of North America, on which Bachman collaborated. Meanwhile yet another bond was tied between the Bachman and Audubon households with the marriage of Victor and Eliza, the frail younger sister of Maria Bachman Audubon.[47]

The octavo edition of *The Birds of America* appeared over a period of four years, the first part late in 1839. To John Audubon fell the task of reducing his father's original paintings. New flowers, trees, and birds were added, errors corrected, and the text improved. The completed work in seven volumes included descriptions of 474 distinct species of American birds, a very substantial increase over Wilson's 262.[48]

The four years during which the first miniature edition of the birds was appearing brought many changes to the Audubon family. Within the space of a few months, in 1840 and 1841, both Maria and Eliza Bachman Audubon died. Weary of city life, which he had always disliked, Audubon in 1841 bought 25 acres of beautifully wooded land overlooking the Hudson,[49] and built a commodious house to which he moved his family the following year.

[47]Ford, *Audubon*, pp. 363–366.

[48]Allen, *History of American Ornithology*, p. 553; but see Herrick, *Audubon*, vol. 2, p. 214, where Wilson is credited with 278, Wilson with Ord 320, and with Bonaparte 382. The miniature edition of *The Birds of America* is again available in a Dover edition (7 vols., New York, 1967). In its miniature format *The Birds of America* was an immediate success, and enjoyed a sustained popularity, nine editions (the later ones without plates) before 1872.

[49]About a mile below the site of the George Washington Bridge. Audubon named his home "Minnie's Land" in honor of his wife, Lucy (Minnie being the Scots form of her name)—Herrick, *Audubon*, vol. 2, p. 235.

The formal prospectus for the *Quadrupeds* was issued, and subscription lists opened for the new project. As Audubon himself continued to age, the bulk of the work on both the *Birds* and the *Quadrupeds* fell to Victor, John, and the invaluable Bachman. Relieved from the workload that had burdened him for so long, Audubon set out once again to fulfill his long-cherished dream of a collecting expedition in the West. In the spring of 1843, he boarded a Missouri River steamer bound for Fort Union, on an expedition that provided little beyond a period of recreation for the "old" gentleman.

The fame of the Audubon name in natural history circles was further enhanced as subscribers began in 1845 to receive their serial issues of the plates that would comprise the two imperial folio volumes, with their three accompanying volumes covering the mammalian quadrupeds of North America, incorporating 150 impressive plates, mostly the work of Victor and John, and a text by Bachman. The reception accorded the first volume of plates in 1846 was encouraging; so encouraging that plans were launched for a miniature octavo edition of the *Quadrupeds*. [50] But of these successes the elder Audubon had little awareness. On a visit to him in May 1848, Bachman was distressed to find his old friend with "his mind all in ruins."[51] Even before the second volume of the *Quadrupeds* plates had been completed and the first of the planned three volumes of the miniature edition had come off the press, John James Audubon had died on January 27, 1851, at his home on the Hudson.[52]

[50]John James Audubon and Rev. John Bachman, *The Viviparous Quadrupeds of North America* (2 vols., folio, Philadelphia, 1845–48, with 3 octavo vols. of text); octavo or miniature edition, *The Quadrupeds of North America* (3 vols., New York, 1854).

[51]Ford, *Audubon*, p. 418.

[52]*Ibid.*, pp. 448–449.

CHAPTER 11

Catlin, Schoolcraft, and Maximilian of Wied

BY 1832, in a now familiar pattern, the Sauks and Foxes, two closely related Algonquin tribes, had been finally expelled from the last of their homes in Michigan and Wisconsin and forced across the Mississippi into the backyard of the warlike Sioux. Their highly respected old chief, Black Hawk, aroused by the latest of the long series of "purchases" and "treaties" of questionable morality and legality by which his people had been expelled from the lands of their fathers, repudiated the terms of a cession arranged with Keokuk, a rival young chief who had been put in power and supported by American authorities, and led his people back across the Mississippi to reoccupy their pristine homeland. The response of the settlers, quick and emphatic—embalmed in history under the euphemistic title of the Black Hawk War, its fame enhanced by young Abraham Lincoln's reluctant involvement—was in fact little more than a shameful indiscriminate massacre of Black Hawk's followers. By mid-September old Black Hawk himself and several of his leaders were in ball and chain in Jefferson Barracks near St. Louis.[1]

The imprisoned Black Hawk and his companions quickly became objects of great interest. One of their earliest visitors was Washington Irving, recently returned to America after many years in Europe, who was in St. Louis preparing to set out for the plains of the Upper Arkansas and his initial acquaintance with the trans-Mississippi

[1]Allan Nevins and Henry Steele Commager, *A Short History of the United States* (New York, 1942), p. 183; Carl Sandburg, *Abraham Lincoln: The Prairie Years* (2 vols., New York, 1926), vol. 1, pp. 150–160.

West.[2] A little later the artist-writer George Catlin, who was back in St. Louis after more than a year devoted to studying, writing about, and painting the Indians of the Missouri River country, made memorable portraits of Black Hawk and five of his fellow captives in their native garb plus the balls and chains of civilized authority.[3] Despite the manifold duties of his office as superintendent of Indian Affairs, General William Clark personally escorted to Jefferson Barracks some of Black Hawk's more distinguished guests. On one such occasion in the early spring of 1833, Clark accompanied Prince Maximilian, newly arrived from New Harmony with the artist Karl Bodmer (often known in America as Charles Bodmer) and the Scottish adventurer-novelist Captain William Drummond Stewart, for an interview with the noted chieftain.[4]

During the previous summer while the Black Hawk War was still in progress and its leader still a free man, 600 miles to the northeast at Sault Ste. Marie, Henry Rowe Schoolcraft, a scholarly U.S. Indian agent who had just returned from an expedition through the northern parts of the Sauk and Fox country to the source of the Mississippi, was busy preparing his official report on the Black Hawk War.

All these men whose paths had fortuitously crossed that of old Black Hawk—Clark, Irving, Catlin, Maximilian, Bodmer, Stewart, and Schoolcraft—played important roles in revealing the American domain beyond the rapidly expanding mid-nineteenth-century frontier and the peoples who sparsely occupied it. Three of them —Catlin, Schoolcraft, and Maximilian—contributed greatly to a field of rising interest, American ethnology, together building upon

[2]In the autumn of 1832 Irving, with three European companions, joined Indian agent Henry L. Ellsworth on an official inspection tour of the Arkansas, Cimarron, Canadian, Verdigris region of what is now Oklahoma, preliminary to the planned removal of the remnants of the Eastern Indian tribes to reservations there. Two years later Irving turned his diary account of that "month's foray beyond the outposts of human habitation" into *A Tour on the Prairies* (Philadelphia, 1835), a slight but entertaining and immensely successful little book, the first on the trans-Mississippi West by a professional writer. It has since seen more than thirty editions in English and twenty in other languages—Washington Irving, *A Tour on the Prairies,* edited by J. F. McDermott (Norman, Okla., 1956), p. xxxii. Subsequent citations are to this edition.

[3]The sitting had been arranged for Catlin by General William Clark, former territorial governor, then superintendent of Indian Affairs of St. Louis. Catlin also painted a full-length portrait of the old general.

[4]Bernard DeVoto, *Across the Wide Missouri* (Boston, 1947), p. 18; Maximilian, Prince of Wied, *Travels in the Interior of North America, 1832–1834,* in Reuben Gold Thwaites (ed.), *Early Western Travels, 1748–1846* (vol. 22, Cleveland, 1906), pp. 228–231.

the foundation provided by Albert Gallatin. After a long and distinguished career in government finance and diplomacy, Gallatin was devoting his later years to following up a suggestion of his friend, Jefferson. He was preparing for publication a notable work, which appeared in 1836 under the title *Synopsis of the Indian Tribes within the United States East of the Rocky Mountains and in the British and Russian Possessions in North America,* [5] an accomplishment soon to be supplemented in 1842 by his founding of the American Ethnological Society.

George Catlin, the first of these men whose work in the Indian country gained wide attention, was born in Wilkes-Barre, Pennsylvania, on July 26, 1796. He grew up there amid tales of the Wyoming Massacre of July 1778, during which his mother and her mother had been carried off by the Indians. Following his father's example, he studied law and practiced for a while, but, finding little appeal in it, abandoned it for the arts. At twenty-five, without formal training, he had become a respected portrait painter in Philadelphia, sufficiently recognized to be elected a member of the Pennsylvania Academy and, two years later, an Academician of the National Academy, and to have attracted prominent sitters, among them Governor DeWitt Clinton and Sam Houston, of whom he did fine miniatures on ivory. Perhaps his most remarkable work was a watercolor in amazing detail of the entire assembly of more than 100 members of the Virginia Constitutional Convention of 1829–30, in which every face was recognizable. Then, just as the road to conventional success in his second profession appeared open before him, an event deflected him to the tortuous, dangerous, and unconventional work that would lead him into distant wildernesses and foreign lands, to fame, disappointment, and ultimate poverty. As Catlin tells it, he was

reaching for some branch or enterprise of the art, on which to devote a whole lifetime of enthusiasm; when a delegation of some ten or fifteen noble and dignified-looking Indians, from the wilds of the "Far West," suddenly arrived in the city, arrayed and equipped in all their classic beauty —with shield and helmet—with tunic and manteau, tinted and tasselled off, exactly for the painter's palette! In silent and stoic dignity, these lords of the forest . . . wrapped in their pictured robes, with brows plumed with the quills of the war eagle

[5] *Transactions of American Antiquarian Society, Archaeologie Americana* (vol. 2, Cambridge, Mass., 1836).

so appealed to Catlin that he was forthwith persuaded that "the history and customs of such a people, preserved by pictorial illustrations," were "themes worthy of the lifetime of one man." He decided that he would become historian to a dying people, "who have no historians or biographers of their own to pourtray with fidelity their native looks and history; thus snatching from a hasty oblivion . . . a truly lofty and noble race."[6]

Now, more than a century later, few will deny him the laurels of success. However, after dedicating himself to his objective, it was three or four years before Catlin set out to paint the Indians beyond the frontiers. During that period, which was largely devoted to accumulating the means he would require for his travels, Catlin seized every opportunity to paint Indians wherever he could find them; some were visitors from the West, others the remnants of the Eastern tribes found on nearby reservations. But all the while, encouraged by his young wife, Clara, he kept a steady focus on his objective. In 1830, leaving her settled in Albany, we find him in St. Louis, the gateway to the West, to which General William Clark, by virtue of his official position, held the master key. Soon, through Clark's friendship, that key was available to the artist. He was invited to witness the frequent visitations of tribal delegations on missions to the superintendent, an opportunity to secure ample subjects for his rapid and insatiable brush. There were expeditions with the general, one of which went up the Mississippi to treaty parleys at Prairie du Chien with the Iowa, Missouri, Sioux, Omaha, and the Sauk and Fox nations. In the fall there were expeditions up the Missouri, one to Leavenworth where Catlin portrayed many representatives of removed Eastern Indians, Delawares, Kickapoos, and Shawnees, one of whom was the Shawnee prophet, the one-eyed brother of the great Tecumseh. An expedition to the Kansas was more to the artist's liking. There for the first time he was able to paint Indians still living in their native state, untouched by European civilization.

During that busy summer Catlin developed the distinctive style he was to employ through the years in portraying Indians. His Philadelphia period had amply demonstrated his ability to produce competent traditional work, the miniatures particularly showing a high

---

[6]George Catlin, *Letters and Notes on the Manners, Customs, and Conditions of the North American Indians* (2 vols., London, 1841), vol. 1, pp. 2–3; Harold McCracken, *George Catlin and the Old Frontier* (New York, 1959), pp. 21–27.

degree of skill and painstaking detail. However, when he was confronted with the exigences inherent in painting, under primitive
conditions, as many factually accurate pictures as possible, Catlin
developed a cartoon style. This permitted him to reduce to a minimum the variety of the colors on his palette, to use little mixing and
blending, and to omit backgrounds and all but token shading.[7]
During that summer of 1830, thanks in no small part to General
Clark, he had gained some mastery of the confusing tribal nomen-
clature and the complex relationships of the numerous Plains peoples, nations, and tribes, as well as of the titles, functions, and social
distinctions of individuals within the villages themselves. Catlin was
well on the way to becoming what Bernard DeVoto calls the "first
painter of the West"—using "first" in the sense of most effective—
and the man with whom "American ethnology may be said to
begin."[8]

In St. Louis again in the summer of 1831, Catlin made plans for
the next summer to ascend the Missouri on Astor's American Fur
Company's new river steamer, *Yellow Stone.* It was her maiden voyage, which, it was hoped, would take her all the way to Fort Union
at the mouth of the Yellowstone River.

In late March 1832 the wide-beamed sidewheeler, with her twin
forward stacks belching the acrid smoke of cordwood-fired boilers,
swung out into the Mississippi and headed up its muddy side into
the tawny Missouri. She was off on "a voyage of nearly three months
from St. Louis, a distance of two thousand miles," according to
Catlin's letter to the *New York Commercial Advertiser,* which, in the
ensuing months, published five detailed and fascinating accounts of
the voyage.[9] Aboard the *Yellow Stone* was a polyglot aggregation of
Company men; mostly French-Canadian river men and American,
Scottish, and half-breed trappers. Catlin himself; Major John F. A.
Sanford, a government Indian agent; and a band of Upper Missouri
Indians returning from Washington under Sanford's chaperonage,
were the only wayfarers intent on their own affairs. Among the
Indians was an Assiniboin warrior of distinction, *Wi-jun-jon* (Pi-

---

[7]Only through such simplifications could he sit in on a conference and have in hand
several portraits at its conclusion, even when he employed the custom of merely
adumbrating on the spot and "finishing," Catlin-style, at a later time. The pictures
he carried back when he returned east for the winter show those characteristics well
developed.

[8]DeVoto, *Across the Wide Missouri,* pp. 392–393.

[9]McCracken, *Catlin,* pp. 40–65.

geon's Egg Head), who had been greatly impressed by what he had seen on his expedition and by his present exalted mode of travel—feelings no doubt much enhanced by his full-dress American regimentals, complete with epaulettes, white kid gloves, and high-heel boots, reputedly a gift from President Jackson, to which he had added a blue umbrella, high-crown beaver hat, and a folding fan. When this warrior was on his way east the previous season, it happened that Catlin had made a full-length portrait of him in all his native finery, full feather headdress, scalp lock fringes, painted tunic embossed with colored porcupine quills, buffalo robe, and long-stemmed red pipe. As the *Yellow Stone* puffed her way upstream while the metamorphosized *Wi-jun-jon* whistled "Yankee Doodle," Catlin again painted the now exalted pilgrim. When they reached the Assiniboin town, the awe and wonderment with which the returnee was greeted soon turned to suspicion as his people heard his "tall tales" of what he had seen; eventually he was completely demoted in tribal esteem when he persisted in his "lying." The tableau of the two paintings of *Wi-jun-jon* going to and returning from Washington was destined to become one of the highlights of Catlin's Indian Gallery.[10]

Beyond Council Bluffs, near the mouth of the Platte barely a third of the way to the mouth of the Yellowstone, the river had never before been navigated by a steamboat. Few natives of the villages above had ever seen one, let alone one that announced her approach with the thunderous voice of cannon, the firing of which became customary at each village as the boat made her way upstream. Delays were frequent and sometimes prolonged—for repairs, or to wait for higher water to release them from sandbar or snag—delays that provided Catlin with welcome opportunities to see much of interest along the way. At one such halt the prospect of moving again appeared so remote that a party, including the artist, set out on foot for Fort Pierre, 200 miles of wild prairie country above the stranded vessel. A week later he was sketching their approach to Fort Pierre: gleaming white in the sun on the flat plain below the knoblike hills, with the fort and the wide Missouri in the background, were the 600 tepees of a large band of Sioux who had come in from the prairies to witness the heralded arrival of "the Great Canoe." To Catlin's eye the Sioux were impressive people,

[10] *Letters and Notes*, vol. 1, pp. 194–200.

"fine and prepossessing, tall and straight," with a striking grace of movement. At least half the men stood 6 feet or more. Among them Catlin found some of the finest-looking Indians in his entire lifetime collection of portraits, and here he painted some of his most striking group action pictures, notably those of their beggars' dance and bear dance. While awaiting the arrival of the *Yellow Stone*, the Indian camp day and night seemed a wild and primitive festival: endless chanting, yelling, and spontaneous dancing to a constant thump of drums. The Sioux head men particularly were most impressive, both physically and in their attire; they had handsome faces, with an unusually strong Oriental cast, beneath coils of carefully groomed, phenomenally long black hair, sometimes sweeping the ground when loosed. Profoundly impressed by the artist's ability to make paper or canvas blossom with a perfect likeness of his subject, they honored him with the title *Ee-cha-zoo-kah-wa-kon*, "The Medicine Painter" ("medicine" in Indian parlance indicating "magic") and danced for him their resplendent "Dance of the Chieftains." They took him on their buffalo hunts, which in his adept sketches veritably breathe the excitement of the chase.[11]

However, drawings and paintings were but part of the record Catlin sought to make in order to preserve—to rescue—the looks and modes "of the red men of North America, as a nation of human beings"; for, as they sadly confessed, "they are fast-travelling to the shades of their fathers, towards the setting sun." He was constantly recording in his journal their beliefs, their philosophy, customs, and "laws." Ever on the alert to acquire more substantial accouterments of their culture, Catlin gathered bows and arrows, shields, war clubs, pipes, vessels, a fine tepee, and on more than one occasion the complete attire of a chieftain from feathered crown and scalp lock-fringed shirt to porcupine-embossed leggings and moccasins.

At Fort Union, at the mouth of the Yellowstone, the steamboat's ultimate destination, which was reached the middle of June, Catlin was delighted to find Indians of many different tribes camped, as at Fort Pierre, on the flat plain beneath the steeply rolling hills near the trading post. There were Blackfeet with cheeks and jaws variously painted, shoulder-length hair with a square-cut forelock dropping down between the eyes to the nosebridge, and headdresses of buffalo horns, and medicine men with their weird equipment of

[11]McCracken, *Catlin*, pp. 47–50.

rattles, animal skins, medicine bags, and masks. There were Crows, Assiniboins, and Crees, each in their way spectacular.[12] Looking back on his journey upriver, Catlin exulted in the opportunities afforded him

to paint a vast country of green fields, where the men are all *red*—where *meat* is the staff of life—where no *laws*, but those of *honour*, are known— where the buffaloes range, the elk, the mountain-sheep, and the fleet-bounding antelope—where the magpie and chattering parroquettes supply the place of the redbreast and the blue-bird—where wolves are white and bears are grizzly—where pheasants are hens of the prairie, and frogs have horns, where rivers are yellow, and white men are turned savages in looks . . . the dogs are all wolves—women all slaves—men all lords.[13]

A few years later, in his great two-volume work *Letters and Notes on the Manners, Customs, and Conditions of the North American Indians,* Catlin made the prescient suggestion that America should "pre-serve . . . [for] the world in future ages! A *nation's Park* containing man and beast in all the wild and freshness of their nature's beauty!"[14]

In his month at Fort Union Catlin painted an almost unbelievable number of pictures. Chiefs and medicine men so clamored for an opportunity to sit for him, and so many others wished to watch the magic process, that guards had to be stationed at his "studio" to keep space and order. But in mid-July, to allow time to paint and sketch along the way and still make it down to St. Louis before winter, the artist loaded his rich store of paintings and his collec-tions into a commodious skiff and started downriver with a crew of two, a French voyageur and a Mississippi frontiersman, and, on a perch at the bow, a "domesticated war-eagle, the noble bird which the Indians so much esteem for its valour and the quills to adorn the heads of chiefs and warriors."[15] Although aided by the current, their progress was slow, partly because of the necessity to live off the land as they went along, but mostly because of Catlin's wish to visit every village along the way to add to his store of paintings and artifacts. Space permits attention to just one of those stops: his memorable visit at the Mandan towns near Fort Clark, 200 miles below Fort Union, where Lewis and Clark had spent their first

[12] *Ibid.,* pp. 65–72.
[13] *Letters and Notes,* vol. 1, pp. 59, 60.
[14] *Ibid.,* p. 262.
[15] McCracken, *Catlin,* p. 81.

winter. It was a week after their embarkation that Catlin's party beached their skiff beneath a high bluff atop which, ensconced in a sharp bend of the river and protected by a log palisade across the neck, stood the closely crowded, mud-covered domes of the Mandan town, a place of which many a campfire tale had been told.

Ever since the sieur de la Vérendrye had visited them in 1737, tales of these hospitable, unwarlike, sedentary tillers of the soil, in the midst of a region of ever-warring, roving hunters with no fixed abode, had been attracting white visitors to the Mandan towns.[16] Through the generations, the widely known intimate hospitality of the attractive Mandan women to their white visitors no doubt accounted for the lighter skins, less uniformly black hair, and eyes of varied shades that encouraged the widespread belief that they were people of a different origin from other Indians,[17] as du Pratz had believed the Natchez to be. There were those who came to believe them descendants of that legendary band of twelfth-century Welsh —a belief Catlin himself later embraced when he detailed the Mandan religious ceremonies in a separate volume titled *O-kee-pa.*[18] It was Catlin's good fortune to find at nearby Fort Clark James Kipp, the American Fur Company's agent, who enjoyed the high regard of his neighbors, and his even greater good fortune to arrive at the place on the eve of the Mandans' most important religious festival, the late July *O-kee-pa* ceremonies.

As a friend of Kipp, the artist was made welcome in the larger Mandan town. Soon he was among the villagers gathered on the dome of one of the ovenlike lodges, with a view of the whole village below and about him, "with its sachems—its warriors—its dogs— and its horses in motion—its medicines (or mysteries) and scalp-poles waving over my head—its piquets—its green fields and prairies, and river in full view. . . ." On the tops of the lodges were groups of

wild and picturesque appearance . . . stern warriors . . . wrapped in their painted robes, with heads decked and plumed with quills. . . . In another

[16]John Bartlett Brebner, *The Explorers of North America, 1492–1806* (London, 1933), pp. 295ff.

[17]George Catlin, *O-kee-pa* (Philadelphia, 1867); Centennial edn., edited by John C. Ewers (New Haven, 1967), pp. 8–10. Future citations are to the Centennial edition.

[18]Bernard DeVoto, *The Course of Empire* (Boston, 1952), pp. 68–70, 373–374; *Letters and Notes,* vol. 1, p. 3; *O-kee-pa,* p. 61. See also Chap. 16 in Charles M. Boland, *They All Discovered America* (New York, 1961).

direction, the wooing lover softening the heart . . . with the notes of his simple lute. On other lodges . . . groups engaged in games. . . . In the centre of the villages is an open space, or public area, of 150 feet in diameter . . . used for public games and festivals . . . and also for their "annual religious ceremonies," which were about to take place. . . .[19]

Arrangements were soon made for Catlin to paint portraits of two of the most distinguished Mandans. When the portraits were done and revealed to the subjects, they clapped their hands to their mouths in amazement, drank fully of admiration for their likenesses, and formally bestowed on the artist a Mandan title, *Te-ho-pe-nee Wash-ee*, "Great Medicine White Man," and the traditional staff with its appended animal parts and rattle, emblems of the profession. But when the canvases were displayed to the townspeople, while "hundreds covered their mouths with their hands and were mute; others, indignant, drove their spears frightfully into the ground. . . ." Most critical were the eclipsed native medicine men, who proclaimed that all who subjected themselves to being painted would soon die, a conviction proved spurious a little later by their own readiness to have their likenesses painted by the interloper. But some fear lingered that the artist had taken part of his sitters' life force and put it in the picture—a superstition shared by other tribes as Catlin, to his great dismay, would later discover. However, the fearful and suspicious were in the minority, and Catlin's prestige soared.[20] As part of the honors accorded to him, when the *O-kee-pa* ceremonies began, he, Kipp, one of his men, and an interpreter were included among the élite group of spectators permitted to witness them. They were the only whites ever known to have witnessed the entire wild, gruesome, sometimes ribald and comical ceremony, which, except for Catlin's record of it, was soon to be swept into oblivion with the practical extermination of the Mandans a few years later by a smallpox epidemic.

The horrendous ceremonies that Catlin reported and graphically illustrated began with the preparatory starvation of the aspiring young men who were to subject themselves to the trial of their merit by ordeal, a requisite preliminary to warrior status. The formal commencement of the ceremonies was signaled by the entrance from the prairie of the symbolic first and only man, which was followed by the gathering of the head men in the great circular

[19]*Letters and Notes*, vol. 1, pp. 87–88.
[20]*Ibid.*, pp. 106–110; *O-kee-pa*, pp. 51–52.

medicine lodge. Outside in the dance plaza, to the accompaniment of rattles and drums, the ritual bull dance was repeatedly performed by fantastically painted men, each covered with an entire buffalo skin, while a black-colored "evil spirit" constantly interfered. Meanwhile, inside the medicine lodge the young men being tested were suffering sticks to be inserted into the flesh of their chests, backs, and legs to which ropes were attached; some were hoisted to swing from the roof, while from their leg skewers buffalo skulls dangled as the bleeding but uncomplaining sufferers continued to swing from the roof beams until, unconscious, the medicine bag and shield each carried in his hands fell to the earthen floor. Only then were they lowered and dragged out by their ropes to the dance plaza, to be dragged around it until the skewers were torn from the flesh. The ceremonies culminated with the symbolic flight of the evil spirit and a ritual sexual orgy with the "buffaloes," designed to attract the real beasts to the neighborhood of the little-roaming Mandans' towns. All this was detailed and most of it illustrated in Catlin's *Letters and Notes,* and later embellished, with few expurgated details, in his *O-kee-pa.* To many people these ceremonies seemed unbelievable; others were skeptical. But the veracity of Catlin's reporting has now been amply confirmed.[21]

Intrigued by the Mandans' unique rituals, strange superstitions, and childlike simplicities, their peaceable ways but cruel tortures, their agrarian society but fantastic courtship of the buffalo, Catlin lingered on after the days of the *O-kee-pa,* until the corn dance festival of the nearby Minnetarees, which marked the ripening of that native American staff of life. Then a touch of frost in the Dakota air warned of the inexorable approach of fall and ice on the river. So with moving farewells and embraces the Mandans' *To-ho-pe-nee Wash-ee* and his two companions deployed his augmented treasures, launched their skiff, and moved off downstream.

When they had gone a little way they were overtaken by a frantic band of Mandan horsemen, who hailed them to report that a girl whose picture Catlin had painted and taken away with him had fallen ill, and that she lay dying because too much of her had gone into the picture. They begged to be permitted to carry the picture back

[21] *O-kee-pa,* introduction, pp. 25–33; John C. Ewers, senior ethnologist at the Smithsonian, has marshaled the evidence vindicating Catlin's account of the ceremonies. Ewers (p. 97) says *O-kee-pa* meant "to look alike," it being the Mandans' belief that the bull dancers should look alike.

to her, a petition readily granted by the artist.[22] Further downstream, among a band of Sioux, the artist was denounced as killer of three of their warriors whose deaths had resulted from a tribal feud that arose out of one of his paintings. Passing near another town where any and all whites were being sought for execution to atone for the loss of three Sioux they alleged had been captured and burned by a reckless band of whites, the three in the skiff floated past at night under the cover of the willows along the bank. Despite these and other hazards (such as being caught in a milling mass of thrashing buffalo swimming the river), the party in due course arrived safely at St. Louis. There the indefatigable Catlin, shortly afterward, added his paintings of the imprisoned Black Hawk to his burgeoning collection.[23]

Catlin and his wife, Clara, went downriver to spend the winter on the Gulf and the following summer at Cincinnati. There he and Judge James Hall[24] saw much of each other. Hall's *Western Monthly Magazine* had announced and highly praised Catlin's initial exhibition there of part of the portrait, landscape, and artifact collection he called his American Indian Gallery. After another winter on the Gulf, Catlin was off again for the Indian country beyond the frontier, this time to the Southwest.

By special authority granted to him by Secretary of War Lewis Cass[25] Catlin joined a regiment of mounted dragoons under Colonel Henry Dodge, who were to visit and negotiate treaties with the Comanche and Pawnee Picts far across the southern plains in territory claimed by Mexico. The expedition was destined to become one of the most disastrous marches in American military history.[26] After arriving at Fort Gibson, whence Washington Irving had set out eighteen months before on his tour of those plains, Catlin had

[22]McCracken, *Catlin*, pp. 114–116.

[23]*Ibid.*, pp. 121–124. According to his biographer, in the eighty-six days of that voyage, while averaging 18 miles a day and participating in many other activities, Catlin executed more than 135 pictures—66 portraits, 36 scenes of Indian life, 25 landscapes, and 8 hunting scenes.

[24]Thomas L. McKenney and James Hall, *History of the Indian Tribes of North America* (3 vols., Philadelphia, 1837). Hall later became an important figure in American ethnology.

[25]General Lewis Cass, for many years territorial governor of Michigan, had while serving as governor prepared and published a survey entitled *Inquiries Respecting the History, Traditions, Languages, Manners, Customs, Religion, Etc. of the Indians Living within the United States* (Detroit, 1823).

[26]McCracken, *Catlin*, p. 134.

an extended wait for the expedition to get under way. The delay provided him the opportunity to paint numerous erstwhile Southern Indians, Cherokees, Creeks, and Choctaws, recently removed from their ancestral homes to the relatively barren Fort Gibson region. He attended their festivities, and among other activities depicted in great detail a mammoth Choctaw ball game, which had the appearance of a wild mêlée but was, in fact, the strictly ordered and formalized favorite game of that nation. He also found numerous subjects among the Osages, natives of the region.[27]

On June 19, 1834, General Henry Leavenworth, senior officer of the expedition, reviewed the dragoons as they set out for the Mexican Indian territory. It was a deceptively grand event, each company distinctively mounted on horses of matching color, blacks, whites, grays, and bays. For more than a third this was their "last roundup," for even as they set out a fever, probably cholera, was daily cutting the muster rolls. Catlin, who with a companion, Joe Chadwick, made a separate company of two, was even more splendidly mounted on a spirited Comanche-trained wild mustang, cream-colored with black mane and tail, which he regarded as the finest mount in that part of the country. The line of march was southwest, toward the Texas Panhandle, across the Canadian River, to the Wichita Mountains and the plains of the Washita and Red River country. No sooner were they under way than the epidemic started decimating the column. On the Washita in western Oklahoma General Leavenworth, fatally ill himself, ordered Colonel Dodge to select a troop of those still in good health to continue the mission to west Texas. Catlin moved out with Dodge's remnant troop of 400, "to penetrate the wild and untried regions of the hostile Comanches." With them also went the infection. A few days later the adjutant recorded: "July 18—Six litters [of sick] including Mr. Catlin."[28]

Despite his illness, the indomitable artist persisted in his private mission. He crawled from his litter whenever opportunities pre-

[27]Irving had sketched a pen picture of these Osages: "stately fellows; stern and simple in garb and aspect. They wore no ornaments; their dress consisted merely of blankets, leggings, and moccasins. Their heads were bare; their hair was cropped close, excepting a bristling ridge on the top, like the crest of a helmet, with a long scalp lock hanging behind. They had fine Roman countenances, and broad deep chests; and, as they generally wore their blankets wrapped round their loins, so as to leave the bust and arms bare, they looked like so many noble bronze figures"— Irving, A Tour, pp. 21–22.

[28]McCracken, Catlin, pp. 143–144.

sented themselves: to do sketches of the dramatic first meeting with a Comanche war party, "one of the most thrilling and beautiful scenes I ever witnessed"; of a Comanche taming a wild horse; of the Comanche tepee town, replete with meat-drying racks, squaws busily dressing hides; and of their 300-pound chief, "The Mountain of Rocks." But the highlight was the superb Comanche horsemanship, exceeding any he had ever seen. He painted a group demonstrating their ability to throw themselves "far down on the sides of their horses while riding at full speed . . . shoot an arrow from under the horse's belly," each rider exposing only one foot atop his mount, and then "throwing himself up again and changing to the other side." This feat was assisted by a horsehair band worn around the neck of the rider's horse and woven into its mane, into which the rider inserted his elbow whenever he dropped to either side of his mount.[29]

When the troop set off for the Pawnee Picts (Wichitas) at the base of the western mountains, Catlin, too ill to travel even by litter, was left behind. He dispatched Chadwick with sketch pad and notebook to record the data for a drawing of the mountain-girt Pawnee Pict town of round, grass-covered huts beside the Red River, surrounded by fields of corn, melons, and beans. These were the "people of Quivira" who three centuries before had drawn a bitterly disappointed Coronado deep into their inhospitable country. When Colonel Dodge returned after their councils were concluded, two of their head men accompanied his column back to the Comanche town. Catlin mustered strength enough to execute striking paintings of them both.[30] Sinking again under the strain of travel on their homeward way, he was critically ill when he was unloaded from an army cart at Fort Gibson. Already more than a third of the entire expeditionary contingent, including its general, had been buried, and as many more were still ill.[31] But, as Catlin began to rally, the "mournful sound of 'Roslin Castle' with muffled drums passing six or eight times a-day . . . to the burying ground" drove him to quit the place regardless of consequences. Although barely able to mount his spirited horse, Catlin set out cross-country for St. Louis, 500 miles away, guiding himself by his pocket compass

[29]*Letters and Notes,* vol. 2, p. 65.
[30]McCracken, *Catlin,* p. 155; Clark Wissler, *Indians of the United States* (New York, 1966), p. 154.
[31]McCracken, *Catlin,* pp. 156–158.

like a mariner at sea across the rolling prairie.[32]

After another winter in the South, early in 1835, "like a bird of passage," Catlin and his wife sailed north again "at the rallying notes of the swan and the wild goose. . . ." But their Mississippi riverboat lagged far behind the birds, for when he next heard their calls, at the Falls of St. Anthony, he found "their nests built—their eggs hatched—their offspring fledged" while the Catlins were making their tortuous way upstream to those beautiful upper reaches of the Mississippi, the land of the Dakota Sioux, Ojibway (Chippewa), Potawatomi, and Sauk-Fox. At the end of a profitable summer doing portraits, collecting information, paraphernalia, and vestments of these people, witnessing their ball games and traditional symbolic dances at Fort Snelling, Clara Catlin descended to St. Louis by steamer while George followed in more leisurely fashion by bark canoe.[33]

Late the following summer, 1836, after a winter at his parents' Pennsylvania home and a spring given to preparing for a full-blown exhibition that would soon become famous as Catlin's Indian Gallery, the artist was again on the Upper Mississippi. He had traveled the Great Lakes route to Prairie du Chien, which gave him the opportunity "of seeing many distinguished Indians among the Chippeways, Menomonies and Winnebagoes . . . not before seen or painted" by him. But the real objective of that late season expedition was a visit to the famed Red Pipestone Quarry, from the sacred ground of which came the material used to make the ceremonial pipes of all the Indians he had met. For years, he had heard talk of the quarry and observed the reverential and secretive attitude of his Indian friends toward the mystery-shrouded place from which had emanated many of the traditional Indian myths.

With an "English gentleman" whom he had met on his way to Prairie du Chien, Catlin ascended the Mississippi to the Falls of St. Anthony, then up the sluggish "St. Peters" (now the Minnesota) almost to its source, thence by horseback across "gracefully rising terraces . . . of green and carpeted plains," to the "ridge between the St. Peters and Missouri Rivers," and on to the "Red Pipe Stone Quarry," near which they bivouacked in late August. To get to this geologically and ethnologically unique place, George Catlin had perhaps taken greater risks and shown more determination than

[32]*Letters and Notes*, vol. 2, pp. 80–82.
[33]*Ibid.*, pp. 129–150.

ever before in his years of wilderness wanderings. Along the way the
two men had received repeated warnings that no white man would
be permitted to go near the place; that they would surely forfeit
their lives if they persisted in the effort. At one point they were
overtaken "by a rascally band of Sioux, and held in *durance vile,* for
having dared to approach the sacred fountain of the Pipe!" They
were told by the chief of their captors that as "this red stone was part
of their flesh, it would be sacriligious for white man to touch or take
it away—a hole would be made in their flesh, and the blood could
never be made to stop running." The Indians went on: "We come
now to ask for what purpose you are going, and what business you
have to go there. 'How! How!' vociferated all of them, thereby
approving what was said, giving assent by the word *how,* which is
their word for yes." Released after this warning, the tourists nevertheless continued on their way without being molested, perhaps
because of an inexorable tradition that no one bearing arms could
approach that "classic ground."

The quarry was a surprising place of enigmatic formations: a cliff
30 feet high and 2 miles long, composed of layers of polished quartz
of various hues, rising from a flat and treeless plain carpeted with
short grass. From the brink of the precipice a creek spilled in a
waterfall to the plain below, to flow out past five gigantic granite
boulders resting one against another in a line. Everywhere were
primitive memorials, mounds, carvings, paintings, and cairns. Near
the course of the brook were deep straight-line trenches, the excavations of generations of red pilgrims retrieving the sacred pipestone
for which they had come. "Here (according to their traditions)
happened the mysterious birth of the red pipe, which has blown its
fumes of peace and war to the remotest corners of the continent.
. . . And here also, the peace-breathing calumet was born, and
fringed with eagle's quills, which has shed its thrilling fumes over
the land, and soothed the fury of the relentless savage." Dozens of
such myths had their origins in this place, and Catlin recorded many
of them.

But to the two trespassers in that savage holy place there were
other features almost as intriguing as its religious associations. The
pipestone itself was one. This rare stone, a grayish-red to a dark
blood red in tone, was soft and easily worked when freshly removed
from the earth, later hardening on exposure. Catlin carried back
specimens both for his Gallery and for geologists to study. They

would pronounce it a new compound, which they named catlinite. Other features of the place provide bountiful food for speculation: the giant granite boulders with no other granite nearby, primeval rocks resting on later forms, the polished surfaces of the cliffs, the geometrical markings across the plain. Catlin did speculate, wondering that any current could exert the force required to polish quartz and move boulders. What a joy it would have been to the inquiring artist-scientist had he hit upon the force of moving ice as the answer to the questions he was posing in his notebook.[34]

With that summer's daring penetration of the Red Pipestone Quarry Catlin concluded his series of wilderness forays to build up his Gallery of illustrations, weapons, garbs, and other paraphernalia of the remaining unspoiled Americans—at least for the moment, until he could manage to relieve his financial difficulties. So far he had visited forty-eight Indian tribes, made twenty transits of the frontier, and devoted the better part of five years to painting his hundreds of pictures and accumulating innumerable Indian objects. He constantly cherished the hope that the government might recognize the importance of his work and purchase his collections to form the heart of a national Indian museum. But to that end a favorable public sentiment must first be created. It was both for financial relief and to build that sentiment that Catlin launched his long series of public exhibitions of the American Indian Gallery. After try-outs in Albany and Troy, the New York showing of Catlin's Gallery was announced in late September 1837, featuring "several hundred portraits," "splendid costumes," "paintings of their villages," "dances," "buffalo hunts," and "religious ceremonies," with the artist-collector presenting explanatory lectures, all for an admission charge of 50 cents. The exhibition was a tremendous hit, if not a total success in Catlin's eyes, for too many visitors questioned his veracity, especially in respect to the Mandan ceremonies, and too many were obviously averse to revising their predelictions to accord with his view that the "North American Indian in his native state is honest, hospitable, faithful, warlike, brave, cruel, relentless—and an honorable and religious human being."[35]

[34]*Ibid.*, pp. 160–174; McCracken, *Catlin,* pp. 173–178. At the time of Catlin's visit to the Red Pipestone Quarry, the concept of glacial transport of boulders was beginning to be discussed in geological circles. Not until more than twenty years later did the North American continental ice cap become accepted as a geological fact.

[35]McCracken, *Catlin,* pp. 184–185.

In early November the show was augmented by live Indians, most notably *Kee-o-kuk* (Keokuk), successor to Black Hawk as chief of the Sauks and Foxes, whom Catlin had represented in all his finery mounted on a splendid steed. The showing continued to prosper until near the end of the year, when Catlin, upon learning of the capture of the Seminole chief Osceola, suddenly closed the exhibition and set out for Charleston where the chief was imprisoned in Fort Moultrie. As leader of a band of Seminoles outnumbered ten to one, Osceola had for two years evaded the army's efforts to transport them from their Florida swamps to the West. His successful resistance had made the army appear ridiculous and himself a folk hero. When it was charged that he had been taken by treachery, while under a flag of truce, Catlin set out to investigate the charge and paint a portrait of the chief. His *Os-ce-o-la* canvas, completed shortly before the chieftain died, is perhaps the finest of all Catlin's Indian portraits. Doubtless it contributed greatly to setting the name of Osceola alongside those of Pontiac, Tecumseh, Black Hawk, Cochise, and Sitting Bull in the pantheon of red heroes.

The success the Gallery had enjoyed in New York was encouraging; but the focus of Catlin's efforts had continued to be on Washington and the Congress. In the spring of 1838 Catlin moved his American Indian Gallery to Washington in the hope of encouraging its acquisition by the government. But Catlin's criticisms of the government's Indian policies and the treatment of the Indians tolerated by the powerful fur companies alienated too many influential men. In consequence, despite the efforts of such admirers as Henry Clay, Daniel Webster, and William Seward, nothing came of the proposal. Disappointed, Catlin moved the Gallery to Baltimore, then to Boston.[36]

Late in 1839, his hopes for recognition disappointed, Catlin decided to take his Gallery to London. There both he and his exhibit quickly became the rage of the day, appealing not only to royalty, nobility, and ordinary folk, but to scientists as well. When his show was enlivened by a visiting band of Chippewa, he and they were invited to Buckingham Palace to entertain the young Queen Victoria and her guests. Two years later his success was crowned by the appearance of his delightful and informative (but disorganized and temporally scrambled) two-volume work, *Letters and Notes on the Man-*

[36] *Ibid.*, pp. 88–89.

ners, Customs, and Conditions of the North American Indians. The book was an immediate success both in England and back in America, going into seven editions within a year; to this day it survives as a classic of its genre. To fill Catlin's cup to brimming, his wife and two small daughters arrived from America to be with him. Encouraged by the favorable reception of *Letters and Notes,* Catlin immediately began plans to publish an extravagant Indian portfolio of colored reproductions selected from his collection. This elegant work, Catlin's *North American Indian Portfolio,* which was published in London in 1844, although much too costly for wide circulation, won high favor among critics.[37]

After three years in London and a tour of the principal British cities, Catlin with his family (now including a son) and the Gallery moved on to Paris. With the help of a band of Iowas, he captivated the sophisticated capital. There were crowds at his shows, invitations to the royal court, and an exhibition at the Louvre. Then, suddenly, the artist's world began to crack and crumble about him. First his wife and then his little son died. As the novelty of the Gallery passed, attendance fell and expenses, swollen by illness and death among the Iowas, mounted, setting off a series of financial difficulties that began to engulf him. There were desperate but fruitless efforts to sell the collections. The French king accepted, but failed to pay him for, several large paintings he had commissioned for the palace. Another effort to sell the Gallery to the American government and another move by Congress to acquire it collapsed with the outbreak of war with Mexico. Word came that a national museum, the Smithsonian, had been established independently of him and with no allusion either to him or his collections.

By 1853 Catlin's world was in ruins, leaving the fifty-seven-year-old artist in broken health and straitened finances, reduced to potboiling as a hack artist for subsistence. After yet another move in Congress to purchase his collections had failed, thanks in part to Henry Rowe Schoolcraft's opposition, Catlin's creditors closed in upon him in Paris, stripping even his modest rooms of everything of value. The crowning blow was the arrival of his wife's parents in Paris, and the departure with them of the little daughters he was no longer able to support.[38]

For a quarter century the paths of Catlin and Schoolcraft had

[37] *Ibid.,* pp. 192–193.
[38] *Ibid.,* pp. 194–198.

crossed many times in many places, and the two were acutely aware of each other, although they never met personally until late in the summer of 1846. Catlin, struggling with mounting difficulties, was on a desperate trip to England in search of financial aid from a wealthy admirer and friend from his palmier English years, when Schoolcraft arrived there with a letter of introduction from Catlin's old acquaintance, General Lewis Cass, who as Secretary of War had permitted Catlin to join the Leavenworth expedition to the Comanche country. Schoolcraft had crossed the Atlantic with the letter for the sole purpose of enlisting Catlin as illustrator of a multi-volume work on the American Indians, for which he was seeking a government subsidy. He hoped that the addition of Catlin's name to the prospectus would assure favorable congressional action. Whether Catlin felt he was being used for political purposes or whether the gulf between the rivals was already too wide, Catlin gave short shrift to the idea. Disappointed and angry, Schoolcraft sailed back to America. A few months later Congress did authorize and commit the requisite funds for the work, enabling its compilers, led by Schoolcraft, eventually to produce the six-volume, lavishly illustrated *History and Statistical Information Respecting the History, Condition and Prospects of the Indian Tribes of the United States.*[39] It was an encyclopedic work, which Alexander von Humboldt, the scientific arbiter of the day, would characterize as "an immense scrap-book."[40] Extant sets, little used today, sit on library shelves as massive monuments to the industrious and prolific Schoolcraft.[41]

Henry Rowe Schoolcraft's long and productive career as a student of the American Indian had fortuitous origins. Three years Catlin's senior, he was born in Albany on March 28, 1793. His father, a glassmaker, induced him to follow his trade, which led the young man to the related fields of mineralogy and geology, interests he furthered by studies at nearby Union College. When the glass works where he was employed failed, Schoolcraft struck out for the West. In 1818 he made an extensive expedition through Missouri and Arkansas, prospecting and inspecting the lead mines of the region. On his return he prepared and published a report of his journey, which came to the attention of the then Western-oriented

[39]Published in Philadelphia, 1851–57.
[40]*O-kee-pa,* introduction, p. 18.
[41]McCracken, *Catlin,* pp. 201–204.

Secretary of War, John C. Calhoun. Calhoun was sufficiently impressed to recommend that, "as a man of industry, ambition and insatiable curiosity," Schoolcraft should be invited by Michigan Territorial Governor Lewis Cass to accompany an expedition, planned for the spring of 1820, to explore in detail the western regions of Lake Superior and the country between Fond du Lac and the Mississippi.

That expedition in company with Cass and a small group of able young men, most of whom were destined for national prominence, was of great moment for Schoolcraft's future. Officially, he was attached to the party as mineralogist and geologist; but the Indians they met along the way so aroused his interest that the journey marked the birth of his career as an ethnologist. At Sault Ste. Marie he watched with fascination numerous Chippewas taking with dipnets great quantities of whitefish from the magnificent rapids boiling down from Superior to Huron. At this time his personal tie with those people was established, for there he met his future wife, Jane Johnson, whose mother was the daughter of a Chippewa chief and whose educated father, John Johnson, had for years been a respected resident Indian trader at that center of Chippewa activity. Upon the return of the expedition at the end of the summer, the industrious Schoolcraft prepared an account of it that was published the following year.[42]

On their expedition Governor Cass had been so impressed by the industry and wide-ranging intelligence of young Schoolcraft that he soon arranged to have him appointed Indian agent at Sault Ste. Marie in charge of the Indians of the Lake Superior region. Doubtless, considering the locale, the people he would be thrown with, and the studious proclivities of the young man, this move cast him in the mold that would shape his future fame.

The next year he and Jane Johnson were married and her services as interpreter of Chippewa ways and legendary tales began. Many of the tales came from Jane's Chippewa mother, who, although unable to speak English, could relate them to Jane for her to interpret to her scholarly husband, until he himself mastered their language. Schoolcraft's nature mandated that he record everything of interest to him. The legends accumulated during the ensuing fifteen

[42] *Narrative Journal of Travels through the Northwestern Regions of the United States Extending from Detroit through the Great Chain of American Lakes to the Source of the Mississippi River in the Year 1820* (Albany, N.Y., 1821).

years became the material for his two-volume *Algic Researches,* published in 1839. It was largely upon those Algonquin tales that Henry Wadsworth Longfellow based *The Song of Hiawatha.*[43] Some of the light from *Hiawatha's* brilliant success reflected on Schoolcraft. The year after the poem appeared, in an attempt to capitalize on its great popularity, a new edition of *Algic Researches* came out under the title *The Myth of Hiawatha and Other Oral Legends,* despite the fact that "Hiawatha" was actually an Iroquois demigod, not the counterpart of the Algonquin "Manabozo"—the hero of the legend Schoolcraft had recorded and Longfellow adapted.[44] The legendary Manabozo and Hiawatha were sometime noble savages, sometime barbarous hounds of hell, much as the Indian in real life had been regarded by Europeans since first they came upon the Indian's shores.

Meanwhile Schoolcraft established another claim to fame by "discovering" the source of the Mississippi. Although in reporting the Cass expedition of 1820, Schoolcraft had claimed ascent to the river's source both in the title to his book and in his claim that he was the only man living (Pike was now dead) who had viewed both the source and the mouth of the river, that expedition had actually reached no further than Pike had done in the winter of 1806. Both Pike and Cass turned back after reaching Red Cedar Lake (now Cass Lake); and both had hailed it as the source of the Mississippi. Obviously by the time he launched his 1832 expedition Schoolcraft had realized his error and was now aware that the true source lay far beyond Red Cedar Lake.

When Schoolcraft's canoes set out from Sault Ste. Marie across Lake Superior to Fond du Lac, the expedition's ostensible objectives were to curb the endemic wars between the Sioux and the Chippewa of the Upper Mississippi region, to gather statistical facts about the Indians there, to investigate their fur trade, and to vaccinate them against smallpox. There is little doubt, however, that in Schoolcraft's mind its foremost objective was to locate the actual source of the river. On all counts the expedition was successful, despite the lack of permanence in the pledges of intertribal peace secured. Moreover, it earned a place in the annals of American

---

[43]Boston, 1855. "Algic" was Schoolcraft's coined adjective for things Algonquin.
[44]Albert Keiser, *The Indian in American Literature* (New York, 1933), pp. 192–198; Roy Harvey Pearce, *Savagism and Civilization* (Baltimore, 1953), pp. 191–194; Mentor L. Williams's introduction to *Schoolcraft's Indian Legends* (East Lansing, Mich., 1956), pp. v–xiv.

exploratory history. It was all accomplished in a five-week dash that posed some of nature's sharpest challenges to impede human passage: canoe travel on a great lake subject to oceanic boisterousness, the ascent of swift rivers and shallow streams through mosquito- and deerfly-infested forests, long portages through dense woods, deceptive channels, and submerged alluvial banks hiding the way through the watery maze of the Minnesota north country, lakes all but choked with tall reeds and wild rice *(Zizania aquatica),* the natives' staff of life, and a final long portage to the little lake that for many years had been known to the *couriers de bois* as Lac la Biche and to their English-speaking successors as Elk Lake: the true source of the Mississippi, 2,400 miles above its subtropical mouth. If not a discovery in the strict sense of the word, it was nevertheless a dramatic revealing of a bit of geography of unique significance to Americans. When Schoolcraft wrote his account of the expedition, he gave Lac la Biche a new name: Lake Itasca, which he devised from the words *veritas caput,* the "true head" (using the last two syllables of the one and the first syllable of the other).[45]

Upon their return to Sault Ste. Marie in mid-August, newspapers carried generous accounts of the exploit that quickly caught the popular imagination. With his usual industry Schoolcraft soon completed his manuscript account. It was published under the title *Narrative of an Expedition Through the Upper Mississippi to Itasca Lake.*[46] Of less popular appeal, but equally important in revealing in detail the regions they had explored and its inhabitants, were the several appendices published with the narrative, mostly the work of Schoolcraft's companions on the expedition. There was much data on the natives, their trade in furs, and the mineral deposits encountered along their way. The commander of the expedition's military escort furnished river data and the most advanced map yet of the Upper Mississippi, from which Schoolcraft derived the maps that appeared in the *Narrative.*[47]

In the late summer of 1846, with the prestige of his half-dozen books (several of popular appeal), a record of service in the Michigan territorial legislature, years of service as Indian agent, and

[45]Philip P. Mason (ed.), *Schoolcraft's Expedition to Lake Itasca* (East Lansing, Mich., 1958), pp. xix–xx. For the botanical significance of the expedition, see S. D. McKelvey, *Botanical Exploration of the Trans-Mississippi West, 1790–1850* (Arnold Arboretum, Jamaica Plain, Mass., 1955), pp. 449–463.

[46]New York, 1834.

[47]Mason, *Schoolcraft's Expedition,* pp. xxi–xxvi.

political influence sufficient to have gotten from Congress a generous subsidy for his proposed definitive Indian cyclopedia, Schoolcraft sailed to England to solicit Catlin's services as illustrator. Catlin's rejection—which would cost him both materially and in reputation—disappointed and infuriated Schoolcraft. On his return
Schoolcraft secured Seth Eastman to fill the position Catlin had
rejected, but the rebuff still rankled. Five years later he used his
influence to defeat a move by Congress to acquire Catlin's Indian
Gallery. Retaliation continued as the six ponderous volumes of the
*Historical and Statistical Information Respecting the History, Condition and
Prospects of the Indian Tribes of the United States* came off the press.
Among other attacks on Catlin contained in the work was one by a
contributor that branded his account of the Mandan religious ceremonies a figment of the artist's imagination, an attack that
prompted old Baron Humboldt to write Catlin (then painting Indians in South America) telling him of the criticism contained in the
work prepared by Schoolcraft for the government. "I have," he
wrote, "often conversed with our illustrious traveler in America, the
Prince Maximilian, of Neuwied, who spent a winter with the Mandans . . . entirely corroborating your descriptions." In due course
the verdict of scholars fully vindicated Catlin's account.[48]

For Prince Maximilian's qualifications to speak on the subject of
Mandan customs, it is necessary to hark back to 1833 and St. Louis,
when the prince, Captain William Drummond Stewart, and the artist Karl Bodmer were the guests of General Clark on a visit to the
imprisoned Black Hawk.

Captain Stewart, later baronet of Grandtully, Scotland, was perhaps the most interesting of all the high-born Europeans who made
the West their playground, a breed of wealthy, reckless, and romantic adventurers.[49] After going on west from St. Louis, Stewart fell
so in love with that big sky country that he later came a second time,

[48]*O-kee-pa*, pp. 18–24, 25–33.
[49]A precedent soon followed by privileged and well-educated young Americans,
notable among them the historian Francis Parkman, who in 1846 at the age of
twenty-three, with a young kinsman, followed in Stewart's footsteps along the Oregon Trail as far as the Rockies before turning south to Bent's Fort on the Arkansas,
to return to St. Louis along the Santa Fé Trail. Parkman's account of his tour, *The
Oregon Trail*, appeared serially in *Knickerbocker Magazine*, beginning in 1847. Later in
book form (New York, 1849) it was warmly received, went into many editions, and
remains a popular youth classic.

bringing with him a highly gifted artist, Alfred Jacob Miller, to sketch the land and its people as a preliminary to painting huge canvases to be hung in Stewart's Murthy Castle. Miller was Stewart's official "photographer," so to speak. Many of the noble scenes and notable landmarks they came upon had never before been depicted: Scott's Bluff, Chimney Rock, Independence Rock, Devil's Gate, the Wind River Mountains, and the Grand Tetons. Although for many years Miller's work had limited viewers, its primacy and excellence earn him a place in this account. Stewart employed his own talents as well in preserving and advertising the Western wilderness in his novels *Altowan* and *Edward Warren*.[50]

In early April 1833, while Stewart followed the Oregon Trail west, Maximilian and Bodmer boarded the *Yellow Stone* as she sailed for her third navigation of the Missouri. So rapidly had big game been exterminated by the westward progress of the frontier that after a month of chugging upstream the impatient naturalist had yet to see a buffalo and Bodmer had found little to inspire his brush. Progress up the Big Muddy was still fraught with interruptions and delays, what with shifting sandbars, elusively twisting channels, sawyers and submerged snags, caving banks and headwinds; all played their part in providing the prince and his illustrator with abundant time ashore for their own enterprises, which, as they moved upstream, heightened in interest. It is tempting to dwell on the enchanted Bodmer's magnificent watercolors and sketches and Maximilian's fascinating word pictures and astute observations on the strange flora and fauna of the countryside, and of the Indians along the way, the Omaha and Sioux. Earlier visitors have substantially preempted the revealing of the Missouri; nevertheless, Maximilian's advances in scientific observations and Bodmer's extraordinary work demand recognition as substantial contributions to the continuing discovery of that region.

After changing to the American Fur Company's newer vessel, the *Assiniboin,* at Fort Pierre, Maximilian and Bodmer continued upriver, past Fort Clark and the Mandan towns, to Fort Union in the Assiniboin country (the furthest reach of Catlin's brush and pen), where the obliging Company official sent them on in a keelboat to Fort McKenzie at the mouth of the Marias. This was the last Missouri post of the Company, deep in the heart of the domain of the

[50]Published in New York, 1846, and London, 1854, respectively.

dangerous Blackfeet. A fellow passenger on the keelboat recorded a brief description of Maximilian, now fifty: an unostentatious man of medium height, wearing "a white slouch hat, a black velvet coat rather rusty from long service, and the greasiest pair of trousers that ever encased princely legs."[51] Delays resulting from the frequent necessity of cordeling the keelboat in the passage of the Dakota Bad Lands permitted Bodmer to portray the weird wind and water sculptures of the earth's strata in their fantastic shapes and equally fantastic colors.

All along the way, wherever natives were encountered, Maximilian avidly studied their ways, and, with the aid of interpreters,[52] listed their vocabularies until he had compiled those of twenty-three tribes. He was intrigued by their sign language, the Esperanto of the Western Indians, on which he was preparing a dissertation. He noted striking similarities and baffling differences between these red men of the Northern Hemisphere and their relatives he had studied in earlier years in the Amazon Basin of Brazil.[53] He made notes on everything of interest, while Bodmer, hawk-eyed and perceptive, sketched illustrations for his studies. But there were days of less quiet and peaceful occupations. One of those was in August at Fort McKenzie when at dawn the old soldier was roused from his slumber by a shout: "Levez-vous, il faut nous battre!" Fortunately, this time the whites were merely audience to a fierce attack by Assiniboins and Crees on the Blackfeet camped about the fort, so Maximilian and Bodmer, in response to the call to arms, could repair to the scene armed only with notebook, sketch pad, and pencils to record the wild and colorful demonstration of savage warriors in their element. Bodmer's depiction of the battle scene, said to be the only painting by an eyewitness of an Indian battle, glows with fierce vitality. Against a background of rugged cliffs and jagged peaks one glimpses the fort with Old Glory flying high; the struggling savages in the foreground, every figure individualized in a combat of deadly ferocity, are brilliantly confirmed in bodily action and facial grimace.[54]

[51]DeVoto, *Across the Wide Missouri*, p. 137.

[52]Among those interpreters was old Touissant Charbonneau, who had served Lewis and Clark.

[53]Maximilian, Prince of Wied-Neuwied, *Travels in the Interior of North America, 1832–1834* (trans., London, 1843); also in Reuben Gold Thwaites (ed.) *Early Western Travels, 1748–1843* (vol. 22, Cleveland, 1906), pp. 16, 19.

[54]DeVoto, *Across the Wide Missouri*, pp. 142–146.

But it was on his way back down the Missouri, among the Mandans at Fort Clark where Maximilian and Bodmer spent the winter of 1833–34, that Bodmer did his most notable American work and the prince made observations that qualified him authoritatively to support Catlin's accounts of the torture rites of those Indians, whose unique culture would soon die of the white man's germs and become merely a record in the white man's books. No shadow of their impending doom haunts the faces in Bodmer's exquisite paintings.[55] Particularly memorable is his portrayal of the interior of a Mandan hut—a richly detailed and accurate ethnological statement on the life of this people. There sits the warrior at home, with his family harmoniously at work, in the single room of the domed lodge that sheltered also his household dogs, his cherished horses, and every essential of savage life: buffalo robes, baskets, spears, canoe paddles, headdresses, and trophy scalps.

In contrast to the tranquil atmosphere of this painting, an eloquent illustration of the Noble Savage at rest, is the frenetic intoxicating rhythm of a Mandan buffalo dance, a painting of barbarous intensity.[56] So vivid is the scene one can almost hear the clamor, the rattles, and the shouts of the dancers, some adorned with buffalo skins or horns, the shrill cries of the watching women and children, the keening pipes, the dull beat of the drums, and the stamping feet, all combined in a cacophony of dissonant sounds.

In all, Bodmer painted over 400 pictures of the West, including his landscapes, which, though not in every case the first depiction of a site, were the first to do justice to the fantastic beauty, variety, and magnificence of those fabulous regions. His paintings and drawings were intended as illustrations for Maximilian's meticulous scientific reports and, as such, they reflect the same precise and careful observations of every detail of his subjects. But Bodmer, who later achieved a distinguished career as a member of the French Barbizon School of painters, was first and last a highly skilled artist, sensitively perceptive. His paintings of the West reflect his personal responses to fearful desolation and emptiness, as well as to the beauty and grandeur of those strange landscapes.

In the summer of 1834 the prince and his party, with well-filled notebooks, portfolios of sketches, and abundant specimens, returned triumphantly to Europe to begin the preparation of his mag-

[55]Thwaites (ed.), *Travels*, vol. 25, Atlas, plate xiv.
[56]*Ibid.*, Atlas, plate xxvi.

nificent work, *Travels in the Interior of North America in the Years 1832–34*[57] in two quarto volumes. It was accompanied by an elephant folio, or "Atlas," of Bodmer's paintings, splendidly reproduced in full color. The accomplished naturalist's readable and informative narrative, in journal form, was much enhanced by Bodmer's illustrations.

Albert Gallatin had laid the foundation for the work of Catlin, Schoolcraft, and Maximilian, who together substantially amplified American ethnology, leaving it to others, most notably, John Wesley Powell, better known for his explorations of the Colorado River[58] to cap the structure.

[57]Published in German, Coblentz, 1839–41. This impressive production was translated into French and English and reissued many times, often in pirated editions; even today it remains a landmark in American natural history. The botanical aspects of the work are discussed in McKelvey, *Botanical Exploration*, pp. 522–558.

[58]See below, Chapter 15.

CHAPTER 12

John Charles Frémont and the American West

I N 1898 the United States Post Office, encouraged by the success
of its philatelic innovation of 1893, when it had issued the first
commemorative postage stamp issue to promote the Columbian
Exposition, issued a second set of commemoratives, this time to
promote the Trans-Mississippi Exposition being staged in Omaha.
Among the stamps of that issue, the one that depicted famed explorer John Charles Frémont in the act of planting a flag atop a
craggy Rocky Mountain peak made an indelible impression on a
generation of young stamp collectors, even as Frémont himself had
evoked the fervor of the romantic and venturesome young nation
during the 1840s and 1850s. No American explorer, before or since,
more successfully transported the imaginations of so many across
the wide reaches of little known lands. Although early in his career
Frémont had come to be known as "Pathfinder of the American
West," in truth he did little pathfinding. Generally others, less articulate, less magnetic, and less romantic, had preceded him along
almost every path he trod. However, Frémont's personal magnetism
and keen sense of drama enabled him to use those paths to lead him
to the pinnacles of fame: fortune, a senator's seat, nomination for
the presidency, a major general's command in the Union army, and
eventually countless honors in social and scientific circles both at
home and abroad. Yet his was a career marked by sharp alternations
of success and failure, honor and disgrace, wealth and poverty, even
as in bold letters he was writing his name across the geography of
a third of the continent.

With Frémont, peak and valley alike were always shrouded in a romantic aura, which reached back even beyond the explorer's birth. While supporting himself as dancing master and French tutor in the fashionable homes and private schools of Tidewater Virginia, his father had eloped with the beautiful, spirited, and highborn young wife of a wealthy Richmond businessman. Of that informal union between the roving Gallic adventurer and the rebellious, independent-minded young descendant of early Virginia settlers, Frémont was born on January 21, 1813, at Savannah, Georgia. After his father's death, about the time he reached school age, his mother moved to Charleston, South Carolina, where the boy attended school and then the tiny College of Charleston where he soon proved himself particularly talented in mathematics. Associates described him as brilliant, passionate, restless, reckless, headstrong—and highly ambitious. They also noted his cavalier disdain for rules, a trait that was to spell grave trouble on several occasions in his later years.

His brilliance and charm brought him to the attention of several of Charleston's most influential residents.[1] By far the most significant of those prominent friends, because of the profound influence he would have in launching the future explorer's career, was the many-faceted Joel R. Poinsett, who had recently returned from his post as American minister to Mexico, bringing with him the flamboyant native flower, *Poinsettia.* Although the widely traveled Poinsett had been formally educated in both law and medicine and was by heritage a planter, it was in other areas—politics, engineering, and the military—that he attained his greatest successes. During the tariff controversy in South Carolina in the early thirties he was a brilliant and outspoken Unionist in a hotbed of Nullification, displaying a political philosophy that was not lost on his young protégé. The esteem was mutual, Frémont's wide-ranging intelligence strongly appealing to the even wider ranging mind of Poinsett.

Through the good offices of Poinsett, at the age of twenty Frémont was made a mathematics instructor on a sloop of war that had put into Charleston on a cruise to South America. Upon his return Poinsett secured him another highly significant appointment as surveyor with the United States Topographical Corps, then engaged in laying out a route through the Carolina and Tennessee mountains

[1]This sketch of the early years of Frémont is based on Allan Nevins, *Frémont: Pathmarker of the West* (New York, 1955), pp. 1–88.

for the projected Charleston, Louisville, and Cincinnati Railroad. In later years Frémont wrote enthusiastically of that stint, calling it a picnic they were all sorry to see come to an end. It led to a further assignment in the same region: a survey of the lands from which the Jackson administration was forcibly removing the Cherokee Indians westward along their "Trail of Tears" to the relatively barren wastes of Indian Territory. That detail was definitely no picnic, performed under pressure in the depth of winter in the home territory of bitterly resentful Cherokees.

When Martin Van Buren became President in 1837, Poinsett became his Secretary of War, whose office then administered the official mapping surveys and explorations. Early the next year he brought Frémont to Washington, had him commissioned second lieutenant in the Topographical Corps, and assigned him to accompany the distinguished French scientist Joseph Nicholas Nicollet, who was about to leave on a scientific survey of the plateau regions between the Missouri and the Upper Mississippi. The assignment provided Frémont with a priceless opportunity to work under the tutelege of Nicollet, with whom he quickly developed warm rapport. For five years after his arrival in America, Nicollet had independently explored wide areas of the country, including the southern Appalachians, the Arkansas River region, and the environs of the Mississippi from its mouth up to, and even beyond, Schoolcraft's Lake Itasca, up an affluent stream now recognized as the actual source of the "Father of Waters." When Nicollet returned from his Itasca expedition, Poinsett enlisted him to head the 1838 survey to which Frémont was to be attached as chief assistant.

The 1838 Nicollet expedition carried them up the Mississippi to Fort Snelling, then up the Minnesota to Traverse des Sioux, and westward to the Couteau des Prairies, the plateau separating the Mississippi tributaries from those of the Missouri, where they visited the Red Pipestone Quarry. There they experienced a prairie thunderstorm so fearful and violent that it almost gave credence to the Indians' belief the place was divinely guarded against all but the redskin fraternity.

The following summer found Nicollet and Frémont again together in the same region, but reached this time from Fort Pierre, more than 1,200 miles up the Missouri, from which they had set out cross-country to the northeast, recording all along the way their observations (including latitude, longitude, and altitude at every river crossing, lake, and mountain) as they moved over to the Red River of the North whose waters find their way to distant Hudson's Bay. When all these observations were tied together with those made the year before, Nicollet had a firm foundation for a reasonably accurate map of that vast, little explored region. On those expeditions Nicollet imparted to his apprentice priceless training in all the branches of science necessary for a successful topographical survey; for in addition to geographical data, the Corps called for the investigation and recording of data on climate, soils, geology, botany, and zoology.[2]

After the Nicollet expedition of 1839, Frémont and his mentor were kept busy with the preparation of the map of the great Mississippi-Missouri quadrant, working together, except when Frémont stole away to pay court to the beautiful and talented Jessie Benton, daughter of the powerful Senator Thomas Hart Benton of Missouri, who was the most vocal and influential advocate in the Senate of an aggressive national expansion policy. Jessie and her father were destined to complete the circle of those whose lives had momentous impact on the vital and ambitious young officer. From the outset the father and his sixteen-year-old daughter were in the throes of an emotional conflict over the young man, whom both had found uncommonly magnetic and congenial. The senator was adamantly opposed to one so young marrying. Jessie was equally determined to become Mrs. Frémont. In a delaying maneuver, Benton appealed to Poinsett, who lent a sympathetic ear to the distraught father. Early in June 1841, Frémont was surprised by orders to repair forthwith to St. Louis to conduct a survey of the lower 200 miles of the Des Moines River. Although there is little doubt that the order was partly designed to checkmate the young couple's marriage, there is no doubt that completion of the survey of the Des Moines was important to Nicollet's map, and therefore legitimate.

The domestic impasse that had precipitated Frémont's despatch to the Des Moines was revived as soon as he arrived back in Washington: the ardent and impatient young couple on the one hand and the autocratic senator on the other. In mid-October the lovers eloped and were secretly married. Their secret was short-lived; even shorter-lived was Senator Benton's fury when the young couple confessed their insubordination. Confronted by the *fait accompli*, he

[2]William H. Goetzmann, *Army Exploration of the American West, 1803–1863* (New Haven, 1959), pp. 69–74.

soon embraced his new son-in-law as warmly (and possessively) as if he had been his own son. Henceforth Benton would occupy the place in Frémont's career that had been successively Poinsett's and Nicollet's. Indeed, Benton seemed to regard this son-in-law as his personal instrument to forward his obsessive devotion to that policy of national expansion we have come to term "manifest destiny." For many years, ever since a visit to Monticello on Christmas Day 1824, Benton had been in thrall to this idea. There the young senator from Missouri and the old sage of Monticello had talked for hours of the West. What the sponsor of the Lewis and Clark and Pike expeditions envisioned for the future of that region was quite apparent. And from that day Benton regarded himself as appointed by Jefferson to encourage the realization of the nation's manifest destiny.[3] Now, in 1841, the forceful senator saw in his new son-in-law a promising instrument to that end.

Benton's power to manipulate was quickly demonstrated. An expedition had been planned, to set out the next spring for the Rocky Mountains to map the Oregon Trail and regions in its proximity; the requisite appropriations had been assured, Frémont's leadership of it arranged, and actual preparations gotten well under way, before Colonel James Abert, now chief of the Topographical Corps, drafted his orders and notification to Frémont directing him to repair to Fort Leavenworth, to make a survey of the Platte up to the head of the Sweetwater and, if time permitted, a similar survey of the Kansas River.[4] It was Benton's belief that more positive steps by the government to encourage the westward trek of settlers were long past due. Logically, the first step in that direction was the preparation of an adequate map of the Oregon Trail, supported by a scientific inspection of the regions through which the Trail presently passed, and possible alternatives to its more difficult stretches. Unofficially, Frémont was about to become Benton's eyes in the vast Western domains now lying fallow in the palsied hands of Spain or the overextended arms of Britain. Eventually, he would become an instrument of Benton's policies, even when those policies were not agreeable to official policies or required straying from orders.[5]

In the late spring of 1842, Frémont was on the boat making its

[3]William H. Goetzmann, *Exploration and Empire* (New York, 1966), p. 240.
[4]Donald Jackson and Mary Lee Spence (eds.), *The Expeditions of John Charles Frémont,* vol. I, *Travels from 1838 to 1844, with Map Portfolio* (Chicago, 1970), p. 121.
[5]Goetzmann, *Army Exploration,* p. 68.

way up the Missouri to the mouth of the Kansas where his expedition was to set out cross-country when he met a man named Christopher Carson, whom he described as being "of medium height, broad shouldered and deep chested, with a clear, steady, blue eye and frank speech and address; quiet and unassuming."[6] This man, better known as Kit Carson, was destined to play a major role in the young explorer's career. Few if any men of his day had more intimate knowledge of wide areas of the West, from the Rocky Mountains to the Pacific, and it was Carson's association with Frémont and the latter's accounts of Kit's exploits in official reports and memoirs that rendered Kit Carson the Daniel Boone of Western American folklore. With Kit enlisted as official guide, Frémont, on June 10, led his column of twenty mounted men, including Senator Benton's twelve-year-old son Randolph, and eight muleteers driving the equipment carts, pack mules, and spare animals, up the banks of the Kansas. With the company traveled Charles Preuss, a German, who would prove himself a versatile, wide-ranging, and learned scientist, a capable cartographer, a conscientious collector of botanical and geological specimens, and a competent artist of value to the three expeditions on which he accompanied Frémont.[7]

Between the north and south forks of the Platte they encountered incredible herds of buffalo. Frémont estimated 11,000 in view in a single herd. A series of other spectacular sights evoked wonder in the men and scientific curiosity in Frémont and Preuss: Chimney Rock, between the North and South Plattes, a famous landmark of the Sweetwater; the Red Buttes, composed of red sandstone and pudding stone and, a little further up the Sweetwater, Independence Rock, which brought them to a halt to read the names cut into the stone, many well known to them. On his return Frémont added a conspicuous cross to the display. At Devil's Gate, where the Sweetwater makes its spectacular way through lofty granite escarpments, they camped for a night, despite the fact that the place was so devoid of timber that to cook their buffalo meat they had to fuel their fires with buffalo chips or, as Frémont more politely called them, *bois de vache.*

[6]Nevins, *Frémont,* p. 94.

[7]For Charles Preuss's account of those expeditions, see Edwin G. and Elizabeth K. Gudde (eds.), *Exploring with Frémont: The Private Diaries of Charles Preuss, Cartographer for John C. Frémont on His First, Second and Fourth Expeditions to the Far West* (Norman, Okla., 1958).

In August 1842 the ragged file made its way over the continental divide through the open and gentle South Pass, surprisingly unlike what one would expect of a pass over a lofty mountain chain. Its mildness so impressed Frémont that he compared it with the ascent of Capitol Hill from the street. Once over the pass, however, as they moved northward along the Wind River Mountains, scene after scene excited the romantic explorer:

Winding our way up a long ravine, we came unexpectedly in view of a most beautiful lake, set like a gem in the mountains. [As we descended to the lake] a view of utmost magnificence and grandeur burst upon our eyes. With nothing between us and their feet to lessen the effect of the whole height, a grand bed of snow-capped mountains rose before us, pile on pile, glowing in the bright light of an August day. Immediately below them lay the lake between two ridges covered with dark pines, which swept down from the main chain to the spot where we stood. Here where the lake glittered in the sunlight, its banks of yellow sand and light foliage of aspen groves contrasted well with the gloomy pines.

And three days later: "again a view of the most romantic beauty met our eyes. . . . We were overlooking a deep valley, which was entirely occupied by three lakes, and from the brink the surrounding ridges rose precipitously five hundred and a thousand feet, covered with dark green balsam pine, relieved on the border of the lake with the foliage of the aspen."[8] They sighted a peak nearby that Frémont was convinced was the loftiest in all the Rockies. He, Preuss, and four companions set out to scale it, carrying the clumsy mercury barometer to determine its height. After a perilous and difficult climb, Frémont reached the summit, a narrow, icy crest about 3 feet in width. Each in turn mounted to that aerie to view the Three Tetons and the sources of the Snake River and the Yellowstone far to the north, and to look down into the valley below at the gathering of the tributary waters of the Green starting on their turbulent way down to the Colorado. They set up the barometer and calculated that they were standing 13,570 feet "above the Gulf of Mexico." Before they started their descent, Frémont's flair for the dramatic carried him back to the narrow peak to unfurl and fix in a crevice a flag bearing thirteen stripes, but with a screaming eagle grasping in its talons a peace pipe and arrows in place of the serene field of stars. Thus, a mountain of the Wind River range became Frémont

[8]Jackson and Spence, *Expeditions*, pp. 255–256, 259–260.

Peak, joining Pike's and Long's, commemorating explorers of the Rockies.[9]

Soon after Frémont's return to Washington in late October, he began, with Jessie as amanuensis, the preparation of his official report, pacing the floor dictating with the aid of his journal and notes, while she employed her gift for words and syntax to improve her "transcription." It was early March 1843 before the finished report was delivered to Colonel Abert, complete with a 26-page botanical catalogue prepared by John Torrey and Asa Gray, and meteorological and geographical tabulations contained in an additional supplement of about the same length.[10]

Even as the Frémonts were preparing the final draft of the report, Senator Benton was busy arranging a far more extensive expedition to be led by his son-in-law. The senator himself even supplied the wording for the orders under which it was to set out, doubtless with Frémont's assistance. Colonel Abert, in his letter telling Frémont of the plans for this new expedition, supplied the details of its proposed route by enclosing a copy of Benton's proposal for an expedition up the Kansas River to its source, thence across to the Arkansas and up to its source, then to cross over the mountains and move northward to the end of Frémont's 1842 route at the Wind River range, then north again to the Flat Head country (in the present Montana), and so westward to the Columbia and Fort Vancouver. There it was to tie its survey with one made to that point by Lieutenant Charles Wilkes in the course of a wide-ranging Pacific exploration and survey expedition of 1838–42. That done, Frémont was to return east by the Oregon Trail. As it turned out, those specifications, under which Frémont's second expedition departed St. Louis in mid-May 1843, bore little resemblance to the expedition's 1843–44 heroic sweep of the West.

[9]*Ibid.*, pp. 267–271. Through some unaccountable error, the peak now known as Frémont Peak is a Wind River range neighbor of that on which Frémont set his flag. For Preuss's account, see *Exploring with Frémont*, pp. 39–47.

[10]Congress readily authorized the printing of 1,000 copies of the *Report*, which despite its heavy overburden of mundane scientific observations and data was to prove a very popular and influential document. Later, it was far more widely distributed in conjunction with the report of Frémont's next expedition, that of 1843–44 —a popularity no doubt largely attributable, in that romantic era, to the image of Frémont as an adventurer and daring leader—*A Report on an Exploration of the Country Lying between the Missouri River and the Rocky Mountains, on the Line of the Kansas and Great Platte Rivers*, Senate Exec. Doc. 243, 27th Congress, 3d Sess., U.S. serial no. 416 (1843).

It was to be the most extensive American land expedition yet. undertaken. Charles Preuss was again Frémont's right-hand man and the expedition's scientist. Among the others in the party of thirty-nine, more than half of whom bore French names, was Jacob Dodson, a Benton slave, and Tom "Broken Hand" Fitzpatrick, one of the most knowledgeable of mountain men, who it had been Frémont's good fortune to enlist as hunter and guide. On the eve of departure from Chouteau's Post the expedition barely missed being countermanded. Banking on his reputation and the Bentons' friendship for General Stephen Watts Kearny, Frémont had secured from the general an order on the St. Louis Arsenal for a howitzer, complete with carriage and harness. On learning of this unauthorized requisition of unorthodox equipment for a scientific survey, and realizing the dangerous implications inherent in setting out to cross foreign territory with such a weapon, Colonel Abert despatched a letter to Frémont peremptorily ordering his immediate return to Washington to account for his serious indiscretion.[11] In later years Jessie confessed that the letter reached her in St. Louis before the expedition set out from Chouteau's, but instead of sending it on to her husband, she despatched an urgent message to him directing him, without explanation, to set forth without further delay. The howitzer, after being hauled all the long way across the plains and Rockies, down the Columbia, and along the eastern flanks of the Sierras, was finally abandoned in the deep snow of an unidentified pass of the Sierras somewhere in the neighborhood of Lake Tahoe.

In crossing the Great Plains to the mountains, Frémont followed fairly closely his routing instructions. Six weeks of travel carried them past the towering, snow-covered bulk of Pike's Peak, of which Preuss made a sketch to be used in Frémont's formal report. On their way up the Arkansas he again enlisted Kit Carson and a younger, but already renowned, mountain man named Alexis Godey. Neither of them had ever heard of a feasible pass in that part of the Rockies. Faced with that frustrating intelligence, Frémont turned his column north toward the South Platte and South Pass,

[11]Neither this nor the Frémont expedition of the previous year was entirely a scientific survey in the strict sense. All his surveys were partly reconnaissance expeditions for knowledge of possible military utility or diplomatic advantage, factually tied to scientific benchmarks and observations—Goetzmann, *Army Exploration*, pp. 103–108.

detaching himself and a few chosen companions to travel close to the mountain flanks in a continuing, but futile, search for a more southerly route than South Pass. The two parties would not be reunited until mid-September, when Frémont's band reached the Snake River at Fort Hall after his detour to examine Great Salt Lake. Meanwhile both groups made their way up to South Pass and over to Green River, which Fremont was astonished to find had an elevation of 6,230 feet where they forded it. From there his group continued on to Bear River, well below the 42nd Parallel, the northern boundary of Mexico.[12]

Bear River, a major source of Great Salt Lake's water, was a feature of a region that for Frémont "possessed a strange and extraordinary interest," and this river one of the most "remarkable features of the country . . . around which the vague and superstitious accounts of the trappers had thrown a delightful obscurity." They followed down the beautiful valley of the Bear to the remarkable Beer Springs, situated in a cedar grove that shaded the rutted course of the Oregon Trail along the north bank of the river where it reverses its course to flow south into the Great Salt Lake. At that popular campsite they found numerous mineral springs, some very hot, one a miniature geyser, and the elevated crater of an enormous inactive one; these impressive phenomena were of great interest to Preuss and Frémont, who made the rounds taking the temperature of the waters and gathering samples for chemical analysis.[13]

After departing Beer Springs in late August, three more weeks were devoted to that region and the Great Salt Lake. There were

[12]Jackson and Spence, *Expeditions*, pp. 466ff., 518.

[13]*Ibid.*, pp. 470–488. One who often used the Beer Springs site for rest and recoupment for his party was Louis Eulalie Bonneville, who on special leave from the army spent more than three years (1832–35) shuttling from the Rockies and Great Basin to the mouth of the Columbia while engaged in a combined fur-trading and military reconnaissance expedition. Bonneville has been remembered in the name of a dam on the Columbia River, an extinct great inland sea (Lake Bonneville) of which Great Salt Lake is a surviving remnant and Bonneville Flats its salt residue, but mostly through the skillful pen of Washington Irving in his work *The Rocky Mountains; or Scenes Incidents and Adventures in the Far West, digested from the Journal of Captain B. L. E. Bonneville, U.S.A., and Illustrated from various other sources* (2 vols., Philadelphia, 1837). Later editions adopted the name *The Adventures of Captain Bonneville, U.S.A. in the Rocky Mountains and the Far West.* My references are to the 1961 University of Oklahoma Press edition, edited by Edgeley W. Todd.

Bonneville became the principal source of our knowledge of such fabled mountain men as John Colter, James Bridger, Jedidiah Smith, Joseph Walker, and the Sublette brothers.

memorable sights all along the way down to the plain surrounding
the lake where the wide, reed-fringed Bear entered that briny inland
sea: the crater of an extinct volcano; "Standing Rock," a tall, free-
standing shaft in the middle of a gorge through which they passed;
benighted Digger Indians, the pitiful Shoshones (Snakes) of the
Great Basin, whose staple fare was roots, supplemented by insects
and lizards; and near the mouth of the river myriads of waterfowl,
pelicans, ducks, gulls, and geese. Crossing to the eastern bank of the
Bear, they continued south along the western base of the lofty
snow-capped peaks of the Wasatch range, rising 4,000 feet above
the plain. A dozen large hot springs, strongly impregnated with iron
and lime, formed a large stream that led them to well-timbered
Weber River, which meandered westward across the plain. A few
miles down the Weber a long butte rose high above the plain, from
the summit of which the romantic captain reported the sight:

Immediately at our feet we beheld the object of our anxious search—the
waters of the Inland Sea, stretching out in still and solitary grandeur far
beyond the limit of our vision. . . . As we looked eagerly over the lake in
the first emotions of excited pleasure, I am doubtful if the followers of
Balboa felt more enthusiasm when, from the heights of the Andes, they saw
for the first time the great Western ocean. . . . Several large islands raised
their high rocky heads out of the waves. . . .[14]

The next day, from their camp on the Weber they set out downstream in the rubber boat on an expedition they thought was to be
"the first ever attempted on this interior sea." Aboard were five of
the party, Frémont, Preuss, Carson, and two crewmen. Toward its
mouth the deep river became "merely a sheet of soft mud," but

[14]Jackson and Spence, *Expeditions*, p. 501. Frémont implies priority of discovery of
Great Salt Lake; however, other explorers had preceded him, among them a contingent of Bonneville's party under Joseph Walker that in the summer and fall of 1833
marched from their trappers' rendezvous on Green River to explore Great Salt Lake,
rumored to be an untapped source of beaver. Finding little but a great briny lake
surrounded by saline deserts, Walker's band continued west to follow down Ogden's
River (the Humboldt) along the way to its Sink (substantially the route of the California Trail of later years), thence across the Sierras near Yosemite Valley into the
Valley of California, which they crossed to the government town of Monterey—
Bonneville, pp. 281–294. Marching south from Monterey, they went back across the
Sierras through Walker Pass, near their southern extremity, then northward along
their desert east flank back to the Humboldt. One of Walker's men provided a more
detailed account of Walker's California expedition; see Zenas Leonard, *Narrative of
the Adventures of Zenas Leonard* (Clearfield, Pa., 1839), and John C. Ewers (ed.), *Adventures of Zenas Leonard, Fur Trader* (Norman, Okla., 1959).

witnessing their "dragging the boat" were "millions of waterfowl," the wide expanse of the river's mouth being "absolutely covered with flocks of screaming plover."[15]

Once afloat again they headed the clumsy craft, which was already leaking air from one of its compartments, toward what appeared to be a volcanic cone rising from the lake about 10 miles away. The water of the lake was "an extremely beautiful bright green color," and "transparently clear"; but its spray on their clothes "was directly converted into a crust of common salt, which covered our hands and arms." The edges of the lake, likewise, were fringed with snow-white borders. As they approached the island that now bears Frémont's name, they waded in with their fragile craft, carrying it to the beach above the rocks, where they noted a strip "10 or 20 feet in breadth, of a dark brown color . . . being composed to the depth of seven or eight or twelve inches, entirely of the *larvae* of insects . . . or the skins of worms, about the size of a grain of oats." No doubt this explained the myriads of waterfowl, particularly the gulls and plover, on the waters of a briny lake entirely devoid of fish life. Frémont identified these larvae as the same he later learned were the staple item of the Diggers' diet.[16]

The island proved disappointing. When first seen from the butte, their imaginations had clothed it with a forest sanctuary teeming with unmolested wildlife. Instead they found a barren, rocky peak, supporting little more than a sparse cover of saline desert shrubs. But there was compensating gratification in disclosing previously unknown geography, and pleasure in the thought that they "were the first who, in the traditional annals of the country, had visited the islands, and broken, with the cheerful sound of human voices, the long solitude of the place."[17] That night, to the rhythm of the waves that began to break heavily on the rocky shore, they slept soundly for the first time in their long journey without posting a watch.

Next day, after battling a boisterous sea in their failing craft, they reached their camp on the Weber. They lingered there another day to make further observations for mapping, and to boil down a quan-

[15]Jackson and Spence, *Expeditions*, pp. 502, 504, and note at p. 502 pointing out that in 1826 others had also preceded Frémont in navigating the waters of the lake —a party with William H. Ashley.

[16]*Ibid.*, p. 506.

[17]*Ibid.*, p. 509.

tity of lakewater to secure residual salts for analysis; it proved to be almost 98 percent sodium chloride, common table salt.

In 1845, when Frémont's *Report* of his 1843–44 expedition was released, it described the region of the Bear River and Great Salt Lake as a place where "the bottoms are extensive; water excellent; timber sufficient; the soil good, and well adapted to the grains and grasses suited to such an elevated region . . . cattle and horses would do well. . . . The Lake will furnish exhaustless supplies of salt." All of which rendered it "truly a bucolic region."[18] It was a description freighted with historical consequences. To Brigham Young, the newly chosen leader of the followers of the Church of Jesus Christ of Latter-day Saints, this "bucolic region" forthwith became the promised land of his people, a land potentially flowing with milk and honey and a sanctuary more protected from the persecutions that had already driven them west as far as the banks of the Mississippi. The next year, 1846, the Mormons would abandon their shattered sanctuary at Nauvoo and resume their westward migration to settle in the Valley of the Saints that Frémont had described.[19]

A week after leaving their camp on the Weber, Frémont's party had made its way back north up the Bear and across to Fort Hall, the Hudson's Bay Company's post on the Snake River,[20] where the main body of his command had been resting, awaiting his return from the lake reconnaissance. From Fort Hall to the Columbia their way lay across "a melancholy and strange looking country—one of fracture and violence and fire," the harsh and unhospitable plateau through which the Snake flows in the spectacular gorges that had caused the overland Astorians so much suffering. Along the now well-worn Oregon Trail they made their way down to Walla Walla and down the Columbia, past snow-capped Mount Hood, roseate in the morning sun, following the Columbia to where the Deschutes, coming in from the south, literally falls into the Columbia "with a roar of falls and rapids." Leaving the main body of his party in Carson's charge, Frémont, with a few companions, including the essential Preuss, continued to Fort Vancouver to tie his geographical observations to Wilkes's survey from the mouth of the river.

[18]*Ibid.*, p. 516.
[19]Ray Allen Billington, *The Far Western Frontier, 1830–1860* (New York, 1956), pp. 193–217.
[20]Businessman turned trapper Nathaniel J. Wyeth, who had built Fort Hall, had sold it to the Company in 1837.

Although many travelers had preceded Frémont and Preuss along that way, they conscientiously busied themselves with recording descriptive details to embellish the scientific knowledge of the region, collecting botanical specimens, spring waters, soils, and stones for later analysis, and determining the location and heights of such notable peaks as Mount Hood, Mount Rainier, and Mount St. Helens. When they reached the fabled forests of the Cascades, they added numerous measurements of forest giants among the rich variety of conifers of the area. They saw Mount St. Helens 50 miles to the north in eruption. A sample of the ash with which the volcano had coated the whole region at the height of its activity the previous year was added to their collections.[21]

In mid-November, Frémont rejoined his men at the mouth of the Deschutes for their "homeward journey." Although homeward, this contemplated "a new route, and a great circuit to the south and southeast, and the exploration of the Great Basin between the Rocky Mountains and the Sierra Nevada," despite the fact that Frémont recognized "it was a serious enterprise, at the commencement of winter, to undertake the traverse of such a region, and with a party consisting only of twenty five." Early in the morning of November 25, under a canopy of stars, with the thermometer standing at 26° F., they set out southward between the eastern ramparts of the Sierras and the turbulent waters of the Deschutes. It was a heavily forested route, where progress was severely slowed by the cumbersome howitzer. Their immediate objective was Lake Klamath, and then perhaps the mysterious Buenaventura River, which some maps represented as breaching the Sierras to flow into San Francisco Bay.[22]

For three weeks they toiled through stupendous evergreen forests they could little enjoy in the bitter cold. The streams were full of ice, and "the trees and bushes glittering white" when the thermometer fell below zero. On the third night out, with the temperature at 20°, they "encamped on a stream after dark aided by the light of fires which some naked Indians were kindling for us on the bank." The scenery was as magnificent as the forest. Whenever they reached an elevated point, great snow-robed peaks, first Mount Jefferson and then the Three Sisters, could be seen rising from heavily forested buttresses. Interesting fossil finds enriched the col-

[21]Jackson and Spence, *Expeditions,* pp. 516–576.
[22]*Ibid.,* pp. 573–577.

lection they were accumulating for study by paleontologists at West Point. The extraordinary forest through which they were traveling added scientific chores—measuring the circumference of the boles of numerous species and securing needles and cones from the lofty branches. For a while the forest stand was dominated by ponderosa pine, the red-colored trunks of some measuring up to 22 feet in circumference and bearing cones 16–18 inches long.[23]

Although they had intended to visit Lake Klamath in southern Oregon, the difficulties of forest travel, particularly with the howitzer, plus the heavy snow and bone-numbing cold prevented any nearer approach than Klamath Marsh, a sometimes flooded savanna area 30 miles to the north. Frémont's company were terrifying visitors at a native village on the edge of the reed-covered marsh; Frémont was intrigued by the amazing adaptability of its inhabitants, "almost like plants . . . growing on what the immediate locality afforded." Their shelters were "large round huts, perhaps 20 feet in diameter, with rounded tops, on which was the door." Huts, clothing, even the shoes of these people were made of matted reeds and woven grasses. Their "singular-looking dogs, resembling wolves, were sitting on the tops of the huts" with their masters. The Indians' main diet was a tiny fish of the marsh, "great quantities of which, that had been smoked and dried, were suspended on strings about the lodge." Frémont added: "Unlike any Indians we had previously seen, these wore shells in their noses."[24]

From Klamath Marsh, Frémont turned east to free his weary band from the hampering mountain snows. The next day, after struggling on through the dark pine forest, made even darker by the falling snow, "towards noon the forest looked clear ahead appearing to suddenly terminate." A few minutes later they found themselves "on the verge of a vertical and rocky wall of mountain. At our feet, more than a thousand feet below—we looked into a green prairie country in which a beautiful lake, some twenty miles in length, was spread along the foot of the mountains," illuminated by sunshine while the storm continued to rage fiercely around them. Standing there "shivering in snow three feet deep," Frémont named the lake below Summer, and the ridge on which his party stood Winter, names they still bear.[25] The bold contrasts he witnessed here in-

[23]*Ibid.*, pp. 578, 583–585.
[24]*Ibid.*, p. 587.
[25]Winter Rim and Summer Lake, south central Oregon.

spired Frémont to make one of the most revealing observations in the history of discovery of the American West:

We were now immediately on the verge of the forest land, in which we had been travelling so many days; and, looking forward to the east, scarce a tree was to be seen. . . . Broadly marked by the boundary of the mountain wall, and immediately below us, were the first waters of that Great Interior Basin which has the Wahsatch and Bear River mountains for its eastern and the Sierra Nevada for its western rim; and the edge of which we had entered upwards of three months before, at the Great Salt Lake.[26]

The map delineating the country explored by Frémont's 1842 and 1843–44 expeditions has this descriptive legend arched across the mostly vacant expanse between the Sierras and the Wasatch:

The Great Basin; diameter 11° of latitude, 10° of longitude: elevation above the sea between 4 and 5,000 feet: surrounded by lofty mountains: contents almost unknown, but believed to be filled with rivers and lakes which have no communication with the sea, deserts and oases which have never been explored and savage tribes which no traveller has seen or described.[27]

When, with great difficulty, they had succeeded in making their way down the mountain wall, what had appeared from its summit a scene of pastoral beauty was cruelly disappointing. The gem they had named Summer Lake was fit for neither man nor beast, being so saline that, although it harbored waterfowl, it supported no fish; while the surrounding green plains were of artemisia (sagebrush), a poor substitute indeed for life-supporting grass. So, with only a brief stop, the little cavalcade, following a "plainly beaten trail," continued southward along the western edge of the Great Basin, a region of "very forbidding appearance, presenting to the eye nothing but sage and barren ridges." The few natives able to scrounge a subsistence from the austere region were miserable Diggers, living on roots and seeds, in "huts open at the top, and loosely built of sage." Almost naked and fleeing like deer from the explorers, they seemed to Frémont "the nearest approach . . . among human beings . . . to mere animal creation."[28] Along the way they came upon several hot springs exceeding even the Bear River outpourings; the basin of one, which had a circumference of several hundred feet, "at intervals, and with much noise"

[26]Jackson and Spence, *Expeditions*, pp. 591–592.
[27]*Ibid.*, map portfolio, map 3.
[28]*Ibid.*, pp. 596–599. The party was now at about the Oregon-Nevada line.

gave forth great quantities of boiling water.[29]

After days more of travel through barren country, early in January 1844 their eyes were gladdened by the sight of a large lake, "set like a gem in the mountains," from the green waters of which rose a pyramid 600 feet high. It "presented a pretty exact outline of the great pyramid of Cheops," inspiring Frémont to name it Pyramid Lake and Preuss to prepare a sketch of it for reproduction in their report. The main source of this lake, beautiful Truckee River, fed it the melting snows of the Sierras and Lake Tahoe's overflow. Both the lake and the river abounded with "salmond trout" (cutthroat trout), a species Frémont declared superior to any fish he had ever known. Here, too, they found ample timber and good forage for the animals. Although the hardships of their way had so reduced their transport that all the surviving animals were fully laden, leaving the men unmounted, the caravan (after only a brief respite) pushed on south from Pyramid Lake and the bountiful Truckee. A fortnight later, the condition of the animals precipitated a sharp alteration of plans. Gathering his men about him, Frémont announced that, at the first opportunity, they would cross the Sierras, along the eastern flank of which they had been traveling for so many weeks, and descend into the Sacramento Valley of California to rest and resupply. This momentous decision "was heard with joy . . . and diffused new life throughout the camp."[30]

That Frémont could boldly undertake to go beyond his orders and on his own initiative lead his armed contingent, unauthorized howitzer and all, into settled alien territory and never suffer even an official reprimand for such blatant transgression, speaks loudly of justification by the unwritten mandate of "manifest destiny," the spirit of which had become a powerful influence although the actual coining of that rallying cry for popular exchange was still two years in the future.[31]

Led by Frémont himself and Carson, the men spent days probing

[29]At Gerlach, Nevada—*ibid.,* p. 603.

[30]*Ibid.,* p. 611.

[31]See Billington, *The Far Western Frontier,* pp. 148–150, for a discussion of the origination of the "pulse tingling phrase" manifest destiny, by John L. O'Sullivan in the *New York Morning News* on Dec. 27, 1845. But the spirit of manifest destiny had been incipient since the early days of the nation. Witness Timothy Dwight in his *Greenfield Hill* (1794): "All hail, thou western world! By heaven designed/The example bright to renovate mankind./Soon shall thy sons across the mainland roam/And claim on far Pacific shores their home;/Their rule, religion, manners, art convey/And spread their freedom to the Asian Sea."

promising-looking entries into the towering mountain mass, in search of possible passes. When a way was finally selected, there were struggles with the howitzer through ever-deepening snows, many hours devoted to pounding down paths through snow banks up to 20 feet deep, day after day of bitter cold and gnawing hunger when their fare was reduced to the seeds of the piñon or nut pine and the carcasses of their starving animals, and of men losing their reason under the weight of their suffering. Even the phlegmatic Preuss wandered off without supplies or arms, only to stumble into camp days later with a report of having resorted to a survival diet of acorns, tiny frogs, and ants. At last, in early March 1844, the weary, gaunt, and tattered caravan staggered out of the hills to the trail down the valley of the westward-flowing American River. It had been a costly six weeks. Left behind in the mountains, in addition to the howitzer, abandoned in an impassable defile, and most of their sixty-seven pack animals, was one of their deranged companions who had wandered off from camp never to be seen again, and the entire, highly valuable botanical collection, the burden of a mule that had slipped from a mountain ledge and fallen into an inaccessible chasm.[32]

As they trudged down the trail along the river after their living death in the mountains, the countryside through which they passed must have seemed to them a veritable Elysian Fields: grazing herds of horses and cattle, bountiful fields of ripening grain with borders aflame with California poppies. As they neared the place where the American River joins the Sacramento, across the fields could be seen the heavy adobe walls of Sutter's Fort, by reputation already well known to Frémont. In the bright spring sunshine, riding out to greet his bedraggled callers, was a ruddy-faced, heavyset German, Captain John Sutter, owner of an enormous estate of which the fort and surrounding fields were the heart. Sutter had come to California from Missouri only four years previously. In that brief span, thanks to his own energy and enterprise and the bountiful region in which he elected to settle, he had developed this immense plantation-ranch, equipped with a dozen mounted cannon acquired from

[32]Despite this loss, and another loss in a flash flood on their homeward way, Frémont's botanical collections in this and his other expeditions were significant enough to justify the publication by John Torrey of his *Plantae Frémontianae*, Smithsonian Contributions (1850). Jackson and Spence, *Expeditions*, pp. 616–650; M. M. Quaife (ed.), *Kit Carson's Autobiography* (Chicago, 1935), pp. 79–81; Preuss, *Exploring with Frémont*, pp. 104–118.

a nearby Russian fur post. Enclosed within its walls, as Frémont would shortly see, were quarters for the fort's uniformed guard of forty Indians, a horse-powered flour mill, smithy, saddlery shop, a distillery, warehouses, and Sutter's personal quarters. Anchored in the Sacramento were his two vessels, one of seagoing size, which traded the produce of his domain to the British and Russians along the Northwest Coast. Of his fields, some of which were irrigated, more than 2,500 acres were given over to wheat alone; out beyond the fields Indian vaqueros tended herds of half-wild horses, cattle, and sheep. When Frémont's *Report* appeared, his account of Sutter's success inspired thousands to head for California for the boundless opportunity it seemed to offer, a movement that soon swelled to a mass migration.[33]

Thanks to Sutter's generous hospitality, it was a rejuvenated but diminished band that, a fortnight later, resumed its homeward travel down the Valley of the Sacramento. Five of the men had elected to stay in California. Those departing with Frémont and Carson formed a well-provided cavalcade of 130 horses, 25 beef cattle, and 5 milk cows, all furnished by the generous Sutter. It had been four months and 1,000 miles of hard travel since their first start for home; yet now they were making this new start from a place even more distant from home, and not yet heading east. Instead, Frémont projected a still wider southward sweep, down almost the length of California, across the Sierras near their southern terminus, then across the deserts to the southern rim of the Great Basin, before crossing the Rockies to the headwaters of the Arkansas or Platte, one of which they planned to follow down to the frontier.

As they made their way southward between the western flanks of the Sierras and the San Joaquin River, Frémont's account of what he saw in California further advertised the abundant promise of its great valley, focusing covetous eyes on its bounty when his widely circulated *Report* was published the following year. The bottomlands of the San Joaquin were, in Frémont's words, "broad, rich and

[33]Nevins, *Frémont*, pp. 161–174; Jackson and Spence, *Expeditions*, pp. 654–658. For more detailed information on Sutter's operations three years later, after the completion of his irrigation system, see Edwin Bryant, *What I Saw in California* (Minneapolis, 1967), pp. 265–274. Bryant's title is misleading. His book is an excellent day-to-day account of the crossing of the country by an immigrant party of which he was a group captain, which reached the Sacramento Valley just in time for him to march with Frémont on his next expedition into California.

extremely fertile; and the uplands shaded with oak trees," whose acorns supplied the Indians of the region with their staple fare. Showy blue lupines, "four or five feet high, and covered with spikes in bloom, adorned the banks . . . and filled the air with" perfume; great clumps of them, "some being 12 feet in height," formed "a giant bouquet" of blue flowers. The trail was "one continued enjoyment" as it led through open groves of liveoaks whose branches swept the ground, through fields of the "California poppy, of a rich orange color," while all along to their left a magnificent array of "rocky and snowy peaks" was constantly in view. Along the Tuolumne were numerous bands of elk, 200 in a single herd, and signs of grizzly bears all around. With the advent of spring, migrating waterfowl came in incredible numbers, so that whenever their trail approached the San Joaquin, they "disturbed multitudes of wild fowl, principally geese," which astonished them by their tameness. Along the Mercid, a stream fed by the melting snows of Yosemite, antelope could be seen here and there, springing across the open areas. Within two years Frémont would be intimately involved in this Mercid River region, establishing and developing his own rich domain that for a while would rival Sutter's vast estate.[34]

By mid-April they had reached the arid regions of southern California and passed over Tehachapi Pass down into the Mojave Desert. As they had now traveled almost the entire length of California on one side or the other of the Sierras, there remained no doubt that despite the authority of some maps showing a river flowing through the Sierras, there was definitely no Rio Buenaventura. Equally emphatically Frémont could now testify to (and would soon proclaim in his *Report*) the incredible bounty awaiting exploitation in California and the raveled ties binding this El Dorado to Mexico—revelations freighted with historical consequences as the spirit of manifest destiny began aggressively to assert itself.

From the Mojave, Frémont's motley column moved northeast among the "stiff and ungraceful" forms of the Joshua trees (*Yucca brevefolia*), moving him to comment that it was "hard to conceive so great a change in so short a distance," and that "one might travel the world over, without finding a valley more fresh and verdant—more floral and sylvan" than California, and then within a few short miles find oneself crossing "a vast desert plain . . . from which the

[34]Jackson and Spence, *Expeditions,* pp. 657–666.

boldest traveller" turns away in despair. Nevertheless, his "half-wild cavalcade" of 124 animals and 21 men—Indian, American, French, German, and Negro—"the whole stretching a quarter of a mile along our dreary path," moved out across the forbidding desert.

By early May they had made it across to the welcome springs of Las Vegas on the Spanish Trail from Los Angeles to Santa Fe. From there, under the expert guidance of mountain man Joseph Walker, they traveled northeast on the Trail, along the Virgin River deep in its canyons, enduring *jornados* of up to 60 miles without a drop of water, until they reached in the Great Basin the Sevier River and Utah Lake.[35]

Now crossing the Wasatch and Uinta mountains, the wildest and least-explored section of the central Rockies, to the Green River, which they forded at the present Dinosaur National Monument, they entered the magnificent park region of the Colorado Mountains, with its welcome herds of buffalo. From this complex source region of the Platte, Rio Grande, Colorado, and Arkansas, their way home was the familiar route from South Park down past Pike's Peak, across the Great Plains, to their departure point at Independence on the Missouri, which they reached before the end of July 1844.

From St. Louis, where Jessie had been anxiously awaiting her husband's return, the Frémonts hastened to Washington, where they were soon again immersed in their felicitous collaboration. Working together methodically, they completed the official report of his 1843–44 expedition in February 1845. The Senate promptly ordered 10,000 extra copies of it to be printed together with the report of his 1842 expedition, as Frémont's *Report of the Exploring Expedition to the Rocky Mountains in the Year 1842, and to Oregon and North California in the Years 1843–44.*[36] A map prepared to accompany the reports, largely the work of Charles Preuss, represented a very substantial advance in Western cartography.[37] Preuss also pre-

[35] *Ibid.*, pp. 667–684; *Carson's Autobiography*, pp. 82–85. Walker had become a well-known mountain man since his expedition with Captain Bonneville in the early 1830s.

[36] Frémont's *Report of the Exploring Expedition to the Rocky Mountains in the Year 1842, and to Oregon and North California in the Years 1843–44*, Senate Exec. Doc. 174, 28th Congress, 2d Sess., U.S. serial no. 461 (1845), was in no sense a typical dry government report. Very soon it became apparent to commercial publishers in both America and England that Frémont's reports made the right book, on the right subject, at the right time; in the ensuing few years many editions, some quite large, responded to the tremendous public interest they evoked.

[37] Goetzmann, *Army Exploration*, accompanying map D; Jackson and Spence, *Expeditions*, accompanying map 3.

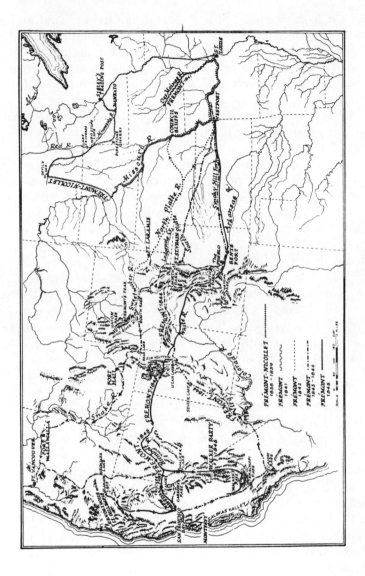

pared a map in seven sections showing the Oregon Trail in detail from the mouth of the Kansas to the confluence of the Walla Walla and the Columbia; the inclusion of pertinent comments from the *Report* all along the route made the map a most valuable companion for immigrants who were heading in mounting numbers for the golden West.[38]

Frémont became the hero of the day. His influence was enormous, his *Report* became the pattern for the long series of Topographical Survey reports in the years to follow. Although Frémont's Far Western expeditions had been only ostensibly predicated upon scientific exploration, neither the romantic turn given them in his *Report* nor their political consequences dampened the Baron von Humboldt's lavish praise of their scientific revelations, and of the "talent, courage, industry and enterprise" demonstrated in Frémont's work.[39]

At this time of mounting acclaim, both the Frémonts were still young—he thirty-two and she but twenty-one—with notably long, varied, and undreamed-of careers in the future. In the ensuing dozen years Frémont's fame would reach new heights; so would his failures and disgraces. With the publication of the *Report* in 1845 and its companion maps, he had virtually shot his explorer's bow. Thanks largely to his work and his personality, the world had been made aware of the rich potentialities of the region of Great Salt Lake, California, and the Oregon country, of the scenic wonders to be found all across the great wide West, and of the mineral riches latent in that vast wilderness. The Pathfinder's next two Western expeditions are less pertinent to this work, despite the fact that his next, that of 1845–46, is by far his most famous. It was to launch him in meteoric careers, both in fortune building and politics, while embroiling him in one of America's most famous court-martial proceedings, which resulted in his conviction for mutiny and disobedience and dismissal from the service, all of which conspired to bring him a major party's nomination for the presidency and a high military post in the Civil War.

---

[38] *Topographical Map of the Road from Missouri to Oregon, Commencing at the Mouth of the Kansas in the Missouri River and Ending at the Mouth of Walla-Walla in the Columbia, in VII Sections* (Baltimore, 1846); Jackson and Spence, *Expeditions,* accompanying map 4, secs. I–VII. This map and Frémont's *Report* immediately became the foundation for numerous emigrants' guides to the West, of which Lansford W. Hastings's famous *Emigrants' Guide to Oregon and California* (Cincinnati, 1845) became the most popular.

[39] Goetzmann, *Army Exploration,* p. 108.

Even as the Frémonts were putting the finishing touches on the *Report* and attending to the preparation of its appendices, Benton, Colonel Abert, and the new Polk administration were formulating plans for yet another Frémont expedition; this one ostensibly designed to be a survey of the Arkansas and Red rivers, "within a reasonable distance of Bent's Fort" on the Arkansas, and to "return during the present year," employing a party of no more than forty men.[40] The newly breveted Captain Frémont marched out of Bent's Fort on August 16, 1845, at the head of a well-armed column of sixty men, largely built around his earlier friends, Alexis Godey, Joseph Walker, and, a little later, Kit Carson also, to which ten Delaware Indians would soon be added. Now Edward M. Kern, a young Philadelphia artist and naturalist, had the place the skillful Preuss had proficiently filled on the two previous expeditions. Obviously the captain had a secret understanding of his new mission, one that little resembled and almost entirely preempted his written instructions. Without hesitating for even a cursory examination of the Arkansas and without a look at the Red, he immediately headed west from Bent's Fort on the Arkansas into and across the Rockies, and then as directly and expeditiously as possible made his way to Utah Lake and on north to Great Salt Lake. He skirted the lake's southern shore, and then, with daring bordering on recklessness, ignoring the warnings of the natives of the area that his column was entering a barren and waterless waste too wide to cross, Frémont set out straight across Great Salt Lake Desert and the Shoshone Mountains to Walker Lake. That crossing provided the expedition with its single significant justification for the ostensible role of making a scientific topographical study, and one of the few of Frémont's treks that actually justified his sobriquet as Pathfinder. Beyond Walker Lake, he divided his party for the awesome wintry crossing of the Sierras. Both made successful crossings but were lost from each other for several weeks, during which Frémont and his companions were again Sutter's guests. All along the way Frémont had been branding lasting names on notable bits of geography: Pilot Peak in northeast Nevada, Hunboldt's name in place of Ogden's on the river that flows west across the Basin to lose itself in saline sinks, Walker's on a river and a lake of western Nevada, among others. Later, Kern was given a namesake river in California.

[40]Col. Abert's orders to Frémont, Feb. 12, 1845, and Abert to Frémont, March 1, 1845—Jackson and Spence, *Expeditions*, pp. 395–396.

Understandably the Mexican authorities, conscious of their feeble hold on the rich province, were greatly disturbed by the presence of this relatively formidable foreign military unit, whatever its ostensible mission. Half expecting word of open war between the United States and Mexico, Frémont's little army played a waiting game, lingering between marches here and there in the valley for near two months, until, stiffened by the growing rumors of war, the governor, with a show of force, demanded their departure. Frémont responded with dilatory movement up the Sacramento into Oregon.[41] It was May before they passed east of Shasta's grand peak and moved out of California to camp near Oregon's Klamath Lake. There, on May 9, 1846, Marine Lieutenant A. H. Gillespie, freshly arrived from Washington via Mexico City and Honolulu, after forced marches following Frémont's trail, finally overtook the dallying American unit. The message the lieutenant had for Frémont at their dramatic wilderness meeting beneath the forest giants bordering the lake remains a mystery; but whatever it was, it prompted Frémont to forthwith prepare to lead his troop back into California. As a matter of fact, even as they sat and talked by the light of their campfire, American armies on the Rio Grande were resting after two sharp battles with Mexican forces. But that news would not reach California for weeks; meanwhile, events began to generate themselves.

News of Frémont's wild-looking file making its way back down the Sacramento Valley sped through the American settlements across northern California, and doubtless served, at least in part, as catalyst of what came to be known as the Bear Flag Revolt. On June 14 a band of American settlers mounted an attack on the moribund Mexican post at Sonoma and seized a substantial supply of munitions and several brass cannon. For their standard, one of the attackers had devised a crude flag bearing the silhouette of a grizzly bear and a single star. With that attack, Mexican authority in northern California quickly withered. Acting in concert with Commodore Robert F. Stockton, who commanded American naval vessels on the coast and who, upon learning of the clash at Sonoma, had raised the American flag at Monterey and San Francisco, Frémont (now elevated by Stockton to the rank of major) in late July rode south at the head of his California Battalion, a nondescript small army built

[41]Nevins, *Frémont*, pp. 217–233.

around his own seasoned band. Before leaving San Francisco on his southward sweep to attack Santa Barbara and Los Angeles, Frémont named another memorable landmark when, in response to his enthusiasm for the magnificent portal of San Francisco's bay, he called it the Golden Gate.[42]

At the close of their successful military operation in the south, Commodore Stockton appointed Gillespie military governor there and Frémont military governor in the north. In late summer a Mexican counter-revolt in the south was near to succeeding when an overland American force under General Stephen Kearny crossed the Colorado into California to turn the tide. With the capitulation of the Mexican leaders in January 1847, Stockton, believing he had the authority, promoted Frémont to civil governor of all of California. He thereby plunged the explorer into the middle of a bitter and prolonged dispute between the commodore and the general, each acting under unclear orders that were mutually irreconcilable. Before the year was out, in a celebrated court-martial trial for disobeying a lawful command and for mutiny, Frémont was found guilty and dismissed from the service in January 1847. That penalty was promptly remitted by President Polk, even as he confirmed the hero's conviction. Indignant, Frémont resigned his army commission.

During his action-packed sixteen months in California Frémont had welded substantial personal ties to the rich new province. He had acquired a home and made arrangements to acquire other property there—most notably the fabulous 70-square-mile Mariposa estate in the foothills of the High Sierras, at the front door of the future Yosemite National Park. Although that estate was destined to make him fabulously rich for a short time, it eventually destroyed him financially for the duration of his life. Meanwhile it would keep summoning him back to California and cementing his bonds there.[43]

[42]*Ibid.*, p. 278. In the winter of 1835–36 Richard H. Dana, aboard the *Alert*, to which he had transferred from the *Pilgrim*, had visited the Bay and viewed it with prescience: "A magnificent bay, containing several good harbors, a great depth of water and surrounded by fertile and wooded country . . . this will be the center of prosperity . . . the excellence of its climate, which is as near to being perfect as anywhere in the world; and its facilities for navigation, affording the best anchoring-grounds in the whole western coast of America—all fit it for a place of great importance"—Richard H. Dana, *Two Years Before the Mast* (Boston, 1895), p. 270.

[43]Nevins, *Frémont*, pp. 339–340, 371–372.

Frémont was never a man to recognize personal defeat. Determined to cling to his career as an explorer, before the year was out after his court-martial conviction and separation from the army, he was off to the West again. This time he was to lead a privately supported expedition to search for a way through the Southern Rockies that could be traveled in midwinter—an expedition that would prove his sternest trial and a tragic nightmare that would haunt the explorer for the remainder of his life. He enlisted an able and experienced band: Godey as hunter, Preuss back again as topographer, Edward Kern who, as artist and leader, had served so well on his last expedition, and "Old Bill" Williams, an experienced mountain man, memorialized in the names of a river, a mountain, and a town in Arizona. With a supporting crew of thirty, Frémont set out on November 24, 1848, in search of a pass over the Sangre de Cristo Mountains to the Rio Grande Valley, near where Pike's frostbitten band had reached refuge.

Confused by deep snow on every trail, the party took one that led deep into the northern San Juans and a maze of lofty peaks where impassable snowbanks, blizzards, incredible cold, and starvation spelled irretrievable ruin to the expedition. Forced to turn back, death stalked their retreat. Some sustained themselves only by eating the frozen cadavers of fallen comrades, others survived on buds and carrion. Eleven died. The remaining twenty-two, although reduced to miserable skeletons, finally reached Taos. Recriminations flared; some, with justification, were directed at their leader. But despite the loss of all his equipment and money in the mountain snows, Frémont had enough loyal friends and admirers in Taos to enable him to mount and equip the handful who chose to continue with him to California by the Gila River route—a southward detour to avoid both the San Juans and the Sierras. Incredibly, despite the failure of his projected winter passage of the Colorado Mountains, Frémont still persisted in his conviction that he had demonstrated the way for a southern route to California. This claim was not merely for public consumption. He expressed his conviction even to Jessie.[44]

As his remnant band was making its way along the Gila River, westward-bound migrants, hurrying toward California, reported the gold discovery at Sutter's Mill. Soon placermen were finding rich

[44] *Ibid.*, pp. 370–371.

gold deposits in the streams of Frémont's Mariposa estate,[45] recovering nuggets by the bucketful, and Frémont's half of the take was being delivered to him in Monterey in 100-pound buckskin sacks worth nearly $25,000 each. Money rolled in so fast that Frémont was soon distracted from its accumulation, and from the protection of its source, by the enticements of California's rough-and-tumble political scene as the territory moved toward statehood. In December 1849 he was elected first United States senator from California and was soon on his way back east to take his seat in the Senate. In the space of less than a year, almost as if by magic, Frémont had been transformed from an impoverished adventurer confronting starvation and death in the frigid passes of the San Juans to a fabulously wealthy tycoon, lord of an imperial estate, well on his way toward the nation's political pinnacle. Then, almost as suddenly, fortune frowned again on the Frémonts.

Although, in the election of its two senators, Frémont had received the most votes, in the selection between them by lot Frémont had drawn the short term. Because of his antislavery views, which were becoming more pronounced and better known, the California Senate denied him a new full term. Soon other events conspired to cloud the Frémonts' days: illness in the family, the death of a child, endless legal troubles in respect to his Mariposa holdings, and the difficulty of supporting the heavy investments that he had thought necessary to work its gold veins as the placer operations exhausted the gold deposits of the stream beds. Then came one of the unkindest blows to Frémont's pride. He was passed over by Secretary of War Jefferson Davis in the selection of leaders for the five expeditions to explore transcontinental rail routes that had been authorized by Congress in 1852. Out of his injured pride the Pathfinder's fifth and final expedition was born.

For years he and Senator Benton had advocated building a railroad across the Rockies between the 37th and 38th parallels. Twice already Frémont had searched for easy passes in that region, most memorably in his attempted winter passage of 1848–49. Now, in the late fall of 1853, at forty still lithe, but sad-eyed and graying, Frémont set out again to find a path for a transcontinental railway. In addition to the eight other whites and ten Delaware Indians who made up the roster of this expedition, Frémont had enlisted, as his

[45]Purchased for him by an agent in February 1847—*ibid.*, p. 371n.

assistants, two men whose own contributions to the revealing of the West were to be significant: Baron F. W. von Egloffstein, a competent artist, who was to serve as official topographer, and S. N. Carvalho, likewise a capable artist, who would be the expedition's photographer, the first official photographer ever to accompany a military or exploring expedition. It is yet another illustration of Frémont's extraordinary magnetism that Carvalho, a Portuguese Jewish emigrant with (like Frémont) a Charleston background, of no experience in outdoor living and never having saddled a horse, should have been so inspired by admiration for the explorer as to leave his wife and young children and risk his life in the same mountains that had cost the lives of so many on Frémont's last expedition.[46]

This time, albeit with great suffering and the loss of one man, they did succeed in making their way from the Rio Grande headquarters, through Cochetopa Pass (where they found only 4 inches of snow), to the Gunnison, a tributary of the Colorado, and then across more mountains to Parowan, a village in the Great Basin where the starving survivors were taken in and nursed back to health by its Mormon settlers. It had been a magnificent effort, but relatively fruitless. To this day no rail line or major highway has followed the path Frémont found and espoused. At Parowan, Carvalho and Egloffstein, both still suffering from their mountain ordeal, left the expedition to convalesce in Salt Lake City. The orthodox Jewish photographer developed a surprisingly warm friendship with Brigham Young, territorial governor of Utah, and his fellow elder, Ezra Benson. After recovering his strength, Carvalho returned to the East; Egloffstein joined the Pacific Railroad Survey party of Lieutenant E. G. Beckwith and continued on to California.[47]

Frémont, who had pushed on to California with the remainder of his party, reaching San Francisco in April 1854, soon returned east, to become presidential nominee of the new but vital antislavery Republican Party at its June 1856 Convention. In the ensuing bitter campaign, with sectional lines sharply drawn, unrestrained personal

---

[46]In title only was Carvalho first. Another artist photographer, John Mix Stanley, was already on his way west with Governor I. I. Stevens, who headed the Railroad Survey of the proposed Northern route as official "artist" of that expedition—Robert Taft, *Photography and the American Scene* (New York, 1938), pp. 261–262. Carvalho's account of this expedition is the principal record of it—S. N. Carvalho, *Incidents of Travel in the Far West* (New York, 1856).

[47]See below, Chapter 14.

attacks on Frémont tarnished the once brilliant image of the explorer. His defeat was the first in a succession that marked the long slide of the Frémonts' fortunes, a slide that began on the day of his nomination and ended only with his death in 1890.

In what measure were the accomplishments of John Charles Frémont significant to American topographical exploration? The man was such a romantic figure that his solid accomplishments are overshadowed by the dramatic features of his career and the high adventures with which it was colored. Nevertheless, there were in Frémont's career achievements of great moment: his epic Western marches provided the material for a proper cartographic view of the Great Basin; he recognized and advertised the potential of the Great Salt Lake region sufficiently glowingly to attract the Mormons to the area. Thanks in large measure to the skill and industry of Charles Preuss, he produced a survey of the Oregon Trail studded with valuable information descriptive of the way. His reports were replete with the observations and collections of an able amateur in the fields of botany and geology. And beyond those achievements, Frémont's explorations bore other fruit. His immense popularity during much of his career served to publicize his "discoveries" so that much of the West became known to many through the eyes and words of the "Pathfinder."[48]

[48]Nevins, *Frémont,* pp. 612–622; Goetzmann, *Exploration and Empire,* pp. 313–314.

CHAPTER 13

The Great Western Surveys

B Y the middle of the nineteenth century Americans could look
back on three and a half centuries of the Western world's persistent dream of finding a westward route to the riches of the Orient,
a dream unabated since Columbus had wishfully misnamed the
Caribs "Indians." As the concept of the breadth of the North American land barrier widened from the narrow sandy islands across
which Verrazzano could glimpse the waters that "flowed around the
shores of India and China," to the few hundred miles that a century
and a half later separated Jamestown from Lederer's "Indian Sea,"
to the 1,000 miles of breadth visualized by both Joliet and LaSalle
when they set out west from La Chine Rapids, New France's gateway
to China, in the hope of navigating the Mississippi to the Vermilion
Sea's Pacific waters, still the Orient, like the elusive pot of gold
beneath the rainbow, moved frustratingly further west. Another
1,000 miles had been added a century later when Jonathan Carver
was planning to find the Pacific's Straits of Anian at the common
source of the Missouri and the other great Western rivers. By the
time Jefferson dispatched Lewis and Clark to locate a northwest
passage by way of the Missouri and a single short portage to the
Columbia, the continent had well nigh reached its full conceptual
growth.

But even after the captains had returned with their discouraging
report of the immensity of the intervening barrier, the lure of the
Oriental pot of gold persisted. That his country, and more importantly, his city might grasp it, Thomas Hart Benton in 1818 pro-

posed a government-constructed canal and roadway to span the West from St. Louis to the mouth of the Columbia. A year later the architect Robert Mills, best known as the designer of the Washington Needle, in the light of plans under way to build a railroad in England, modernized Benton's proposal by substituting rails for the senator's canals and roads. For more than three decades sectional rivalries and local jealousies effectively stymied any substantial action toward accomplishing those proposals and the later, more specific proposal of the dynamic and persistent promoter Asa Whitney. Whitney, a wealthy New England merchant, in 1841 launched his futile but long-sustained campaign to induce Congress to permit him to build a railroad from Lake Michigan to the Pacific, to be financed by land sales from a strip of land to be granted him along the route. It was Whitney's plea that America should reach "out one hand to all Asia and the other to all Europe," and establish herself in trade in "the spices, teas, precious woods and fabrics of Cathay."[1]

Although for himself Asa Whitney's campaign came to naught and was even disastrous, it was by no means fruitless for the nation. As the dream of a way to the Orient progressed from canal and portage, to canal and roadway, and finally to railroad, the inevitability of a transcontinental railroad had become apparent. For twenty years the mounting drumbeat of its approach defied the dissonances of sectional and local divisiveness. By 1852, what with the settlement of the Oregon question, the acquisition of California and New Mexico, and gold discoveries in the West, the essentiality of a government-sponsored railroad to the Pacific was so universally recognized that a sectionally riven nation could agree it had become too important to be delayed by regional jealousies. Six distinct routes between the Mississippi and the Pacific, each with its vociferous supporters, were vying for congressional approval: one, long advocated by Asa Whitney, contemplated a line connecting Lake Michigan with the mouth of the Columbia, utilizing the Oregon Trail route through South Pass; the second, supported by Senator Benton, would run from St. Louis to San Francisco, via a pass yet to be found in the region of the headwaters of the Arkansas; the third, also projected from St. Louis, would utilize South Pass; the fourth, advocated by many Southern leaders, would run from Memphis to

[1]Robert West Howard, *The Great Iron Trail* (New York, 1962), pp. 41–42; George L. Albright, *Official Explorations for Pacific Railroads, 1853–1855* (Berkeley, 1921), pp. 10–18. My citations are to a facsimile reprint (New York, 1974).

San Diego by El Paso; the fifth, supported by Robert Mills, was much the same, but included a three-way branching at Fort Smith, to provide eastern terminii at St. Louis, Memphis, and Vicksburg; and the sixth, very similar to the Mills plan, ran directly from Vicksburg to El Paso, thence to San Diego.[2]

Although it had long since become obvious that no one of those routes could muster majority support in Congress, the members individually were all but unanimously convinced of the overriding necessity of a transcontinental railway to bind the emerging Far Western provinces to the East and the seat of the national government. Moreover, it had become generally recognized that the immensity of the project would require massive federal support, either directly or through land grants, or both. After several sessions of acrimonious debate, in March 1853 Congress enacted the Pacific Railroad Survey Act, which directed the Secretary of War to have field surveys made under the supervision of the army's Topographical Corps of all feasible routes across the trans-Mississippi West to the Pacific, "to ascertain the most practicable and economical route." These surveys were not intended to lay out mile by mile or even project the exact routes to be followed. Rather, they were to be topographical surveys in the fullness of its meaning, which encompassed a wide gamut of observations: climate, soils, rocks, and minerals; distances, grades, and elevations; economic potentials; the availability of water and timber. These investigations were all embraced in the information each survey party was expected to garner and report to the Secretary who, on the basis of the data thus compiled, would then determine "the most practicable and economical route."[3] In view of the widespread interest that had been generated during the interminable debates in Congress, the years of editorial enthrallment with the issue, and the intense partisan interests involved in the various Pacific railroad proposals, it was assured in advance that these surveys and their reports would receive wide and profound attention.

To inspect the several tentative railroad routes a variety of specially trained personnel, unmatched on earlier expeditions, would be required. In addition to its military escort and the usual accompaniment of guides, interpreters, carpenters, smithies, hunters, and

[2]Albright, *Official Explorations*, pp. 27–28.

[3]*Ibid.*, pp. 37–40; William H. Goetzmann, *Army Exploration in the American West, 1803–1863* (New Haven, 1959), pp. 274–275.

muleteers, each of the four initial survey parties hurried into the field included men with field survey experience, and others trained in medicine, astronomy, meteorology, botany, geology, and natural history. Each also included a cartographer and one or more artists to provide pictures of the notable sights along the way and to delineate the specimens collected. Never before had any significant area of the country been so thoroughly and systematically subjected to the inspection of so many trained observers.

With astonishing despatch, three of the survey parties were organized and in the field before the summer of 1853; and a fourth, to cover the southernmost-proposed routes, was launched from California early in 1854. Meanwhile other parties had been organized to attack the formidable location problems for rail lines between California's three principal towns, San Diego, Los Angeles, and San Francisco, and a northward route from San Francisco to Fort Vancouver on the Columbia. Those Western teams were also directed to seek feasible passes through the Sierras for each of the east-west routes. Of the six proposed routes from the Mississippi to the Pacific, Secretary Davis believed there was already in hand sufficient information on the Oregon Trail-South Pass route to weigh its merits *vis-à-vis* the others. And, with all the fresh information garnered in the Mexican War and the ensuing boundary surveys, much the same was true of the two proposed Far Southern routes; as these duplicated so much of their way, a single survey team was assigned to that area.[4]

Isaac I. Stevens, the newly appointed territorial governor of Washington Territory, was selected to head the largest of all the survey parties, that assigned to seek a feasible route from St. Paul to Fort Vancouver. The energetic, ambitious, and efficient Stevens, a West Point man, veteran of the Mexican War campaigns, with experience in the Coast Survey, was to prove a most effective leader in his dangerous and difficult investigations across the least well-known reaches of the nation. Stevens had little advance information of much of the vast mountain area other than that provided by Lewis and Clark. In those northern latitudes he was instructed to

[4]The reports of these surveys, including a massive array of scientific data, were published between 1855 and 1861 under the title *Reports of Exploration and Surveys to Ascertain the Most Practicable and Economic Route for a Railroad from the Mississippi River to the Pacific Ocean* (12 vols., Washington, D.C., 1855–61). Better known as *Pacific Railroad Reports*, they will be cited so hereafter.

examine carefully the passes of the several mountain ranges, the geography and meteorology of the whole intermediate region, the character, as avenues of trade and transportation, of the Missouri and Columbia rivers, the rains and snows of the route, especially in the mountain passes, and, in short, to collect every species of information bearing upon the question of railroad practicability,

including the natives encountered along the way.[5]

To accomplish these wide objectives Stevens launched four separate survey teams, two from the Mississippi and two from the West Coast. Of the two working west, one under his personal direction marched overland from St. Paul; the other went up the Missouri to rendezvous with Stevens at Fort Union at the mouth of the Yellowstone, from where they continued together to Fort Benton (Fort McKenzie of earlier days) within view of the Rockies. A similar plan was employed by the parties moving east from Fort Vancouver under the direction of Captain George B. McClellan, later to become notable as an over-cautious Union army commander. McClellan himself led an expedition from Fort Vancouver northeast across the Cascades, thence to Fort Spokane to investigate possible passes through the Bitterroot Range to a general rendezvous of all four parties in the valley east of that towering range. To supply the rendezvous, he despatched his other party up the Columbia to Fort Walla Walla, from where it was to continue straight east across the mountains to the projected rendezvous. Considering the difficulties of communication between the several parties, the lateness of the season, and the rough, little known terrain, it was a complex plan. In practice it proved even more complex, for in order to cover as much as possible of the entire area under Stevens's purview, all four parties repeatedly detached reconnoitering bands to make investigatory circuits north and south of their main line of travel. At least four of these explored well up into Canada, and others as far south as Fort Hall on the Snake and the Oregon Trail, and the Flathead camp below the Yellowstone. All in all, it was an incredibly dispersed but remarkably correlated performance.

The plains across which Stevens led his survey team west from St. Paul had long since been revealed by Carver, Catlin, Nicollet, and numerous others, so Stevens's journey from the Mississippi to the mountains will not be described here. It was at Fort Benton that the

[5]Unless otherwise noted, this brief account of Stevens's survey is based upon Albright, *Official Explorations*, Chap. 4.

crucial part of his survey began. Stevens left an able contingent at the fort to make winter-long meterological observations, and to note the accumulations of snows in the passes over the continental divide beyond. From Fort Benton west the location of passes, the grades of their approaches, and the likelihood of their being blocked by snow became the chief concern of the survey. The very nature of the inhospitable climate, the season, the series of serried mountain ranges and narrow valleys that made indirect routes, willy nilly, essential, all imposed other obstacles and limitations in the months ahead. It was already September, wintry in that latitude, when Stevens left Fort Benton in search of passes over the Lewis range. Several were located and studied, among them that at the head of the Sun River that Captain Lewis had found on his return trip, and Cadotte's Pass, over which Stevens led his party to Bitterroot Valley and the planned rendezvous. By early October three of his four parties and several reconnoitering details had converged at Fort Owen, their appointed meeting place, on a tributary of the Bitterroot, from which "right and left" the serried ranges of mountains "were very rough and rugged, many peaks being jagged."[6]

Since each of these parties included surveyors and other technical personnel who had been busy along their several routes to Fort Owen, Stevens's basic survey was virtually completed when they met up at Fort Owen, except for such information as McClellan might add about possible passes over the Cascades to Puget Sound. But there remained much, in the way of detail, to fill in, and numerous alternate possibilities to investigate. Compression of the accounts of the several Pacific Railroad surveys into a single chapter permits few details, but here and there observations and sidelights demand our attention, however brief. Among these, in the case of Stevens's survey, were his Indian activities. All the way across the plains and into the mountains, with dual intent, he had sought out the natives of the area: to determine their disposition toward white intrusions, a requirement of his instructions; but also to make their acquaintance as a means to promoting intertribal peace councils. Most of the Indians he had met with on the plains—representatives of the same nations that, a half century earlier, had evoked the admiration of Lewis and Clark, and a generation later of Catlin— had in Stevens's view, sadly degenerated into dirty, miserable beg-

[6]*Pacific Railroad Reports,* vol. 1, p. 518.

gars. On the other hand, he found the Pend d'Oreilles and their neighboring tribes, who were relatively isolated in the valleys beyond the mountains, still a proud and independent people. Although they too had come under the influence of whites a dozen years back, theirs was the gentle guidance of the famous Father de Smet, at whose mission they had received and profited by instruction in agriculture and other arts; and they had been spared the evil influences of the traders and trappers suffered by less secluded peoples.[7]

When Stevens, after only a few days of rest and deployment, set out again in late September, he left behind one of his most valued lieutenants, John Mullan, that he might monitor the Indian peace parley they had scheduled to be held there next season. Among his deployments before departure was that of a reconnaissance of all possibly usable passes over the rugged Bitterroot Range, including Lewis and Clark's Lolo. After Stevens's departure Mullan spent a profitable and busy winter in the mountains keeping tabs on snow accumulations in the important passes of the area and undertaking valuable reconnaissances in every direction from his Bitterroot post, one of which took him all the way south to Fort Hall on the Snake. Although the achievements of Mullan's and some of the other detached units were remarkable, even amazing, none exceeded that of Dr. George Suckley, Stevens's chief naturalist. In mid-October he set out in a canoe down the unknown and unmapped Bitterroot River, aiming to follow its waters to the Pacific. His tiny craft carried him down the circuitous course of the Bitterroot, past Clark's Fork and Pend Oreille Lake, and finally to the Columbia itself, a distance of 1,059 miles, with but 60 miles of portage. He completed that feat in fifty-nine days, without neglecting to make entries in the diary of his voyage or failing to gather and preserve an extensive botanical collection.

Stevens and the main party had made their way north down the Bitterroot, crossed the Bitterroot Range, and followed a trail to an active mission of Father de Smet's followers on Coeur d'Alene Lake, from which they continued west to Spokane House, an abandoned trading post. Learning from some Spokane Indians that McClellan was only a few hours journey north at Fort Colville, Stevens joined him there to receive his report and tie their surveys together. The

[7]*Ibid.*, vol. 1, p. 518.

lateness of the season and the poor condition of their animals dissuaded them from continuing west into the Cascades. Instead, they repaired south to Walla Walla; from there they followed the riverside path to Fort Vancouver, and then moved north to Olympia to search for an acceptable pass over the mountains to the east of Puget Sound.

Despite all the energy, effort, and talent invested in the survey of the Northern route, when Stevens's report appeared in Volumes 1 and 2 of the *Pacific Railroad Reports,* it was flawed in several respects. Most damaging was Stevens's ill-concealed bias in favor of his own route. His enthusiasm was too blatant to inspire confidence in his findings—an impression compounded by an obvious underestimate of construction costs in comparison with the estimates for other possible routes. The cautious McClellan contributed additional doubts when twice he turned back from passes through the Cascades east of the Sound, doubts that persisted even after civilian engineers announced the discovery of a feasible route through Snoqualmoo Pass. To cap it all, it became apparent that Stevens's enthusiasm was not shared by some of his own personnel, one of whom submitted a dissenting report recommending the Oregon Trail-South Pass approach to the Northwest.[8] Thus, despite the fact his was the only survey under one man's direction all the way to the coast, and became the first of the several *Pacific Railroad Reports* to be published, Stevens practically eliminated the Northern route from serious consideration.

In addition to the attention gained by its priority, Stevens's report added dimensions to the concept of the American Northwest through numerous impressive illustrations (including thirteen magnificent plates) reproducing the drawings and paintings of John Mix Stanley, chief artist of the expedition. Enthralled by the West from boyhood, Stanley at twenty had left his native New York for Detroit, Chicago, and then Fort Snelling, where he began to create an Indian Gallery on the order of Catlin's. Like Catlin, to add to its variety, he later moved down to Fort Gibson in Indian Territory to paint Indians transported there from the East as well as the native denizens of the southern plains. At Santa Fe, in 1846, he had joined General Stephen Watts Kearny's Army of the West as artist, on its march to California and the Stockton-Frémont confrontation. Re-

[8]Goetzmann, *Army Exploration,* pp. 281–283.

cruited by Stevens to serve as chief artist for the Northern survey, he was soon doubling as Stevens's deputy, leading at least one of the reconnaissance expeditions. Moreover, when he used the daguerreotype equipment he had brought along, he became the earliest photographer of a Western expedition.[9] Among Stanley's most notable works on the survey was his sketch of the Minne-ha-ha or Laughing Water, in southeast Dakota, immortalized by Longfellow. Another was his "Herd of Bison, Near Jessie Lake," which is perhaps the most effective painting ever done of a buffalo herd, giving the viewer some idea of the incredible numbers of those beasts still roaming the prairies of North Dakota after a half century of profligate decimation.[10]

It was inevitable that citizens of St. Louis and San Francisco should believe that a route from one to the other across the belt line of the country was the logical location for the country's first transcontinental railway. For decades Senator Benton had campaigned, first for a national road, and then for a railroad to run across the waistline of the West and join those two cities. He had mustered wide support. By mid-century, with sectional antagonisms ensuring bitter opposition to both the Northern and the Southern routes, political realities seemed to enhance the chances of his central route. Consequently, intense attention was focused on the survey of the route between the 38th and 39th parallels. Secretary Davis— well aware that many suspected him of having already prejudged the findings of the surveys in favor of one of the Southern routes—was scrupulous in his selection of the survey leaders, as indicated by his choice of Captain John W. Gunnison to lead the survey of this central route. Gunnison, a forty-one-year-old rural New Englander with extensive experience in the Seminole Wars and on topographical surveys in the Great Lakes country and the Northwest, had already achieved a national reputation.[11]

[9]Robert Taft, *Photography and the American Scene* (New York, 1938), p. 261; Robert Taft, *Artists and Illustrators of the Old West, 1850–1900* (New York, 1953), pp. 8–21, 269–275. See also W. Vernon Kinietz, *John Mix Stanley and His Indian Paintings* (Ann Arbor, Mich., 1942).

[10]Taft, *Artists and Illustrators,* pp. 14–16. Although approaching winter hastened their passage through the mountains to Fort Vancouver, Stanley somehow found time and subjects enough in those rugged regions to provide another thirty illustrations depicting that little known section of the country.

[11]Gunnison had also had experience in the West as assistant to Captain Howard Stansbury's outstanding information-gathering expedition to the Great Basin in

With Lieutenant E. G. Beckwith as his second-in-command, Gunnison's wagon train set out on June 23, 1853, from the mouth of the Kansas on the Santa Fe road. With him went an able complement of engineers and scientists, among them James Schiel, a German geologist; Frederick Ceutzfeldt, a German botanist; and R. H. Kern, topographer, who, with his two brothers, Benjamin and Edward, physician and artist, five years before had been with Frémont on his disastrous foray through western Colorado. Under a July sun Gunnison's wagons creaked across the prairie toward the headwaters of the Arkansas, specifically seeking its tributary, the Heurfano, to lead them across the towering Sangre de Cristo Mountains, through which Pike's band had suffered, into San Luis Valley and the headwaters of the Rio Grande.[12]

After effecting a painful crossing of those mountains, Gunnison's party set out to search up the San Luis Valley north and west for a feasible route for a rail line to follow from the valley, across the intervening confusion of peaks and disorderly ranges separating the valley from that of the Grand River (now the Upper Colorado). Carefully avoiding the inviting gap in the mountains to the west that had lured Frémont's party to disaster, Gunnison's party pushed on northwest to discover a trail with an encouragingly easy grade to Cochetopa Pass and the continental divide. But the approach proved deceptive. When they started down its west slope, they found the gradient far too steep. On descending from the pass to the river that now bears Gunnison's name, they discovered that it and its tributary streams flowed through deep gorges that would present major construction difficulties for a rail line. Reaching the mouth of the Gunnison, the party crossed the Colorado to its north bank and set out westward over extremely difficult terrain to where the Spanish Trail crossed the Green River. From there, through "country destitute of wood," "desolate and disheartening in the extreme," the Spanish Trail took them along the east flank and then

1849–50, a crucial section of the central route—Howard Stansbury, *Exploration and Survey of the Valley of the Great Salt Lake of Utah*, Senate Exec. Doc. 3, 32d Congress, Spec. Sess., U.S. serial no. 608 (1851); also commercial editions, Philadelphia and London (1853). While wintering among the Mormons, Gunnison gathered the material for a book on the Deseret theocracy that had further enhanced his reputation— John W. Gunnison, *The Mormons or Latter Day Saints in the Valley of the Great Salt Lake, a History of their Rise and Progress, Peculiar Doctrines, Present Conditions and Projects* (Philadelphia, 1852).

[12] *Pacific Railroad Reports*, vol. 2, pt. 1, p. 34; Albright, p. 89, and Chap. V, generally.

across the Wasatch range[13] to the valley of the Sevier River, which flows north as if to fall into Great Salt Lake before reversing direction to flow into Sevier Lake. Approaching that "bucolic valley," and imagining at least a temporary surcease of hardship, Gunnison exulted that "the great mountains have been passed and a new wagon road open(ed) across the continent—a work which was almost unanimously pronounced impossible" by those who knew these parts.[14]

With almost two months remaining before the arrival of winter, Gunnison decided to reconnoiter the Sevier River region. Accordingly, he set out with a small party for desert-girt Sevier Lake, where the river sacrifices its waters to desert sands. But before they reached the lake, early in the morning of October 26 while they were still asleep in their riverside camp, a band of revenge-seeking "Pah-Utahs" (Pai-Utes or Parvante) attacked, slaughtering and mutilating almost the entire party. Among the eight slain were Creutzfeldt, Richard Kern, and Gunnison himself, "pierced with fifteen arrows." Lieutenant Beckwith assumed command and marched north for Salt Lake City a few days later, following Gunnison's original plan to winter there while making inspections of possibly usable passes through the Wasatch range east of the lake.[15]

In the course of the winter of 1853–54 Beckwith prepared a report and sent it off to Washington. In it he calculated that from the mouth of the Kansas they had covered 1,560 miles, along which, "at enormous expense," he thought a railroad could be built. While awaiting his instructions in Salt Lake City, Beckwith had the good fortune to enlist an addition to his party who would add greatly to the survey of the route on to California, and especially to Beckwith's report in its published form. He was Baron F. W. von Egloffstein, Frémont's topographer, who had arrived from Parowan—the village Frémont's party had reached in near-starving condition after their winter crossing of the mountains. Following the breakup of the Frémont expedition, Egloffstein had sought refuge in Salt Lake City, where Beckwith persuaded him to take Kern's place as artist and topographer of his survey.[16]

---

[13]Albright, *Official Explorations*, p. 92; *Railroad Reports*, vol. 2, pt. 1, p. 61.
[14]*Railroad Reports*, vol. 2, pt. 1, p. 70.
[15]Albright, *Official Explorations*, p. 94n; Goetzmann, *Army Exploration*, pp. 285, 310. Suspicions of Mormon involvement in the raid put further strain on the already tense relations between the Deseret settlers and Washington.
[16]Taft, *Artists and Illustrators*, pp. 263–264.

While awaiting his own instructions from Washington, Beckwith launched an expedition east up the canyon of the Weber and on across the Wasatch range to Fort Bridger on a small tributary of the Green River, the southwest Wyoming home of the mountain man Jim Bridger, who had discovered Great Salt Lake in 1824 and guided Stansbury's 1850 expedition to the Great Basin. On his return across the Wasatchs Beckwith led his survey team by way of the Echo and Weber canyons, the eventual route of the Union Pacific Railroad. He also determined that, further south, Timpanogos Canyon could provide a practicable way through the range.[17]

On May 3, 1854, having received his instructions, Beckwith headed west across the Great Basin and the salt deserts to Pilot Mountain, thence to the Sierras in the latitude of Pit River and volcanic Mount Lassen, where in the west rose Mount Shasta's magnificent snow-capped cone. Exploring the Sierras to the south, Beckwith surveyed Madeline Pass and Pit River, which is edged by canyons that prevented passage of his wagons and compelled him to take Lassen's road through Noble's Pass in the Honey Lake region; from there he went on to the Sacramento at Fort Redding, which he reached on July 22.[18]

Lieutenant Beckwith's two reports, which appeared the following year in Volume 2 of the *Pacific Railroad Reports,* made clear that the difficulties presented would render the route he and Gunnison had followed impractical. Its impact was therefore predominantly negative. An important exception was Beckwith's reassurance of the feasibility of a direct approach through Weber River Canyon to Great Salt Lake from the east.

Of inestimable value, however, were the illustrations accompanying the Gunnison-Beckwith part of the *Reports.* They provided outstanding revelations of Far Western places and people seldom or never before pictured. After John Mix Stanley had finished his own

[17]Albright, *Official Explorations,* pp. 95–96; *Pacific Railroad Reports,* vol. 2, pt. 2, Chaps. 2–5. After wintering in Salt Lake City, in the spring of 1850 Captain Howard Stansbury of the Topographical Corps had surveyed the Weber River-Echo Creek route through the Wasatchs. It was Stansbury who first recognized the marks indicating the existence in earlier geological times of a great inland sea occupying the Great Basin—Stansbury, *Exploration and Survey;* Richard Bartlett, *Great Surveys of the American West* (Norman, Okla., 1962), p. 176.

[18]Albright, *Official Explorations,* pp. 97–100; *Railroad Reports,* vol. 2, pt. 2. The report Beckwith prepared for Gunnison and the Kern-Stanley illustrations appeared in vol. 2, pt. 1.

work for Stevens's report, using field sketches left by Kern, he prepared twelve full-page color plates, mostly landscapes, for the Gunnison-Beckwith report. Equally illuminating were the illustrations by Egloffstein in Part 2 of Volume 2. They were invaluable in providing a properly impressive picture of the immensity of Western landscapes and the gargantuan problems to be faced when it came to building a railroad across the harsh topography of the geologically raw mountains of the West. Perhaps Egloffstein was more scientist than artist. In any case his maps were superb. His panoramas could almost serve as armchair reconnaissances for a railroad location engineer, while the rock formations in his foregrounds were detailed enough to illustrate a geology text. His striking drawing of the Weber River Canyon, with the river winding deep in its sinuous gorge, is both an exciting work of art and an accurate enough portrayal to forewarn the location men of the Union Pacific of the problems they would face in the Wasatch range. One of Egloffstein's four striking foldout panoramas is a "wide-angle" view, looking west from Noble's Pass in the Sierras, with horsemen in the foreground filing along a trail through rocky, sparsely vegetated country; the figures lend perspective to the meticulously delineated, seemingly impassable escarpments fronting the wide sweep of serried mountain crests to the skyline, except where the magnificent snowy cone of Mount Shasta provides elegant accent to the immensity of the scene.

The third route to be studied was that along the 35th Parallel. The part of the corridor between the Mississippi and Santa Fe had already attracted more attention from explorers and writers than any other part of the trans-Mississippi region, except for the Missouri–Kansas–Platte River region. It was into this Old Southwest that the first organized scientific exploration under Major Stephen Long had been sent in 1820. To this region the naturalist Thomas Nuttall had journeyed in 1818. Washington Irving came there in 1832; and, soon afterwards, Catlin and Stanley with their palettes and brushes. In 1839 and 1840 the fascinating Dr. Josiah Gregg, who a few years later would become famous on two continents for his engrossing book *The Commerce of the Prairies,*[19] had blazed a supe-

---

[19]2 vols., published in New York and London, 1844. In addition to numerous subsequent editions, Gregg's work was reprinted in Reuben Gold Thwaites (ed.), *Early Western Travels, 1748–1846* (vols. 19 and 20, Cleveland, 1905). My citations are

rior trade route, almost entirely within a degree of the 35th Parallel, along the Canadian River from Fort Smith to Santa Fe, and marked it out on his superior map of the Southwest.

In 1849 political pressures to transform Gregg's trail into a Fort Smith-Santa Fe emigrant road had mounted to the point that a most ambitious reconnaissance—the joint enterprise of the army and the Topographical Corps—had been launched across the region. The survey team was under the command of Captain Randolph B. Marcy, an infantry officer, and army engineer Captain George McClellan, who was doubling as military escort for almost 500 California-bound emigrants.[20] Perhaps it was the wide diversity of recorded impressions, good and bad, some irreconcilable, that suggested to both Secretary Davis and Colonel Abert that another look at that corridor was needed—that, unlike the South Pass route, the information already accumulated was not sufficiently stable to support a decision as to its merits as a rail route.

To lead the new 35th Parallel survey, Secretary Davis selected yet another native of the Northeast, Lieutenant Amiel Weeks Whipple, who was an able and scientifically oriented scion of an old Massachusetts family, with a background of almost ten years experience with the Northeastern Border Survey and the Mexican Boundary Survey.[21] The group of scientists, artists, and technicians selected to accompany him was second only to Stevens's party in numbers and talent.

Yet, with so much attention focused on the area in the past, there was little that Whipple's party could add in the way of significant new impressions of the country until it left the Mississippi Valley. At least that would have been the case had not the Whipple team included Heinrich Balduin Möllhausen, the young German artist, who had been attached to the party in the capacity of topographer

to the abridged University of Nebraska Press edition, edited by Milo Milton Quaife (Lincoln, Nebr., 1967).

[20]Captain Marcy's report was published as Senate Executive Document 64, 31st Congress, 1st Sess., U.S. serial no. 562 (1850). His report was generally favorable except for the lofty Texas Llano Estacado, "in places two hundred miles wide, without a tree or running stream throughout its entire surface," which presented, in his judgment, "an impassable barrier" for wagon road or railway—Grant Foreman (ed.), *Adventure on Red River: Report on the Exploration of the Headwaters of Red River by Captain Randolph B. Marcy and Captain G. B. McClellan* (Norman, Okla., 1937), pp. 180–181.

[21]Albright, *Official Explorations,* p. 104. Except as noted, the account here of Whipple's expedition is based on Albright, Chap. 6.

although he styled himself a "naturalist." Möllhausen kept a diary that later, when he returned to his native Germany, he turned into a romantic odyssey, while the dramatic paintings he made along the way, many of which were utilized to illustrate the published report of the expedition, leavened the pedestrian, factual account of its laconic leader.[22]

It was torrid mid-July before Whipple's file of wagons creaked west out of Fort Smith, more than a month after the expedition's leaders, engineers, scientists, and two German cooks had arrived at the fort by steamboat from St. Louis. Almost immediately they entered Indian Territory and the reservation of the transplanted Choctaws. They soon reached the Shawnee towns, where a guide was enlisted. Then they passed, successively, settlements of the Delaware and Kickapoo, also forcibly transplanted from east of the Mississippi but already displaying progress in reestablishing themselves as farmers, while still retaining the distinct and varied cultural traditions that had attracted first Catlin and then Stanley to the region.[23]

Beyond the Indian settlements, Whipple's column entered the notorious Cross Timbers, which stretched 40 miles along the watershed between the Canadian and Washita; it was a strange and savage region of extensive scrubby forest, meagerly supported on a terrain frequently cleft by "deep ravines . . . the beds of temporary streams," a region Irving had described as "rough and cheerless country" and progress across it "like struggling through forests of cast iron."[24] Gregg, knowing its reputation, when he traveled this

[22]Taft, *Artists and Illustrators*, pp. 22ff. Möllhausen's book, which contains his diary of the Whipple expedition, was entitled *Diary of a Journey from the Mississippi to the Coasts of the Pacific with a United States Government Expedition* (trans., 2 vols., London, 1858). This was the German's second venture into the American West. The first was up the Missouri where, despite harsh experiences, after wintering among the Otoes he confessed to having been tempted to wed a half-breed and cast his lot with her people. In later years Möllhausen used the material of his American experiences and observations for a long string of popular novels that earned him the title of a German Fenimore Cooper.

[23]Twenty years earlier, before these Eastern Indians had been settled here, Washington Irving had been impressed by this region where the Arkansas was "a broad and rapid stream, bordered by a beach of fine sand, overgrown with willows and cottonwood trees. Beyond, the eye wandered over a beautiful champaign country, of flowery plains and sloping uplands, diversified by groves and clumps of trees, and long screens of woodlands—Washington Irving, *A Tour on the Prairies*, edited by J. F. McDermott (Norman, Okla., 1956), pp. 36, 41.

[24]*Ibid.*, p. 152.

way crossed to the north side of the Canadian to avoid it.[25] Hot on the heels of the Cross Timbers ordeal came a new hazard for Whipple's men, a great prairie fire, set by the Indians to bring on new grass. To the men the fierce conflagration looked like Hell itself as it swept across the country, with a noise "like the distant hollow trembling of the earth when thousands of buffalo are tearing and trampling over it with heavy hooves." Afterwards, for days they crunched across the charred stubble in the blackened path of the fire, with kerchiefs pulled down over their faces against the smoke and suffocating clouds of dust raised from the ash by the wagon train.[26] Dr. Gregg, who in the same long grass region had endured a similar experience, reported that the "terror which the prairie conflagrations are calculated to inspire when the grass is tall and dry" is "sufficient to daunt the stoutest heart."[27]

After that ordeal, it was easy going along the wide valley of the Canadian all the way to the Antelope Buttes, at the hundredth meridian. Whipple saw those buttes scientifically as merely the ragged fringes of the notorious Llano Estacado or Staked Plains, the inhospitable Texas plateau Captain Randolph Marcy had branded "the Zahara of North America."[28] Strangely enough, in that same repellant region less than two decades earlier Dr. Gregg had found "buffalo, deer and the fleet antelope," and "the graceful and majestic mustang" sweeping "across the naked country," as well as numerous "dog-towns, so often alluded to by prairie travelers."[29] Here too was the beginning of the traditional domain of the Kiowa and Comanche, fierce kinsmen of the Aztecs,[30] a proximity that added fear of those marauding wild horsemen to the expedition's discomfiture. Reflecting Gregg's feeling of kinship between prairie country and the open sea, Möllhausen was moved by these empty plains to think of the sea, where one "looks round the horizon for a sail" and rejoices if one is sighted; but on the Llano, one seeks "in vain for such a consolation; no tree or shrub breaks the montony of the plain," and while the ocean's heavings "show it to be still alive, the Llano Estacado is dead, and varied only by the deceitful mi-

[25]Gregg, *Commerce of the Prairies*, p. 321.
[26]H. Craig Miner, *The St. Louis-San Francisco Transcontinental Railroad* (Lawrence, Kans., 1972), p. 9.
[27]Gregg, *Commerce of the Prairies*, p. 306.
[28]Goetzmann, *Army Exploration*, p. 217.
[29]Gregg, *Commerce of the Prairies*, p. 196.
[30]Clark Wissler, *Indians of the United States* (New York, 1940), pp. 235–237.

rage." Some of those mirages were spectacular. One so magnified an antelope in flight before a prairie fire that the creature seemed to fill half the sky, only to split into two galloping animals, one upside down.[31] On those same plains an earlier traveler, already prudently uneasy in the environs of the Kiowa and Comanche, was greatly disconcerted by a mirage in which the figure of a mounted Indian "swept along the horizon," looking "very giant," and then quickly "another and another burst upon our view, on every side, which led us to believe we were surrounded."[32]

As the survey continued westward through this home of the jack rabbit and the coyote, the Canadian River, frequently in view, became increasingly outlandish. Whipple read in Dr. Gregg's book that it wore a perpetual snowcap on its head in the distant Rockies and had its mouth in the Arkansas 900 miles to the east. Strange and erratic, the river bore little resemblance to the decorous New England streams of Whipple's boyhood, or to those of Möllhausen's Germany, flowing gently between neat green banks. Dr. Gregg had reported that at a place 80 miles from its source it was still but "a rippling brook," while one of its minor tributaries, sometimes flowing out of the Llano Estacado, had a bed "at least 2000 yards wide without a vestige of water," and the Canadian itself sometimes went dry 400 miles from its source.[33] But it was flowing now, and presented a magnificent sight as its waters wound through a picturesque valley guarded by majestic cliffs, weirdly sculptured and cleft in places to reveal mesas in the process of creation.

At Tucumcari Creek they left the river, whose course had guided them for some 800 miles, to follow Gregg's old trading path southwest across the Pecos, at Anton Chico, thence down into the Rio Grande Valley to Albuquerque, which they reached in early October.[34] They settled down in that old Mexican town for a month's rest and preparation for the greater challenges that awaited them further west. In addition to the commonly expected hazards of travel across long reaches of arid wilderness, rough terrain, and deserts few had dared to cross, it was well known that they would run the risk of encounters with several decidedly disaffected groups of na-

[31]Miner, *St. Louis-San Francisco Railroad,* p. 10.
[32]Goetzmann, *Army Exploration,* p. 125, quoting Lt. James W. Abert.
[33]Gregg, *Commerce of the Prairies,* pp. 96, 307.
[34]Grant Foreman (ed.), *A Pathfinder in the Southwest: The Itinerary of Lieutenant A. W. Whipple During His Exploration for a Railway Route from Fort Smith to Los Angeles in the Years 1853 & 1854* (Norman, Okla., 1941).

tives. Whipple had with him a tracing of a map that Captain Lorenzo Sitgreaves and his cartographer, R. H. Kern, had recently completed for Sitgreaves's forthcoming report, covering an expedition he had led across the same region in the fall of 1851.[35] Here and there Whipple had garnered considerable other information as to the country they were about to penetrate, but nothing on the order of what he had been heir to on his route from Fort Smith. Besides, since Sitgreaves had been seeking a route for a wagon road, the more exacting specifications for a rail route might call for a far different route from that Sitgreaves had found feasible, particularly in a geologically young country characteristically devoid of gentle slopes and widely spaced contour lines.

Early in November Whipple's wagons snaked their way out of Albuquerque and into the mountains to the west, aiming for the famous Zuñi pueblo beyond the continental divide, 150 miles away. Sitgreaves had brought back a drawing of a festival in progress in the plaza at Zuñi. In the background, like a giant stairway rising from the plaza, was Zuñi's many-storied masonry structure, impressive enough to have given rise to accounts that, in 1540, attracted Coronado to the place in his search for the mythical Seven Cities of Cíbola. Disappointed in finding Zuñi no golden city, Coronado had despatched one of his lieutenants to search further north, an assignment that led to something far more wonderful but equally disappointing to gold-distracted conquistadors—the awesome chasm of the Grand Canyon of the Colorado.[36]

The trail from Albuquerque to Zuñi, after making its way through forbidding great lava beds and crossing the continental divide in the Zuñi Mountains, passed near El Moro, the "Inscription Rock" of earlier explorers,[37] a great fortress-like rock that for ages past the Indians had utilized to display their arcane figures and ritual glyphs. Beneath it, and on the walls of a neighboring butte, seventeenth-century Spaniards had played their Ozymandian parts, chiseling their messages to posterity, which the fascinated Whipple and Möllhausen tried to transcribe.[38] When the Whipple party reached

[35]*Report on an Expedition Down the Zuñi and Colorado Rivers*, Lorenzo Sitgreaves, Senate Exec. Doc. 59, 32d Congress, 2d Sess., U.S. serial no. 668 (1853).

[36]Herbert E. Bolton and Thomas M. Marshall, *The Colonization of North America* (New York, 1920), pp. 44–45; David B. Quinn, *North America from Earliest Discovery to First Settlements* (New York, 1977), pp. 197–200.

[37]Albright, *Official Explorations*, pp. 110–111; *Pacific Railroad Reports*, vol. 3, pt. 1, pp. 63–65.

[38]Goetzmann, *Army Exploration*, pp. 242–243.

Zuñi,[39] the pueblo was in the grip of a smallpox epidemic. Except for requisite formalities, the stop there to await the arrival of one of its reconnaissance teams was mostly devoted to studies of nearby ruins of old pueblos, with the expectation of identifying the Zuñi culture with that of the Aztecs.

Here Whipple was entering upon the crucial stage of his survey. Thus far, the route investigated offered a relatively good way for a railroad. But now, across the semi-desert country of cliffs and canyons, it would be far more difficult to locate a feasible route. Since a dependable water supply was essential to a suitable way, Whipple led his party down Rio Puerco, a westward-flowing tributary of the Colorado Chiquito (now the Little Colorado). The Puerco led them through the amazing Petrified Forest, where for miles the sparsely vegetated, sandy ground was strewn with fractured columns, the broken shafts of giant trees up to 200 feet in height, which had flourished when this semi-desert was a lush, well-watered country in Mesozoic times until some incredibly violent catastrophe suddenly leveled and buried them, to be transformed through nature's alchemy into beautiful columns of jasper, chalcedony, and onyx. To Whipple and Möllhausen, and particularly to Jules Marcou, the expedition's Swiss geologist, this was one of the great wonders of the world of science.[40]

When the Puerco joined the Colorado Chiquito, they continued on along the canyon of the latter until it became too difficult for the wagons. Realizing that the possibility of finding a practical rail route along the rim of the deepening canyons of the Colorado Chiquito and the Colorado itself was remote, Whipple turned his caravan more to the west and crossed the mountains between Bill Williams Mountain and the San Francisco Peaks, near the present Flagstaff, Arizona. On Christmas Eve, when they camped during the mountain crossing, a nostalgia prompted the men to celebrate by setting fire to nearby isolated pines, a magnificent setting for the songs ringing through the camp. Once over the mountains and seeking another river to follow, Whipple chose the Verde, a tributary of the Gila; but he abandoned it when he recognized his error, and struck

[39]Möllhausen painted a view of many-storied Zuñi nestled on a mesa, showing about a dozen levels of its stairlike structure—*Pacific Railroad Reports*, vol. 3, pt. 1, p. 67.

[40]Now the Petrified Forest National Park in eastern New Mexico. One of the fallen giants Whipple measured was 10 feet in diameter—*Pacific Railroad Reports*, vol. 3, pt. 1, p. 74.

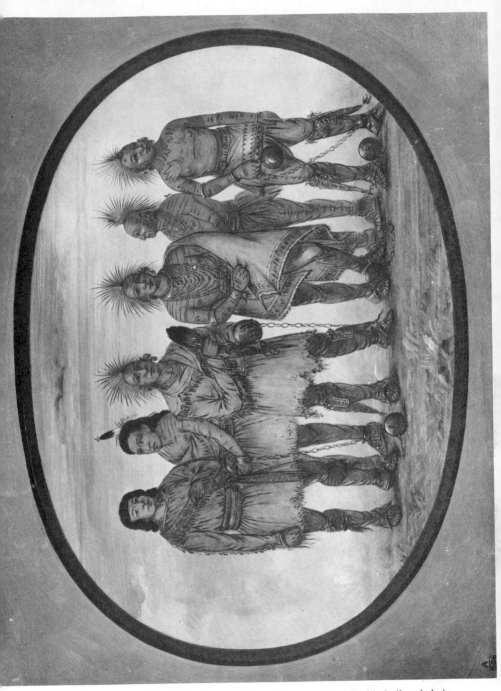

26. "Black Hawk and Five Other Sauk and Fox Prisoners," sketched in ball and chain, by George Catlin, at Jefferson Barracks, Missouri, in 1832.

(National Gallery of Art, Washington, D.C., Paul Mellon Collection.)

27. "Black Rock," an oil on canvas painting of a prairie chief, illustrating artist George Catlin's cartoon style of portrayal.

(National Collection of Fine Arts, Smithsonian Institution.)

28. "Comanche Village, Women Dressing Robes and Drying Meat," painting by George Catlin (1834).

(National Collection of Fine Arts, Smithsonian Institution.)

29.   Camp on the Missouri, from a painting by Karl (also known as Charles) Bodmer, artist accompanying Prince Maximilian of Wied on his 1833–34 expedition to the West.

(Thomas Cooper Library, University of South Carolina.) *(Jacket photo)*

30. Interior of a Mandan hut, after a painting by Karl Bodmer.

(Thomas Cooper Library, University of South Carolina.)

31. Battle between the Assiniboins and Blackfeet Indians before the palisades of Fort McKenzie, as portrayed by Karl Bodmer, who made his sketches for the painting while the battle was in progress.

(Thomas Cooper Library, University of South Carolina.)

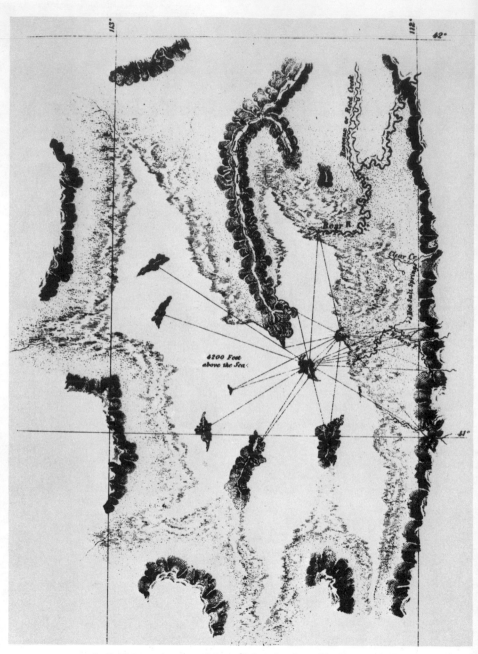

32. J. C. Frémont's map of Great Salt Lake, from his *Report* of 1845.
(University of South Carolina Information Services photograph.)

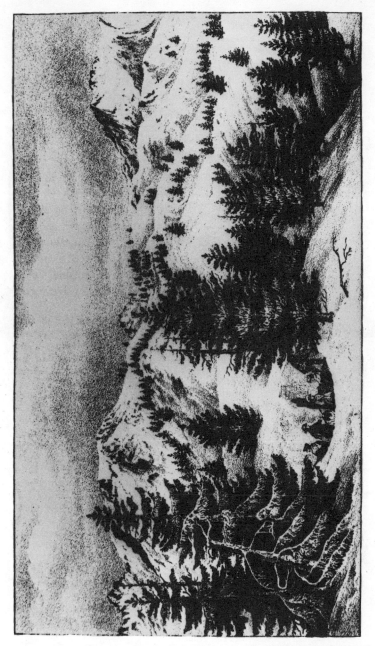

33. Pass in the Sierra Nevada of California, as depicted during Frémont's winter crossing of the range by his topographer, Charles Preuss.

(University of South Carolina Information Services photograph).

34. The pueblo of Zuñi in New Mexico, from a drawing by R. H. Kern, for Alonzo Sitgreaves' 1853 *Report*.

(The Beinecke Rare Book and Manuscript Library, Yale University.)

35. Buffalo near Lake Jessie in North Dakota, a painting by artist photographer John Mix Stanley, who accompanied Isaac I. Stevens on the 1853–54 survey of the most northern route proposed for a Pacific railroad.

(Thomas Cooper Library, University of South Carolina.)

36. First view of Grand Canyon, as drawn by F. W. von Egloffstein, and engraved by J. J. Young, for J. C. Ives' *Report on the Colorado River of the West.*

(The Beinecke Rare Book and Manuscript Library, Yale University.)

37. Mount of the Holy Cross in Western Colorado, from a drawing by William H. Jackson, photographer-artist with the 1873 Ferdinand V. Hayden expedition of 1873.

(The Beinecke Rare Book and Manuscript Library, Yale University.)

38. Granite Falls, Kiabab Division, Grand Canyon, from a drawing by Thomas Moran, from J. W. Powell's *Exploration of the Colorado River and its Canyons.*

(University of South Carolina Information Services photograph.)

39. "The Grand Canyon of the Yellowstone," a painting by Thomas Moran.

(Courtesy of the National Collection of Fine Arts, Smithsonian Institution; lent by the U.S.

40. Mammoth Hot Springs, Yellowstone Park, in an 1872 photograph by W. H. Jackson. The figure in the picture is artist Thomas Moran.

(Courtesy of the National Park Service.)

41. "The Chasm of the Colorado," an 1873 painting by Thomas Moran.

42. "Yosemite Falls," an 1855 pencil and chalk sketch of Yosemite Valley and Falls by Thomas Ayres.

(National Park Service Photo, Yosemite Collection.)

43. "Giant Redwood Trees of California," an 1868 painting by Albert Bierstadt. (Berkshire Museum).

out instead across arid highlands and the Aquarius range, to Big Sandy Arroyo. In crossing that country their compasses lost all direction among the magnetic hills, and mules died for lack of forage. But, following the arroyo, they eventually reached Bill Williams Fork and finally, at its mouth, in a desolate region, the great Colorado itself. On February 20, 1854, they gazed across the wide expanse of its "chocolate colored" waters.[41]

Where three sharp peaks they named the Needles rose from a spur of the mountains close to the river, they found a feasible crossing place. There, with the assistance of a band of Mojaves using their light craft made of tightly bound rushes, a crossing was effected over the half mile of swift current. The Mojaves, fascinated by the whites, with whom they had had little contact, guided Whipple's column along the Pai-Ute path across the desert to the Mojave River, "a beautiful stream of fresh water, from ten to twenty feet wide and a foot deep." The party followed down to where it disappeared into the desert sands. From there they made their way through Cajon Pass to Los Angeles.

Because of the possibility that the 35th Parallel route might serve as a compromise location, special attention had been focused on Whipple's assignment and his report was awaited with great interest. When it appeared, it carried Whipple's assertion without reservation "that, for the construction of a railway, the route we have passed over is not only practicable but in many respects eminently advantageous." That it was indeed practical time would prove when most of the 1,952 miles Whipple's survey had covered became the route of the Atchison, Topeka, and Santa Fe.[42]

The survey of the southernmost-proposed route for a Pacific railroad differed markedly from those of its rival routes in that it was the product of several investigations without temporal or physical continuity. The report covering that corridor was a composite creation. By mid-century there was already in hand a vast store of information touching on the route, garnered in the Mexican War campaigns and the boundary surveys that followed. Generally speaking, a reinvestigation focusing on problems peculiar to railroad construction was all that was deemed necessary.

[41]*Ibid.*, pp. 82–85, 109.
[42]Goetzmann, *Army Exploration*, pp. 288–289; Whipple's *Report* appeared in vols. 3 and 4 of the *Pacific Railroad Reports*.

The development of the 32nd Parallel survey started in the early months of the Mexican War, when General Stephen Kearny was directed to march from Fort Leavenworth to southern California. In December 1846 Kearny's army of a hundred dragoons, with a topographical unit of fourteen men under Lieutenant William H. Emory, reached the headwaters of the Gila River and followed it westward down to the Colorado. Marylander Emory, one of the brightest stars of an exceptionally able Topographical Corps, was an engineer of ability with a broad scientific mind, boundless energy, and powerful social and political connections. However, the conditions of a military unit, rushing through enemy territory on a critical mission to California, provided a far from ideal setting for the conduct of a first-class topographical survey. Early on he was visualizing a railroad crossing the continent along their line of march, declaring in his journal that the road from Santa Fe to Fort Leavenworth "presents few obstacles for a railway." But by the time the party started down the Gila Valley, the urgency of its westward pace had been reduced by a meeting with Kit Carson, heading east on the trail as Frémont's courier to Washington with the news of the success of the Bear Flag Revolt. A protesting Carson was compelled by Kearny to turn back to serve as guide to the expeditionary force.

Emory found much of interest in the way of life of the Pima villages along the Gila, where the people continued peacefully in their simple agricultural pursuits despite periodical raids by roving Apaches. He was impressed by the Pimas, noting that they were a "nation of what are termed wild Indians, surpassing many of the Christian nations in agriculture, little behind them in the useful arts, and immeasurably before them in honesty and virtue"—an opinion reinforced as he rode past more than 15 miles of carefully cultivated fields. The management of these fields inspired another interesting observation: that an agricultural operation dependent upon irrigation, "wherever practiced in a community with any success, or to any extent, involves a degree of subordination and absolute obedience to a chief repugnant to the habits of our people"—a principle about to be illustrated again by the success of the Mormon settlements in the Great Basin to the north under the absolutism of its hierachy.[43] Most of Emory's report on the Gila River area was excerpted for

[43]Goetzmann, *Army Exploration,* pp. 128–138.

inclusion in the *Pacific Railroad Reports* covering the 32nd Parallel survey.[44]

When the several Pacific Railroad Survey parties were being despatched into the field, public and diplomatic attention was again focused on the Gila River country that Emory had hurriedly examined in 1846–47. In December 1853 the Gadsden Purchase was arranged, by which the proposed Mexican boundary along the Gila River was moved 100 miles south, to secure for the United States territory thought to be essential to the location of a railroad across the desert Southwest. Moreover, although not included in the *Pacific Railroad Reports*, a mass of unpublished material had been in the process of accumulation by the Mexican Boundary Survey Commission since its creation in 1850, despite the internecine turmoil and dissension that almost constantly swirled about the Commission and periodically inundated it.[45] Often at the center of controversy was the director of the survey during most of its existence, John Russell Bartlett. Bartlett, a native Rhode Islander, and a bibliophile who operated a New York bookstore where many of the prominent scientists and writers of the day often lingered, was without qualifications to justify his political appointment to the position. He spent his survey years roaming far and wide, deep into Mexico and far up into California, gathering material for his *Personal Narrative of Explorations and Incidents in Texas, New Mexico, California, Sonora and Chihuahua.* [46] He hoped his opus would be as momentous a success as the current sensations of his friend John Lloyd Stephens, one of the habitués of his bookstore, whose two *Incidents of Travel* had sensationally revealed the antiquities of Central America and Yucatán.[47] As it turned out, Bartlett's profusely illustrated two-volume *Personal Narrative,* although less spectacular in its revelations, was a fitting companion for Stephens's works, and remains today one of the classic works on the American West. Until the official report of the Boundary Survey appeared in 1846, Bartlett's work was the principal published source of factual knowledge of the southwest border regions.

[44]*Pacific Railroad Reports,* vol. 2, pt. 6.

[45]Among those assisting in accumulating that data were both Emory and A. W. Whipple.

[46]The title continues: *Connected with the United States and Mexican Boundary Commission During the Years 1850, '51, '52 and '53* (New York, 1854).

[47]*Incidents of Travel in Central America, Chiapas and Yucatan* (2 vols., New York, 1841); *Incidents of Travel in Yucatan* (2 vols., New York, 1843).

After Emory's contributions both with Kearny and the Border Survey, the next expedition to become an adjunct of the 32nd Parallel survey was the search for routes from Fort Yuma, where the Gila joined the Colorado, to San Diego, Los Angeles, and San Francisco. While the several east-west surveys were in progress, solutions were being sought to the geographical difficulties presented by the north-south direction of the Coastal and Sierra ranges, and particularly by the merging of these ranges in southern California. Responsibility for the search for feasible ways to surmount these barriers was given to Lieutenant R. S. Williamson, with Lieutenant J. G. Parke serving as his assistant. Before they were done, their West Coast surveys would extend north all the way to the Columbia and south to Mexico. Their first objective, when they set out from San Francisco Bay in the summer of 1853, had been to locate feasible routes both from the Needles and Fort Yuma to Los Angeles and San Diego and into the San Joaquin Valley. They were soon successful in finding a reasonably direct approach to Los Angeles, and in establishing the feasibility of Tehachapi Pass[48] as a rail route from the Mojave Desert into San Joaquin Valley. But no feasible direct approach to San Diego could be discovered on American soil. Eventually, when a railroad into San Diego from the east was built, it was found necessary to route it partly below the border in Mexico.

After six months with Williamson's California investigations, Lieutenant Parke was directed to lead a new survey along the 32nd Parallel route from Fort Yuma to the east, retracing Emory's steps through the Gila Valley and on to El Paso. His principal concern was the availability of sufficient water and wood along the otherwise highly advantageous route.

While Parke was still making his way east to the Rio Grande in mid-February 1854, Captain John Pope was setting out from Dona Ana, on the Rio Grande a little upstream from El Paso, to cover the easternmost section of the proposed route. Pope's assignment carried him over harsh country, sparsely inhabited by dangerous, roving Apaches. As he progressed east to the Pecos, risking Indian attacks, Pope employed numerous reconnaissance details to find usable passes through the Hueco and Guadalupe mountains and to investigate thoroughly the southern reaches of that dreadful *terra*

[48]Found by Frémont on his first visit to California in April 1844.

THE GREAT WESTERN SURVEYS

incognita of west Texas, the Llano Estacado. On one occasion Indians set grass fires in an attempt to destroy his command. On another it was threatened by a band of Kiowas, heading toward the Llano Estacado on their way back from a plundering expedition into Mexico. Nevertheless, Pope was happy with his expedition's results. When he reached Fort Smith he was lavish in his praise of the 940-mile route he had surveyed from El Paso to Fort Preston on the Red River, much of it (some 350 miles) being through fertile, well-watered, and well-timbered country in the Upper Brazos and Trinity valleys.[49]

In 1854 the reports of the railroad survey leaders and their scientific companions, covering the several military-scientific expeditions, began to pour into the War Department. The next year, with the basic reports in hand, Secretary Davis rendered Congress a three-volume preliminary report, unillustrated and devoid of the accumulating masses of scientific data. It became immediately obvious, however, that if there were any in Congress who still harbored real hope that the surveys would provide conclusive factual data for a determination of the "most practicable and economical route for a railroad from the Mississippi to the Pacific Ocean," that hope would soon be dashed. In the climate of sharply mounting geographical and partisan differences by which the nation was riven in the mid-fifties, the surveys merely served to provide additional ammunition for verbal battles over the issue.[50] Nevertheless, Congress continued to support the great project to its conclusion. Late in 1855 the first of the thirteen massive, elegant, and impressive volumes of the *Pacific Railroad Reports* appeared, with successive volumes following until the final volume in 1860. The cost of publication of this monumental compilation of the complete reports, enhanced with numerous illustrations, beautiful color plates, and excellently executed maps, was over $1 million—more than twice the cost of the surveys themselves.[51]

Although the *Reports* failed to resolve the congressional impasse over the location of the first Pacific railroad, they were definitely not

[49]Albright, *Official Explorations,* pp. 133–144, 119–122, 124–129; Goetzmann, *Army Exploration,* pp. 289–295; *Pacific Railroad Reports,* vol. 5, pt. 1, vol. 2, pt. 5, vol. 2, pt. 4.

[50]Albright, *Official Explorations,* pp. 156–158; Goetzmann, *Army Exploration,* pp. 295ff.

[51]Taft, *Artists and Illustrators,* pp. 5–8.

without momentous consequences. In the ensuing decades, when practical men of business and engineers undertook the construction of rail lines to the Pacific, they generally followed the routes laid out in the *Pacific Railroad Reports*. Governor Stevens's route became substantially that of the Northern Pacific and Great Northern; the Central Pacific and Union Pacific utilized most of Stansbury's and Beckwith's route to win the rail race west, when, on May 10, 1869, the famous golden spike was driven at Promontory Point, Utah, the meeting point of those two converging lines. Whipple's route near the 35th Parallel became almost exactly that of the Atchison, Topeka, and Santa Fe; while Secretary Davis's recommended route, that of Pope, Emory, Parke, and Williamson, became substantially the location of the Southern Pacific and the Texas Pacific.[52]

The observations, descriptive information, statistical compilations, scientific illustrations, and classifications prepared by the 106 men of science who took part in the surveys comprised a scientific compendium of the American West probably unmatched anywhere in the history of scientific geography. The surveys provided, moreover, the warp and woof for a new and far more detailed mapping of the region. Using that data, the Topographical Corps engineer Lieutenant G. K. Warren and topographer-artist Egloffstein prepared the most important map of the trans-Mississippi West yet produced to accompany the *Reports*.[53] Warren's map left few extensive areas undetailed. Only the geography of those regions east of the Three Forks of the Missouri, including Yellowstone Park, parts of the Salmon River country, and Snake River Plateau; the Grand Canyon itself, and the Utah plateau country north of the canyon; and parts of the Llano Estacado of Texas, remained conjectural. Only in those areas were there natural wonders as yet unrevealed.

In the last analysis, however, the most consequential heritage of the Pacific Railroad Surveys was the stimulus they provided for further investigations of the West in more depth. The surveys of the fifties had been the culmination of a military-scientific partnership in romantic adventuring on a grand scale in search of a common pool of knowledge for each partner in enterprise—the pattern of which had been developing since Major Stephen H. Long led his

[52]J. D. Galloway, *The First Transcontinental Railroad* (New York, 1950), pp. 38–45.
[53]*Pacific Railroad Reports*, vol. 2; Goetzmann, *Army Exploration*, pp. 313–316. Also Appendix C, in which Goetzmann reprints Warren's account of the compilation of the map; a copy of Warren's map accompanies Goetzmann's volume.

coterie of scientists southwest to the "Great American Desert" in 1819–20. In the intervening years the military continued to enjoy a good press and much reflected glory for its part in these wilderness adventures, while for many eminent men of science the surveys provided providential opportunities to adventure at government expense and with army protection on field trips that often advanced them tremendously in their professions. For other scientists, safely ensconced in their ivy halls, the accumulating masses of specimens were likewise invaluable in a period when collecting and classification was a veritable scientific mania. A product of that military-scientific partnership, the Topographical Corps, from its formation on July 1, 1838, had been evoking wide public interest and garnering prestige, as expedition after expedition was launched into the romantic West. Then came the *Pacific Railroad Reports,* pregnant with political rivalries and economic consequences that enhanced the impact of their revelations. Even before the magnificent volumes of the *Reports* had come from the presses, the stream of wonders revealed by those expeditions had become a heady diet for public consumption. The nineteenth-century public had developed a taste and a seemingly insatiable appetite for descriptions and pictures of awesome mountains, belching volcanoes, magnificent waterfalls, black plateaus of the lava of the volcanic violence of earlier ages; of cruel deserts and incredible gorges; of trees unmatched elsewhere in the world, of cacti, the saguaro *(Cereus gigantea),* and lilies *(Yucca arborescens)* of tree size; of forests of stone; of the ancient cities of vanished people, some storied masonry structures, others perched high on ledges and in crevices of canyon walls; of romantic roving natives stubbornly rejecting the white man's ways and often antagonistic toward his approach; of untold stores of mineral riches, gold, silver, copper, and coal; of geysers and boiling springs, seas and deserts of salt, and a vast array of wildlife as varied as the land itself. All these marvels and many more had been carefully studied, measured, classified where susceptible to classification, and competently illustrated in the *Reports;* yet they were but the fruit of the traverse lines along which the topographical engineers and scientists had made their investigative ways. What wonders, what treasures might lie unrevealed in the vast virgin areas between those corridors, still awaiting disclosure by similarly organized teams of investigators?

In response to that persistent question, during the ensuing

decades expedition after expedition, of increasing refinement and specialization, set out not merely to shed light on the unexplored territories shown on Warren's map, but also to study in greater depth and detail every facet of even those deemed already explored. In 1857, even as Warren's map was being completed and dated, with UNEXPLORED lettered across the Grand Canyon region, Lieutenant Joseph Christmas Ives, who had served as Whipple's assistant on the 35th Parallel survey, was preparing to set out for the Colorado on a voyage that would give some inkling of its tremendous canyons. Artists Möllhausen and Egloffstein would impressively depict its fantastic gorges, while John Strong Newberry, the first geologist to view the canyon, read its geological history in the colorful strata of its walls and provided the means to tie its creation to the geological history of regions as far away as the Bad Lands of the Upper Missouri.

Even the trauma of war failed to halt this process. In 1860 Josiah Dwight Whitney, the first of a stream of outstanding scientists emanating from Yale, where they had been galvanized by Benjamin Silliman,[54] was appointed state geologist of California. There Whitney undertook an ambitious and elaborate survey of the marvelous resources of the burgeoning young state, and in the course of his work developed the triangulation survey method, which would soon become standard procedure for the mounting stream of similar government-sponsored surveys all across the West. Whitney and his chief assistant Clarence King—who in later years would lead many such surveys including the most ambitious of all (across a wide swathe from California to Nebraska) and become a highly effective writer of the West—were to play important roles in the eventual preservation of Yosemite, one of the world's greatest parks.[55]

During the postwar years, consonant with a romantic nation's enthrallment with the romantic West, to take part in a Western expedition became almost a *sine qua non* of the scientist of the day. Given the prominence of some who set out for the West, and the brilliance of others joining with the hope of speeding their climb up the scientific ladder, it was inevitable that scientists would gradually become the dominant partners in the structure of these surveys and

[54]Founder of Yale Medical School and principal figure in the establishment of Sheffield Scientific School; immensely popular in his field, Silliman was the most influential scientific man in America during the first half of the nineteenth century.
[55]Bartlett, *Great Surveys*, pp. 132–135.

investigative expeditions. Equally inevitable was their tendency to become more and more specialized. Perhaps the clearest illustration of both these trends were the several expeditions of Professor Orthaniel C. Marsh, whose paleontological collecting expeditions by 1870 had become sensational throughout the scientific world. On his extensive 1869 expedition, protected by a cavalry troop provided by General William T. Sherman and guided by William Cody (Buffalo Bill), the civilian arm was made up almost exclusively of his own graduate students. Its narrow focus produced sensational results, from fossil remains of tiny primitive horses and camels to the gigantic bones of a mastodon in the eroded strata along a North Platte tributary. Later in the season, in northern Colorado, Marsh's band of scientific hunters chipped from their resting places the remains of ancient turtles, giant dinosaurs, and the strange oreodon.[56] Marsh's already sensational fossil equine display—which graphically revealed the development of the horse from the toed, jack rabbit-sized *eohippus,* to the majestic hoofed *equus* reintroduced to America by the Spaniards ages after becoming extinct in the Western hemisphere—was rounded out to provide persuasive documentation for Darwin's thesis at the height of the controversy it had aroused.

While Marsh was leading his students on their grand transcontinental field trips, a classmate at Yale, the able and incredibly energetic Clarence King, whom Henry Adams regarded as "the most many-sided genius of his day" and the "best and brightest man of his generation," after a three-year apprenticeship under Whitney in California, had returned east to seek and secure an appointment to conduct a survey of his own. Under specifications he himself had prepared, the twenty-five-year-old King soon had in his pocket an appointment signed by Secretary of War Stanton, and with it a warning that there were "four major-generals that want your place." King's team was to survey and map in detail a wide section near the 40th Parallel, to include the routes of the advancing rails of the Union Pacific and Central Pacific railroads. The immense swath he was to cover extended across the Far West from the Sierras to the Rockies, included most of northern Nevada and Utah, part of Idaho, and large sections of Wyoming and Colorado—a vast territory to be carefully surveyed, mapped, its geology and all existing mines ex-

[56]Goetzmann, *Exploration and Empire,* pp. 425–427.

amined, mineral resources, especially coal deposits, sought, water, soil, and weather information gathered, and a natural history collection gathered. In short, in all that vast area he was "to examine and describe the geological structure, geographical condition and natural resources"; and he was to accomplish the examination in two seasons.[57]

It was mid-July 1867 before King's hurriedly recruited band of professionals and their assistants left their mustering point at Sacramento and were in the field beyond the Sierras. Nevertheless, King laid out as the season's task: to cover a band of the Great Basin 100 miles wide extending eastward to the Shoshone Mountains—an area of 1,500 square miles. To accomplish this, he broke his party into separate teams to cover the wide front while keeping the entire survey coordinated by employing Whitney's triangulation process. Even so, it would be almost five years before the field work was complete all the way to the continental divide 750 miles to the east, and another eight years before its results were fully compiled.[58]

As Secretary Stanton had indicated in his remark to King, his appointment was followed by great rivalry for similar appointments in the West. The launching of King's survey was soon followed by others modeled to a substantial degree on his. By 1869 Lieutenant George M. Wheeler was in the field to the south of King's province, beginning a survey that eventually covered most of the area below the 40th Parallel survey almost to the Mexican border. Dr. Ferdinand V. Hayden led surveys of Nebraska and areas to the north of King's province; and Major Wesley Powell covered the Grand Canyon and Green River regions. We shall meet the latter two again in later chapters. Together these surveys substantially completed the detailed discovery of that vast, sparsely populated region between the Sierras and the Rockies, south of Oregon and Montana—an important indirect consequence of young Clarence King's enterprise.[59]

[57]Bartlett, *Great Surveys*, pp. 141–155.

[58]*Ibid.*, pp. 438–464; an excellent account of King's 40th Parallel survey, enlivened with anecdotes, may be found in Thurman Wilkins, *Clarence King* (New York, 1958), pp. 93–172. See also Bartlett, *Great Surveys*, pp. 156–186.

[59]Goetzmann, *Exploration and Empire*, pp. 466, 544. Dr. Hayden had conducted several surveys before King's 40th Parallel survey, but they were not of the same order in size, extent, organization, or support as that known as the Hayden Survey, which began its field work in 1870—Bartlett, *Great Surveys*, pt. I. Bartlett details Wheeler's survey in pt. 4, pp. 333–372.

One more individual achievement of King's richly varied career deserves mention. In the course of his 40th Parallel explorations, he continued to pursue the problem presented by the rounded valleys often encountered in both the Sierras and the Rockies. After concentrating for years on the geology of the great middle belt of the West covered by his official survey, while gradually developing in his mind a more cosmic view of his field, he again investigated Mount Shasta's towering cone. This time he approached the peak from a different direction than that usually taken, and there discovered the first active glacier to be found in the nation. Its very presence, being "caught in the act" of shaping the bed of rock over which it crawled, provided King with substantive support for his long-standing disagreement with his former chief, Josiah Whitney, over the origin of Yosemite's spectacular U-shaped valley,[60] and many others similarly shaped.

Clarence King's final noteworthy contribution to the discovering of America in depth and detail was the establishment, in 1879, of the United States Geological Survey (with himself its first director and Powell as its second). The dramatic era of discovery in the West drew to a close as the new Geological Survey began its systematic and pedestrian, but monumental, task of mapping in detail the entire surface of the nation.

[60]Wilkins, *Clarence King*, pp. 135–137, 143–144, 230–243; Bartlett, *Great Surveys*, pp. 179–181; Goetzmann, *Exploration and Empire*, pp. 449–450.

CHAPTER 14

Powell and the Colorado

I N the year 1868, the village of Green River City, Wyoming, was born, flourished, and all but died when the Union Pacific completed its trestle across the Green and moved its work crews further west to their most formidable challenge, the crossing of the Wasatch range through Echo and Weber canyons. On the morning of May 24, 1869, most of its remaining residents gathered on the riverbank a little below the trestle to witness a new moment of glory in Green River City's brief history. There, at one of Green River's uncharacteristically quiet reaches, where the tree-lined stream made its way through a spectacular array of treeless pyramids, most surmounted by massive cathedral-like summits of eroded sandstone, four small boats were drawn up on the bank. Several days previously they had arrived by rail from Chicago accompanied by their designer, Major John Wesley Powell, professor of natural history at an obscure little Illinois college. Now the professor was displaying his military background as he busily directed his nine companions in the enterprise of deploying their duffel and stowing their supplies—tins, oilcloth-packed and rubber-bagged—against possible disaster, enough to support the ten-man party for the ten months Major Powell calculated they might be out of reach of replenishment.

But that was no scientific calculation, for the Green and the Grand, and the Colorado which they formed, flowed deep in mysterious canyons, cut through an immense, high, and arid plateau, throughout most of their way to the Gulf of California, 2,000 miles and more than 6,000 feet below the brave little flotilla preparing to shove off from Green River City that morning in May. Knowledge of the river was meager, except for its sources in the perpetually snow-capped peaks of the Wind River and Wyoming ranges of Wyoming, and the Medicine Bow range and Park country of Colorado, and its lower reaches in the torrid deserts of Arizona, California, and Mexico. Through the years, fears and suspicions born of the river's deep mysteries, the inhospitable territory through which it coursed, and the equally inhospitable natives who sparsely peopled its environs, had conspired to give the Colorado a bad name. It had become a river of ill repute, sinister and dangerous, while yet still virgin waters for any would-be navigator. The launching of those four little boats that May morning provided the opening paragraph of what was to become the most dramatic and exciting adventure story in the annals of American exploration.

There had been attempts to unveil the Colorado's mysteries and even to navigate its course, but not enough to provide sufficient hard facts to gainsay the designation UNEXPLORED inscribed across the Grand Canyon Region by Warren and Egloffstein on their great map of the West. In 1540, three and a quarter centuries before Powell's men launched their little fleet in the waters of the Upper Green, a band of Coronado's treasure seekers had peered down on the Colorado, which, a mile below the canyon rim on which they stood, seemed but a muddy brook draining the bottom of the immense chasm. After a futile effort to descend to the river, they had returned to report the region a "useless piece of country."[1] Then the recorded visits of outsiders to Grand Canyon skip all the way from Coronado's day to the year of American independence, when a Franciscan padre, Francisco Garcés, with a Havasupai companion, climbed down into the depths of the lower canyon to visit his guide's people who resided there in a little paradise of several hundred acres where the canyon briefly widens sufficiently to provide enough arable land and sunlight for crops. That same season two other Franciscan fathers, Silvestre de Escalante and Francisco Dominguez, searching for a more northern way from Santa Fe to Monterey in the course of a vain attempt to cross the Great Basin to California, succeeded nevertheless in crossing the gorges of the

[1]Herbert E. Bolton and Thomas M. Marshall, *The Colonization of North America, 1492–1783* (New York, 1920), pp. 44–45; Frederick S. Dellenbaugh, *The Romance of the Colorado River* (New York, 1902), pp. 32–35; David B. Quinn, *North America from Earliest Discovery to First Settlements* (New York, 1977), pp. 199–200.

Gunnison, the Grand, and the Green, and journeyed on to Utah Lake before turning back toward Santa Fe. The place they found to cross the Colorado itself, between Glen and Marble canyons, memorializes their exploit by its name: "Crossing of the Fathers."[2]

In the first half of the next century, when trappers roamed the West seeking every likely beaver stream, doubtless many a curious mountain man investigated the great river and descended into its gorges; but such knowledge as they gained died with them. One unusual follower of that wilderness profession, General William Henry Ashley, who in his day accumulated a fortune through the fur trade, had once embarked with a few daring companions in bull-boats with the intent of navigating the Green River Canyon, but was forced to abandon his attempt at "Ashley Falls" of Red Canyon (in the northeast corner of Utah). There he inscribed his name and the date, 1825, on a rock, where the inscription lasted to be read by Powell in 1869.[3]

After Ashley's abortive navigational effort, there is an interval of another three decades before the record of Colorado explorations resumes with Lieutenant Joseph Christmas Ives's 1857–58 investigations of the Lower Colorado, and Grand Canyon itself. The twenty-nine-year-old Ives of the Topographical Corps, who was familiar with the Lower Colorado as a result of being Whipple's assistant in 1853, accepted his assignment enthusiastically. He was directed to explore the navigability of the Colorado primarily to determine the utility of the region as an access route to the Great Basin, where relations between the federal government and the Mormon settlers were becoming increasingly strained. Although the objectives of Ives's expedition were commercial and military, its retrospective significance lies in its scientific and graphic revelations.[4] Its most fruitful accomplishments were the product of Dr.

[2]Bolton and Marshall, *The Colonization of North America*, pp. 390–393; William H. Goetzmann, *Exploration and Empire* (New York, 1966), pp. 11, 69; and a more full account of the Franciscans in Dellenbaugh, *Romance of the Colorado*, pp. 86–105.

[3]Dellenbaugh, *Romance of the Colorado*, pp. 107–112. Goetzmann states that Ashley continued much further downstream through Flaming Gorge, Ladore, and Split Mountain canyons to Ashley's Fork—*Exploration and Empire*, pp. 122–124.

[4]My summary of the Ives expedition is derived from William H. Goetzmann, *Army Exploration of the American West, 1804–1863* (New Haven, 1959), pp. 378–394; Edward S. Wallace, *The Great Reconnaissance* (Boston, 1955), pp. 175–203; Dellenbaugh, *Romance of the Colorado*, pp. 156–170; and Joseph C. Ives, *Report on the Colorado River of the West*, HR. Exec. Doc. 90, vol. XIV (1860), 36th Congress, 1st Sess., U.S. serial no. 1058 (1861).

John Strong Newberry of the Smithsonian Institution, physician and geologist of the expedition. Dr. Newberry was the first scientist to view the Colorado's great canyons and to see displayed there the colorful and dramatic pages of a modern version of the first chapter of Genesis. A more popular impact of the expedition was provided by Möllhausen, who had hastily returned from Germany for his third American foray, this time as artist, collector, and Humboldt's ambassador to the expedition. Augmenting Möllhausen's work was that of his compatriot, Egloffstein, topographer of Ives's party, who appears to have been too enthralled with the American West to long abandon it.

The costly and impractical *modus operandi* employed by Ives in making his study of the navigational potential of the Colorado was dependent on the steamboat *Explorer,* a prefabricated, shallow draft, 54 feet long, stern-wheel craft which had been specially designed, constructed, assembled, and tested in the relatively tame waters of the Delaware. Disassembled, she was shipped to Panama, hauled across the Isthmus, transshipped to San Francisco, then back down around Lower California to the mouth of the Colorado. There, under a torrid sun, after she was painfully reassembled and launched, the *Explorer* slowly steamed and was intermittently hauled upstream by tow ropes until she was wrecked on a rock concealed beneath the river's chocolate waters. The vessel sank just as she was entering Black Canyon (the site of Hoover Dam), far short of the mouth of the Virgin River, which was said to have been previously reached by a commercially operated steamer. Undeterred by the *Explorer*'s disaster, Ives manned a skiff and continued upstream as far as the Vegas Wash, through the sheer walls of Black Canyon, which rose 1,000 feet from the water's edge. There, thinking he had reached the mouth of the Virgin and observing the mute warning of driftwood lodged in cliffs 50 feet above the water, Ives deemed it discreet to consider the navigational aspect of his mission completed. He turned back downstream to join his land caravan, which was making its way up along the river from Fort Yuma.

Frustrated in his hope of exploring the canyon by water, Ives, accompanied by Dr. Newberry, Möllhausen, and Egloffstein, set out with the pack train to investigate the gorge by land. A few days later, guided by a Hualpai Indian, they descended the complex side canyon, cut by Diamond Creek, visited the abject kinsmen of their guide who had huddled their miserable huts in its defiles, and scrambled on down to the floor of the great canyon itself. In his official report, recalling the emotions aroused by that descent, Ives in vivid and evocative prose wondered at

the increasing magnitude of the colossal piles that blocked the end of the vista, and the corresponding depth and gloom of the gaping chasms into which [they] were plunging, [which] imparted an unearthly character to a way that might have resembled the portals of the infernal regions. Harsh screams issuing from the aerial recesses in the canyon sides, and apparitions of goblin-like figures perched in the rifts and hollows of the impending cliffs, gave an odd reality to this impression.[5]

At Havasupai or Cataract Creek another attempt was made to descend to the river. Some 40 feet from the base of the canyon Egloffstein discovered a primitive ladder with thong-bound rungs. When he undertook to put it to use it gave way, jettisoning him to the canyon floor, albeit without serious injury—the first white visitor since Father Garcés's visit of 1776. The baron was rescued by rope without great difficulty. From Havasupai Creek, Ives's caravan continued eastward across the Little Colorado and thence northeast across the Painted Desert, to visit the towns of the little known Moqui (Hopi) before disbanding at nearby Fort Defiance.

With the possible exception of Frémont, no engineer or leader of a survey of the Topographical Corps was more adept with words than Joseph Ives. His romantic, often Dantesque imagination and facile prose, combined with Baron von Egloffstein's Dorésque drawings, the romantic exaggerations of Möllhausen, and Dr. Newberry's new creation story,[6] all melded to make his report an impressive and revealing work.[7]

Although Warren's renowned map had not yet been published when Ives returned to Washington in 1858 and submitted his preliminary report, it was too late to have the map reflect the expedi-

[5]Ives, *Report*, p. 100.

[6]In 1859, the year after the Ives expedition, Dr. Newberry accompanied Capt. John N. McComb to the region of the confluence of the Grand and the Green but was unable to descend to the river from the incredibly tortured sage plains over which they were toiling; they did find there parts of a large dinosaur's skeleton—Goetzmann, *Army Exploration*, pp. 394–397; Dellenbaugh, *Romance of the Colorado*, pp. 170–173.

[7]Ives, *Report*. While the *Report* was being printed, Ives was making his decision in respect to the crisis of the day. Although his antecedents, birth, and education were Northern, he threw in his lot with the Confederacy and became a member of President Davis's staff. He only briefly survived the Confederacy.

tion's discoveries. However, it is doubtful that Ives's three-point contacts with the great canyon would alone have been sufficient for him to describe the canyon region as explored. There remained hundreds of miles as yet unseen by European-Americans, miles of mystery fraught with frightening possibilities. In preparing for his own undertaking to visit those unvisited reaches, Major Powell had the benefit of most of the information gathered by his predecessors in the area, and other scraps of helpful knowledge he had himself garnered during two seasons of exploring in the region of the Green and the Grand.[8]

Powell's preparation for the expedition had fortuitous beginnings in rural Ohio to which, in one of a series of westward moves, his English-born evangelical parents had taken their family four years after John Wesley's birth near Palmyra, in rural New York, in 1834. When he made his move to Ohio, John Wesley's father, a tailor by trade but an itinerant lay preacher by choice, and devoted follower of his elder son's namesake, settled his family at the raw frontier village of Jackson.[9] Among their first acquaintances was an enormously fat Wesleyan, George Crookham, the community's intellectual. When young Wesley was hounded out of the local school because of his family's abolitionist views, the boy was taken into Crookham's home. For the next few years, with Crookham as tutor, exemplar, and companion on countless field trips to caves, mines, quarries, woods, ponds, and Indian mounds in the area, the boy received the foundation upon which he avidly built his scientific education, just as his beloved mentor had done.

When the boy was twelve, the restless elder Powell moved his family westward again, to a farm in northern Illinois. The boy's self-education, mostly pursued at night after sun-to-sun labor on the farm, sufficiently advanced him, at seventeen, to qualify for a teaching post at a rural school. A decade of intermittent teaching,

[8]Ashley's account was the only extant information of which Powell was unaware; it was not published until 1918—Wallace Stegner, *Beyond the Hundredth Meridian* (Boston, 1953), p. 380n.

[9]Coincidentally, it was also near Palmyra that, a few years before, Joseph Smith had reported finding the golden tablets inscribed with the Book of Mormon, originating a sect with which Powell was to have much association during the most significant years of his life—William C. Darrah, *Powell of the Colorado* (Princeton, 1951). My account of Powell's life prior to his first Western expedition is derived from Darrah. A less full biographical account of Powell's background for his Colorado expedition is available in Richard A. Bartlett, *Great Surveys of the American West* (Norman, Okla., 1962), pp. 219–236.

brief periods of attendance at little Ohio Valley colleges, and extensive collecting expeditions, usually alone and by boat, up the Mississippi to the Falls of St. Anthony, down it to New Orleans, to the mountains of Pennsylvania and the mines of Missouri, continued to advance the young Powell's scientific training. In the course of that decade, he accumulated extensive collections that gave him a regional reputation as a naturalist: a 6,000-specimen herbarium, plus prizewinning conchology and respectable geology collections.

Then came the war, an abrupt termination of his teaching and solo rambling, and the beginning of a new, more orderly way of life, opening out into new opportunities, new stimuli, and new associations that would later prove most useful. At the first call, student-pedagogue John Wesley Powell became Private Powell, Company H, Twentieth Illinois Volunteer Infantry, only to abandon his lowly rank a few days later when his comrades elected him sergeant major. As commonly happens in war, events of moment in Powell's life were telescoped. In the course of a year, thanks to a warm friendship with General Grant, he was given a week's leave to go to Detroit to marry his cousin, Emma Dean, won a captain's commission, and lost his right arm at Shiloh. Upon his recovery, in February 1863, he rejoined his battery in Louisiana just in time to take part in Grant's campaign across Mississippi, which culminated in the capture of Vicksburg on July 4, 1863. During the siege Powell found distraction by hunting for fossils and geological specimens in the entrenchments, sending his collections back to his natural history society in Illinois. After more campaigning in the Gulf region he was advanced in rank to major, but was soon returned home for his discharge in January 1865.

Later that year Powell accepted the professorship of geology at Illinois Wesleyan University at Bloomington. One of the principal attractions of the post was the proximity of nearby Illinois State Normal University, where the Illinois State Natural History Society, to which he had donated most of his collections, was located. Within a year his title was broadened to professor of natural science. Nevertheless, very soon he was hungering for wider ranges, and visions of what he might find in the Rockies and beyond began to tempt his imagination.

It was alien to Powell's nature long to harbor dreams without responding to them. By mid-spring of 1867 he had secured a state appropriation for the Illinois Natural History Society, his own appointment as its curator, and other assistance for a collecting expedition to the mountains of Colorado, including a loan of instruments from the Smithsonian, free transportation from the railroad and express companies, and, thanks to General Grant, the right to draw rations and protective escorts from military posts. Before the summer of 1867, Powell's party of twelve, including several of his students, were heading west from Council Bluffs. Carefully arranged publicity back home, extraordinary success in both the quantity and variety of the collections brought back, a successful climb to the summit of Pike's Peak, and particularly Emma Dean Powell's priority as the first woman to make the climb,[10] practically assured a sequel. After the expedition had been disbanded, the Powells stayed on in the West for two months to investigate the canyons of the Upper Colorado, then known as the Grand. He determined that the following season's expedition would concentrate upon the Colorado and its mysteries.

The next party of twenty men and Mrs. Powell included more scientific men. In early July 1868 they set out on the trail leading from Cheyenne to Denver, mounted on unruly, only partly broken horses and mules. At Denver, six days later, several of the hunters and guides of the 1867 expedition again volunteered their services. From Denver the party made its way west across the continental divide to Hot Sulphur Springs, where a base was established for investigations in the Colorado Basin. As summer waned, and Powell's determination to navigate the Green and Colorado through their canyons waxed, they continued their reconnaissance northward up along the Green to the mouth of the White River, where the Powells and a few companions built cabins for winter quarters. Nearby, a band of unspoiled Utes, still dependent upon their bows and arrows, had established their winter quarters, thus immersing Powell in yet another topic, the ethnology of the American Indian, which was destined to be one of the most fruitful interests of his varied and highly productive life.

Major Powell's nine companions in daring, who had volunteered to pit their mettle and skills against whatever might await them down the canyoned 1,000 miles of the almost unknown river, were: Powell's younger brother, Walter, who had served as a captain in the

[10]Stegner, *Beyond the Hundredth Meridian*, pp. 18–19. Mrs. Powell is generally credited with this priority, but apparently erroneously—see Goetzmann, *Exploration and Empire*, pp. 535–536.

Union army and been wounded in the service; Oramel G. Howland, a Denver printer, thirty-six, eldest of the group and a companion of Powell the previous year; Oramel's brother, Seneca; George Bradley, another Union veteran, a New Englander with valuable boating experience; Andy Hall, youngest of the group, a Scottish scapegrace with four years of Western adventuring behind him; Frank Goodman, a pink-faced English adventurer who begged to join the expedition as they were preparing to embark; and John Sumner, William Dunn, and William Hawkins, all three with wide Western wilderness experience as trappers, and with Powell on his earlier expeditions. When, on May 24, 1868, the little band took their places aboard and pushed off downstream, the river at first dealt gently with them.[11] For a while the delights of the magnificent scenery and comradeship in venture dominated the spirited group. That day out they stopped early to permit Powell to climb to the canyon's rim to view the Green River badlands of "sandstones and shales, gray and buff, red and brown, blue and black strata . . . shaped by fantastic carving . . . suggesting rude but weird statuary." The next day was marked by a fat young mountain sheep providing a gay afternoon feast; on the third day they glided "quietly down the placid stream past the carved cliffs of *mauvais terres* . . . where occasionally deer are started from the glades among the willows," and several wild geese were brought down for another feast of game. They rode the current on into Flaming Canyon, "a flaring brilliant red gorge" where the Green cuts its way through the Uinta Mountains that run east and west squarely across the river's course.[12] Although here Powell refers to the canyon, with walls 1,200 feet high, as having been cut through the "great mass of the mountain ridge . . . as if the river thought a mountain range no formidable obstruction," he later explains that the river, having been there long before the mountains rose, had by its rushing silt-laden waters simply ground its way through the mountains as they rose, much as a log is cut by the whirring saw as it is brought against the cutting teeth. Likewise, all the canyons below were sawed through the great plateau as it rose,

[11]In the course of the party's passage down the river, unless otherwise noted, all citations are to John Wesley Powell, *The Exploration of the Colorado River* (Chicago, 1957). This available edition is a republication of the river expedition portion of Powell's *Exploration of the Colorado River of the West and Its Tributaries* (Washington, D.C., 1875). A more concise account of Powell's first navigation of the Colorado canyons is available in Bartlett, *Great Surveys*, pp. 237–265.

[12]Powell, *Exploration*, pp. 2–5.

leaving the powerfully resistant river further and further below the surrounding country, in its pristine channel.[13]

Riding the swift current, they passed through Flaming Gorge to a place where the towering walls for a short distance moved back from the river to form a small park. Soon, however, they were between even higher walls, as the river rushed down among great rocks; Powell, standing on the deck of his little wave-tossed flagship, sought a way among the rocks while the untried fleet rushed on "with exhilarating velocity, mounting the high waves, whose foaming crests dash over" them. Horseshoe Canyon, Kingfisher Park, and Kingfisher Canyon followed, before surcease and campfire at Beehive Point, "where hundreds of swallows have built their nests" and, flitting about the cliffs, gave "the appearance of a colossal beehive." This camp marked the final day of their first week on the river. It was eight days after their embarkation before they were forced to try their hands at letting the boats down over the rapids with ropes held by the men while they, in tug-of-war stance, gave ground along the boulder-strewn bank. Back in the boats they sped downstream "at a wonderful rate," as the river rushed into a narrow gorge where impeding rocks rolled it into "great waves, and the boats go leaping and bounding over these like things of life," like "herds of startled deer bounding through forests beset with fallen timber." Then, mercifully, a calm stretch, where the ominous roar of a waterfall below called for camp and rest in preparation for the first of the countless portages they would be forced to endure in the weeks to follow.[14]

Next morning, while they were investigating the source of that ominous roar and preparing a portage path along the narrow, rock-filled gorge, down which navigation was obviously out of the question, one of the men noticed a boulder upon which was etched, "Ashley 1825," prompting them to honor this unknown predecessor by naming the rapids there Ashley Falls.[15] Downstream from those rapids, from time to time, the river flowed through "beautiful parks," where "mule deer and elk abound; grizzly bears, too, are abundant; wild cats, wolverines and mountain lions are" at home and the forest aisles "filled with the music of birds" and "decked with flowers. Noisy brooks meander through them; ledges of moss-

[13]Stegner, *Beyond the Hundredth Meridian*, pp. 152–155.
[14]Powell, *Exploration*, pp. 10–11.
[15]At the time they could not be certain of the third digit of the date.

covered rocks are seen; and gleaming in the distance are the snow fields and the mountain tops. . . ." This was Brown's Park, a short distance below Ashley Falls.[16] Powell noted that there, where the Vermilion comes in from the east, Frémont on his way home to a hero's welcome in 1844 after his foray into California effected his crossing of the Green by means of a bullboat ferry over the expanse of "several hundred yards."[17] The peaceful beauty of the place, its bountiful game and fish, and a comfortable camp beneath a giant cottonwood held them in that little Eden for several days. "At daybreak," Powell writes, "I am awakened by a chorus of birds. It seems as if all the feathered songsters of the region have come to this old tree. Several species of warblers, woodpeckers, and flickers above, meadow larks in the grass and wild geese nearby"—this more than 1,000 feet beneath the surface of the surrounding desert plateau.[18]

Two weeks after setting out, the party reached the portal of the canyon they called Lodore, the first of a long series of canyons awaiting their little fleet. "The cañon opened up," wrote Powell, "like a beautiful portal to a region of glory. Now as I write the sun is going down, and the shadows are setting in the cañon. The vermilion gleams and the rosy hues, the green and gray tints, are changing to sombre brown above, and black shadows below. Now 'tis a black portal to a region of gloom."[19] Lodore was the first real test of the mettle of Powell's band. Their first day in that narrow canyon was but an arduous series of lining down the boats, of portages of boats and cargo, and of running terrific rapids in which the stupendous waves were the great hazard, several times during the day upsetting the boats, spilling crews and cargo into the rushing brown flood. Powell explains why these waves in the rapids were so much more dangerous than comparable waves at sea: "The water

[16]Today a navigator of the Green would cruise across the still surface of Flaming Gorge Reservoir almost the entire distance from Powell's point of embarkation to Brown's Hole.

[17]Donald Jackson and Mary Lee Spence (eds.), *The Expeditions of John Charles Frémont* (2 vols., Urbana, Ill., 1970), vol. 1, p. 707, and map 3.

[18]Powell, *Exploration*, pp. 13–15.

[19]Stegner, *Beyond the Hundredth Meridian*, pp. 62, 174–184. In later years, when *Scribner's Monthly* published Powell's first account of the expedition, his friend Thomas Moran, a superb Romantic artist, particularly of the Western scene, impressively portrayed the Gate of Lodore in all its exalted gloom. In Powell's subsequent published variations on the theme, this and other Moran illustrations immensely enhanced the impact of his story—Powell, *Exploration*, p. 16. See Chapter 15 for a more detailed introduction of Moran.

of an ocean wave merely rises and falls; the form only passes on. . . . A body floating on such waves merely rises and sinks. But here, the water of the wave passes on, while the form remains." In rapids the water itself keeps plunging down and springing back up, rendering navigation through such waves extremely hazardous as the boat "leaps and plunges along with great velocity."[20]

Next day there were more back-breaking portages. In rowing for shore to prepare for yet another, one of the boats, with the two Howlands and Goodman aboard, was swept downstream and broken in two on the rocks below; and moments later the forward section, to which the men clung, struck another rock and dashed to splinters. Hazardous rescue operations saved the men, the barometers, and a keg of whiskey clandestinely stored in the decked-over stern compartment.[21] At the mouth of the Yampa, which marked the completion of the Green's passage through the Uinta Mountains, Powell looked back on its passage as "a chapter of disasters and toils," of scenic interest "beyond the power of the pen to tell . . . the roar of its waters unceasing . . . but its walls and cliffs, its peaks and crags, its amphitheaters and alcoves, tell a story of beauty and grandeur that I hear yet—and shall hear."[22]

The mouth of the Yampa served as a punctuation point after the strenuous monotony of Lodore. There they camped for several days while Powell explored the gorges and cliffs around the camp. It was among these cliffs that the expedition came literally within a drawers' length of losing its leader. In the course of one of their climbs, Powell jumped a crevice, only to find himself on a narrow ledge above an 80-foot drop from which he could neither retreat nor advance, and even to stay there required him to stand on his toes and hold fast to an angle of the wall. In a desperate do-or-die performance Bradley stripped off his drawers and, from a safe ledge above, dangled them within reach of the major's quick grasp, so

[20]Powell, *Exploration*, p. 17.

[21]*Ibid.*, pp. 19–22. "Disaster Falls," so named after finding in the rocks a wrecked stove, presumably Ashley's.

[22]Dellenbaugh, *Romance of the Colorado*, pp. 387–389. Frederick S. Dellenbaugh accompanied Powell on his second expedition down the river, when he attempted to tabulate the falls and rapids of the Green and Colorado and was forced to skip 20 miles of Lodore, it being "so nearly one continuous rapid that it is difficult to count the special drops"—Powell, *Exploration*, p. 26. Lodore Canyon and that of the Yampa below are in Dinosaur National Monument, the richest known deposits of dinosaur remains, exposed here where the river has cut through Mesozoic strata.

hoisting him to safety.[23] From the Yampa they coursed down Whirl-pool Canyon, to a confrontation with a series of rapids down which they had a headlong ride, shooting past rocks and islands, like "riding a fleet horse over the outstretched prairie," to a beautiful island in a broad park. And again, after a rough passage down Split Mountain Canyon, they reached a gently flowing stretch of river, where it made its leisurely way through meadows and groves beneath which herds of antelope browsed.[24]

For a week they halted there to permit an expedition 20 miles up the Uinta to the Uinta Indian Agency to despatch and pick up mail and replace their kitchen equipment, lost to the muddy stream in a freak accident. Here Frank Goodman, who had had his fill of this sort of adventure, decided to escape the party's hazardous, self-imposed imprisonment between canyon walls.[25] Early on June 6 the little fleet, now diminished by a boat and a man, resumed its tortured cruise.[26] The next ten days carried them to the mouth of Grand River (now known as the Colorado all the way to its source in Rocky Mountain National Park) where "these streams," the Grand and the Green, "unite in solemn depths more than one thousand two hundred feet below the general surface of the country." It had been a strenuous ten days of almost constant struggle, of frequent upsets, soaked supplies, instruments and guns broken or lost, smashed oars requiring replacements sawed or hacked from driftwood. The pervading gloom was memorialized when they named Gray Canyon and Canyon of Desolation, "where the lamented Gunnison crossed" in 1853. Further down, the sharp twisting of the gorge suggested the name of Labyrinth for one of the canyons passed before reaching the spectacular buttes of Tower Canyon, the Indian's Land of Standing Rock, and the Gorge of the Grand where it joined the Green to form the Colorado.[27]

[23]Powell, *Exploration*, p. 29–31: an illustration of the liberties taken by Powell in his published accounts of the expedition—others of the party reported this episode further down on July 8. Here we follow his account, which in numerous instances takes liberties with time, place, and other nonessential facts. He also reported events that did not occur until his second expedition down the river; however, it was his account, with all its insignificant inaccuracies, that provided the world with the first proper picture of the Colorado and its canyons—Darrah, *Powell of the Colorado*, p. 131; Stegner, *Beyond the Hundredth Meridian*, p. 72.

[24]Powell, *Exploration*, pp. 33–38.

[25]*Ibid.*, pp. 38–41.

[26]Bradley's rescue of Powell actually occurred the next day, a little below the mouth of the Uinta.

[27]Powell, *Exploration*, pp. 47–55.

Major Powell, investigating the environs of this significant point in their exploration, succeeded in reaching a point of rock from which he had a view of the Green, the Grand, and the Colorado, "a world of grandeur": to the west, cliffs "from which the gods might quarry mountains," which, if set on a plain, would make a lofty range, no mere cliffs "where the swallow builds its nest, but cliffs where the soaring eagle is lost to view ere he reaches the summit." All about were walls, pinnacles, and towers of sandstone in bands of red, buff, and gray, where "curious caves and channels . . . and royal arches" had been carved.[28]

On July 21 they resumed their contest with the river and its seemingly endless challenges. So continuous were the rapids that the canyon below the Grand River's mouth was named Cataract Canyon. In its depth one day they progressed less than a mile, owing to the "rocks, in chutes, whirlpools, and great waves," the water sometimes heaping "up in mounds, and even in cones," or dizzily swirling in pools, one of which caught Powell's light craft and held it so tenaciously that it was extricated with great difficulty. As they fought these mad torrents, the men could only wonder what the river would be like if the water were running 75 or 100 feet higher in the gorge, where they could see driftwood wedged in crevices, and the gorge filled up from wall to wall, the rocks in places even overhanging the water so as to "almost shut out the light." Down through the gloom they coursed, swiftly and helplessly, toward any waterfall that might suddenly appear before them.[29]

In Glen Canyon, into which they were swept soon after passing the mouth of malodorous Dirty Devil River, Powell devoted hours to studying the mortar-bound stone masonry remains of Indian dwellings discovered on the ledges of the canyon walls, and arcane etchings on the walls themselves. He was intrigued and moved: "Here I stand, where these now lost people stood centuries ago, and look over this strange country."[30] Below the mouth of the San Juan, where they had made an unsuccessful attempt to climb out of the

[28] *Ibid.*, pp. 58–61. Stegner, *Beyond the Hundredth Meridian*, pp. 195–196, observes that in the Grand Canyon, which has been called a "mountain-range-in-a-ditch," subordinate buttes, vestiges of the cleft plateau, are commonly larger than any mountain east of the Mississippi.

[29] Powell, *Exploration*, pp. 61–68. Now Cataract Canyon is flooded by the waters of Lake Powell, which extends downriver some 160 miles to its dam near the mouth of Glen Canyon and the head of Marble Canyon, an installation deplored by many as a rapidly silting catch basin. For an eloquent protest, see Eliot Porter's epilogue in *Down the Colorado* (New York, 1969).

[30] Powell, *Exploration*, pp. 70–71.

canyon to investigate the plateau, they found "a curious ensemble of wonderful features—carved walls, royal arches, glens, alcove gulches, mounds and monuments." Of these features the green glens of entering gorges suggested the name Glen Canyon, through which, during the first ten days of August, they coursed relatively easily to even more beautiful Marble Canyon, where polished limestone comprised almost 1,000 feet of the half-mile depth of the canyon. Massive buttresses ran down to the river, giving the appearance of supporting those exalted walls. In the recesses between these projections they found quiet bays. And in one were "fountains bursting from the rock, high overhead, and the spray," forming gems, bedecked the walls, while the rocks below were "covered with mosses, and ferns, and many beautiful flowering plants." This memorable place they named Vasey's Paradise, in honor of Powell's botanist of the previous season. One of Thomas Moran's memorable illustrations shows Marble Canyon in all its grandeur.[31]

Two months and twenty days after their departure from Green River City, they were camped near the mouth of the Little Colorado after yet another attempt to climb to the canyon rim had failed. A deeply disturbed Powell confided his concerns to his journal while the men prepared the boats to push off into the upper portal of Grand Canyon itself:

We are now ready to start on our way down the Great Unknown, Our boats, tied to a common stake are chafing each other, as they are tossed by the fretful river. They ride high and bouyant, for their loads are lighter than we could desire. We have but a month's rations remaining. The flour has been resifted through the mosquito-net sieve; the spoiled bacon has been dried, and the worst of it boiled; the few pounds of dried apples have been spread in the sun, and reshrunken to their normal bulk; the sugar has all melted, and gone on its way down the river; but we have a large sack of coffee. The lightening of the boats has this advantage; they will ride the waves better, and we shall have but little to carry when we make a portage.

We are three quarters of a mile in the depths of the earth, and the great river shrinks into insignificance, as it dashes its angry waves against the walls and cliffs, that rise to the world above; they are but puny ripples, and we but pigmies, running up and down the sands, or lost among the boulders.

We have an unknown distance yet to run; an unknown river yet to explore. What falls are there, we know not; what rocks beset the channel, we know not; what walls rise over the river, we know not. . . .[32]

[31]*Ibid.*, pp. 78–79, 56.
[32]*Ibid.*, p. 83.

Later, Powell employed more graphic terms to dramatize the immensity of the gorge ahead. "Pluck up Mt. Washington by the roots to the level of the sea," he wrote, and "drop it headfirst into the Grand Canyon, and the dam will not force its waters over the walls. Pluck up the Blue Ridge and hurl it into Grand Canyon, and it will not fill it."[33]

On August 14 they were swept into a granite gorge.[34] Here the canyon was narrower and the water swifter than any so far encountered. In places where fallen boulders made lateral dams they were forced to chance a run down a chute, hoping for the best. More than once there were places where, though the rapids and rocks mandated a portage, there were no banks to permit one, forcing the choice between abandoning the boats and attempting to find a way out of the canyon or taking their chances on the ominous torrent. In each instance they cast their fate with the river, and made it through without loss of life or boat, but with further levy on their meager provisions, leaving them with a Spartan supply for only a few more days. And their progress was alarmingly slow. One difficult day it was but 2 miles. Twice the boats had to be let down by lines carried along the shelves of cliffs high above the water. Those unremitting hardships took a heavy toll of morale. There was a night spent huddled without a fire on a bank too narrow to afford sleeping space, and another hunched on a ledge while cold rain chilled them to the bone. No one was fully clothed and some even lacked a blanket. Clouds filled the canyon, adding to the continuous gloom, only briefly relieved by a day of sunlight and the discovery of Bright Angel Creek, in the heart of today's Grand Canyon National Park. But the Colorado is a capricious river and the country through which it makes its way is a region of extremes. The next day, although they were on waters of melted snows a mile deep in the sunless gorge, their thermometer rose to 115 degrees before plummeting at night, when they again shivered in an "especially cold rain." But mostly it was uncertainty that plagued them. They had little idea as to how much river lay ahead of them; the last of the barometers was broken, leaving them without means to calculate the fall of the river

[33]J. W. Powell, *The Exploration of the Colorado River and Its Canyon* (New York, 1961), a reprint of *Canyons of the Colorado* (Meadville, Pa., 1895), p. 390.

[34]Powell erroneously uses the term "granite" for the dark Archaean gneiss and schist of the lower strata of the canyon—Stegner, *Beyond the Hundredth Meridian*, p. 84.

between where they were and where Ives's data had ended.

On the day that they advanced only 2 miles, Powell, hoping to allay that pervading anxiety, had left the men who were engaged in a difficult portage to climb as far as he could, seeking a clear view ahead. He gained the top of the granite stratum, crossed one of rust-colored sandstone and another of greenish-yellow shales, only to be stopped at the foot of a marble wall. Below, the men and boats were lost in the depths and the dashing river appeared but a rippling brook, although there was still more canyon above him than below. "All about me," he wrote, "are interesting geological records. The book is open and I can read as I run. . . . I can see below only a labyrinth of deep gorges. . . . But somehow I think of the nine days' rations, and the bad river, and the lesson of the rocks, and the glory of the scene is but half seen."[35]

Two days later they ran out of the abhorred granite and back into limestone, permitting good progress for several days. On August 25 they came upon a place of amazing geological wonders, where the familiar strata sequence of the canyon walls had broken along a clear line of cleavage, and fallen 800 feet below their matching strata upstream. From this fault, in relatively recent geological times, a volcanic cone had arisen, from which lava had flowed down the canyon wall in a waterfall, to be frozen there in place. "Just imagine a river of molten rock," wrote Powell, "running down into a river of melted snow. What a seething and boiling of the waters; what clouds of steam rolled into the heavens!" Across the river, mammoth saline springs gushed "from the fissure and fell between one and two hundred feet down to the river, with a flow quite equal in volume to the little Colorado." Next day they reached the Havasupai irrigated fields in a wide place in the canyon, the first white visitors to the place since Baron von Egloffstein; but their owners were nowhere to be seen. Pleading justification in their great need, they helped themselves to a generous supply of squash. Good progress and a brief surcease from their monotonous fare made the day a good one.[36]

But the following morning the river turned south and again entered the dreaded granite and rapids "much worse than any . . . yet met with in all the course." Although it was still early, they went into camp to ponder their predicament. That evening, after supper, for

[35]Powell, *Exploration*, pp. 83–93.
[36]*Ibid.*, pp. 98–100.

which the last sack of flour was opened, the elder Howland took Powell aside and told him that he, his brother, and Dunn were convinced that it would be suicidal to attempt to run the awful rapids ahead. In their opinion, in view of the worsening of the river, the weakness of the men, and the paucity of their larder, they should attempt to climb out of the canyon and make their way cross-country to the Mormon settlements on the Virgin River. After a tormented night, before daylight Powell polled the others, all of whom elected to stay with the boats. Each group obviously thought the other was making a suicidal choice. Shortly after daybreak the three defectors set out with guns and ammunition, but refused any part of the stores. The remaining six, leaving the small boat on the bank, boarded the other two craft and pushed out into the furious brown current. In a mad ride they were quickly carried through the worst of the series of rapids, to a stopping place where they fired guns to signal their success and waited in the hope that those left behind would take the little boat and join them. But there was no change of mind and the boatmen pushed on. Very soon they faced even worse rapids, so swift and boisterous that, in the attempt to line down one of the boats with Bradley aboard to ward it off the rocks, the stem post, to which the line was tied, was ripped from the bow and Bradley set adrift in the worst of the mad torrent. Miraculously, both he and the boat were pitched into an eddy from which he was rescued when the others, in desperation, dared to follow him down the furious stretch.

Those rapids, the worst of the entire venture, were the last of consequence. By noon the next day, August 29, the two battered craft with their six bedraggled, half-starved crewmen emerged from Grand Canyon at the Grand Wash.[37] In the unfamiliar quiet that evening, Powell could relax the tension that had gripped him for so long and permit his journal to reflect his relief. "Now the danger is over; now the toil has ceased; now the gloom has disappeared; now the firmament is bounded only by the horizon; and what a vast expanse of constellations can be seen! The river rolls by us in silent majesty; the quiet of the camp is sweet; our joy is almost ecstasy."[38]

Next day they were greeted by three Mormons, sent by Brigham Young to watch the river for wreckage or bodies of the members of the expedition thrice reported dead. After a brief stop for rest

[37]Now submerged by the headwaters of Lake Mead.
[38]Powell, *Exploration*, pp. 107–108.

and resupply at the hands of the hospitable Mormon settlers, Powell and his brother set out for Salt Lake City.[39] On their way, word reached them that the Howland brothers and Dunn were dead. They had succeeded in finding a way out of the canyon to the forested plateau north of the gorge; but while the three slept beside a waterpocket, they were attacked by a band of Shivwits and riddled with arrows.[40]

The Powells hastened on to Salt Lake City and then back east, where a hero's welcome awaited the major. The drama inherent in the daring expedition had been further enhanced by the deaths of three of their number, and by frequent reports of the death of all the party, one having been broadcast by an imposter who plausibly represented himself as the sole surviving member of the expedition based on his assumption that no one survived to belie his tales. In Illinois plaudits were showered on their hero, their own self-educated scientist, suddenly rocketed from homespun celebrity to national fame. It was a frenetic fall of '69 and winter and spring of '70 for Powell as he strove to keep up with a busy lecture series while concentrating his efforts on arrangements for a second expedition.

He was dissatisfied with the scientific results of the first expedition. To remedy this, he determined to lead another, better-planned expedition down the Colorado. To allow the time necessary for a proper scientific survey of the canyons would require two seasons, supply points along the way, scientifically trained personnel, and better-designed boats, all of which would entail much greater expense. Obviously, a government-sponsored study was the answer, a study along the lines of those that had been supported for decades past and were still being fielded, most notably at the time those of Clarence King and Ferdinand V. Hayden. Before mid-year 1870, Powell and his supporters had secured commitments for sponsorship of a Geographical and Topographical Survey of the Colorado River of the West, which, anomalously, was placed under the Department of the Interior with close ties to the Smithsonian Institu-

[39]The other four continued on downstream in the boats. Bradley and Sumner left the river at Fort Yuma, leaving only Hawkins and Hall to round out the expedition at tidewater.

[40]Stegner, *Beyond the Hundredth Meridian*, pp. 110–112, 131–132. Powell later learned from the Shivwits themselves that the Howlands and Dunn had been the victims of mistaken identity at the hands of a band seeking a party of prospectors who had molested and shot a Shivwit squaw.

tion, permitting more independence than other surveys enjoyed.[41] By August, Powell was back in Utah with his brother-in-law A. H. Thompson, another school man with a good scientific foundation. Their principal objective was to locate practical approaches to the river that might serve as interim supply points for the second river expedition. It was in the course of that search that Powell became acquainted with the Shivwits and learned the full story of the death of his three men. Intrigued by these primitive people, he soon developed an interest in them, their customs and traditions, that persisted and grew as his scientific interests began to concentrate more and more on ethnology.

The next two seasons, 1871 and 1872, were devoted to the second navigation of the Green and Colorado.[42] This time Major Powell's fleet numbered only three boats, but they were somewhat larger than those of 1869 and much improved by the addition of decked-over center compartments. To one of these a high chair was lashed, from which Powell might better observe and guide the flotilla through the rough waters or serve as entertainer with poetry and other uplifting readings during the quiet water. His ten companions, except for a photographer who proved none too satisfactory, were again all amateurs but mostly uncommonly able ones. His brother-in-law, Thompson, served as topographer of the expedition; a cousin of Thompson's, Frederick Dellenbaugh, who years later would publish a classic account of the expedition in his *Romance of the Colorado River,* was the expedition's artist and later one of its photographers, while a fellow geologizer of Powell's in the trenches before Vicksburg, J. F. Steward, was its geologist.

Their start on May 22, 1871, was again from Green River City, which in the two years since the first departure had shrunk until it was almost nonexistent. They left the river to winter at the Mormon settlement of Kanab, and on September 9, 1872, abandoned the expedition short of its mark, at Kanab Wash, less than halfway through Grand Canyon. In many ways this repeat performance was as exciting and harrowing as the first, despite improved equipment, better planning, and superior personnel. Powell himself missed much of the river voyage, leaving for plateau explorations, and for two trips to Salt Lake City, one to visit his wife, and the other to

[41]Darrah, *Powell,* p. 152; Stegner, *Beyond the Hundredth Meridian,* p. 114.

[42]The careful preparations for Powell's second Colorado expedition and that expedition are recounted in Bartlett, *Great Surveys,* pp. 266–301.

escort her and their new daughter to their winter quarters at Kanab; he left again, from February to August 1872, for a trip east, in the course of which he displayed his confidence in his career by purchasing a home in Washington. During those absences Thompson proved himself a most capable leader. To him goes credit for the discovery of the Henry Mountains (named for Joseph Henry of the Smithsonian) and the Escalante River, both missed by the first expedition—the last mountain range and last river of consequence to find their places on the map of the contiguous states of the Union. In revealing the great gorge the expedition's contributions were substantial, thanks mainly to the numerous photographs and sketches made possible by its superior equipment and slower pace. In the years that followed, millions saw the canyons in breathtaking full perspective through the stereopticon pictures brought back in 1872.[43]

Although Powell continued for years to study and to blaze new scientific trails across the arid lands of the West, the completion of his second Colorado expedition, the publication of his account in *Scribner's Monthly,*[44] and of his *Exploration of the Colorado River of the West and Its Tributaries* (1875) marked the high-water mark of the major's popular reputation. The greatest contributions of Wesley Powell's richly innovative life, however, were reserved for the years to come.

Those contributions were mostly made beyond the time frame of this work—well after the Far West had become accessible by rail and telegraph, and its last river and last mountain range named, when fact had substantially replaced fable and fancy. But Powell's later career is too important for any Procrustean truncation.

At the height of his public popularity Powell used his influence to persuade Congress in 1879 to consolidate all the rival bureaus engaged in overlapping and competing surveys into the United States Geological Survey, and to place it under the Department of the Interior. By the same Act Powell's own survey, which was becoming increasingly involved with American Indian ethnology, was established as the Bureau of Ethnology. A decade later, Powell

[43]Many of those photographs and sketches became illustrations that accompanied Powell's own account, ostensibly of the first expedition, but actually a medley of the two.

[44]"The Cañons of the Colorado," *Scribner's Monthly*, IX(1874), 293–310, 394–409, 523–537.

the self-made scientist had become the most powerful scientific figure in the world, holding in his hands the largest scientific budget of any nation on earth—"in his hands" because his was an anomolous "lump sum" rather than a "line item" budget, which enabled him to allocate funds to those projects he approved. In that period of burgeoning influence of science, the incorrigibly purposeful Powell was regarded by some as even more powerful than the President himself.[45] His administration was marked by great planning and substantial accomplishments, most notably the commencement of the topographical and geological mapping of the entire nation— a stupendous undertaking that, after almost a century, is yet far from complete.

As for Powell himself, honors were heaped upon him. For the homespun scientist there were honorary degrees from major American universities and even from Heidelburg, the scientific center of the Old World, and positions of leadership in the most prestigious societies. But riding high inevitably involves hazards; and Powell came a cropper when he undertook to tilt at the ponderous windmills of entrenched bureaucracy by championing reforms in the homestead laws to reflect the views he had put forth in his greatest work, the *Report on the Arid Region of the United States*.[46] That famous paper advocated revolutionary modifications in the Homestead Act of 1862, its administration, and the common-law doctrines of riparian rights to the use of water. In the arid regions Powell wanted riparian rights to the use of water to be replaced by laws tying water rights to lands susceptible to irrigation, whether or not those lands were adjacent to the watercourse. He further advocated laws to encourage cooperative unions and irrigation districts, in order to accomplish the development and operation of irrigation works. He sought a reduction in the size of land allotments in irrigable areas, and an increase of those in non-irrigable areas of the arid regions. All these innovations called for drastic reforms in the survey and allotment system of the General Land Office.[47] Such ideas were

[45]Stegner, *Beyond the Hundredth Meridian*, pp. 239–251, 272–274; Bartlett, *Great Surveys*, pp. 327–328.

[46]Published in Washington, D.C., 1878. The full title was *Report on the Lands of the Arid Region of the United States, with a More Detailed Account of the Lands of Utah*. My references are to the Harvard University Press edition (Cambridge, Mass., 1962), edited by Wallace Stegner.

[47]Stegner's introduction to Powell's *Arid Region*, pp. xxiii–xxv; also Bartlett, *Great Surveys*, pp. 321–327.

far-sighted and revolutionary proposals, as bold as the major's 1869 dash through the canyons of the Colorado. Their wisdom is well recognized now, and they have through sheer necessity been put substantially into practice, albeit painfully and at awful cost, vindicating the foresighted brilliance of their early champion.[48] But when Powell pushed them, the forces of special interest groups, aided and abetted by rivalries and jealousies born of a long and vigorous career, moved in concert to unhorse the high-riding innovator.

Mounting pressures finally forced Powell in 1894 to resign his directorship of the United States Geological Survey. But he managed to stay on as head of the Bureau of American Ethnology, his other great governmental creation, which he continued lovingly and productively to nurture until his death in 1902.[49]

[48]Stegner's introduction to Powell's *Arid Region,* pp. xxiii–xxv.
[49]Stegner, *Beyond the Hundredth Meridian,* pp. 258–259, 345–350; Bartlett, *Great Surveys,* pp. 327–328.

CHAPTER 15

Yellowstone and Yosemite

THE first three-quarters of the nineteenth century was the Munchausen era in America, a time of tall tales and mythical heroes. Around the evening fires in the logging camps of Maine and the western Great Lakes there were tales of gargantuan Paul Bunyan and his fabulous blue ox, Babe; stories of the fantastic feats of Pecos Bill gave zest to lonely evenings on the isolated cattle spreads of the Southwest; and in the railroad construction camps the prowess of black John Henry and his 12-pound sledgehammer rang out in song. Less formalized, but kindred, were the tall tales of hunting exploits and Indians of the Far West. Two among the Western mountain men, John Colter and Jim Bridger, were widely renowned, in part for their authenticated exploits, but mostly for their fertile imaginations and engaging tall tales.

In 1806 when Colter secured his discharge from the homeward-bound Captains Lewis and Clark and turned back up the river, he was already well provided with tales of Western adventure that needed no embellishment. The next few years multiplied his eyebrow-lifting repertoire. There was, for example, the famous escape, when he outran all the Blackfoot warriors who had gathered to participate in his execution, to make his way naked and unarmed to the safety of a fur post 200 miles away. But even before that harrowing experience Colter was regaling listeners with accounts of wonders: fountains periodically bursting from the earth and jetting 200 feet into the air, seething and spluttering mud springs, boiling water bubbling up in an icy lake, wondrous waterfalls thundering into painted canyons, all in close proximity where the Snake, the Yellowstone, the Madison, and the Gallatin find their source waters, some to be carried to the Pacific, others to the Gulf and Atlantic. Colter's descriptions of those marvelous phenomena, which he had been the first white man to gaze upon, left his hearers incredulous. Three years after his 1807–8 exploration of the area known today as Yellowstone Park, a newspaper humorously dubbed the place "Colter's Hell."[1] John Colter's efforts to reveal the wonders of that unique region were little more successful than were the loggers' tales of Paul Bunyan in convincing the world of the actual existence of that giant.

Jim Bridger, mountain man of the next generation, who had trapped and campaigned across the Yellowstone country, vouched for Colter's claims and launched his own efforts to broadcast Yellowstone's wonders; but again with little success.[2] In later years there were many other futile attempts to convince a skeptical world, accustomed to hearing tall tales, of the wonders of Yellowstone. Thus, Lieutenant John Mullan, Governor Stevens's wide-ranging scout, during his survey of the northern railroad corridor in September 1853, while on his mission to visit the Flathead Indians on the Musselshell River, learned from them of "the existence of an infinite number of hot springs at the headwaters of the Missouri, Columbia and Yellowstone rivers, that hot geysers . . . exist at the head of the Yellowstone." In his 1863 report to the War Department covering a later survey of the region, Mullan said he had confirmed these reports through his own explorations.[3] Before the Topographical Corps became a casualty of the Civil War, an expedition, under the command of Captain William F. Raynolds, set out in 1859 to explore the Upper Yellowstone country and the area westward beyond the Big Horn Mountains,[4] across which Warren had found it necessary on his great map, then in preparation, to inscribe UNEXPLORED.[5] However, so deep was the snow in the passes in the summer of 1860 that even with Bridger as guide Raynolds was

[1]Robert Scarff, *Yellowstone and Grand Teton National Park* (New York, 1966), p. 2.
[2]F. Cecil Alter, *Jim Bridger* (Norman, Okla., 1962), pp. 76–77.
[3]Nathaniel Pitt Langford, *The Discovery of Yellowstone Park*, p. xxix (originally privately printed in 1905). This and subsequent citations are to the University of Nebraska edition of 1972, foreword by Aubrey W. Haines.
[4]William H. Goetzmann, *Army Exploration of the American West, 1803–1863* (New Haven, 1959), pp. 407–408.
[5]See Chapter 13 above, p. 308.

unable to cross the mountains between the Wind River and the Upper Yellowstone, and had to content himself with "listening to the marvelous tales of burning plains, immense lakes, and boiling springs," without being able to verify them.[6] Meanwhile Jim Bridger never tired of bending any willing ear to proclaim the hidden wonders of that region, which Indian mythology considered an unfinished bit of creation.[7] In the new towns of Montana, north and west of the park area, he found many interested, but few with sufficient temerity to brave the terrain and the dissident Indians of the region and to sally forth to see for themselves such wonders as "a column of water as large as his body spout as high as the flagpole in Virginia City."[8]

But by 1869, rancher David E. Folsom and his partner C. W. Cook had become sufficiently tantalized to set out to test for themselves the sources of Jim's tall tales. Armed to the teeth, they made a quick circuit up the Yellowstone, along its canyon and past its falls to Yellowstone Lake, then over to and down the Firehole and Madison rivers, before returning to confirm Bridger's stories of Colter's Hell.[9] So impressed was Folsom that, despite the exploitive temper of the postwar period and his own entrepreneurial bent, he was one who proposed that the area should be set aside as a national park.[10] Folsom's word-of-mouth account of his foray quickly stirred a lively interest. Friends in Helena invited him to recount to a group what he and Cook had seen on their tour; but, according to Nathaniel P. Langford, who was his successor in exploring the region and his colleague in the effort to create a park of it, when Folsom's audience was gathered, "there were so many present who were unknown to [him] that he was unwilling to risk his reputation for veracity, by a full recital . . . of the wonders he had seen."[11] Obviously Folsom was quite aware of the reception commonly given to Bridger's and

[6]Alter, *Bridger*, p. 287.

[7]Goetzmann, *Exploration and Empire* (New York, 1966), p. 405.

[8]Langford, *Discovery*, p. xxix; Alter, *Jim Bridger*, p. 326.

[9]There had been other early visitors to the area, most notably that of trapper and erstwhile surveyor Warren Angus Ferris, in 1833—see Aubrey L. Haines, *Yellowstone National Park, Its Exploration and Establishment* (Washington, D.C., 1974), pp. 10–11ff; for a full account of the Folsom expedition, see pp. 47–56.

[10]There is confused priority for the proposal. Probably Folsom's was the first, but without knowledge of it, Cornelius Hedges, one of the Washburn party, was the first (Nov. 9, 1870) to publish such a proposal—Langford, *Discovery*, xliii–xliv; Haines, *Yellowstone National Park*, p. 56.

[11]Langford, *Discovery*, p. xxxiv.

Colter's tales of the place. Nevertheless, his account galvanized into action a long-planned but chronically deferred Montana expedition known as the Washburn Expedition, which was destined to name and proclaim exploration of the area.

The prime mover of this first full-scale exploration of the future park area was Langford, who for some time had been president of a wagon road company that several years before had employed Jim Bridger. He counted himself among the few nonbelievers in the old saw, "Here *Lies* Bridger." General Henry D. Washburn, ex-congressman, now surveyor general of Montana, was elected leader of the thirteen-man group, which included several other leading citizens: Cornelius Hedges, a young lawyer and future judge; Samuel T. Hauser, banker and engineer; Walter Trumbull; and Truman C. Everts, who was destined to add high suspense to the expedition.[12] Although a military escort had been promised them, when the time came the nearby Crow bands were proving so threatening on the trails that the post commander at Fort Ellis, the nearest military post to the park region, could spare no more than a token escort of five soldiers, under Lieutenant Gustavus C. Doane, a capable young officer with training in geography and geology, valuable to the expedition. With supplies for thirty days for their planned twenty-five-day tour, the column marched out of Fort Ellis on August 22, 1870.

From the outset, numerous signs of skulking Crows made apprehension a constant companion as they moved eastward to the north-flowing Yellowstone, and thence up to its stupendous canyon and on to the wonderful 308-foot[13] plunge of the Lower Falls into the richly colored gorge below, finding all along the way a bounty of wonders: a tributary stream memorable for its hot sulphur springs, rock spires and towers, and an exquisite waterfall called Tower Falls. Near the river, rising from the west side of the canyon was the most notable mountain they would encounter. From its summit (10,243 ft.) most of the present National Park area could be seen, including its scenic jewel, Yellowstone Lake. To this peak they gave General Washburn's name. Further along, for a sulphur spring boiling up from a 20-foot orifice and exuding offensive gases, they thought Hell Broth Springs an appropriate name. Nearby were a dozen or more of these weird effusions, flowing into a creek whose

[12]A richly documented account of the Washburn Expedition appears in Haines, *Yellowstone National Park*, pp. 59–99.
[13]Half again higher than Niagara Falls.

rim they followed for some 3 miles to where it entered the river, 1,500 feet down in its canyon. Although its tumultuous rapids could be clearly seen, they were so deep that no sound of their roar reached the canyon rim. Later on, when the men camped on a stream they called Cascade Creek, they were amazed to find themselves in the immediate presence of the Lower Falls, for there had been no forewarning sound, even the roar of the falls being "smothered by the vast depth of the cañon into which they plunge." Seeking to reach the river itself below the falls, they scrambled down through the creek gorge, past cascades they called Crystal Falls whose beauty rivaled the far more grand falls toward which they were making their way. Below Crystal Falls the narrow gorge displayed "a thousand fantastic shapes," huge masses of obsidian and other volcanic matter, tracks of grizzly bears—the whole suggesting "nothing earthly nor heavenly," but in their opinion deserving the name the Devil's Den.[14]

Langford confessed the impossibility of giving "the faintest conception" of the beauty and majesty of the cataracts of the Yellowstone and its immense canyon, "through which the river descends, which perhaps more than the falls is calculated to fill the observer with feelings of mingled awe and terror." Some of the party located Inspiration Point and were awestruck by the superb spectacle the falls and canyon presented. The "hues of abundant vegetations . . . crowned with a vesture of evergreen pines," verdant meadows, "remarkable volcanic deposits, wonderful boiling springs, jets of heated vapor, large collections of sulphur, immense rocks and petrifications . . . in great profusion"; a river "filled with trout, and bear, elk, deer"; and mountain lions roaming the vicinity, all added to the "stupendous climax" of Yellowstone's wonders, the awe-inspiring falls themselves.[15]

Reluctantly they left this place of marvels to resume their southward route to the lake they had seen from Washburn's summit. Along the way, 6 miles above the falls, they came to the place now known as Hayden Valley, the locale of a variety of sulphur springs. In places the hollow sound of their horses' tramp gave warning of cavernous depths concealed below the surface. And in the vicinity was Mud Volcano, where the ground itself resounded with "dull, thundering, booming sounds." Among the numerous boiling mud

[14]Langford, *Discovery,* pp. 27–28.
[15]*Ibid.,* pp. 27–36.

springs nearby, the most astonishing was Mud Geyser, which was declared the "greatest marvel" yet seen. Its crater, 30 feet in diameter, rose 35 feet above the surrounding ground, which "shook and trembled as from successive shocks of an earthquake," while from the crater itself came explosions of sulphurous gases that could be heard a half mile away. Mud on the topmost branches of nearby trees 150 feet tall indicated that recent eruptions had cast it up 300 or 400 feet. The quantities of exuding sulphur in the area fouled the water all about and tarnished the party's watches.[16]

On the evening of September 3 they camped on the shore of Yellowstone Lake, which Langford was confident was "the most beautiful body of water in the world," with sandy beaches like the ocean, projecting rocks, emerald islands, deep inlets, and crystal-clear water, to which "two of the three Tetons" provided a magnificent backdrop.[17] At this point the decision was made to head east along the north side of the lake and continue round clockwise to its southwest bay, visible from their campsite and marked by columns of steam rising from hot springs in the lake. It proved an extremely arduous seven-day journey, much of the way through dense forests encumbered by undergrowth and fallen timbers so numerous that the pack animals sometimes had literally to be lifted across them. Langford and Lieutenant Doane climbed a peak on the east side of the lake. From its summit they had a memorable view of the Absaroka range to the east, the Tetons to the southwest, and the exquisite lake in full outline below them to the west, providing Langford with the opportunity to prepare the first reasonably accurate portrayal of the lake's irregular shoreline and islands. In the course of their struggle through the dense forest, Truman Everts became separated from the party and lost his way. Several days were devoted to a systematic search for him before a heavy snowfall and dwindling supplies forced them to abandon him to his fate and move on with greatly dampened spirits.[18] As it turned out, after thirty-seven days of wandering and near starvation, Everts found his way out of the Yellowstone wilderness to recount his

[16]*Ibid.*, pp. 38–47. The Mud Geyser subsided soon after these observations—see note pp. 48–49 and Gustavus C. Doane, *Report of Lieutenant Gustavus C. Doane upon the So-called Yellowstone Expedition of 1870*, Senate Exec. Doc. 51, 41st Congress, 3d Sess., U.S. serial no. 1440 (1871).

[17]Langford, *Discovery*, p. 50; N. P. Langford, "The Wonders of the Yellowstone," *Scribner's Monthly*, II, no. 2 (May–June 1871), 114.

[18]Langford, *Discovery*, pp. 54–93.

harrowing ordeal in a gripping *Scribner's* article, "Thirty-seven Days of Peril."[19]

The latter part of the search for Everts was conducted from a campsite at the southwest extremity of Yellowstone Lake—an area of thermal activity known as the Thumb, the principal features of which are the Paint Pots and numerous hot springs displaying a variety of colors. Among the ninety or more springs many were of boiling mud in a variety of colors, white, lavender, and pink; even more wonderful were the water "springs of various colors, in some cases dark red, in others scarlet, in others yellow, and in still others green." Although clustered in close proximity, the varying levels of these springs indicated that none flowed from a shared source beneath the surface.[20]

From the Thumb they struck out westward to find Firehole River, where Bridger and Folsom had reported concentrations of wonders, and a route to the Madison and their homeward trail. Five miles below where they reached the Firehole, they entered an area of extravagant phenomena to which they were fittingly welcomed by "an immense body of sparkling water projected suddenly and with terrific force into the air to the height of over a hundred feet." In the valley below "were a thousand hot springs of various sizes and character, and five hundred craters jetting forth vapor," many with "beautiful encrustations." During the twenty-two hours of their stay they counted twelve geysers in action. One of these, which erupted regularly every sixty to sixty-five minutes, General Washburn named Old Faithful. Neighboring marvels included the Castle, an encrusted crater, its summit resembling "the ruins of some tower with its broken down turrets"; the unfathomable basin of an ultramarine spring in front of the Castle; the Giant, a geyser that steadily, for more than an hour, shot a stream 3 feet wide 140 feet into the air; the Fan, which radiated two 60-foot jets; and the Beehive, which, for their breakfast entertainment, shot up a column of water 219 feet high and sustained it long enough for the height to be measured by instrument and triangulation. But most spectacular of all was the Giantess, a geyser within a geyser, which reached skyward 250 feet "amid a thousand rainbows." They

[19] *Scribner's Monthly*, III, no. 1 (November 1871), 1–17; Langford, *Discovery*, Haine's Foreword, p. xii, and note pp. 100–101.

[20] Langford, *Discovery*, pp. 93–95; *Scribner's Monthly*, Nos. 1 (May 1871) and 2 (June 1871), 120–121.

judged it "the greatest wonder of our trip."[21]

That night Cornelius Hedges suggested that the whole area should be made into a national park, thus adding their dedication to that of Folsom and Cook.[22] Despite the fact that the expedition arrived back in Virginia City without knowledge of many other marvels, upon their return its leaders lost no time in joining a concerted drive for legislation to set aside the Yellowstone area for use as a park. To that end Langford prepared and sent to *Scribner's Monthly* an account of their expedition, which appeared in the May-June 1871 issue. It had been one of the main regrets of the expedition that there was no artist or photographer to picture the wonders they saw. Trumbull had tried his hand at sketching some of the geyser craters, and one of Doane's soldiers tried his on the falls of the Yellowstone. With these and Langford's descriptions as guides, a rising young artist, Thomas Moran, was able to create very creditable illustrations for the *Scribner's* article. It was an assignment with a destiny, for when Moran learned of plans for a new Yellowstone expedition under Ferdinand Hayden, he arranged to join it and became an important element in its success. Everts followed up the Langford account with his "Thirty-seven Days of Peril" in *Scribner's* November issue.[23] Nevertheless, skepticism persisted: one reviewer of Langford's account concluded that its author "must be the champion liar of the Northwest." But the National Park protagonists were part of an ascendant movement, rapidly gaining adherents. A member of the United States Geological Survey, just returned from a look at the area, reported that "Langford did not dare tell one-half of what he saw." Doane's official *Report* to the War Department added substantial weight to the movement. Professor Hayden, leader of the 1871 expedition, voiced his opinion that "for graphic description and thrilling interest," Doane's *Report* "has not been surpassed by any official report since the times of Lewis and Clark."[24] Langford's ardent advocacy of the park idea soon gained him the sobriquet "National Park" Langford. As a result of this campaign, Congress in the spring of 1871 provided for a full-scale investigatory expedition under the Interior Department's Geologi-

[21]Langford, *Discovery*, pp. 106–112; *Scribner's Monthly*, no. 2 (May-June 1871), 123–127.

[22]Langford, *Discovery*, pp. 117–118.

[23]III, no. 1, November 1871, 1–17.

[24]Langford, *Discovery*, pp. lx, xlii.

cal and Geographical Survey of the Territories, under the direction of its head, Professor Hayden; and the army too responded by ordering a team to survey and map the region. Both expeditions made speedy preparations to enter the area during the 1871 season.[25]

Constrained to suppress their basic rivalry in order to take advantage of Hayden's substantial military escort, the army survey team under John Whitney Barlow and David Porter Heap set out in mid-July together with Hayden's well-equipped party of thirty-four, exclusive of its escort, to make their respective detailed examinations of Yellowstone's reported wonders. In the course of their seven-week survey, the engineers secured the data for a detailed map of the environs of Yellowstone River, the lake, and the trails leading over to the thermal areas of the Firehole. Except for an exploration up the Gardner River, a tributary stream that enters the Yellowstone near the north boundary of the park, the combined party covered much the same portions of the area as the Washburn Expedition. However, Hayden made a considerably more extensive and detailed investigation of the geyser basins along the Firehole. It was on its Gardner River variance from the Washburn trail that the 1871 expedition disclosed one of Yellowstone's greatest marvels, Mammoth Hot Springs. The revelation of the beautiful, tinted, "frozen" waterfalls of Yellowstone's great hot springs, and the work of Moran and of the photographer William H. Jackson during their six weeks in Yellowstone, destined Hayden's expedition for an important place in this last chapter of the story of the revealing of America.[26]

Thomas Moran, born in Lancashire one of three artist sons of a hand-loom weaver, had grown up in the United States but at thirty-four had only recently returned from art studies in England when the opportunity to join Hayden's Yellowstone expedition presented itself.[27] Artist-photographer Jackson, twenty-eight at the time of his recruitment as photographer of the expedition, had seen a year of service with the Union army in Virginia as an official artist; he had left his native Vermont to adventure in the West, and photographed the route of the new Union Pacific all the way to Promontory Point, which he reached two months after the gala Golden Spike ceremo-

[25]Goetzmann, *Exploration and Empire,* pp. 406–407.

[26]*Ibid.,* pp. 502–509; Richard A. Bartlett, *Great Surveys of the American West* (Norman, Okla., 1962), pp. 37–73.

[27]Thurman Wilkins, *Thomas Moran, Artist of the Mountains* (Norman, Okla., 1966).

nies in May 1869. Convinced that photography was a new and exciting art form of immense potential, Jackson dedicated himself to its development, with the West as his principal subject. It was on his 1869 photographic expedition that Jackson and Professor Hayden met and the seed of years of cooperation between the master geologist and the master photographer was planted.[28]

At Mammoth Hot Springs Moran and Jackson found a subject for their arts the like of which the world had never seen. The terrace-like deposits of calcareous sediments laid down by the waters from these high mountain springs were described by Hayden in *Scribner's Monthly* as forming "a high white mountain looking precisely like a frozen cascade. . . . The surface covered by the deposits comprises from three to four square miles. The springs now in active operation cover an area of about one square mile . . . and create a series of reservoirs or bathing-pools, rising one above the other, semi-circular in form, with most elegantly scalloped margins composed of calcareous matter. . . ." The diversity of pastel tints and the grace of the frozen cascades were captured by Moran in his beautiful watercolors, while the light effects, contrasts, and softly graceful lines were perfect subjects for Jackson's impressive photographs, in some of which, to provide a measure of scale, Moran is posed against the alabaster background of one of the frozen waterfalls. Before leaving these marvelous expressions of nature, Hayden noted with concern that they were already threatened by commercialism. Two men had staked out claims that covered 320 acres of the active springs and, in compliance with the homestead laws, were preparing to erect "improvements" on their claims. Already attracted by the springs were a number of invalids, who were camping nearby, and who were enthusiastic about the therapeutic virtues of the springs.[29]

From Mammoth Hot Springs the Hayden and Barlow parties moved east to the Yellowstone, up which they followed much the same way as had the Washburn group. But there were longer hesitations at the canyon and the falls to allow Jackson to make his magnificent first photographic prints and Moran to capture in watercol-

[28]This account of Jackson's early career is based on Clarence S. Jackson, *Picture Maker of the Old West: William H. Jackson* (New York, 1958).

[29]F. V. Hayden in *Scribner's Monthly*, "The Wonders of the West, II, More About the Yellowstone," III, no. 4 (February 1872), 389–396. The article was impressively illustrated by Moran.

ors the glories of those scenes. Although, according to Hayden, the artist had despairingly exclaimed that they were quite beyond the reach of human art, Moran's watercolors nevertheless would later guide him in the preparation of his gorgeous canvas, "The Grand Canyon of the Yellowstone," bought by Congress to hang in the nation's Capitol.[30] Later, for a companion piece, Congress also purchased Moran's equally beautiful and dramatic Grand Canyon painting, "The Chasm of the Colorado," done at Powell's behest in 1873.

While a detailed survey of Yellowstone Lake was being made, Hayden, with a small party including Jackson with his ponderous equipment, set out for the notorious Firehole Basin, across the high divide and through a "rocky and densely wooded region" of fallen trees, "lodged upon each other" and piled in networks "presenting insurmountable obstacles" to the progress of the traveler. During the five days spent in the Firehole region, they estimated there were 1,200 to 1,500 active springs and geysers in an area 5 miles square. Jackson photographed many of these, including their outstanding find, the Great Geyser, which then every thirty-two hours ejected "a column of hot water eight feet in diameter to a height of two hundred feet," for a duration of about fifteen minutes.[31]

With Moran's watercolors, Jackson's photographs, and his own wide reputation as a scientific explorer to back him, Hayden hastened back to Washington to join the Yellowstone Park protagonists in their struggle against time to preserve the area unspoiled for park purposes. He hurriedly prepared his *Scribner's* article and Moran its illustrations, both corroborating all that Langford had claimed for the place, while adding more to its catalogue of wonders. Moran's paintings were put on exhibit for the members of Congress. Key members were presented bound folio volumes of Jackson's most striking Yellowstone photographs. Stereopticon views of many of its outstanding features were distributed among the members of Congress and influential people all across the country, so that soon hundreds of thousands were seeing Yellowstone's strange and wonderful phenomena in three-dimensional perfection. Faced with such formidable evidence, skepticism was finally vanquished; opposition

[30]*Ibid.*, p. 392; Wallace Stegner, *Beyond the Hundredth Meridian* (Boston, 1953), pp. 177–180.

[31]Hayden, in *Scribner's Monthly*, III, no. 4 (February 1872), 394–395; Goetzmann, *Exploration and Empire*, pp. 507–508.

crumbled, and Hayden was asked to supply a description of the boundaries the park should have. On March 1, 1872, President Grant put his signature to the bill establishing Yellowstone National Park—the world's first National Park.[32]

Unlike the marvels of Grand Canyon and Yellowstone, knowledge of Yosemite filtered out, bit by bit, for three decades before there was any general awareness of its matchless scenic wonders. For two generations after the settlement in 1770 of Monterey on the coast opposite Yosemite, there was no knowledge of the existence of the wonders hidden in the High Sierras: the snow-capped peaks of the eastern skyline beyond the San Joaquin Valley where the Sierras reach for the sky, with Mount Whitney's 14,495-foot peak leading an array of near rivals for the altitude record for the contiguous states. Then, in the fall of 1833, Joseph Walker's rough band of mountain men, despatched from Captain Bonneville's Green River rendezvous for an investigatory foray into California, struggled across the Sierra barrier for three terrible weeks before emerging on its western flank, in the Yosemite–Hetch Hetchy region, where they found trees "eighteen fathoms round the trunk," and looked down from "precipices . . . more than a mile high," as they made their way down the backbone of the lofty ridge separating the Tuolumne and Mercid rivers.[33] Apparently their reports were given as short shrift as were Colter's and Bridger's stories of Yellowstone.[34] Nobody was inspired to investigate. In fact, the next recorded glimpse of Yosemite's scenic offerings by any outsider was almost two decades later—and accidental.

In the neighborhood of Frémont's Mariposa estate an exceptional frontier merchant had for several years prior to 1850 operated a highly prosperous mercantile establishment that had grown to include several locations. The miners, mostly resident Indians who worked the several placer mines of the region, regularly used these

[32]Robert Taft, *Photography and the American Scene* (New York, 1938), pp. 298–301; Jackson, *Picture Maker*, pp. 145–158; Goetzmann, *Exploration and Empire*, p. 508; *National Parks and the American Landscape* (Washington, D.C., 1972), pp. 86ff.

[33]Walker's exact route is open to some speculation, but there is no question that he saw ample to invite investigation—Carl P. Russell, *One Hundred Years in Yosemite* (Berkeley, 1932), pp. 5–8. The trees they reported were probably *Sequoia gigantea* of the Tuolumne Grove—*ibid.*, p. 8.

[34]Bernard DeVoto, *Across the Wide Missouri* (Boston, 1947), pp. 146–149; Goetzmann, *Exploration and Empire*, pp. 150–155.

trading posts of James D. Savage to exchange their bags of gold dust for merchandise. However, in the fall of 1850 relations with the Indians of the Sierra Valley deteriorated. Savage's establishments at Mariposa and Fresno suffered surprise attacks by bands of native raiders led by the mountain people. At Fresno all his white employees were killed. His store on the Mariposa was burned, its attendants killed, and his Indian wives carried off. Quickly, volunteers launched a punitive expedition against the raiders, the U-zu-ma-ti (Yosemite), or "grizzly bear" people of the Sierras. Under the command of Savage, this "Mariposa Battalion" set out in March 1851 to chastise the offending U-zu-ma-ti in their home in the upper valley of the Mercid.[35]

The route the Mariposa Battalion followed into the valley of the Mercid closely approximated the present Wawona Road into Yosemite. When it reached Inspiration Point, one of the party, deeply moved, recalled the effect: "Haze hung—light as gossamer—and clouds partially dimmed the higher cliffs and mountains . . . a peculiar exalted sensation seemed to fill my whole being, and I found my eyes in tears with emotion." While camped that night in view of Bridalveil Falls, a youth, stirred by the magnificent valley ahead, proposed that it be called Yosemite for the tribe whose home it was and from whom they were intent on wresting it. The next day, following along the south bank of the Mercid, they passed beneath the shadow of Cathedral Rocks and came within view of El Capitan's 3,600-foot sheer granite wall, rising in grandeur from the north side of the valley. The intermittent groves of magnificent conifers were in sufficiently open stands to permit the view across the river to the Three Brothers, and further on the valley's gem, Yosemite Falls, in its successive leaps of 1,430 feet and 675 feet. They set up camp opposite where Indian Canyon comes in from the north, between Castle Cliffs and the great Royal Arches. Finding no enemy, the Mariposa Battalion's scouting parties turned explorers. One group penetrated Tenaya Canyon[36] beyond Mirror Lake, a placid mirror in the valley. Another ascended Mercid Canyon to be rewarded with Vernal Falls, the steep dome of Liberty Cap, and Nevada Falls. But most impressive of all was Half Dome, a great 8,800-foot-high granite dome with its south half missing, leaving a sheer parabolic face

[35]Russell, *One Hundred Years*, pp. 15–25.

[36]*Ibid.*, p. 146. Tenaya was named for the chief of the Yosemites—Goetzmann, *Exploration and Empire*, p. 369.

looking down on the Mercid's superb valley, the other half in ages past having fallen away along vertical fracture lines, and the resulting talus having been carried off by stupendous glaciers that for countless ages ground their way down all these narrow valleys, carving and shaping their confining walls into shapes that provide scenic marvels.[37]

Finding no trace of the Indians they sought, empty-handed but otherwise enriched, the battalion turned back for home. Later in the spring, after two more expeditions into the valley, it was cleared of dissident natives. However, few, other than those purposeful groups, were curious enough to undertake the very difficult way leading to the valley's wonders. A handful of prospectors braved it, but found little there to interest them. Yosemite continued to be rarely visited until 1855, when wider interest was aroused by several first-hand accounts of the valley, written by members of the military expeditions and published in the San Francisco papers. Their descriptions of Yosemite's wonders, especially that of a 1,000-foot-high waterfall, inspired James M. Hutchings, a San Francisco journalist, to investigate with an eye to its tourist potential. With two Yosemites as guides, the Hutchings party entered the valley in June 1855; Thomas Ayres, an artist, accompanied them with pencils, chalk, and composition boards. After "five glorious days" of "scenic banqueting," they emerged from the valley to proclaim the marvels they had seen. At Mariposa, gateway to the valley, Hutchings supplied the newly established Mariposa *Gazette* with a glowing description of that "banquet," an account soon noted and copied the country over, while Ayres's portrayals of the valley's most notable sights soon became the basis for widely distributed lithographic reproductions. Hutchings and Ayres had launched tourist travel to fabulous Yosemite.[38] By 1856 entrepreneurs had seized the opportunity to reap a pecuniary harvest, easing the difficult access by means of an improved Wawona toll trail and a wayfarer's camp in the Mariposa Big Tree Grove. Stockmen seeing the lush meadows along the Mercid brought their sheep (which John Muir would later castigate as "hoofed locusts") and built their herdsmen's camps. Hotel men soon followed, setting up crude hostelries for which everything but

[37]Harriet E. Huntington, *The Yosemite Story* (New York, 1966), pp. 64–65; Russell, *One Hundred Years*, pp. 25–48.

[38]Russell, *One Hundred Years*, pp. 48–50; *National Parks and the American Landscape*, pp. 102–107.

the timber had to be brought in on muleback over the difficult and dangerous access trail. Homesteaders staked out claims and began their "improvements." The exploitation of Yosemite burgeoned.

The *California Magazine,* founded by Hutchings the year after his expedition into the valley, soon became almost a promotional organ for Yosemite. In 1859 it ran the earliest photographs of its notable features, adding another medium for broadcasting the valley's extravagant offerings.[39] By that year Hutchings's continuing promotion was beginning to show results, especially among Californians; but Easterners too, in increasing numbers, dared Yosemite's difficult access. Notable among these was the editor Horace Greeley, who had popularized the advice to the young of his day to go west. Upon his return east after a tour of Yosemite, Greeley added the powerful voice of the *New York Tribune* to the mounting acclaim. "I know of no single wonder of nature on earth which can claim superiority over Yosemite,"[40] he wrote enthusiastically. To promote Yosemite as a tourist attraction Hutchings moved into the valley, acquired a hotel, and set up a saw mill at the foot of the falls to get the lumber needed for its expansion and improvement.[41]

Soon, however, a concerted effort was launched to preserve Yosemite from private exploitation. The newly created California Geo-

[39]Russell, *One Hundred Years,* p. 56; Holway R. Jones, *John Muir and the Sierra Club* (San Francisco, 1965), pp. 5–7; Taft, *Photography and the American Scene,* pp. 269–270, 494.

[40]On his Western journey in 1859 nothing had more impressed Greeley than Yosemite Valley. In one of his despatches to the *Tribune* he told of descending into the valley by moonlight to stand "by the rushing, roaring waters of the Mercid. . . . Can I ever forget it? The valley here is scarcely half a mile wide while its northern wall of mainly naked, perpendicular granite is at least four thousand feet high. . . . But the modicum of moonlight that fell into this awful gorge gave to that precipice a vagueness of outline, an indefinite vastness, a ghostly and weird spirituality. Had the mountain spoken to me in audible voice . . . I should hardly have been surprised" —*An Overland Journey from New York to San Francisco* (New York, 1860); edited by Charles T. Duncan (New York, 1964), pp. 256–258. Greeley was almost as impressed by the Mariposa sequoias, believing them to have been "of very substantial size when David danced before the Ark, when Solomon laid the foundations of the Temple" —*ibid.,* p. 265.

The impact of Greeley's despatches, later embodied in his *Overland Journey,* appearing at the height of the great journalist's fame and popularity, is difficult to overestimate. Earlier writers may have said, in effect, "Go West, young man, go West!" When Greeley said it, thousands listened.

[41]Among the workers at Hutchings's saw mill in 1868 was a newly arrived Scot named John Muir, a man whose voice and pen were to become powerful forces for the preservation and development of the area into one of the world's best known and most admired national parks—Russell, *One Hundred Years,* pp. 57–58.

logical Survey of 1860–74, under the direction of Josiah D. Whitney, lent its support. When Whitney's studies reached the southern Sierras and his scientific team saw the regions of the present Yosemite, Kings Canyon, and Sequoia national parks, the impact of the splendors hidden in those mountains was profound. As the survey reached Yosemite, one of Whitney's assistants, Professor William H. Brewer, declared the area "one of the most remarkable in the world." Whitney agreed, and began urging legal enactments to preserve it for public enjoyment.[42] While the Civil War raged in the East and events moved toward their 1864 climax, in California a different sort of struggle was deciding the destiny of Yosemite and the big trees of the Sierras. Advocates seeking their preservation for public enjoyment were mounting a clamor for action. To their assistance in 1863 came the Romantic German-American artist Albert Bierstadt, a product of the famed Düsseldorf Academy. Following a visit to the area, Bierstadt produced a series of superb, evocative, and deeply moving canvasses of Yosemite, perhaps unmatched in the annals of American landscape painting.[43] A bill to grant the state of California an area of almost 50 square miles embracing Yosemite Valley and the nearby Mariposa Big Tree Grove, to be preserved "for the benefit of mankind," was signed into law by President Lincoln on July 1, 1864, and the state accepted the grant in September "as a public pleasure ground."

Although Whitney and the California Geological Survey had played an important role in California's success in securing the grant of Yosemite to the state, among the legislators there was rising resentment against the survey for importing its scientists and engineers from the East to the exclusion of Californians. Even as Congress was in the process of passing the legislation for the Yosemite grant, the state's appropriation for the Geological Survey was reduced by half. Despite that body blow, Whitney and his dedicated group carried their work forward without interruption. In fact, 1864 became outstanding in the annals of the survey. As soon as winter's snows released their grip on the High Sierras south of Yosemite, in the area of the present Kings Canyon and Sequoia national parks, Whitney had an able team on its way into those almost unknown alpine regions.[44] Led by Professor Brewer, with

[42]Goetzmann, *Exploration and Empire*, pp. 368–370.

[43]Paul A. Rossi and David C. Hunt, *The Art of the Old West* (New York, 1971), pp. 193–195; *National Parks and the American Landscape*, plates 75–80.

[44]Goetzmann, *Exploration and Empire*, pp. 370–372.

young Clarence King as one of his assistants, in May the party had set up camp in a grove of forest giants, "pines two hundred and forty feet high," with "straight fluted trunks smooth and without a branch for a hundred feet." This grove of *Sequoia gigantea* characteristically occupied a granite spur between the Kaweah and Kings river canyons at an elevation of between 5,000 and 7,000 feet, above or below which they do not grow in the Sierras.[45] In the region were other stupendous, previously unexplored groves. To the east beyond, strenuous and dangerous exploratory expeditions were undertaken during the spring and summer, and many of the highest peaks of the contiguous states rose to challenge the mountaineering skills of the party.

When Brewer's group returned to San Francisco at the season's end, word of the approval of the Yosemite grant had arrived. Despite the lateness of the season, the survey team was forthwith despatched into the field again to make a boundary survey of the grant as required by the Act, and to conduct studies of the area in greater detail than had been done in its preliminary Yosemite survey.[46]

These 1864 activities of the California Geological Survey provided much of the material for two important books, both of which contributed immensely to the authoritative revealing of the phenomenal geography of the regions of the High Sierras. In 1869 the survey chief himself, Josiah Whitney, published a book under the deceptively limited title of *The Yosemite Guide-Book;* in addition to justifying its guidebook status, this contained a mass of material on the Sierra surveys of 1864, not only in Yosemite but also in the Kings Canyon, Kaweah, and Kern river regions and the Sierra peaks beyond. It also provided the most scientific and complete disclosure of the Sierra sequoias yet published, with detailed reports covering the Calaveras and Mariposa groves and those now preserved in Sequoia National Park. Whitney's book went into many editions, some reduced to pocket size for use as a field handbook.

Two years later Clarence King, Whitney's assistant and companion on many an expedition into the Sierras and other parts of California, wrote a series of sketches that appeared as articles, mostly

[45]Clarence King, *Mountaineering in the Sierra Nevada* (Boston, 1872), p. 30, and Chaps. 3 and 4; Josiah D. Whitney, *The Yosemite Guide-Book* (Cambridge, Mass., 1869), pp. 112–138, 152–155.

[46]Goetzmann, *Exploration and Empire*, pp. 377–378; Bartlett, *Great Surveys*, pp. 135–140.

in the *Atlantic Monthly*, relating his experiences in the Sierras and an expedition to Mount Shasta. In 1872 *Mountaineering in the Sierra Nevada* appeared in book form. King's book played a major role in revealing the wonders of the southern Sierras, now attested to by the presence there of three of the nation's outstanding national parks. King's work was an immediate and immense success, going into numerous editions, and remains today a firmly established classic of Western exploration, secure in its place alongside Irving's *Astoria*, Frémont's *Narrative*, and Powell's *Colorado*.

On site in the Yosemite Valley in October 1864 King had managed to secure for himself the responsibility for the internal study, leaving to others the rigorous and restricted task of laying out the boundaries of the grant—a division of duties that eventually also returned rich dividends to readers of his Ruskinesque descriptions of Yosemite. It is appropriate in conclusion here to quote from these to illustrate the flavor of his significant contribution.[47]

King describes his introduction to the big trees of the Sierras:

Passing from the glare of the open country into the dusky forest, one seems to enter a door, and ride into a vast covered hall. The whole sensation is of being roofed and enclosed. You are never tired of gazing down long vistas, where in stately groups, stand tall shafts of pine. Columns they are, each with its characteristic tinting and finish, yet all standing together with an air of relationship and harmony. Feathery branches, trimmed with living green, wave through the upper air. . . .

Then the sequoias; one

a tapering, regularly round column of about forty feet in diameter at the base, and rising two hundred and seventy-four feet, adorned with a few huge branches, which start horizontally from the trunk, but quickly turn down and spray out. The bark, thick but not rough, is scored up and down at considerable intervals with deep, smooth grooves, and is the brightest cinnamon color mottled in purple and yellow. [Nothing can] link the past and today with anything like the power of these monuments of living antiquity, trees that began to grow before the Christian era, and, full of hale vitality and green old age, still bid fair to grow broad and high for countless centuries to come.[48]

[47]Goetzmann, *Exploration and Empire*, pp. 377–378.
[48]King, *Mountaineering*, pp. 28–29, 41, 43. King is here describing a grove some 70 miles southeast of Yosemite in Sequoia National Park, but his description could as well apply to the Mariposa Grove in Yosemite Park. At about the same time that King's *Mountaineering* was published, in 1872, an article appeared in *Scribner's Magazine* III, no. 3 (January 1872), 261–277, entitled "Wonders of the West I." This

When King's party came in view of the valley, "that splendid afternoon shadow which divides the face of El Capitan was projected far up and across the valley, cutting it in halves—one a mosaic of russets and yellows with dark pine and glimpses of white river; the other a cobalt blue zone, in which the familiar groves and meadows were suffused with shadow-tones." There was a marked contrast to his June sighting of the same scene. Then, "through slumberous yet transparent atmosphere, you look down upon emerald freshness of green, upon arrowy rush of swollen river, and here and there, along pearly cliffs, as from the clouds, tumbles white silver dust of cataracts. . . . All stern sublimity, all geological terribleness, are veiled away behind magic curtains of cloud-shadow and broken light."[49]

Now, in October,

the shattered fronts of walls stand out sharp and terrible, sweeping down in broken crag and cliff to a valley . . . of autumnal death. . . . In this cold, naked strength, one has crowded on him the geological record of mountain work, of granite plateau suddenly rent asunder, of the slow, imperfect manner in which Nature has vainly striven to smooth her rough work and bury the ruins with thousands of years' accumulation of soil and *debris.*

Seeing Yosemite's bones showing through its nakedness, the geologist in King visualized this place being shaped through hundreds of millions of years: first "the slow gathering of marine sediment within the early ocean," then "in the early Jurassic period this level sea floor came suddenly to be lifted into the air and crumpled in folds, through whose yawning fissures and ruptured axes outpoured wide zones of granite," and then a "volcanic age of fire and steam," followed by a relatively recent age of 2 million years ago, a "glacial period, when the Sierras were one broad field of snow, with huge dragons of ice crawling down its slopes, and wearing their armor into the rocks," to transform it to its present beauty and majesty of line and shape.

Today their burnished pathways are legibly traced with the history of the past. Every ice-stream is represented by a feeble river, every great glacier cascade by a torrent of white foam dashing itself down rugged walls, or spouting from the brinks of upright cliffs. The very avalanche tracks are

article, enriched by Thomas Moran's illustrations and the wit of its author, Isaac Bromley, was a rich portrayal of Yosemite's Mariposa Grove.

[49]King, *Mountaineering,* p. 133.

darkened by clustered woods, and over the level pathway of the great Yosemite glacier itself is spread a park of green, a mosaic of forest, a thread of river.[50]

King and a companion climbed to the crest of El Capitan:

This grandest of granite precipices is capped by a short forehead of stone sweeping down to level, severe brows, which jut out a few feet over the edge. A few weather beaten, battle twisted and black pines cling in clefts, contrasting in force with the solid white stone. . . . The rock fell under us in one sheer sweep thirty-two hundred feet. . . . Directly beneath, outspread like a delicately tinted chart, lay the lovely park of Yosemite, winding in and out about the solid white feet of precipices. . . . Deep in front the Bridal Veil brook made its way through the bottom of an open gorge and plunged off the edge of a thousand foot cliff, falling into white water dust and drifting in pale, translucent clouds out over the tree-tops of the valley.

Directly across from El Capitan

rose the great mass of Cathedral Rocks,—a group quite suggestive of the Florence Duomo. But our grandest view was eastward, above the deep sheltered valley and over the tops of those terrible granite walls, out upon rolling ridges of stone and wonderful granite domes. Nothing in the whole list of irruptive products, except volcanoes themselves, is so wonderful as these domed mountains. They are of every variety of conoidal form, having horizontal sections accurately elliptical, ovoid, or circular, and profiles varying from such semicircles as the cap behind the Sentinel to the graceful infinite curves of the North Dome.

Finally, the valley's most special offering, its centerpiece:

As you stand at the base of those cool walls of granite that rise to the clouds from the green floor of Yosemite, a beautiful park, carpeted with verdure, expands from your feet. . . . An arch of blue bridges over from cliff to cliff. From the far summit of a wall of pearly granite, over stains of purple and yellow—leaping, as it were, from the very cloud—falls a silver scarf, light, lace-like, graceful, luminous, swayed by the wind. The cliffs' repose is undisturbed by the silvery fall whose endlessly varying forms of wind-tossed spray lend an element of life to what would otherwise be masses of inanimate stone. The Yosemite is a grace. It is an adornment. It is a ray of light on the solid front of the precipice.[51]

To conclude the story of the legal evolution of the Yosemite grant into Yosemite National Park, it is necessary to hark back to 1864.

[50] Ibid., pp. 134, 4–5, 153.
[51] Ibid., pp. 136–137, 196–197.

After notification of President Lincoln's approval, the grant covered only the Yosemite Valley up to the surrounding ridge crests and the separated Mariposa Big Tree Grove. It had been formally accepted by the California legislature in September, and to develop and administer the area as a public pleasure ground a commission had been established under the direction of Whitney and Frederick Law Olmstead. Olmstead became its chairman and chief executive officer.[52]

From the outset the commission was beset with controversy and dissension, with the result that after two years Olmstead resigned in frustration and returned to the more park-conscious East. Hampered by private holdings within the reserved area, encroachments on its perimeter, the trespasses of intransigent herdsmen, and other claimants of special privileges; by inadequate support, both financial and political; and by its own flaccidity in dealing with these problems, the commission was slow in its progress toward realizing the dreams of Olmstead and a new devotee, John Muir.[53] Prodded by Muir's inspiration and influential Eastern support, Congress in 1890 surrounded the state-controlled Yosemite and Mariposa Grove with a five-times larger area of "reserved forest lands." Thus Yosemite National Park came into being without its heart, Yosemite itself.

Eventually Muir's effective pen, with the assistance of the Sierra Club (in the organization of which he had been a prime mover), met with success. In 1905 California turned its Yosemite and Mariposa Grove grants back to the federal government, curing the anomaly of a Yosemite National Park without the wonders of that unique valley and its superlative grove of big trees.[54]

After another decade and a half, with the creation of Grand Canyon National Park in 1919, the glorious triad of Yellowstone, Yosemite, and Grand Canyon was complete—a three-pointed crown surmounting the bounty of America's natural wonders.

[52]Whitney, *Yosemite*, pp. 10–11; Russell, *One Hundred Years*, pp. 148–149.
[53]Jones, *Muir*, pp.29–35.
[54]Russell, *One Hundred Years*, pp. 149–155; Jones, *Muir*, pp. 44ff.

Bibliographical Essay

1. Retrospect, 1700

For this retrospective chapter on the period of European discovery and settlement of America before 1700, David B. Quinn's *North America from Earliest Discovery to First Settlements* (New York, 1977) and John Pomfret and Floyd M. Shumway's *Founding the American Colonies, 1583–1660* (New York, 1970), both in this series, are valuable reference works. Other comprehensive and useful studies in this field are Herbert E. Bolton and Thomas M. Marshall, *The Colonization of North America, 1492–1783* (New York, 1920); John Bakeless, *The Eyes of Discovery* (Philadelphia, 1950); J. Bartlett Brebner, *The Explorers of North America, 1492–1806* (New York, 1933); Herbert I. Priestley, *The Coming of the White Man, 1492–1848* (New York, 1929); Samuel Eliot Morison, *The European Discovery of America* (New York, 1971). For this and subsequent chapters up until the time of American independence, the following richly illustrated brief history is a useful reference: W. P. Cumming, S. E. Hillier, D. B. Quinn, and G. Williams, *The Exploration of North America, 1630–1776* (New York, 1974).

Theodore de Bry's engravings of the paintings of Jacques le Moyne and John White's watercolors are beautifully reproduced in Stefan Lorent, *The New World* (New York, 1946), which contains reprints of the reports and narratives of Le Moyne, Nicholas le Challeux, Arthur Barlowe, Ralph Lane, John White, and Thomas Harriot. There is a facsimile reprint of Thomas Hariot, *A Briefe and True Report of the New Found Land of Virginia* (London, 1588; Ann Arbor, Mich., 1931).

The writings of Captain John Smith will be found in Edward Arber, ed., *Travels and Works of Captain John Smith* (2 vols., Edinburgh, 1910). John Lankford, ed., *Captain John Smith's America* (New York, 1967), contains a useful selection and introduction by the editor. William Wood, *New En-*

gland's Prospect (London, 1634), is now available in a modern reprint (Amsterdam, 1968). The best modern edition of William Bradford's *Of Plymouth Plantation, 1620–47* is Samuel Eliot Morison, ed. (New York, 1952). For a general study of colonial literature, the excellent work of Louis B. Wright, *The Cultural Life of the American Colonies* (New York, 1957), in this series is invaluable.

For early exploration of the Southeast, see C. W. Alvord and Lee Bidgood, *First Explorations of the Trans-Allegheny Region by the Virginians 1650–1674* (Cleveland, 1912); and W. P. Cumming, "Geographical Misconceptions of the Southeast in the Cartography of the Seventeenth and Eighteenth Centuries," *Journal of Southern History*, IV, no. 4 (1938), 476–493; a useful collection is J. F. Jameson, ed., *Original Narratives of Early American History* (19 vols., New York, 1906–17; reprinted, New York, 1952).

The Discoveries of John Lederer (London, 1672) has been reprinted, William P. Cumming, ed. (Charlottesville, Va., 1958).

The literature on the French exploration of the Mississippi Valley is extensive. Reuben Gold Thwaites, *The Jesuit Relations and Allied Documents: Travels and Explorations of the Jesuit Missionaries in New France, 1610–1791* (73 vols., Cleveland, 1896–1901), is an inexhaustible source for the work of these remarkable men.

Useful also are John Gilmary Shea, *Early Voyages Up and Down the Mississippi* (2 vols., Albany, 1861), and *Discovery and Exploration of the Mississippi Valley: With the Original Narratives of Marquette, Allouez, Membré, Hennepin, and Anastase Douay* (New York, 1853). More readily available are Louise Phelps Kellogg, ed., *Early Narratives of the Northwest, 1634–1699* (New York, 1917); Edna Kenton, ed., *The Jesuit Relations and Allied Documents* (New York, 1925); Francis Borgia Steck, *The Jolliet-Marquette Expedition, 1673* (Ann Arbor, Mich., 1971); Agnes Repplier, *Père Marquette, Priest, Pioneer, and Adventurer* (New York, 1929); Jean Delanglez, *Some La Salle Journeys* (Chicago, 1938); and Francis Parkman, *The Jesuits in North America in the Seventeenth Century* (Boston, 1908), and *La Salle and the Discovery of the Great West* (Boston, 1869). Timothy Severin, *Explorers of the Mississippi* (New York, 1968), is a useful recent study.

Available material on the American Indian is so extensive that only a selection can be given. Works used in the preparation of this book will be listed under the chapter headings for which they are most relevant. Here Wilcomb E. Washburn, *The Indian in America* (New York, 1975), in this series, and Alvin M. Josephy, ed., *The American Heritage Book of Indians* (New York, 1961), have proved useful. For further consideration of the traders, Verner W. Crane, *The Southern Frontier, 1670–1732* (Ann Arbor, Mich., 1929; reissued, 1956), is especially illuminating, and Henry Savage, Jr., *River of the Carolinas, The Santee* (New York, 1956), has a brief sketch of these intrepid men.

2. Robert Beverley and John Lawson

Valuable background reading for this chapter are the following: Louis B. Wright, *Cultural Life of the American Colonies* (New York, 1957), in this series; Richard S. Dunn, "Seventeenth Century English Historians of America," in James Morton Smith, ed., *Seventeenth-Century America* (Chapel Hill, N.C., 1959); Moses Coit Tyler, A *History of American Literature During the Colonial Period* (2 vols., New York, 1897); and Louis B. Wright, *The First Gentlemen of Virginia* (San Marino, Calif., 1940).

Robert Beverley's *The History and Present State of Virginia* (London, 1705) has been beautifully edited, with a scholarly introduction and notes, by Louis B. Wright (Chapel Hill, N.C., 1947), which I have used throughout. Wright's introduction is an excellent source of biographical material on Beverley. There is also a brief biographical sketch of Beverley in John McGill, *The Beverley Family of Virginia* (Columbia, S.C., 1956).

An interesting look at the Virginia colony by a contemporary of Beverley's will be found in Hugh Jones, *The Present State of Virginia* (London, 1724; reprinted, Chapel Hill, N.C., 1956), edited by Richard L. Martin.

The Secret Diary of William Byrd of Westover, 1709–1712, edited by Louis B. Wright and Marion Tinling (Richmond, Va., 1941), gives a vivid picture of its author and his times, and has glimpses of many of his contemporaries, including his brother-in-law Robert Beverley. Louis B. Wright has also edited *The Prose Works of William Byrd of Westover* (Cambridge, Mass., 1966), and William Byrd's *The Natural History of Virginia* (Richmond, Va., 1940), both of which are useful supplementary reading for this chapter. Biographical data on William Byrd will be found in the introductions to Louis B. Wright's editions of his works and in Richmond C. Beatty, *William Byrd of Westover* (Boston, 1932). See also Richmond C. Beatty and William J. Mulloy, *William Byrd's Natural History of Virginia* (Richmond, Va., 1940).

I have used the edition of John Lawson, *A New Voyage to Carolina, etc.* (London, 1709), with an introduction and notes by Hugh Talmage Lefler (Chapel Hill, N.C., 1967). Lefler's introduction includes a sketch of Lawson's life and career in this country. Henry Savage, Jr., *Lost Heritage* (New York, 1970), contains material on Lawson's life and his 1701 expedition in the Carolinas.

There is an informative and useful sketch of Lawson's patron and his circle: Raymond P. Stearns, "James Petiver, Promoter of Natural Science," in *Proceedings of the American Antiquarian Society,* new series, LXII (1952).

The definitive work on the Indians of the Southeast is the indispensable reference work, John R. Swanton, *The Indians of the Southeastern United States* (Washington, D.C., 1946). For this and subsequent chapters, Roy Harvey Pearce, *Savagism and Civilization, A Study of the Indian and the American Mind* (Baltimore, 1967), is interesting supplementary reading.

3. The Discovery of the Mississippi 1720–1776

The bibliography suggested above for Chapter 1, for the exploration of the Mississippi Valley by Jesuit and other early explorers, is also recommended here as useful supplementary reading for this chapter. W. J. Eccles, *France in America* (New York, 1972), in this series, is also helpful.

I have used the Caxton Club reprint (2 vols., Chicago, 1923) of the London edition of Pierre François Xavier de Charlevoix, *Journal of a Voyage to North America* (2 vols., Paris, 1744; English edn., London, 1761).

Some of the du Pratz history appeared in *Mémoires sur la Louisiane* (2 vols., Paris, 1753) by Georges Butel Dumont, who had access to the du Pratz manuscript before its publication by the author a few years later: Antoine Simon Le Page du Pratz, *The History of Louisiana* (Paris, 1758; London, 1763). For this chapter, I have used the facsimile edition of the London edition of the du Pratz history (New Orleans, 1947).

Jonathan Carver, *Travels Through the Interior Parts of North America in the Years 1766, 1767, and 1768* (London, 1778), has been reprinted (Minneapolis, 1956); I have used this latter edition. Recently Carver's travel diary, which had rested unpublished for two centuries in the British Museum, has been published by the Minnesota Historical Society: *The Journals of Jonathan Carver and Related Documents, 1766–1770*, under the editorship of John Parker, who has included in the volume a biographical sketch of Carver with much new material (Minneapolis, 1976). There is also a very interesting study of Carver and his explorations by John Parker, *The Great Lakes and the Great Rivers: Jonathan Carver's Dream of Empire* (East Lansing, Mich., 1965).

Further discussion of Carver and consideration of some of the disputed facts about his life and work may be found in the following articles: E. G. Bourne, "The Travels of Jonathan Carver," *The American Historical Review*, XI (1906), 287–302; William Browning, "The Early History of Jonathan Carver," *Wisconsin Magazine of History*, III (1920), 291–305; and Louise Phelps Kellogg, "The Mission of Jonathan Carver," *ibid.*, XII (1928), 127–145.

I have used the latest reprint (New York, 1968) of James Adair's *The History of the American Indians* (London, 1775).

The following Indian studies are especially useful supplementary reading for this chapter: Benjamin Bissell, *The American Indian in English Literature of the Eighteenth Century* (New Haven, 1925); Horace Neale Fairchild, *The Noble Savage, A Study in Romantic Naturalism* (New York, 1928); Albert Keiser, *The Indian in American Literature* (New York, 1970); Robert N. Lowie, *Indians of the Plains* (New York, 1954); and Père Lafitau, *Moeurs des Sauvages Américains Comparées aux Moeurs des Premiers Temps* (Paris, 1724).

4. The Eighteenth-Century Natural History Circle

As this chapter deals with the many naturalists who discovered and revealed the flora and fauna of America during the eighteenth century, a general survey of the scientific background of the period is valuable as supplementary reading. Two books highly recommended for this purpose are Raymond Phineas Stearns, *Science in the British Colonies of America* (Urbana, Ill., 1970), and Brooke Hindle, *The Pursuit of Science in Revolutionary America, 1735–1789* (Chapel Hill, N.C., 1956). For an understanding of the cultural life of the times, Louis B. Wright, *The Cultural Life of the American Colonies* (New York, 1957), and Russell Blaine Nye, *The Cultural Life of the New Nation* (New York, 1960), both in this series, are very useful.

Two books indispensable for comprehension of the essential role played by Thomas Jefferson in the scientific discovery of America are Edwin T. Martin, *Thomas Jefferson, Scientist* (New York, 1952), and Henry Steele Commager, *Jefferson and the Enlightenment* (New York, 1975).

The three magnificent eighteenth-century folio editions of Mark Catesby, *The Natural History of Carolina* . . . (2 vols., London, 1731–43, 1754, 1771), are now very rare. Recently the Beehive Press published a limited portfolio edition with an introduction by George Frick and notes by Joseph Ewan (Savannah, 1974). The definitive biography of Catesby by George Frederick Frick and Raymond Phineas Stearns, *Mark Catesby, The Colonial Audubon* (Urbana, Ill., 1961), is a scholarly and comprehensive study, and a valuable reference work for scientific progress during Catesby's lifetime. For a brief and lively sketch, see Robert Cantwell, "Mark Catesby, a Legend Comes to Life," *Sports Illustrated*, XIII, no. 18 (October 1960). William Byrd's impressions of Mark Catesby will be found in Louis B. Wright and Marion Tinling, eds., *The Secret Diary of William Byrd of Westover, 1709–1712*, cited above, an entertaining and intimate glimpse of Byrd and his times.

Elsa G. Allen's scholarly study, "The History of American Ornithology Before Audubon," *Transactions of the American Philosophical Society*, XLI (Philadelphia, 1951), is an incomparable mine of information about early ornithologists and includes a biography and scientific appraisal of Mark Catesby.

Edmund Berkeley and Dorothy Smith Berkeley have produced three illuminating biographies, with much new material, in the field of eighteenth-century natural history: *John Clayton, Pioneer of American Botany* (Chapel Hill, N.C., 1963); *Dr. Alexander Garden of Charles Town* (Chapel Hill, N.C., 1969); and *Dr. John Mitchell, The Man Who Made the Map of North America* (Chapel Hill, N.C., 1974). John Clayton's discoveries in botany are included in Jan Frederick Gronovius, *Flora Virginica* (Leyden, 1739, 1743).

As Cadwallader Colden was a leader for many years in both scientific and political circles, *The Letters and Papers of Cadwallader Colden, 1711–1775* (New York, 1918–37), is a useful reference source for the progress of natural history during this period. Brooke Hindle, *The Pursuit of Science in Revolutionary America*, cited above, gives an excellent appraisal of Colden and his career. The only full-length biography of Colden, Alice Mapelsden Keys, *Cadwallader Colden, a Representative Eighteenth Century Official* (New York, 1906), is disappointingly inadequate. Colden's *The History of the Five Indian Nations* (Pt. I, 1727, Pt. II, 1747), has been reprinted in a modern edition (Ithaca, N.Y., 1958).

The first English version of Peter Kalm, *Travels in North America, etc.* (Warrington, 1770), reprinted, edited, and with an introduction by Adolph Benson, contains a brief biography of Kalm (2 vols., New York, 1937; 2 vols., paperback, New York, 1966). There is also an imprint of the 1772 English edition, Ralph Sargent, ed. (Barre, Mass., 1775).

Donald Culross Peattie gives a sympathetic picture of Carl Linnaeus and his disciples, Kalm among them, in *Green Laurels* (Garden City, N.Y., 1938) —a book that is, in fact, excellent supplementary reading for this whole chapter. There is a beautifully illustrated and well-organized recent biography of Linnaeus: Wilfred Blunt, with the assistance of William T. Stearn, *The Compleat Naturalist: A Life of Linnaeus* (London, 1971). Sir James Edward Smith, ed., *A Selection of the Correspondence of Linnaeus and Other Naturalists* (2 vols., London, 1821), contains much valuable material.

John Bartram's "Diary of a Journey Through the Carolinas, Georgia, and Florida," has been edited and annotated by Francis Harper, *Transactions of the American Philosophical Society*, XXXIII, new series (Philadelphia, 1942). There has been a recent reprint (Barre, Mass., 1973) of his report of his journey to Lake Ontario: *Observations on the inhabitants, climate, soil, rivers, productions, animals, and other matter worthy of notice. Made by Mr. John Bartram, in his travels from Pennsylvania to Onondago, Oswego, and the Lake Ontario in Canada . . .* (London, 1751).

John Bartram's published reports, as Peter Kalm remarked, do not do justice to his botanical lore. The best source for records of his discoveries and for a true impression of his character is the correspondence between Bartram and Peter Collinson, covering all the years of Bartram's botanical explorations. This delightful collection, edited by William Darlington, *Memorials of John Bartram and Humphrey Marshall* (Philadelphia, 1849), contains not only letters of Collinson and Bartram but other naturalists as well, with brief biographical sketches of each, and has been made available in a recent facsimile reprint with introduction by Joseph Ewan (New York, 1967).

E. G. Swem, *Brothers of the Spade* (Barre, Mass., 1957), the correspondence between Peter Collinson of London and John Custis of Virginia, is a more limited but valuable collection, with useful annotation and bibliography. It also contains a vivid word picture of John Bartram. An eloquent description of Bartram and his household can be found in Hector St. John de Crèvecoeur, *Letters from an American Farmer* (London, 1782; New York, 1957).

There is no adequate full-length biography of John or William Bartram. Ernest Earnest, *John and William Bartram, Botanists and Explorers* (Philadelphia, 1940), and Josephine Herbst, *New Green World* (New York, 1954), contain useful biographical data, and Henry Savage, Jr., *Lost Heritage,* cited above, includes chapters on both Bartrams.

The only book-length biography of Collinson is Norman G. Brett-James, *The Life of Peter Collinson* (London, 1925); Richard Kingston Fox, *Dr. Fothergill and His Friends* (London, 1919), is a useful supplement.

Lewis Evans, who accompanied John Bartram to Oswego, published his famous map a few years after Bartram's report of the journey: Lewis Evans, *A General Map of the British Colonies in America* (Philadelphia, 1755). A comparative study of the ten different editions of this map published between 1755 and 1807 is the subject of Henry N. Stevens, *Lewis Evans, His Map of the Middle Colonies in America* (London, 1905). The only biography of Evans is Laurence H. Gipson, *Lewis Evans* (Philadelphia, 1939).

William Bartram, *Travels Through North and South Carolina, Georgia, East and West Florida* . . . (Philadelphia, 1791), has been superbly edited, annotated, and indexed by Francis Harper (New Haven, 1958). William Bartram's drawings and paintings are beautifully reproduced from the British Museum Collection: Joseph Ewan, ed., *William Bartram, Botanical and Zoological Drawings* (Philadelphia, 1968). Selections from the writings of John and William Bartram may be found in Helen Gere Cruickshank, ed., *John and William Bartram's America* (New York, 1957).

A study of the influence of William Bartram's *Travels* on Coleridge and Wordsworth is included in John Livingston Lowes's fascinating work, *The Road to Xanadu* (Boston, 1927). The influence of Bartram's *Travels* on the work of Chateaubriand, especially *Atala* and *René* (Berkeley, 1952), is evaluated by Gilbert Chinard in *Exotisme Américain dans l'Oeuvre de Chateaubriand* (Paris, 1918). Richard Switzer (ed. and trans.), *Chateaubriand's Travels in America* (Lexington, 1969), is interesting supplementary reading.

André Michaux's work on American oaks was published in Paris in 1801, *Histoire des Chênes de l'Amérique* . . . , and his *Flora* two years later, *Flora Boreali-Americana* (Paris, 1803). The inimitable daily journal of his travels and discoveries, edited and with an introduction by C. S. Sargent, was published in French in *Proceedings of the American Philosophical Society,* XXVI (Philadelphia, 1889). A part of this journal, translated and edited by R. G. Thwaites, can be found in *Early Western Travels,* a 32-volume collection of original narratives (Cleveland, 1904–7; all 32 vols. reprinted New York, 1966), with notes, illustrations, and index, a series indispensable to any student of Western American history. See vol. 3 (Cleveland, 1904).

There is no full-length biography of André Michaux. Soon after Michaux's death his friend, M. de Leuze, published in France a memorial biographical sketch, which appeared in translation as *A Brief Narrative of the Life and Travels of André Michaux,* in the *City Gazette* in Charleston, where Michaux had his Southern nursery (Charleston, S.C., July 20–27, 1804). Henry Savage, Jr., *Lost Heritage,* also has a study of Michaux, with emphasis on his American career. There is an illuminating discussion of André Michaux by Gilbert Chinard: "André and François-André Michaux and Their Predecessors," in *Proceedings of the American Philosophical Society,* I, no. 4 (August 1957).

5. The Discovery of the Old Northwest

The original edition of John Filson, *The Discovery, Settlement and present State of Kentucke: and An Essay towards the Topography, and Natural History of that important Country* . . . (Wilmington, Del., 1784; map, Philadelphia, 1784) has been reprinted in facsimile: John Filson, *The Discovery and Settlement of Kentucke* (Ann Arbor, Mich., 1966). The only biography of Filson is John Walton, *John Filson of Kentucke* (Lexington, Ky., 1956).

Biographical data on Thomas Hutchins may be found in the introduction by Joseph Tregle, Jr., in the reprint (Jacksonville, Fla., 1968) of Thomas Hutchins, *An Historical Narrative and Topographical Description of Louisiana, and West Florida* (Philadelphia, 1789). See also Thomas Hutchins, *Topographical Description of Virginia, Pennsylvania, Maryland, and North Carolina* (London, 1778).

Biographical data and critical discussion of Gilbert Imlay is included in Ralph M. Wardle, *Mary Wollstonecraft* (Lincoln, Nebr., 1951), and Elsa G. Allen, "The History of American Ornithology Before Audubon," *Transactions of the American Philosophical Society,* XLI (Philadelphia, 1954). Gilbert Imlay, *A Topographical Description of the Western Territory of North America* . . . (3 vols., London, 1793), has been reprinted recently (New York, 1968).

There are two modern, annotated editions of Thomas Jefferson, *Notes on the State of Virginia* (Paris, 1782, 1785): William Peden, ed. (New York, 1954) and Thomas Perkins Abernathy, ed. (New York, 1964), both with useful introductions.

Supplementary reading for the background and development of Jefferson's dispute with Buffon is provided in Guillaume Thomas Raynal, *A Philosophical and Political History* . . . (4 vols., London, 1776); Georges Louis Le Clerc de Buffon, *Histoire Naturelle* (9 vols., Paris, 1791); Henry Steele Commager, *Jefferson, Nationalism, and the Enlightenment* (New York, 1975), and *Was America a Mistake?* (Columbia, S.C., 1968). The definitive biography of Jefferson is Dumas Malone, *Jefferson and His Time* (5 vols., Boston, 1948–76). Also useful are Bernard Mayo, ed., *Jefferson Himself* (Boston,

1942); Edwin T. Martin, *Thomas Jefferson: Scientist* (New York, 1952); and P. L. Ford, ed., *The Writings of Thomas Jefferson* (10 vols., New York, 1892–99).

The first geography published in the United States was Jedediah Morse, *Geography Made Easy* (New Haven, 1784), which he quickly followed with *The American Geography* (Elizabeth Town, 1789), *The American Universal Geography* . . . (Boston, 1796), and *The American Gazetteer* (Boston, 1797). The only book-length biography of Morse is W. D. Sprague, *The Life of Jedediah Morse* (Boston, 1874).

An account of the visit of the Cherokee Indians to England in 1762 will be found in *The Memoirs of Lieutenant Henry Timberlake* (London, 1765; reprint, edited by Samuel Cole Williams, Johnson City, Tenn., 1927). Chapman J. Milling, *Red Carolinians* (Chapel Hill, N.C., 1940), and Benjamin Bissell, *The American Indian in English Literature of the Eighteenth Century* (New Haven, 1925), offer valuable insights into Indian culture.

6. The Expedition of Lewis and Clark

Other than newspaper reports, the first published account of the Lewis and Clark expedition appeared the year after the triumphant return of the Corps of Discovery. The journal kept by Sergeant Patrick Gass throughout the expedition, after being converted into flowery English by a country schoolteacher, was published in Pittsburgh in 1806. Now known as Gass's *Journal*, its voluminous title begins as *A Journal of the Voyages and Travels of a Corps of Discovery under the command of Capt. Lewis and Capt. Clarke* . . . Sadly inadequate to the preeminent and most fascinating exploration expedition in the annals of America, Gass's account nevertheless stood alone for seven years before the 1814 publication in Philadelphia of Nicholas Biddle's classic two-volume *History of the Expedition under the command of Captains Lewis and Clark,* etc. However, publication of the captains' complete journals had to await the incredible industry of Reuben Gold Thwaites, whose eight-volume *Original Journals of the Lewis and Clark Expedition* was published in New York in 1904–5. Meanwhile Dr. Elliott Coues had prepared a new scholarly annotated edition of Biddle's *History,* published by Francis Harper in New York in 1893.

Because they are readily available volumes, in the preparation of my Lewis and Clark account I relied heavily upon and made most of my citations to the three-volume Dover edition of Dr. Coues's reissue of Biddle's *History* (New York, 1965) and to Bernard DeVoto's condensation of Thwaites's edition of the captains' journals, *The Journals of Lewis and Clark* (Boston, 1953). For information concerning the captains themselves, a joint biography by John Bakeless, *Lewis and Clark, Partners in Discovery* (New York, 1947), is invaluable. There is a more recent biography of Lewis by Richard Dillon, *Meriwether Lewis* (New York, 1965). Anyone interested in the expedition's route in terms of modern geography will find Albert and Jane Salisbury, *Two Captains West* (New York, 1950), a useful guidebook.

Those with a special interest in the natural history aspects of the Lewis and Clark expedition will find helpful: Paul Russell Cutright, *Lewis and Clark: Pioneering Naturalists* (Urbana, Ill., 1969); Susan D. McKelvey, *Botanical Exploration of the Trans-Mississippi West, 1790–1850* (Arnold Arboretum, Jamaica Plain, Mass., 1955); and Raymond Darwin Burroughs, *The Natural History of The Lewis and Clark Expedition* (East Lansing, Mich., 1961). For more light on the Indians encountered along their way, see George Catlin's works (bibliography for Chapter 11); Robert H. Lowie, *Indians of the Plains* (New York, 1954); Philip Drucker, *Indians of the Northwest Coast* (New York, 1955); and Chap. 3 of Walter Prescott Webb, *The Great Plains* (New York, 1931).

The Lewis and Clark expedition is the subject of Chap. 24 of John Bartlett Brebner, *The Explorers of North America, 1492–1806* (London & New York, 1933); Chap. 20 of John Bakeless, *The Eyes of Discovery* (Philadelphia, 1950), and Chap. 11 of Bernard DeVoto, *The Course of Empire* (Boston, 1952).

7. Zebulon Montgomery Pike

In his official account of his expeditions, Pike fared both better and worse than Lewis and Clark with theirs. Soon after his return to the States from the Mexican detention, he succeeded in making arrangements for the publication of his accounts of both his Mississippi and his Southwestern expeditions. However, the chaotic state of Pike's manuscript and accompanying data and the retention by the Spanish authorities of valuable portions of his journals, notes, and maps all contributed to his own dull prose in making his volume difficult for any reader. Nevertheless, it was finally published under the ponderous title of *An Account of Expeditions to the Sources of the Mississippi, and Through the Western Parts of Louisiana to the Sources of the Arkansaw, Kans, La Platte, and Pierre Jaun, Rivers; Performed by Order of the Government of the United States During the Years 1805, 1806, and 1807. And a Tour Through the Interior Parts of New Spain in the Year 1807* (Philadelphia, 1810). Another eighty-five years passed before a much-improved edition, bountifully edited with supplemental matter by Dr. Elliott Coues, appeared under the title *The Expeditions of Zebulon Montgomery Pike to the Headwaters of the Mississippi River, through Louisiana Territory, and in New Spain, During the Years 1805–6–7* (2 vols. and atlas, New York, 1895). Dr. Coues's work has been reprinted in a two-volume format (Minneapolis, 1965).

In recent years with much new material, some discovered after Coues's work and some finally returned from impoundment in Mexico, Donald Jackson edited the whole into a superior work: *The Journals of Zebulon Mont-*

gomery Pike with Letters and Related Documents (2 vols., Norman, Okla., 1966). Other published works on Pike's Southwestern expedition are Milton Quaife, *The Southwestern Expedition of Zebulon Pike* (Chicago, 1925), and Stephen H. Hart and Archer B. Hulbert, eds., *Zebulon Pike's Arkansas Journal* (Denver, 1932). The latter and Donald Jackson both disagree with Coues's belief that Pike was involved in spying for Wilkinson and Burr.

Dr. Coues supplied a biographical sketch of Pike. Longer and more recent biographies are W. Eugene Hollon, *The Lost Pathfinder, Zebulon Montgomery Pike* (Norman, Okla., 1949), and John Upton Terrell, *Zebulon Pike: The Life and Times of an Adventurer* (New York, 1968).

Brief accounts of Pike's explorations may be found in Timothy Severin, *Explorers of the Mississippi* (New York, 1968), and William H. Goetzmann, *Exploration and Empire* (New York, 1967). For more on Pike's invaluable civilian companion, Dr. John H. Robinson, see "Dr. John Hamilton Robinson," *Louisiana Historical Quarterly,* XXV, 644–669. For authoritative accounts of the several Indian nations encountered by Pike on his expeditions, see Clark Wissler, *Indians of the United States* (New York, 1940, revised edn., edited by Lucy Wales Kluckhorn, 1966); Robert H. Lowie, *Indians of the Plains* (Garden City, N.Y., 1954); and Chap. 3 of Walter Prescott Webb, *The Great Plains* (Boston, 1931).

For a popular account of Pike's Mississippi expedition, see Walter Havinghurst, *Upper Mississippi* (New York, 1937). For early descriptions of the regions of Pike's explorations, there is Henry Rowe Schoolcraft, *Narrative of an Expedition Through the Upper Mississippi to Itaska Lake* (New York, 1834), and Josiah Gregg, *Commerce of the Prairies* (2 vols., New York, 1844), also in Thwaites, ed., *Early Western Travels,* vols. 19–20 (Cleveland, 1905), and M. M. Quaife, ed., *Josiah Gregg's Commerce of the Prairies* (Lincoln, Nebr., 1967); and finally, a dozen years after Pike, the Arkansas country was described by S. H. Long, Edwin James, *et al.,* in their *Account of an Expedition from Pittsburgh to the Rocky Mountains* (2 vols., Philadelphia, 1823); also in Thwaites, vols. 14–17.

Those interested in the origin and development of the fable of the "Great American Desert," seeded by Pike and cultivated by the Long *Report,* will find it fully treated in Chap. V of Webb's *The Great Plains.* See also Ralph C. Morris, "The Notion of a Great American Desert East of the Rockies," *Mississippi Valley Historical Review,* XIII (1926–27).

8. The Astorians and the Oregon Trail

The overland journey of the Astorians, their sea voyages to the mouth of the Columbia River, and their experiences during the short-lived enterprise on the West Coast were well documented by various members of the expedition, whose original narratives, plus Astor's records, were brought together in masterly synthesis by Washington Irving in *Astoria*, his classic account of the ill-fated undertaking.

Irving's use of these historical sources is fully documented in the introduction and notes by Edgeley Todd, in his scholarly edition of Irving's book, which I have used throughout this chapter: *Astoria, or Anecdotes of an Enterprise Beyond the Rocky Mountains* (Philadelphia, 1836; Norman, Okla., 1964).

For further critical discussion, see Hiram M. Chittenden, "Astoria, Its Author and the Sources of His Inspiration," in Andrew B. Myers, ed., *A Century of Commentary on the Works of Washington Irving* (Tarrytown, N.Y., 1976).

Two of the original narratives by Astorians, Wilson Price Hunt's journal of his overland journey to Astoria and Robert Stuart's account of his return journey east, are included in Philip Ashton Rollins, ed., *Discovery of the Oregon Trail: Robert Stuart's Narratives* (New York, 1935). See also Kenneth Spaulding, ed., *On the Oregon Trail: Robert Stuart's Journey of Discovery, 1812–1831* (Norman, Okla., 1953).

Two contemporary accounts, whose authors joined Hunt and his companions for part of their overland journey, are useful supplementary reading: John Bradbury, *Travels in the Interior of America* (Liverpool, 1817), and Henry Marie Brackenridge, *Journal of a Voyage up the River Missouri* (Baltimore, 1815). Both of these narratives are included in Thwaites, *Early Western Travels*, vols. 5 and 6, cited above.

Two of the Astorian clerks who sailed on the voyage of the doomed *Tonquin* wrote eloquent accounts of their experiences: Gabriel Franchère, whose original edition in French (Montreal, 1820) has been translated and edited by Hoyt C. Franchère: *Gabriel Franchère, Adventures at Astoria, 1810–1814* (Norman, Okla., 1967), and Alexander Ross, *Adventures of the First Settlers on the Oregon or Columbia River, etc.* (London, 1849; also in Thwaites, ed., *Early Western Travels*, vol. 7).

As further supplementary reading for this chapter, the following books are useful: Ray Allen Billington, *The Far Western Frontier* (New York, 1956), in this series; William H. Goetzmann, *Exploration and Empire* (New York, 1966); Bernard DeVoto, *The Course of Empire* (Boston, 1952).

For those interested in the complex history of the fur companies of the West, Bernard DeVoto's lively classic of the fur trade, *Beyond the Wide Missouri* (Boston, 1947), is highly recommended, as is Hiram M. Chittenden's comprehensive study, *A History of the American Fur Trade of the Far West* (3 vols., New York, 1902; revised edn., New York, 1935). See also Robert G. Cleland, *This Reckless Breed of Men: The Trappers and Traders of the Southwest* (New York, 1950), for a vivid picture of the men engaged in this dangerous trade, and Alexander Ross, *The Fur Hunters of the Far West* (2 vols., London, 1855; modern edition edited by Kenneth Spaulding, Norman, Okla., 1956).

Van Wyck Brooks, *The World of Washington Irving* (Philadelphia, 1945), is unsurpassed for a comprehensive view of the period. The definitive biography of Washington Irving is the excellent study by Stanley T. Williams, *The Life of Washington Irving* (2 vols., New York, 1935). John Francis McDermott has edited with introduction and annotations: Washington Irving, *A Tour on the Prairies* (Norman, Okla., 1956), and *The Western Journals of Washington Irving* (Norman, Okla., 1944).

9. Bearers of the Natural History Torch: Nineteenth Century

The discoverers discussed in this chapter, many of whom were associated with each other, ranged over the length and breadth of the country during the first forty-odd years of the nineteenth century. The most wide ranging of them, geographically and scientifically, was Thomas Nuttall. Jeannette E. Graustein's definitive biography of Nuttall, *Thomas Nuttall, Naturalist: Explorations in America, 1808–1841* (Cambridge, Mass., 1967), is not only indispensable for any student of Nuttall's work but illuminating background reading for the whole progress of natural history during the first half of the century.

The remarkable scientific museum, founded in Philadelphia by Charles Willson Peale at the beginning of the nineteenth century, which served for decades as a center of natural history interests, is vividly described in Charles Coleman Sellers's biography, *Charles Willson Peale* (2 vols., Philadelphia, 1947).

Chronologically, the first naturalist included here is François André Michaux, who left America for the last time the year of Nuttall's arrival in this country. Michaux's lucid report of his American travels appeared first in Paris in 1804: *Voyage à l'ouest des Monts Alléghenys* . . . It was translated into English and edited with an introduction by Reuben Gold Thwaites and included in vol. 3 of his *Early Western Travels* (Cleveland, 1905); there is a recent reprint (New York, 1966).

Michaux followed his *Travels* with *Mémoires sur la naturalisation des arbres de l'Amérique Septentrionale . . . Comparées avec ceux que produit la France* (Paris, 1805). His greatest contribution to American natural history, *Histoire des arbres forestiers de l'Amérique Septentrionale* . . . (3 vols., Paris, 1810–13), appeared in an English edition as *The North American Sylva* (3 vols., Paris, 1818–19).

As in the case of his father, André, there is no full biography of François André Michaux. The most complete biographical data available can be found in Henry Savage, Jr., *Lost Heritage,* and in Rodney H. True, "François André Michaux, The Botanist and Explorer," *Proceedings of the American Philosophical Society,* LXXVIII, no. 2 (Philadelphia, 1937). See also the introduction to Thwaites's edition of the *Travels.* There is an illuminating study of Michaux by the French scholar, Gilbert Chinard, "André, and François-André Michaux and Their Predecessors," in *Proceedings of the American Philosophical Society*, CI, no. 4 (August 1957).

A list of Thomas Nuttall's published works reflects his versatility. *A Journal of Travels into the Arkansas Territory, During the Year 1819* (Philadelphia, 1821) was recently reprinted (Ann Arbor, Mich., 1966). The *Genera of North American Plants* . . . (Philadelphia, 1818) was published the year following his *Journal*. His popular ornithology, *A Manual of the Ornithology of the United States and of Canada* (2 vols., Cambridge & Boston, 1832–34), had three subsequent editions (Boston, 1891, 1896, 1903). Nuttall's final work in American natural history, his three-volume supplement to Michaux's *Sylva:* Thomas Nuttall, *The North American Sylva, etc.* (Philadelphia, 1842–49), was reprinted six times within the century.

The second Wyeth expedition to the Pacific coast, of which Nuttall was a member, is graphically described in Bernard DeVoto, *Across the Wide Missouri* (Boston, 1947), and told from a naturalist's point of view by John K. Townsend, Nuttall's companion on the journey, in J. K. Townsend, *Narrative of a Journey Across the Rocky Mountains to the Columbia River, etc.* (Philadelphia, 1839; London, 1840), a classic of Western travel, included also in Thwaites, ed., *Early Western Travels*, vol. 21.

Richard Henry Dana, Jr., in *Two Years Before the Mast* (Boston, 1840), gives a refreshing description of Nuttall met by chance on the coast of California, as well as his own memorable impressions of that then almost unknown region.

Several of the naturalists in this chapter were associated in one way or another with the experimental Utopia, New Harmony, about which much has been written. The most comprehensive and illuminating account of the community and its member scientists is George B. Lockwood, *The New Harmony Movement* (New York, 1905; 1971). A. E. Beston, Jr., *Backwoods Utopias* (Philadelphia, 1950), is useful in placing New Harmony in context with other similar experiments.

Lockwood's book contains biographical data on Robert Owen and his sons, William Maclure, Charles Alexandre Lesueur, and Thomas Say, among others. The only full-length biography of Say, Harry B. Weiss and Grace M. Ziegler, *Thomas Say, Early American Naturalist* (Springfield, Ill., 1931), includes biographical data on William Maclure and Lesueur also, and a perceptive description of New Harmony and its associates. See also J. T. E. Hamy, *Travels of the Naturalist, Charles Alexandre LeSueur in North America 1815–1837* (Kent, Ohio, 1968).

Both the Say biography and the Lockwood book describe two of New Harmony's most picturesque visiting scientists, Maximilian, Prince of Wied, and Constantine Rafinesque.

Maximilian, noted naturalist and traveler who stopped by New Harmony on his way west, is described also, unforgettably, in DeVoto, *Across the Wide Missouri*. The prince's erudite report on his Western travels, Maximilian, Prinz zu Wied, *Reise in das innere Nord-Amerika in den Jahren 1832 bis 1834* (Coblentz, 1839), can be found in translation as *Travels in the Interior of North America*, in Thwaites, ed., *Early Western Travels*, vols. 22–25.

Constantine Rafinesque wrote a brief autobiography detailing the bizarre circumstances of his early life: *A Life of Travels and Researches in North America and Southern Europe* (Philadelphia, 1836). T. J. Fitzpatrick, *Rafinesque: A Sketch of His Life with Bibliography* (Des Moines, 1911), is a useful and sympathetic biography with a critical appraisal of Rafinesque's scientific career.

Ray Allen Billington, *The Far Western Frontier, 1830–1860* (New York, 1956), in this series, is valuable as background reading for this chapter.

Susan D. McKelvey, *Botanical Exploration of the Trans-Mississippi West, 1790–1850* (Arnold Arboretum, Jamaica Plain, Mass., 1955), is a constantly useful scientific reference work.

10. Alexander Wilson and John James Audubon, Ornithologists

Ornithologist Alexander Wilson's great monument, *American Ornithology* (9 vols., Philadelphia, 1808–14), was later published in an edition of 3 octavo volumes, with an atlas of 76 hand-colored plates (New York and Philadelphia, 1828–29). By this time the supplement to Wilson's ornithology, prepared by the French scientist Charles Lucien Bonaparte, had already begun to appear: *American Ornithology, or the Natural History of Birds Inhabiting the United States Not Given by Wilson* (4 vols., Philadelphia, 1825–33). Three subsequent editions of the Wilson and Bonaparte ornithologies, published in the British Isles in the 1830s, apparently stimulated by the prospect of Audubon's projected ornithology, are discussed in Francis Hobart Herrick, *Audubon, The Naturalist* (2 vols., New York, 1917; Dover edn., New York, 1968).

The ninth volume of the original edition of Wilson's *Ornithology*, prepared after Wilson's death by his friend and fellow naturalist George Ord, contained a biographical sketch of Wilson by Ord. James Southall Wilson, *Alexander Wilson, Poet Naturalist, etc.* (New York, 1906), combines biography and literary criticism, and includes a selection of Wilson's poems. The most satisfactory full biography of Wilson is Robert Cantwell, *Alexander Wilson, Naturalist and Pioneer* (Philadelphia, 1961), a carefully researched and illuminating work, with much new material. Beautifully illustrated with reproductions from Wilson's ornithology, it contains also a portrait of Wilson, a full bibliography, and useful appendices. Robert Plate, *Alexander Wilson, Wanderer in the Wilderness* (New York, 1966), is a competent biography but has nothing new to add. There is a useful study of Wilson, essentially an appraisal of his contribution to American ornithology, in Elsa G.

Allen, "The History of American Ornithology Before Audubon," *Transactions of the American Philosophical Society,* XLI (Philadelphia, 1951).

Wilson's 2,018-line verse epic *The Foresters,* describing his walking tour to Niagara and back, was published a few years before his death (Philadelphia, 1809–10). A two-volume collection of his literary works appeared in his native Paisley, Scotland, in 1876: *The Poems and Literary Prose of Alexander Wilson,* edited by the Reverend Alexander B. Grosart.

John James Audubon's original production of *The Birds of America* first appeared in magnificent double-elephant folio (4 vols., London, 1827–38), with the text to accompany *The Birds* issued separately as *Ornithological Biography* . . . (5 vols., Edinburgh, 1831–39), followed by *A Synopsis of the Birds of North America* (London, 1839), a methodical catalogue of the birds of North America then known and described.

The miniature edition, *The Birds of America* (7 vols., Philadelphia, 1840–44), combined the text with the plates, reduced in size, but omitted the "Episodes" or "Delineations of American Scenery and Manners," which had been part of the original ornithological biography. This miniature edition is now available again in a Dover reprint (7 vols., New York, 1967). *Delineations of American Scenery and Character,* by John James Audubon, has been published separately, edited by Francis H. Herrick (New York, 1926).

In the preparation of *The Viviparous Quadrupeds of North America* (2 vols., New York, 1846–54) Audubon had the competent assistance of his faithful friend and collaborator, the Reverend John Bachman. This was followed by a miniature edition, *The Viviparous Quadrupeds of North America* (3 vols., New York, 1846–54).

A full Audubon bibliography will be found in the excellent and scholarly biography, Frances H. Herrick, *Audubon, The Naturalist,* cited above, which is indispensable for any student of Audubon. Much new material, especially about Audubon's background and early life, has been added by Alice Ford in a recent biography, *John James Audubon* (Norman, Okla., 1964), a work that contains a full up-to-date bibliography. Both the Herrick and the Ford biographies are generously illustrated. There are many romanticized biographies of Audubon, of which Constance Rourke, *Audubon* (New York, 1936), is a fair example.

The naturalist's granddaughter Maria B. Audubon brought out in 1898, with the aid of Dr. Elliott Coues, *Audubon and His Journals* (2 vols., New York, 1898; Dover edn., New York, 1960), which remains a major source of information on Audubon's life and character. This has been supplemented by Alice Ford, ed., *The 1826 Journal of John James Audubon* (Norman, Okla., 1967), a well-annotated edition of Audubon's journal account of his first journey to England and Scotland to promote his great project.

Selections from the naturalist's writings are available with commentaries by the editors in Donald Culross Peattie, ed., *Audubon's America, The Narra-*

tives and Experiences of John James Audubon, with reproductions in color from Audubon's paintings (Boston, 1940), and Alice Ford, ed., *Audubon by Himself* (Garden City, N.Y., 1969).

The earliest biography of Audubon's faithful friend and collaborator John Bachman is C. L. Bachman, *John Bachman* (Charleston, S.C., 1888). Claude Henry Neuffer, ed., *The Christopher Happoldt Journal* (Charleston, S.C., 1960), contains a useful biographical sketch of Bachman, with an account of his association with Audubon, letters between the two, and a portrait of Bachman.

11. Catlin, Schoolcraft, and Maximilian of Wied

Since George Catlin's fame is mostly derived from his portrayals of the American Indian and the West, a bibliography of his work is most fittingly begun with his surviving drawings and paintings and the bibliography of his work as an artist. The principal Catlin collections are now at the Smithsonian Institution and the American Museum of Natural History. A full bibliography of the printed material relating to his paintings may be found in Harold McCracken, *George Catlin and the Old Frontier* (New York, 1959), an excellent, beautifully illustrated biography. Another biographical work is Lloyd Haberly, *Pursuit of the Horizon* (New York, 1948). See also Marvin C. Ross, ed., *George Catlin* (Norman, Okla., 1959). Now recognized not only as an artist but also as a major contributor to the field of American ethnology, Catlin's writings are important both for the autobiographical material they contain and the light they shed on the American Indian's customs and manners. Most important of these is *Letters and Notes on the Manners, Customs, and Conditions of the North American Indians* (2 vols., London & New York, 1841; republished in 1973 in New York, Toronto, & London). His most sensational and controversial work is *O-Kee-pa; A Religious Ceremony; and other Customs of the Mandans* (London & Philadelphia, 1867), reissued in a Centennial edition, John C. Ewers, ed. (New Haven & London, 1967). Ewers has also provided a study of Catlin's pictures of the Indians: John C. Ewers, "George Catlin, Painter of Indians and the West," *Annual Report for 1955, Smithsonian Institution* (Washington, D.C., 1956). And of course Robert Taft, *Artists and Illustrators of the Old West, 1850–1900* (New York, 1953), is essential to any review of the art of the American West. See also the magnificent volume of Paul A. Rossi and David E. Hunt, *Art of the Old West* (New York, 1971).

The focal interest of this chapter being the Indian, to those Indian reference works suggested for Chapters 6 and 7 the following may be added: a wider general reference work, John R. Swanton, *The Indian Tribes of North America* (Washington, D.C., 1952, 1959); another by an anthropologist, Harold E. Driver, *Indians of North America* (Chicago, 1970); and a popular beautifully illustrated work, Alvin M. Josephy, Jr., ed., *The American Heritage Book of Indians* (New York, 1961), which includes among its illustrations examples of the work of most of the Western explorer-artists met with in this volume. Bernard DeVoto's *Across the Wide Missouri* (Boston, 1947) provides an unexcelled picture of the Indian in his early contact with the whites as they encroached on his pristine domain. For more on the legendary origin of the Mandans, see Charles M. Boland, *They All Discovered America* (New York, 1961).

Other works related to or providing background for the subjects of this chapter include Thomas H. McKenney and James Hall, *History of the Indian Tribes of North America* (3 vols., Philadelphia, 1837); Washington Irving, *A Tour on the Prairies* (Philadelphia, 1835), and a new edition, J. F. McDermott, ed., (Norman, Okla., 1956); Van Wyck Brooks, *The World of Washington Irving* (Philadelphia, 1945); Lewis Cass, *Inquiries Respecting the History, Traditions, Languages, etc. of the Indians Living within the United States* (Detroit, 1823); Marvin C. Ross, *The West of Alfred Jacob Miller* (Norman, Okla., 1967); Edgeley W. Todd, ed., *The Adventures of Captain Bonneville, U.S.A.* by Washington Irving (Norman, Okla., 1961); Albert Keiser, *The Indian in American Literature* (New York, 1933); and Roy Harvey Pearce, *Savagism and Civilization* (Baltimore, 1953).

Of the more than twenty full-length volumes written by Henry Rowe Schoolcraft on the Indian and his own explorations beyond the frontier, only a few have been republished to be readily available. Among these are Philip R. Mason, ed., *Schoolcraft's Expedition to Lake Itasca* (East Lansing, Mich., 1958), originally published as a *Narrative of an Expedition Through the Upper Mississippi to Itasca Lake* (New York, 1834); Mentor L. Williams, ed., *Schoolcraft's Narrative Journal of Travels . . . to the Sources of the Mississippi River in the Year 1820* (East Lansing, Mich., 1953), originally published as *Narrative Journal of Travels from Detroit, etc. to the Source of the Mississippi River in the Year 1820* (Albany, 1821). This same editor gathered other works of Schoolcraft in *Schoolcraft's Indian Legends from Algic Researches, the Myth of Hiawatha, Onéota, the Red Race in America, and Historical and Statistical Information Respecting . . . the Indian Tribes of the United States* (East Lansing, Mich., 1956), taken from *Algic Researches, Comprising Inquiries Respecting the Mental Characteristics of the North American Indians* (2 vols., New York, 1839), *The Red Race of America* (New York, 1847), and *The Myth of Hiawatha, and other Oral Legends . . . of the North American Indians* (Philadelphia, 1856). Yet two more works of the prolific Schoolcraft call for inclusion in this list: his *Personal Memoirs of a Residence of Thirty Years with the Indian Tribes of the American Frontiers* (Philadelphia, 1851), and his monumental *Historical and Statistical Information Respecting the History, Condition and Prospects of the Indian Tribes of the United States* (6 vols., Philadelphia, 1851–57).

Finally, mention must be made of the republication of an 1890 scholarly edition, beautifully illustrated by Frederick Remington, of Henry Wadsworth Longfellow's *The Song of Hiawatha* (New York, 1968), which, in its introduction, traces the origin of the legend.

In marked contrast to that of Schoolcraft's works the relevant bibliography of Maximilian, Prince of Wied-Neuwied, is spare indeed. His account of travels in the North American West was originally published in Coblentz, 1839–41. An English translation published in London in 1843 became the text for Maximilian's *Travels in the Interior of North America* in Thwaites, ed., *Early Western Travels*, vols. 22–25. Vol. 25 is an "Atlas" containing Karl Bodmer's magnificent Western paintings—see Robert Taft's *Artists and Illustrators of the Old West*, cited above. Bernard DeVoto in *Across the Wide Missouri* provides lively word pictures of the prince and his artist companion and in an appendix, pp. 401–406, a brief biographical sketch and critical review of Bodmer's contributions to Western art.

12. John Charles Frémont and the American West

There is a plethora of published material dealing with John Charles Frémont and his explorations—far too much for use in a brief summary such as that presented in this volume. For those interested in exploring farther the fascinating character and dramatic career of the man, there are excellent modern biographies: Allan Nevins, *Frémont: The West's Greatest Adventurer* (2 vols., New York, 1928), and his one-volume *Frémont: Pathmarker of the West* (New York, 1955). There is also the first of two projected volumes of the explorer's autobiography, covering the earlier part of his life, *Memoirs of My Life, etc.* (Chicago & New York, 1887), and Frederick S. Dellenbaugh, *Frémont and '49* (New York, 1914). Since Frémont's life and career were so intimately involved with Senator Thomas H. Benton and daughter Jessie, the explorer's wife, the senator's memoirs *Thirty Years' View, etc.* (2 vols., New York, 1854–57), and Catherine Coffin Phillips, *Jessie Benton Frémont: A Woman Who Made History* (San Francisco, 1935), contribute important background material to Frémont's life saga.

For biographer and bibliographer alike, the centerpiece of the life and career of Frémont was and is his *Report of the Exploring Expedition to the Rocky Mountains in the Year 1843 and to Oregon and North California in the Years 1843–44* (Senate Exec. Doc. 174, 28th Cong., 2d Sess., U.S. serial no. 461, 1845). As stated in the title, the 1845 *Report* included his previously published *Report on an Exploration of the Country Lying between the Missouri River and the Rocky Mountains, on the Line of the Kansas and Great Platte Rivers* (Senate Exec. Doc. 243, 27th Cong., 3d Sess., U.S. serial no. 416, 1843). These accounts saw many republications, both in America and abroad, as the explorer's popularity continued to rise. In recent years they have been published again with the addition of much other pertinent material in the form of correspondence and documents relating to all those expeditions and his scientific reports and maps: Donald Jackson and Mary Lee Spence, eds., *The Expeditions of John Charles Frémont*, vol. 1, *Travels from 1838 to 1844, with Map Portfolio* (Chicago, 1970), vol. 2, *The Bear Flag Revolt and the Court-Martial*, Supplement, *Proceedings of The Court-Martial* (Chicago, 1973). A third volume is projected.

Since Frémont made no formal reports covering his last three expeditions such as those made and published covering his earlier ones, the historian is heavily dependent upon his autobiography, as far as it went, and the reports of others, companions on those expeditions, to reconstruct them for the record. Because of the dramatic events involving Frémont's 1845 intrusion into California there were many reporters, not only of the Bear Flag Revolt and the ensuing conquest of California, but of the expedition itself. Vol. 2 of the Jackson and Spence work mentioned above, and the sources they cite, as well as those cited by Ray Allen Billington in his account of Frémont's California saga in a volume of the New American Nation Series, *The Far Western Frontier, 1830–1860* (New York, 1956), provide a more complete bibliography than can be justified here. George H. Goetzmann in both his *Army Exploration of the American West, 1803–1863* (New Haven, 1959) and *Exploration and Empire* (New York, 1966) provides summary accounts of all Frémont's expeditions, and his numerous sources of these accounts. Important among these are Edwin Bryant, *What I Saw in California* (New York, 1848); reprinted, Minneapolis, 1967); E. M. Kern in J. H. Simpson's *Report of Explorations Across the Great Basin, etc. in 1859* (Washington, D.C., 1876); John A. Sutter, *The Diary of Johann Augustus Sutter* (San Francisco, 1932); and M. M. Quaife, ed., *Kit Carson's Autobiography* (Chicago, 1935).

Similarly, we are heavily dependent upon others for much of the certainties we have on Frémont's disastrous subsequent winter expeditions into the Colorado Rockies. For his tragic 1849 attempt to find a way west for a rail line across the mountains, we have Charles Preuss's diaries: Edwin G. and Elizabeth K. Gudde, eds. and trans., *Exploring with Frémont: The Private Diaries of Charles Preuss, Cartographer for John C. Frémont on His First, Second and Fourth Expeditions to the Far West* (Norman, Okla., 1958), and the considerable other documentary evidence reviewed by Nevins in his *Frémont*. For the fifth expedition (1853–54) we have Solomon Nunes Carvalho, *Incidents of Travel and Adventure in the Far West* (New York, 1857; reprinted, Philadelphia, 1954).

Finally, since much of the West covered by Frémont had already been explored, but little revealed to the outside world, by the mountain men, mostly trappers and traders, long before Frémont's ventures into their domain, Washington Irving's *Adventures of Captain Bonneville, U.S.A.* (New York, 1837; republished, edited, and annotated by Edgeley Todd, Norman,

Okla., 1961), and DeVoto, *Across the Wide Missouri*, are essential to the whole picture.

13. The Great Western Surveys

The long series of great Western surveys was launched in the late 1840s. At first their purpose was to locate improved wagon roads, an aim that gradually gave way to the growing belief in the possibility of a transcontinental railroad. Objectives, diverse in other respects, increased the ambivalence of those explorations as the burgeoning nation sought to intellectually and physically take possession of its newly acquired Southwestern empire while at the same time it was seeking political dominance in the disputed Northwest territories. Frémont's expeditions had launched the series. In 1849 Captain Randolph B. Marcy with Lieutenant James H. Simpson studied the country between Fort Smith, Santa Fé, and El Paso. Their official reports were *Report of a Route from Ft. Smith to Santa Fe*, Senate Exec. Doc. 64, 31st Cong., 1st Sess., U.S. serial no. 562 (1850), and *Report and Map of a Route from Ft. Smith, Arkansas, to Santa Fe, New Mexico*, Senate Exec. Doc. 12, 31st Cong., 1st Sess., U.S. serial no. 554 (1850), respectively. Captain Howard Stansbury and Lieutenant John W. Gunnison were dispatched to the Great Basin on a most successful expedition reported as *Exploration and Survey of the Valley of the Great Salt Lake of Utah*, Senate Exec. Doc. 3, 32d Cong., Spec. Sess., U.S. serial no. 608 (1851). Captain Lorenzo Sitgreaves's 1850 expedition crossed the Southwest, carrying Marcy's survey on into California: *Report on an Expedition Down the Zuñi and Colorado Rivers*, Senate Exec. Doc. 59, 32d Cong., 2d Sess., U.S. serial no. 668 (1853). The country southward from there, along the Mexican border, was thoroughly studied by the Mexican Boundary Commission during its long-drawn-out negotiations. The most revealing source of knowledge of that region is John Russell Bartlett, *Personal Narrative of Explorations and Incidents in Texas, Mexico, etc. Connected with the United States Boundary Commission, etc.* (New York, 1854). On the route across the plains to Santa Fe there was a rich store of information in Josiah Gregg, *The Commerce of the Prairies*, first published in 1844 and since continued through numerous editions, among them Milo Melton Quaife, ed., *Commerce of the Prairies* (Lincoln, Nebr., 1967).

Meanwhile, the clamor for action toward achieving a Pacific railroad had continued to mount from the skepticism that prevailed when Asa Whitney first made a specific proposal for the construction of one, to widespread enthusiasm. See Nelson H. Loomis, "Asa Whitney, Father of Pacific Railroads," *Mississippi Valley Historical Review*, VI (1912); Robert S. Cotterill, "Early Agitation for a Pacific Railroad, 1845–1850," *ibid.*, V (1919); Robert S. Cotterill, "The National Railroad Convention in St. Louis, 1849," *Missouri Historical Review*, XII (1918), and Robert S. Cotterill, "Memphis Railroad Convention, 1849," *Tennessee History Magazine,* IV (1918). For generalized accounts of the Pacific railroad development and construction, see John Debo Galloway, *The First Transcontinental Railroad* (New York, 1950); Robert West Howard, *The Great Iron Trail: The Story of the Trans-Continental Railroad* (New York, 1962); Gerald M. Best, *Iron Horses to Promontory* (San Marino, Calif., 1969); and H. Craig Miner, *The St. Louis-San Francisco Transcontinental Railroad* (Lawrence, Kans., 1972).

On the Pacific Railroad Surveys themselves, the problem is mostly a surfeit of material. Although the original *Reports* themselves, *Reports of Explorations and Surveys to Ascertain the Most Practicable and Economic Route for a Railroad from the Mississippi River to the Pacific Ocean* (12 vols., Washington, D.C., 1855–61), are usually only available under the restrictions of rare bookrooms and their sheer volume of content is formidable, there are many brief summaries of the *Reports:* George Leslie Albright, *Official Explorations, 1853–1855* (Berkeley, 1921; reprinted, New York, 1974); Edward Wallace, *The Great Reconnaissance* (Boston, 1955); and in the excellent volumes of George H. Goetzmann, *Army Exploration of the American West, 1803–1863* (New Haven, 1959) and *Exploration and Empire* (New York, 1967). In both of these Professor Goetzmann gives emphasis to scientific revelations of the surveys.

The artists, illustrators, and cartographers who accompanied the expeditions added immensely to the impact of the *Reports.* Robert Taft, *Artists and Illustrators of the Old West, 1850–1900* (New York, 1953), enhances our knowledge of all the noteworthy artists who accompanied the expeditions. Some of these have been the subjects of books: W. Vernon Kinietz, *John Mix Stanley and His Indian Paintings* (Ann Arbor, Mich., 1942), and Preston-Albert Barba, *Badwin Möllhausen, The German Cooper* (Philadelphia, 1914). So have some of the leaders of the surveys: Grant Foreman, ed., *Pathfinder in the Southwest: The Itinerary of Lieutenant A. W. Whipple, etc.* (Norman, Okla., 1941), and Möllhausen's own journal of that expedition, *Diary of a Journey from the Mississippi to the Coasts of the Pacific, etc.* (trans., 2 vols., London, 1858).

For more on the great Western surveys subsequent to the *Railroad Surveys,* see Richard Bartlett, *Great Surveys of the American West* (Norman, Okla., 1966), and the Goetzmann books cited above; also Thurman Wilkins, *Clarence King* (New York, 1958); Edwin Tenney Brewster, *Life and Letters of Josiah Dwight Whitney* (Boston, 1909); and Charles A. White, "Memoir of Ferdinand Vandiveer Hayden, 1829–1887," *National Academy of Sciences, Biographical Memoirs,* vol. 3 (Washington, D.C., 1893).

14. Powell and the Colorado

As an overall work on the Colorado River from its first discovery by Europeans to the twentieth century, none is superior to Frederick S. Dellenbaugh, *The Romance of the Colorado River* (New York, 1902). From the early glimpses of it by the Spaniards and the brief encounters in effecting crossings over it by such as Frémont and Gunnison (which can be ignored in this bibliography), through the exploration of its lower reaches by the Ives expedition, and the dramatic revealing by Powell of the river's great canyons and incredible geology, the story is all there.

The Lower Colorado was covered in detail by Lieutenant Joseph C. Ives, *Report on the Colorado River of the West, explored in 1857 and 1858,* 36th Cong., 1st Sess., U.S. HR. Exec. Doc. 90, serial no. 1058 (1861)—well summarized by George H. Goetzmann in *Army Exploration of the American West, 1804–1863,* as is also a later expedition staffed by some of his party, most importantly Dr. Newberry, but led by a fellow officer to study the river above Grand Canyon, Captain John McComb, *Report on the Exploring Expedition from Santa Fe, New Mexico, to the Junction of the Green and Grand Rivers etc. in 1859* (Washington, D.C., U.S. Eng. Dept., 1876). See also Edward S. Wallace, *The Great Reconnaissance* (Boston, 1955).

This brings us to the man whose name is indelibly linked with the Colorado River, John Wesley Powell. There are two modern biographies of him, both excellent: William C. Darrah, *Powell of the Colorado* (Princeton, 1951), and Wallace Stegner, *Beyond the Hundredth Meridian* (Boston, 1953), the latter giving more emphasis to Powell's scientific activities and achievements. Richard A. Bartlett in his *Great Surveys of the American West* provides a brief and adequate summary of the accomplishments of Powell's Great Basin and arid regions studies.

Powell's own writings pertinent to this volume include his *Report on the Exploration of the Colorado River of the West and Its Tributaries* (Washington, D.C., 1875); this *Report* appears in somewhat revised form under the title *The Canyons of the Colorado* (Meadville, Pa., 1895), and still later in a Dover edition entitled *The Exploration of the Colorado River and Its Canyons* (New York, 1961). More recently, his Colorado diary of his first trip down the river has been published in a lavishly illustrated volume, *Down the Colorado,* with photographs and epilogue by Eliot Porter (New York, 1969). There is also a republication of the river portion of his *Exploration* under the shortened title, *The Exploration of the Colorado River* (Chicago, 1957). And there is Powell's later great work, *Report on the Lands of the Arid Region of the United States, with a More Detailed Account of the Lands of Utah* (Washington, D.C., 1878), and a later edition of that report edited by Wallace Stegner (Cambridge, Mass., 1962).

For more on Thomas Moran, the artist most often associated with the canyons of the Colorado and Powell, see Stegner's *Beyond the Hundredth Meridian,* Pt. II, Chap. 9, and Thurman Wilkins, *Thomas Moran, Artist of the Mountains* (Norman, Okla., 1966). Earlier delineators of the lower reaches of the Colorado, Barons F. W. von Egloffstein and H. B. Möllhausen, are dealt with by Robert Taft, *Artists and Illustrators of the Old West, 1850–1900* (New York, 1953).

15. Yellowstone and Yosemite

The partly legendary account of the discovery of Yellowstone Park begins with trappers John Colter and Jim Bridger. Despite the paucity of hard facts relating to much of their lives, they have both become subjects for biographers: Burton Harris, *John Colter: His Years in the Rockies* (New York, 1952), and F. Cecil Alter, *Jim Bridger, Trapper, Frontiersman, Scout and Guide* (Salt Lake City, 1925). A new, revised edition of the latter has been published under the title of *Jim Bridger* (Norman, Okla., 1962). An earlier biography of Colter is that of Stallo Vinton, *John Colter, Discoverer of Yellowstone Park* (New York, 1926). There is enough legend in the early stories coming out of the area to open to question even the likely sounding story of "Colter's Hell." See Merrill J. Mattes, "Behind the Legend of Colter's Hell: The Early Exploration of Yellowstone Park," *Mississippi Valley Historical Review*, XXXVI, no. 2, 251–282.

Moving on chronologically in order of publication, other first-hand reports of the phenomena of Yellowstone are: Nathanial P. Langford, "Wonders of the Yellowstone," *Scribner's Monthly*, II (May–June 1871), 113–128; Truman Evarts, "Thirty-seven Days of Peril," *Scribner's Monthly*, III (November 1871), 1–17; Walter Trumbull, "The Washburn Yellowstone Expedition," *Overland Monthly*, VI (1871), 431–437, 489–496; Gustavus C. Doane, *Report of Lieutenant Gustavus C. Doane upon the So-called Yellowstone Expedition of 1870*, Senate Exec. Doc. 51, 41st Cong., 3d Sess., U.S. serial no. 1440 (1871); Ferdinand V. Hayden, "Wonders of the West—II; More About Yellowstone," *Scribner's Monthly*, III (1872), 388–396; Ferdinand V. Hayden, "The Yellowstone National Park," *The American Journal of Science and Arts*, III (1872), 294–297; and several of Hayden's official reports: The Fifth (1872), Sixth (1873), and Twelfth (1883) "Annual Reports of F. V. Hayden," in the *Annual Reports of the Geological and Geographical Survey of the Territories* (Washington, D.C., 1868–83). Tardy reports of earlier explorations of the area were that of David E. Folsom, "The Folsom-Cook Exploration of the Upper Yellowstone in the Year 1869," *Contribution to the Historical Society of Montana* (1904), 349–394, and that of Nathaniel Pitt Langford, *Diary of the Washburn Expedition to the Yellowstone and Firehole Rivers in the Year 1870* (St. Paul, 1905); republished with foreword by Aubrey L. Haines (Lincoln, Nebr., 1972).

Hiram Chittenden, *The Yellowstone National Park* (Cincinnati, 1895; republished, Richard Bartlett, ed., Norman, Okla., 1964), and Langford's introduction to his *Diary*, cited above, are early histories of the exploration and establishment of Yellowstone Park. A more recent detailed and excellent account is Aubrey L. Haines, *Yellowstone National Park, Its Exploration and Establishment* (Washington, D.C., 1974). More brief accounts may be found in Richard A. Bartlett, *Great Surveys of the American West*, Pt. 1 (Norman, Okla., 1962), and William H. Goetzmann, *Exploration and Empire* (New York,

1966). Wider-ranging stories of Yellowstone are Richard A. Bartlett, *Nature's Yellowstone* (Alberquerque, 1974), and Robert Scarff, ed., *Yellowstone and Grand Teton National Parks* (New York, 1966).

Artists and illustrators played major roles in the establishment of Yellowstone Park. For their important part, see Robert Taft, *Artists and Illustrators of the Old West* (New York, 1953); Robert Taft, *Photography and the American Scene* (New York, 1938; Dover edn., 1964); Thurman Wilkins, *Thomas Moran: Artist of the Mountains* (Norman, Okla., 1966); and Clarence Jackson, *Picture Maker of the Old West: William H. Jackson* (New York, 1948).

A most useful account of the discovery and history of development of Yosemite National Park is Carl Parcher Russell, *One Hundred Years in Yosemite* (Berkeley, Calif., 1932). For a brief account none is better than that to be found in Goetzmann's *Exploration and Empire.* For the geology of the park in easily understood language and illustrations, an excellent presentation is Harriet E. Huntington, *The Yosemite Story* (Garden City, N.Y., 1966).

Early in the history of the park, the geologist Josiah D. Whitney prepared a comprehensive description of Yosemite Valley and the big trees of California, his *Yosemite Guide-Book* (Cambridge, Mass., 1869), while his assistant, Clarence King, provided memorable accounts and graphic descriptions of the area in *Mountaineering in the Sierra Nevada* (Boston, 1872; reprinted, with introduction by James M. Shebl, Lincoln, Nebr., 1970). Horace Greeley's influential contributions revealing Yosemite's wonders can be found in his *Overland Journey from New York to San Francisco in the Summer of 1859* (New York, 1860), of which there is a modern edition edited by Charles T. Duncan (New York, 1964). The story of the involved evolution of the area from threatened wonderland wilderness to preservation as a National Park is told in Holway R. Jones, *John Muir and the Sierra Club* (San Francisco, 1965).

Index